# CHRIST KILLERS

# CHRIST KILLERS

### THE JEWS AND THE PASSION
### FROM THE BIBLE TO THE BIG SCREEN

JEREMY COHEN

UNIVERSITY PRESS

2007

# OXFORD
UNIVERSITY PRESS

Oxford University Press, Inc., publishes works that further
Oxford University's objective of excellence
in research, scholarship, and education.

Oxford   New York
Auckland   Cape Town   Dar es Salaam   Hong Kong   Karachi
Kuala Lumpur   Madrid   Melbourne   Mexico City   Nairobi
New Delhi   Shanghai   Taipei   Toronto

With offices in
Argentina   Austria   Brazil   Chile   Czech Republic   France   Greece
Guatemala   Hungary   Italy   Japan   Poland   Portugal   Singapore
South Korea   Switzerland   Thailand   Turkey   Ukraine   Vietnam

Copyright © 2007 by Jeremy Cohen

Published by Oxford University Press, Inc.
198 Madison Avenue, New York, New York 10016

www.oup.com

Oxford is a registered trademark of Oxford University Press

Library of Congress Cataloging-in-Publication Data
Cohen, Jeremy, 1953–
Christ killers : the Jews and the passion from the Bible
to the big screen / Jeremy Cohen.
p. cm.
Includes bibliographical references and index.
ISBN 978-0-19-517841-8
1. Jesus Christ—Passion—Role of Jews.   2. Judaism (Christian theology)—
History of doctrines.   3. Christianity and antisemitism—History.
4. Christianity and the arts.   I. Title.
BT431.5.C64 2006
261.2'6—dc22       2006012194

1 3 5 7 9 8 6 4 2

Printed in the United States of America
on acid-free paper

# ACKNOWLEDGMENTS

*Christ Killers* originated in a course that I have taught over the last twenty years at universities in the United States and Israel, and I am grateful to my students for their interest, their ideas, and their feedback, all of which have helped to steer my work in the direction it has taken. As the book itself has taken shape, I have benefited from the assistance of numerous individuals and institutions. My good friends and colleagues Ora Limor, Marc Raphael, Michael Signer, and Israel Yuval read and commented on all or parts of the manuscript, and their wise and candid suggestions, both general and specific, proved most helpful. Numerous other colleagues and friends—among them Elisheva Baumgarten, Naomi Cohen, Hasia Diner, Rebecca Edwards, John Gager, Ed Greenstein, Page Laws, Joel Levy, Sara Lipton, David Nirenberg, Aharon Oppenheimer, Linda Raphael, Adele Reinhartz, Irven Resnick, David Rosen, Miri Rubin, James Shapiro, Yossi Shain, Kenneth Stow, and Heather Valencia—graciously allowed me to share my ideas with them and responded generously to my questions and calls for assistance. My research assistant Avital Davidovich contributed much to this project with her characteristic dedication and congeniality, as did John Matsui during the months before I submitted the manuscript for publication; they, too, read the manuscript in its entirety and offered sound advice.

Profound thanks are due the Goldstein-Goren Diaspora Research Center and its excellent staff for their constant support and encouragement, and the Department of History and the Program of Jewish Studies at Johns Hopkins University, which hosted me as a visiting professor as my project reached its completion. I thank the Israel Academy of Arts and Sciences, the University of Notre Dame, the College of William and Mary, Georgetown University, and the European Association for Jewish Studies, where I had the opportunity to present portions of my work and to benefit from criticism and conversation in advance of this book's publication. And I am indebted to the librarians of the Sourasky and Wiener Libraries at Tel Aviv University, the Jewish National and University Library in Jerusalem, the Bodleian Library in Oxford, the Bibliothèque Nationale in Paris, and the Library of Congress in Washington (and especially to the former head of its Hebrew Section, Michael Grunberger) for facilitating my access to their collections as I pursued my research. My appreciation extends to museums, libraries, and art collections, too numerous to list here, for their help in amassing the illustrations.

I was able to bring this project to its conclusion owing to generous support from various sources: the Memorial Foundation for Jewish Culture; the Spiegel Family Foundation Chair for European Jewish History, the Goldstein-Goren Diaspora Research Center, and the Yaniv Fund for Scholars in the

Humanities at Tel Aviv University; the Crane Foundation Visiting Professorship in Jewish Studies at Johns Hopkins University; and the Abrams Chair for Jewish Thought and Culture and the Center for Medieval Studies at the University of Notre Dame.

I am especially grateful to my agent Jim Rutman of Sterling Lord Literistic and to Cynthia Read, Julia TerMaat, Stacey Hamilton, Norma McLemore, and their colleagues at Oxford University Press for their good-natured efforts and highly professional assistance in seeing this project through to its conclusion.

More than words can tell, my family has always been a source of love, encouragement, and inspiration.

# CONTENTS

# ILLUSTRATIONS

# CHRIST KILLERS

# INTRODUCTION

This book is not a whodunit. Unlike the countless investigators who have set out on a quest for the historical Jesus, hoping to determine who *really* crucified the Christian messiah, I shall not explain the death of Jesus, condemn anyone for it, or exonerate anyone. Were I to do so, I would invariably repeat what others have already done. Almost every opinion imaginable—and many that we might consider unimaginable!—have appeared in reconstructions of Jesus' last days. Furthermore, students of history often discover that the greater the number of answers to a particular historical question, the more unanswerable that question is. Given the limited evidence at our disposal today, we simply cannot know definitively who killed Jesus. And, perhaps even more important, I believe that historians should strive to understand how and why the past has developed and gradually given way to the present, much more than they need try to determine moral guilt or innocence. As this book will argue, the "facts" of Jesus' execution do not account for much of the impact that the Christ-killer myth has had over the course of history.

Instead, *Christ Killers* will demonstrate that Christianity needed the Jews to serve as the killers of Christ and repeatedly cast them in that role, regardless of what may or may not have happened to Jesus during his last, fateful days in Jerusalem. The book will develop this argument by proceeding in three related directions:

- by tracking the image of the Jew as the killer of the messiah and God, from its origins to some of its most recent expressions;
- by establishing that the history that we can learn from this story has much more to do with those who told and received it, and much less to do with its main characters (Jesus, Judas, the high priests of the temple, Pilate, the Jews of Jerusalem); and
- by appreciating the far-ranging effect that this myth has had on Western culture in all its breadth: from religion to politics, from philosophy to literature, and from the visual to the performing arts.

One very balanced study of Jesus' life recently acknowledged how precious few "absolutely secure historical facts" we know concerning his death: He was crucified by the Roman prefect Pontius Pilate in Jerusalem, during the season of the Jewish Passover holiday. And though the punishment of crucifixion indicates that Pilate executed Jesus as a political subversive, he evidently imposed no similar penalties on Jesus' disciples.[1]

Our own investigation departs from a third historical fact: Within forty or fifty years of the Crucifixion, Christians held the Jews and their leaders responsible for the death of their savior. By the end of the first century or the first years of the second, all four of the New Testament's Gospels shared the same basic story line: the Jewish leaders saw Jesus as a threat to their own power and authority. They commissioned Jesus' disciple Judas Iscariot to betray his master and engineer his arrest. They condemned Jesus in a kangaroo court. They and the mob that they incited prevailed upon Pilate to crucify him.

Tracing the career of this Christ-killer myth, we must recognize the role of *interpretation* in human memories—including those memories that we record as history. One can neither remember events nor transmit such memories to posterity without subjecting them to one's own interpretation—that is, to a distinctive "take" on their meaning. Simply put, there is no *uninterpreted* record of past events—neither those of Jesus' last days nor those of any other historical episode. Unraveling the Jewish role in the Crucifixion as understood from New Testament to modern times, I focus precisely on this encounter between interpreters and their past, studying the historical realities that conditioned interpreters to see and understand as they did. I try to identify the memories they found embedded in sources available to them, and I consider their successors who then received, transmitted, and even modified their various interpretations.

Thus told and retold, the story of the Jewish Christ killer has never ceased to affect the lives of real men and women. We shall see how a second-century bishop used it to fuel the hatred of Judaism among Christians in his community, how crusaders invoked it in attacking Jews before they ever left Europe for the Holy Land, how Jews of thirteenth-century Paris were dumbstruck with fear when it appeared on the agenda for a religious disputation, and how it was reflected in countless works of Western literature and art. Modern Jews, too, have not successfully shed the stigma of the deicide. Growing up in New York City during the 1930s, my mother was sandbagged on Halloween by youths seeking to punish the Christ killers. During the same years in Peoria, Illinois, my mother-in-law had to plead her innocence before her schoolmates: how could she have killed Jesus if she had never known him! Adolf Hitler viewed two performances of the Oberammergau Passion Play, renowned for its condemnation of the Jews, and he extolled the play for its Germanic virtues. Even among Christians who opposed the Nazis—the great theologian Karl Barth, for one—the Christ-killer myth endured. Singled out for recognition on Israel's Holocaust Remembrance Day in 2005, the Jewish survivor Robert Finaly recounted how Catholic nuns in Grenoble hid him and his brother in a nursery school during the last years of World War II. But when the war ended, the director of the nursery refused to release the children to their family—and actually had them baptized as Catholics—because their relatives, as she put it, "belonged to the religion that had killed Jesus."[2] As Christian churches still wrestle with the Christ-killer myth and its legacy in the wake of the Holocaust, neither the decree of an ecumenical council nor the courageous leadership of a well-minded pope can do away with mythology that has sunk so deep into our civilization's mind-set over the centuries. Even in the twenty-first century, one hears the rhetoric of ritual murder accusations and blood libels—themselves offshoots of the Christ-killer myth—fanning the flames of anti-Semitism in state-sponsored propaganda. Reflecting on his own Catholic upbringing, author and journalist James Carroll still remembers how he and others were conditioned to internalize the Jews' refusal to believe in Jesus. "Their denial has had tremendous power over Christians. At some deep psychological level, it has felt like nothing less than crucifixion: The Jews who crucified our Lord crucify us."[3]

The stormy controversy triggered by Mel Gibson's film *The Passion of the Christ* offers wonderful testimony to the ceaseless power of the story—on the screen, in the news media, and in our society at large. Long in advance of its release, the film commandeered public attention far beyond reasonable expectations, and the broad spectrum of opinion—along which Christians (Catholics and Protestants of varying sorts) and Jews (Reform and Orthodox, liberal and conservative) divided in almost every possible combination—underscores the stake that people still have in the Crucifixion story. Many readers of the Bible have championed "historical accuracy" and condemned "historical revisionism" without really understanding what either term means. Christians have used the film to battle over whose Christianity is genuine, and Jews have struggled to respond as they believe a religious minority living in the modern Christian world should respond.

My point here is simple but crucial: If diverse readers of the Passion story betray so much emotional and ideological partisanship in our own day, why should we have different expectations of Christians who remembered the Crucifixion one thousand or even nineteen hundred years ago? If the Crucifixion story can serve as a barometer of the social and religious climate in our society, it should also function as a window to the historical experience of our forebears in earlier times. Their culture typically valued religion more than the study of history, with no modern sense that church and state should separate. Just as with Gibson's *Passion of the Christ*, their Passion stories served their purposes. They inform us chiefly about their own experiences, and relatively little, in some cases not at all, about those of Jesus.

Part I of the book will examine the origins of the Jewish Christ killer. I turn first to the Passion narratives of the four Gospels, seeking to understand how, when, and why the story of Jesus' death as told by first-century Christians assumed its anti-Jewish character. Here one must focus not only on ancient Christian tradition but on modern methods for studying New Testament accounts of the Passion. The power of the cross still determines the manner in which many scholars read the Gospels and directs their gaze, moving them to judge the biblical text differently from any other ancient document. I look back from the New Testament to the Hebrew Bible, confronting some of the ancient Jewish traditions that nourished the Crucifixion story. Though it is Christians who imagined the Jews as killers of Christ, the interaction and exchange between Judaism and Christianity has endured throughout the last two thousand years of history; and we shall encounter this mutuality again and again as our story unfolds here. I then move forward in time, turning to one of the earliest Christian condemnations of the entire people of Israel for killing their God. Celebrating Easter in the second century, Melito of Sardis's poem *On the Pascha* lashed out at the Jews openly, collectively, and ruthlessly. In so doing, it set an ominous precedent for things yet to come.

Part II carries the story from ancient times until the present. I review discussions of the intentions of the Jewish Christ killers—Did they or did they not know what they were doing?—during the Middle Ages, exploring the direct effect that theology had on the treatment of Jews in Christian lands. I study the ritual murder charges, the Host-desecration desecration libels, and the accusations of ritual cannibalism leveled against European Jewry, all of them byproducts of the Christ-killer myth in popular Christian culture. I then show how the Christ-killing Jew rears his head repeatedly in a broad array of historical contexts, from the Middle Ages to modern times: from the Crusades and the popular piety of medieval Europe, to the anti-Catholic sermons of Martin Luther, to the Dreyfus case and other episodes of modern political history. I turn yet again to the voices of Jews, who devised various strategies for defending themselves against charges of deicide and, at the same time, for claiming somehow that Jesus and the Crucifixion story in truth belonged to them. Having arrived at the twentieth century, I discuss the Second Vatican Council's landmark decree *Nostra Aetate*, which, in the shadow of the Holocaust, sought to undercut the dangerous power of the Christ-killer myth. Exactly what does the decree say, what does it not say, and what difference has it really made?

Part III dwells exclusively on the visual and dramatic arts: the religious iconography of the Middle Ages, illustrations in early printed books, Passion plays in general and the German play at Oberammergau in particular, and the cinema. How have these different media given expression to the Christ-killer myth and, at the same time, contributed to its meaning? How does the Christ killer work for both the creators and the consumers of these art forms, that is, for both the artists and their audiences?

The cross is ubiquitous in Western culture, and no book about the Crucifixion could hope to be all-inclusive. I have been highly and deliberately selective; mine is but one possible approach (among many) to a fascinating and delicate subject. I recognize how difficult it is to remain dispassionate when it comes to the Passion. Yet I hope that, even as they might challenge long-standing assumptions, the chapters and scenes that I have selected from the long history of the Christ-killer myth will stimulate thought and interest across an array of traditional boundaries: between academic and nonacademic, Christian and Jew, religious and secular. Moreover, adapting a course that I have taught at different universities over the last twenty years, I have worked hard to make this story accessible to both the academic and the nonacademic reader, and I hope that I have done so without neglecting the legitimate concerns of either one. On the one hand, I have kept notes to a minimum and relegated them to the end of the book. And although I rely heavily on the scholarship of hundreds of other investigators, I have generally cited their work in my suggestions for further reading (mostly in English) preceding the notes to every chapter, rather than in the notes themselves. My colleagues will understand, I trust, that this in no way lessens my debt to them. On the other hand, the documentation should suffice to direct an interested reader to the sources I have consulted, both primary and secondary. Should the book awaken reaction in various quarters, I would welcome any constructive discussion that might ensue. There is no last word to be had in relating this story, at least so long as Jews and Christians go on living side by side. Its painful subject notwithstanding, if *Christ Killers* contributes in any way to mutual understanding between them, it will amply fulfill my hopes and expectations.

# THE ARREST, TRIAL, AND CRUCIFIXION OF JESUS (SELECTIONS FROM MARK 14–15)

(1) It was now two days before the Passover and the feast of Unleavened Bread. And the chief priests and the scribes were seeking how to arrest him by stealth, and kill him; for they said, "Not during the feast, lest there be a tumult of the people. . . ." Then Judas Iscariot, who was one of the twelve, went to the chief priests in order to betray him to them. And when they heard it they were glad, and promised to give him money. And he sought an opportunity to betray him.

(2) And on the first day of Unleavened Bread, when they sacrificed the Passover lamb . . . , the disciples set out and went to the city . . . , and they prepared the Passover. And when it was evening he came with the twelve. And as they were at table eating, Jesus said, "Truly, I say to you, one of you will betray me, one who is eating with me. . . ." And as they were eating, he took bread, and blessed, and broke it, and gave it to them, and said, "Take; this is my body." And he took a cup, and when he had given thanks he gave it to them, and they all drank of it. And he said to them, "This is my blood of the covenant, which is poured out for many. Truly, I say to you, I shall not drink again of the fruit of the vine until that day when I drink it new in the kingdom of God. . . ." And they went to a place which was called Gethsemane; and he said to his disciples, "Sit here, while I pray." And he took with him Peter and James and John, and began to be greatly distressed and troubled. And he said to them, "My soul is very sorrowful, even to death; remain here, and watch." And going a little farther, he fell on the ground and prayed that, if it were possible, the hour might pass from him. And he said, "Abba, Father, all things are possible to thee; remove this cup from me; yet not what I will, but what thou wilt. . . ."

(3) While he was still speaking, Judas came, one of the twelve, and with him a crowd with swords and clubs, from the chief priests and the scribes and the elders. Now the betrayer had given them a sign, saying, "The one I shall kiss is the man; seize him and lead him away under guard." And when he came, he went up to him at once, and said, "Master!" And he kissed him. And they laid hands on him and seized him. But one of those who stood by drew his sword, and struck the slave of the high priest and cut off his ear. And Jesus said to them, "Have you come out as against a robber, with swords

and clubs to capture me? Day after day I was with you in the temple teaching, and you did not seize me. But let the scriptures be fulfilled." And they all
forsook him, and fled. . . .

(4) And they led Jesus to the high priest; and all the chief priests and the
elders and the scribes were assembled. . . . Now the chief priests and the whole
council sought testimony against Jesus to put him to death; but they found
none. For many bore false witness against him, and their witness did not agree.
And some stood up and bore false witness against him, saying, "We heard
him say, 'I will destroy this temple that is made with hands, and in three days
I will build another, not made with hands.'" Yet not even so did their testimony agree. And the high priest stood up in the midst, and asked Jesus, "Have
you no answer to make? What is it that these men testify against you?" But
he was silent and made no answer. Again the high priest asked him, "Are
you the Christ, the Son of the Blessed?" And Jesus said, "I am; and you will
see the Son of man seated at the right hand of Power, and coming with the
clouds of heaven." And the high priest tore his garments, and said, "Why do
we still need witnesses? You have heard his blasphemy. What is your decision?" And they all condemned him as deserving death. And some began to
spit on him, and to cover his face, and to strike him, saying to him, "Prophesy!" And the guards received him with blows. . . . And as soon as it was
morning the chief priests, with the elders and scribes, and the whole council
held a consultation; and they bound Jesus and led him away and delivered
him to Pilate.

(5) And Pilate asked him, "Are you the King of the Jews?" And he answered him, "You have said so." And the chief priests accused him of many
things. And Pilate again asked him, "Have you no answer to make? See how
many charges they bring against you." But Jesus made no further answer, so
that Pilate wondered. Now at the feast he used to release for them one pris-
oner for whom they asked. And among the rebels in prison, who had committed murder in the insurrection, there was a man called Barabbas. And the
crowd came up and began to ask Pilate to do as he was wont to do for them.
And he answered them, "Do you want me to release for you the King of the
Jews?" For he perceived that it was out of envy that the chief priests had
delivered him up. But the chief priests stirred up the crowd to have him release for them Barabbas instead. And Pilate again said to them, "Then what
shall I do with the man whom you call the King of the Jews?" And they cried
out again, "Crucify him." And Pilate said to them, "Why, what evil has he
done?" But they shouted all the more, "Crucify him." So Pilate, wishing to
satisfy the crowd, released for them Barabbas; and having scourged Jesus, he
delivered him to be crucified.

(6) And the soldiers led him away inside the palace (that is, the praetorium); and they called together the whole battalion. And they clothed him in

a purple cloak, and plaiting a crown of thorns they put it on him. And they began to salute him, "Hail, King of the Jews!" And they struck his head with a reed, and spat upon him, and they knelt down in homage to him. And when they had mocked him, they stripped him of the purple cloak, and put his own clothes on him. And they led him out to crucify him. And they compelled a passer-by, Simon of Cyre'ne, who was coming in from the country, the father of Alexander and Rufus, to carry his cross. And they brought him to the place called Golgotha (which means the place of a skull). And they offered him wine mingled with myrrh; but he did not take it. And they crucified him, and divided his garments among them, casting lots for them, to decide what each should take. And it was the third hour, when they crucified him. And the inscription of the charge against him read, "The King of the Jews." And with him they crucified two robbers, one on his right and one on his left. And those who passed by derided him, wagging their heads, and saying, "Aha! You who would destroy the temple and build it in three days, save yourself, and come down from the cross!" So also the chief priests mocked him to one another with the scribes, saying, "He saved others; he cannot save himself. Let the Christ, the King of Israel, come down now from the cross, that we may see and believe." Those who were crucified with him also reviled him. And when the sixth hour had come, there was darkness over the whole land until the ninth hour. And at the ninth hour Jesus cried with a loud voice, "Elo-i, Elo-i, lama sabachthani?" which means, "My God, my God, why hast thou forsaken me?" And some of the bystanders hearing it said, "Behold, he is calling Elijah." And one ran and, filling a sponge full of vinegar, put it on a reed and gave it to him to drink, saying, "Wait, let us see whether Elijah will come to take him down." And Jesus uttered a loud cry, and breathed his last. And the curtain of the temple was torn in two, from top to bottom. And when the centurion, who stood facing him, saw that he thus breathed his last, he said, "Truly this man was the Son of God!"

The above is taken from the Revised Standard Version, which I have used for almost all biblical quotations throughout this book. The Revised Standard Version is available online at http://etext.lib.virginia.edu/rsv.browse.html.

# PART

# I

# THE MYTH AND ITS ORIGINS

# THE GOOD NEWS

The story of the Crucifixion begins and ends with the Gospels. These first four books of the New Testament—Matthew, Mark, Luke, and John—provide the foundation for Christian teaching concerning the life and death of Jesus. The word gospel (*evangelion* in Greek) means "good news," and in the four canonical Gospels of Christian Scripture, this means the news that Jesus, the divine messiah, came to inaugurate the kingdom of heaven, dying on the cross so that those who would believe in him might be saved. The Gospels are fascinating, remarkably complex documents, and their importance in the history of Christianity and the world, together with the vast field of scholarship that has grown up around them, has only added to their complexity. Hardly any passage in the Gospels has failed to provoke extensive discussion among academics, theologians, and laypersons alike, yielding virtually every interpretation imaginable—and then some! Here I can devote only a single chapter to the texts of the Gospels themselves, and so I must define my agenda very selectively, explaining my premises and objectives at the outset.

## GOSPELS, HISTORY, AND MYTH

What kind of texts are the Gospels? Because no other sources relate as much of Jesus' life story, readers have understandably appreciated them as biographies of the Christian savior. And because Christianity recognizes Holy Scripture as the word of God, Christians have traditionally considered their authority unimpeachable. Indeed, they contain "gospel truth." Nevertheless, despite their immeasurable value for historians, the Gospels are not books of history, certainly not in the modern sense, and we cannot fairly expect them to offer an accurate, factual report of historical events.

Three factors underlie this presupposition. First, the evangelists, the writers of the Gospels, did not have historical reporting as their goal. Rather, they used the stories, traditions, and memories of Jesus at their disposal to teach Christianity within their recently founded Christian communities, proclaiming the good news of salvation in Christ. Such an appreciation of the Gospels now typifies the instruction of the most established Christian churches. As a prominent Catholic biblical scholar explains, "The evangelists narrated the

words, deeds, and signs of Jesus, not to excite curiosity but to awaken faith."[1]
A similar approach appears in a recent publication of the Society for Promoting
Christian Knowledge, perhaps the oldest Protestant missionary organization
still in existence today. The Gospels, in a word, are

> the Christian faith put in narrative form. That is to say, whatever
> their literary shape, their aim is not biographical in the usual mod-
> ern sense. They do not tell the tale of the life simply for the sake of
> the story. . . . The aim of the Gospels is then perfectly expressed by
> the ending . . . of the Gospel of John: "These [things] are written that
> you may believe that Jesus is the Messiah, the Son of God, and that
> believing you may have life in his name" (John 20:31). They were
> not written for entertainment or for educational reasons, but with
> theological intent and for an evangelistic purpose.[2]

The Gospels, then, teach theology in their storytelling. But perhaps,
calmly and carefully, we can proceed yet further along this line of thought.
Much as the opening books of the Hebrew Bible (particularly Genesis and
the first half of Exodus) do in the case of Judaism, these first books of the
New Testament convey the foundationally important myths of Christianity.
And here I must add quickly and emphatically: *Myth* in this sense does not
mean a falsehood. Quite the opposite, a myth is a story that expresses the
ultimate truths and values of a community. Today we moderns might not
necessarily consider these truths historical or factual, but that makes them
no less important, no less "true." In the sense that I refer to a *myth* here, its
factual accuracy makes little difference. It may or may not be factual, but this
hardly concerns the believer, whose commitment to the story's mythical truth
generally can withstand the most potent historical, archeological, or scientific challenge. If critical historians could possibly prove, for instance, that
Moses and Muhammad did not live when we think they did, I strongly doubt
that many believing Jews and Muslims would abandon their faith. Just as we
ought not to read poetry as prose or a columnist's editorial as a simple news
dispatch (not that one can vouch for the objectivity of news reporting, either),
so, too, should we refrain from imposing our own agenda on the Gospels,
expecting them to respond to questions that did not necessarily occupy the
evangelists.

Second, not only may we not classify the Gospels as historical writing,
but we must also recognize that intellectuals in the classical world did not
place the same high value on the accurate recording of historical events that
we generally do today. The judgment of Aristotle in his work on literature,
the *Poetics*, set the tone for the dominant approach to historical reporting
for many centuries to come.

> It is not the function of the poet to relate what has happened, but
> what may happen—what is possible according to the law of prob-
> ability or necessity. The poet and the historian differ not by writing
> in verse or in prose. The work of Herodotus might be put into verse,
> and it would still be a species of history, with meter no less than
> without it. The true difference is that one relates what has happened,
> the other what may happen. *Poetry, therefore, is a more philosophi-*
> *cal and a higher thing than history: for poetry tends to express the*
> *universal, history the particular.*[3]

By poetry, Aristotle meant literary fiction in general, and plays written for
the theater in particular. His judgment, which views fiction as more serious
and worthy than nonfiction, also helps us to understand why historians in
the ancient world—from the Athenian Thucydides to the first-century Jew
Josephus and beyond—took considerable poetic license, especially in their
rendition of speeches that give past events their meaning. Thucydides explained
in the introduction to his *Peloponnesian War*, "my method has been . . . to
make the speakers say what, in my opinion, was called for by each situation."[4]
Josephus Flavius, a Jewish contemporary of the evangelists, also crafted
speeches as he deemed appropriate, and, to the extent that he really did strive
to preserve a record of the past, his historian's aspirations were themselves
exceptional. As a leading present-day historian reminds us, "It would be
almost fifteen centuries before another Jew would actually call himself a historian."[5] Even when they did preserve historical memories for posterity, Christian writers of the Middle Ages similarly testified to Aristotle's judgment. They
transmitted information about the past when it served a higher purpose, and
in a manner that promoted those interests.

The evangelists were neither Aristotelian philosophers nor even self-
styled historians, but preachers with an urgent theological message to proclaim. Yet the classical perspective does enable us to understand how they
might consider other kinds of truth higher, nobler—truer, perhaps—than the
simple facts of past events. And if the truth of biblical narrative were simply
historical—that is, if it depended on its factual accuracy—one could easily
reach the rather cynical conclusion voiced by the great American philosopher
Arthur Lovejoy a hundred years ago: "Can a proposition about the happening of a particular incident at a certain time in a little corner of the earth really
be one of the fundamental verities which every man ought to know and believe for his soul's health?"[6]

Does the Bible deserve such a peremptory reading? If the formation of
the cosmos took more than seven days and nights, must we consider the
Genesis creation story devoid of truth? Should we read the opening verses of

John's Gospel—"In the beginning was the Word, and the Word was with God, and the Word was God"—as mere history? I submit that such a reading does both ourselves and the Bible a disservice.

Third, though they tell of the life of Jesus, which ended around the year 30 C.E., the texts of the Gospels belong to a very different historical context. None of the evangelists—whom we conveniently call by the names of their books but whose personal identities elude us—knew or interacted with Jesus during his lifetime. None of them numbered among Jesus' original disciples. Though they may well preserve traditions and memories of the first generations of believers in Jesus, the overwhelming consensus of New Testament scholars dates the texts of the Gospels only from the last third of the first century: Mark from around 70 C.E., Matthew from over the course of the next decade or so, then Luke, and John from the last years of the first century or the first years of the second.

More significant than the number of years between Jesus and the evangelists is the difference between his world and theirs. The intervening decades had seen the career of the apostle Paul, perhaps the real founder of the Christian religion as we know it, whose teachings opened up the new "Jesus movement" to non-Jews on an equal footing with Jews, something which the historical Jesus appears never to have imagined. Though Jesus seems never to have dreamed of leaving Judaism to found a religion of his own, the "parting of the ways" between Judaism and Christianity had begun by the time the evangelists wrote the Gospels, even if the Gospels themselves reveal that this process still had a long way to go. The historical Jesus had also not anticipated the Romans' destruction of the Second Temple in Jerusalem in the year 70, an event that rocked the foundations of the Jewish—and Jewish-Christian—world, leaving new crises, interest groups, and power struggles in its wake, developments that thoroughly reconfigured Jewish society. No less important, many, perhaps most, of the very first generation of Christians had died before the return of their messiah—the Second Coming of Christ—which they firmly expected to experience during their own lifetimes. This challenge, too, demanded new and creative responses on the part of the earliest church.

When the evangelists related stories about Jesus to teach *their* Christian theology in *their own* historical context, they worked within a historical reality very different from that of the day of Jesus' crucifixion. Jesus might play the leading role in the drama that the evangelists relate, but that drama testifies first and foremost to *their* day and environment, not his. For the student of history, the reality of any historical narrative—its "social logic," as a prominent historian has termed it[7]—is primarily that of its "inscription": the moment, the context, the constellation of circumstances when it was recorded. Granted, the glaring similarities between all four Gospels' Passion stories do demand recognition. The evangelists clearly drew on an earlier source or sources for their accounts of the Crucifixion. But the basic methodological principle stands: Stories teach the historian chiefly about the historical context in which they were told, recorded, and received—that is, about the storytellers and their audiences. The historical accuracy of the stories' contents and characters is much more difficult, often impossible, to ascertain. The historian has no reason to privilege the Gospels in this regard more than Genesis, Homer's *Odyssey*, or any other ancient text that might not strike the Western reader as containing "gospel truth."

Where does this leave us with regard to the Crucifixion? In the limited space at my disposal, I cannot determine what actually happened or did not happen during Jesus' last days, nor do I seek to pinpoint the responsibility for Jesus' death. This book, as I noted in the introduction, is not a "whodunit." Rather, I approach the Crucifixion story as precisely that: a story, the product of particular historical and religious circumstances in which it wielded immense power, a myth proclaiming Christian truths much more crucial than what actually happened. My interest lies particularly in the blame that the stories cast for the Crucifixion and in the Jewish role as Christ killer from then until our own day.

## THE PASSION NARRATIVE AND THE EVENTS OF THE PASSION

A picture of conflict between Jesus and the Jewish leadership (Pharisees, scribes, priests) develops over the course of all four gospel narratives, suggesting that the evangelists consciously sought to highlight the rift between the Jewish religious establishment and the new Jesus movement. Even as Jesus' popularity grew among the people, their leaders rejected both his authority and his message. As we well know, the story of this conflict culminates in a conspiracy of the chief priests against Jesus, and in a detailed account of Jesus' last days, the Passion narrative.

Time and space do not allow for a systematic comparison of all four Passion narratives, a task that many New Testament scholars have already undertaken. For the moment, one should note that all the evangelists follow the basic story line of Mark's Gospel: (1) the priests conspire against Jesus and enlist Judas to betray him; (2) Jesus and his disciples gather for the Last Supper (a Passover seder in the synoptic Gospels of Matthew, Mark, and Luke) and then adjourn for the night to the garden of Gethsemane, where (3) Jesus is arrested; (4) the chief priests put Jesus on trial, fabricate testimony against him, allow him to be beaten, and deliver him to the Roman procurator Pontius Pilate; (5) Pilate confronts Jesus and offers to release him, but the Jews opt for the release of a criminal named Barabbas instead; the Jews clamor for Jesus' crucifixion, Pilate gives in, and (6) Jesus suffers a painful, humiliating execution, slain by Pilate's Roman soldiers, mocked by Jews and Romans alike, but vindicated by darkening skies at noon.

The other Gospels do depart from Mark's account in various details. Each evangelist understands the timing and the number of Jewish judicial proceedings against Jesus somewhat differently. Matthew, as we shall soon see, portrays the Jews as accepting collective responsibility for the Crucifixion for all time. Luke's Pontius Pilate sends Jesus to Herod Antipas, Jewish ruler of the Galilee, for trial. John depicts the Crucifixion as occurring on the eve of the Passover (rather than on the festival itself) as Jews prepared to offer their paschal sacrifice, such that the Last Supper could not have been a Passover seder, and he emphasizes, more than any other evangelist, Pilate's desire to free Jesus.

But just as the four Gospels share the same story line in their accounts of the Passion, so, too, do they pronounce the same verdict: Pilate authorized Jesus' crucifixion, and Romans may have performed the physical act of nailing Jesus to the cross. But the Jewish leaders and the Jewish mob bear the responsibility for his death. They rejected him and his teaching. They conspired against him, inducing even his trusted disciple Judas—whose name (meaning Jew or Judea) bespeaks the collective identity of the Jewish people—to betray him for money. They tried Jesus in one kangaroo court or another. And they did not rest until Pilate crucified him.

Laying the groundwork for the remainder of this book, and proceeding according to the guidelines that I have set out, I propose to draw on the work of several key players in the vast academic discussion of the Gospels' Crucifixion story. Though this book cannot hope to solve the central problems underlying the birth of the Christ-killer myth, it can, perhaps, clarify some of them, adding to our understanding of the New Testament's condemnation of the Jews for Jesus' death.

At the heart of our concerns lies a debate over the distance between the Gospels' stories of the Crucifixion and the events they relate, a debate in which many have participated. Here, Raymond Brown and John Dominic Crossan stand at the forefront and serve as enlightening examples. Both these investigators share an awareness of the tragic legacy of the Christ-killer tradition in recent generations. Brown, a distinguished Catholic priest and scholar who taught for decades at the liberal Protestant Union Theological Seminary in New York, openly acknowledges: "Given the history of anti-Semitism in the 20th century, even whole books devoted to two millennia of anti-Jewish attitudes derived from the Passion Narratives are inadequate."[8] Crossan, a lapsed Catholic priest who taught (even after leaving the priesthood) at the Catholic DePaul University in Chicago, declares even more categorically:

> The passion-resurrection stories . . . have been the seedbed for Christian anti-Judaism. And without that Christian anti-Judaism, lethal and genocidal European anti-Semitism would have been either im-

possible or at least not widely successful. What was at stake in those passion stories, in the long haul of history, was the Jewish Holocaust.[9]

Yet despite their common awareness of the power of biblical texts and their interpretations to mold human behavior, and despite their mutual recognition of the theological character of the Gospels, as well as their late first-century origins, Brown and Crossan differ sharply over how to read and appraise the stories of the Crucifixion.

In his monumental, rightfully acclaimed two-volume commentary on the Passion narratives, Brown takes steps to narrow the gap between the events of Jesus' last days and their accounts in the Gospels. First, in seeking to establish "what the evangelists intended and conveyed to their audiences" in their Passion narratives, Brown postulates "a general correspondence between what the author intended and what he conveyed."[10] Albeit subtly, Brown thus moves to level some of the different varieties of meaning that a narrative text like the Crucifixion story might have. If the picture of the events plainly evident in the text is that which the evangelists intended, less room remains for ambivalent—or ambiguous—interpretations of the same passage. Now, if the evangelists in fact conveyed the impressions that they intended to convey, how reliable was their reporting? Brown considers the Gospels "distillations of earlier Christian teaching and preaching about Jesus."[11] How far back did these extend? Though the evangelists themselves did not witness the Crucifixion, Brown does affirm that "ultimately there were eyewitnesses and ear-witnesses who were in a position to know the broad lines of Jesus' passion." And, especially in view of the public nature of Roman crucifixion, "from the earliest days available raw material could have been developed into a Passion Narrative extending from the arrest to the burial."[12]

This key sentence demands our attention. Although Brown allows for evolution in the Passion narrative between the events and their gospel narrators, he wishes to present that evolution as essentially direct and uninterrupted. *From the earliest days*, the pristine, uninterpreted *raw material* sufficed to nourish a Crucifixion story structured along the very lines that it has retained in the New Testament, *from the arrest to the burial*. Moreover, this sentence betrays another, equally potent methodological principle in Brown's commentary: Because the earliest testimony *could have* developed into a Passion narrative of the sort we now have, Brown proceeds as if it did. He strives to make the possible appear plausible, and such plausibility generally suffices for credibility. Refusing to abandon his critical academic perspective, Brown warns his readers not to equate history with tradition. Even if we can establish a pre-gospel tradition that brings us back to the years immediately following Jesus' death, it does not "necessarily" establish what occurred in 30 or 33. It does, however, minimize the distance remaining between us and the events in question.

In the very next sentence, Brown offers a range of possible appraisals for the particulars of the gospel narrative: "certain, very probable, probable, possible, not impossible." Every time I read these words, I cannot suppress my surprise: Where is the "impossible"? For Brown, evidently, it does not figure significantly in the discussion. The least probable elements in the Crucifixion story are, at worst, *not impossible*, and the Passion narratives as a whole are characterized by plausibility, or what Brown calls "verisimilitude": "the kind of thing" that someone would have done in that situation.[13] He then applies this plausibility/verisimilitude principle throughout the commentary. For example, with regard to physical abuse of Jesus by his captors on the night of his arrest, "such abuse is not at all implausible historically."[14] Or, concerning the demands of the Jewish mob that Pilate execute Jesus, "as for whether historically such an outcry of crowds occurred during the trial of Jesus by Pilate, we can speak only of verisimilitude."[15] For Brown, however, verisimilitude suffices to preserve the integrity of the narrative. Similarly, while some critics view the reliance of the Gospels on themes, traditions, and texts from the Hebrew Bible as evidence against the factual accuracy of its narrative, Brown argues that these may well reflect Jesus' own self-understanding no less than the creative interpretations—or midrash—of the evangelists. Again: "I admit that certitude may not be possible; but in the matter of historicity[,]probability or likelihood is an important factor, protecting the picture of Jesus from the distortions and unlikelihoods produced by too rigorous a quest for certitude."[16]

Brown's prominence, his "liberality" as a Catholic, and the Herculean accomplishment of his commentary notwithstanding, one cannot leave his book without a sense that he privileges the Gospels—that is, that he approaches them less critically than he might approach other ancient texts. As much as he possibly can, Brown sets out to judge the Gospels as historically convincing, protecting a picture of Jesus from distortions and unlikelihoods produced by too rigorous a quest for certitude. In Brown's case, such an approach certainly suits the official position of the Catholic Church expressed by the Second Vatican Council in its *Dogmatic Constitution on Divine Revelation: Dei Verbum* (The Word of God): "The sacred authors wrote the four Gospels, selecting some things from the many which had been handed on by word of mouth or in writing, reducing some of them to a synthesis, explaining some things in view of the situation of their churches and preserving the form of proclamation but always in such fashion that they told us the honest truth about Jesus."[17] Though hardly a fundamentalist reading of Scripture, Brown's reading begins with the premise that the Gospels tell the honest truth about Jesus. His commentary therefore affords an illuminating example of how thoroughly prior assumptions concerning the historical accuracy of the Crucifixion story—precisely because it is Holy Scripture—have dominated both popular and scholarly opinion.

John Dominic Crossan has attacked Brown's assessment of the Passion narratives vehemently, often stridently. For Crossan, they are not *history remembered*—that is, essentially accurate historical reporting as filtered down through several generations of early Christian memory—as they are for Brown, but *prophecy historicized*. By this, Crossan means that the first Christians grappled with, made sense of, and explained Jesus' death by resorting to the teachings of the Hebrew Bible. "The first Christians were all Jews, and, in trying to understand what had happened to Jesus and themselves, they turned to their sacred writings, the Hebrew Scriptures, which they studied in Greek and would eventually call their Old Testament, as distinct from the New Testament they themselves had created."[18] In other words, they reconciled themselves to the fact of Jesus' crucifixion by appreciating it as the fulfillment of biblical prophecy. They painted a picture of their savior's last days against the background of various biblical precedents, several of which I shall explore in the next chapter. As he reviews the evidence—the scapegoat of Leviticus 16, the tragic daytime darkness of Amos 8, and the conspiracy of the powerful in Psalm 2—Crossan clamors for the thorough dependence of the Crucifixion story on Old Testament prophecy: from Jesus' crime and arrest, to his trial and abuse, to his execution and burial. At the end of the day, he arrives at a striking conclusion:

> I cannot find any detailed historical information about the Crucifixion of Jesus. Every item we looked at was prophecy historicized rather than history recalled. There was one glaring exception. The one time the *narrative passion* broke away from its base in the *prophetic passion* . . . was to assert Jewish responsibility and Roman innocence. But those motifs were neither prophecy nor history but Christian propaganda, a daring act of public relations faith in the destiny of Christianity not within Judaism but within the Roman Empire. In a way that *was* history, not past history but future history.[19]

I shall soon return to Crossan's allusion to Roman imperial politics and propaganda. For the moment, let us focus on the diametric opposition between Crossan's position and Brown's. If, for Brown, the least historical component of the Passion narrative is not impossible, for Crossan, that narrative provides no detailed historical information about the Crucifixion of Jesus. Thoroughly grounded in the Bible, the Passion narrative for Crossan expresses not Jesus' own biblical self-understanding, as Brown might contend, but the post-Crucifixion reading of biblical messianic prophecy on the part of Jesus' disciples, their earliest Christological midrash.

Why, then, do the Gospels read like historical narrative, especially in their treatment of Jesus' last days? Crossan himself offers an explanation for the transition from midrash to Passion narrative. In order to communicate

the new Christian interpretation of Jesus' crucifixion to the ordinary, uneducated, even illiterate believer, an anonymous Christian author performed an
act of religious genius, blending key passages from Hebrew Scripture "into a
coherent story with those prophetic texts as a now hidden substratum."[20] Such
a narrative of the Passion served the needs of the uneducated, just as it enabled
their teachers to draw them into the world of their theological discussion, ad-
vancing their religious ideology and strengthening their young Christian community. Crossan dates the composition of this earliest "Cross Gospel" to the
middle of the first century, and he finds some of its essential elements preserved in the apocryphal Gospel of Peter, a gospel never accepted into the
canon of the New Testament. All four evangelists, he argues, drew upon this
source, just as Matthew, Luke, and John relied upon Mark, which helps to
explain the impressive similarity between all four versions of the Crucifixion
story.

One must ponder the implications of Crossan's argument, for these
extend far beyond the simple issue of chronology to the very substance and
character of the Passion narrative. He parts company with Brown, who contends that an essentially reliable tradition of early Christian historical memory,
based on the testimony of eyewitnesses, made its way from the foot of the
cross to the late-first-century evangelists. (Brown also views the Gospel of
Peter as a second-century text, which would put its composition later than
that of the four canonical gospels.) Instead, Crossan believes that the kernel
of the Crucifixion story elaborated in the New Testament originates with the
mid-first-century author of the Cross Gospel. He deems this story a distilla-
tion of Christological (that is, Christ-oriented) interpretations of biblical
prophecies, not the memories of historical events and reliable testimony to
them. No less important, he understands the Passion narrative as a text composed for theological, ideological, and pedagogic reasons: to allow early
Christian preachers to capture and direct the loyalties of the uneducated. The
Passion narrative thus sheds light primarily on the historical circumstances
of those who composed, developed, and transmitted it, not those of the characters within it—a radical departure from standard Christian belief.

Not surprisingly, Crossan has some sharp words for Brown's appeal to
verisimilitude, which he considers grossly unethical. No doubt his judgment
derives from more recent historical experiences, such as the Holocaust. "The
passion narratives are a section of the Christian New Testament where sec-
tarian intra-Jewish polemics ('the Jews' as all those *other* Jewish groups besides *our* Jewish group) prepared the ground for theological anti-Judaism,
which prepared the ground, in the terrible fullness of time, for genocidal anti-
Semitism." This said, he appeals directly to his readers' common sense: "Think
for a moment about the ethics of judging events as having 'verisimilitude' or
the morality of judging happenings with double negatives such as 'not im-

plausible.' Think of ourselves in court and judged by those standards; we all go straight to jail."[21] Though considered radical and iconoclast by many New Testament scholars—whereas Brown exemplifies a centrist or "mainline" stance—Crossan deserves our attention. Readers opting for Brown's approach might find themselves in good scholarly company, but all can learn from Crossan's take on the place of ideology in the origins and legacy of historical narrative.

## THE PASSION NARRATIVE AND ITS HISTORICAL CONTEXT

The question of distance between the events of Jesus' death and their Passion narratives leads invariably to another: In what historical context did the Crucifixion story take shape? What political, social, and economic realities gave rise to the earliest versions of our story? Many read the Gospels against the background of conflict between the Jews of Judea and their Roman rulers that erupted into armed rebellion late in the 60s of the first century. When Rome quashed the rebellion, destroying Jerusalem and its temple in 70, Christian writers including Mark (who may well have lived in Rome) reworked the earliest Christian traditions about Pontius Pilate's execution of Jesus so as to minimize "the scandal of the Roman cross"—that is, to suppress memories of Roman guilt in Jesus' death. Although the church soon became the target of Roman imperial persecutions, distancing the Christian community from the Jews following Rome's "Jewish war" may well have struck the evangelists as a sound strategic ploy—especially if radically anti-Roman Jewish zealots numbered among Jesus' original disciples, as some investigators have claimed.[22]

One can also focus profitably on what Crossan called the *intra-Jewish polemics* that plagued the Jewish world throughout much of the first century as Roman legions left Judea embattled, Jerusalem and the temple in ruins, the Jewish priestly aristocracy deprived of its former authority, and other interest groups embroiled in a struggle for souls and power. Perhaps more than the synoptic Gospels, the Gospel of John has lent itself to such an approach. The hostilities that it portrays between Jesus and the Jews have long been read as a reflection of Christian and Jewish experience late in the first century. Yet one can read all four Gospels in such a manner, and many have. In her book *The Origins of Satan*, Elaine Pagels considers all the evangelists as Jews who wrote in a Jewish context. Precisely the intimate closeness and kinship between Jews in and outside the new Christian faith community intensified the harsh identification of the Jewish *other* with demonic forces in the Passion narratives. Still others have ventured into the social world of the first Christians, both Jewish and non-Jewish, investigating how the circumstances of everyday life in different communities affected the gospel narratives.

From this last perspective of early Christian sociology, I have learned much from the efforts of various investigators to appreciate the first Christians as a millennial community in the immediate aftermath of a "crisis of nonmaterialization." Drawing on works by social scientists, such as Leon Festinger's now-classic *When Prophecy Fails* and Kenelm Burridge's *New Heaven, New Earth*, these New Testament experts reason as follows. Millennial or messianic movements that look forward to an imminent end of human history as we now know it typically undergo such a crisis—indeed, the end of time has yet to come!—which shatters the greatest hopes of the community. When this crisis of nonmaterialization occurs, as in the death or the defection of a messianic leader, many of the movement's adherents surely abandon hope and seek ways to repair the fractured foundations of their world. Yet some often remain steadfast in their beliefs, ushering their community into a qualitatively new phase in its life cycle. As psychologists have explained, believers must now struggle with the cognitive dissonance generated by their traumatic crisis, the gap between reality as they perceive it and as it appears to most others ("as it is," many would surely say). For the world at large has fallen out of sync with how it is supposed to be. Over the course of time, most such millennial movements have receded into historical oblivion, their followers generally written off by mainstream society as marginal or deranged. Yet a few millennial communities have made profound contributions to history and culture. These survived for centuries after their crises of nonmaterialization, owing largely to the commitment of their adherents, the resolve of their leaders, and the creative genius of their prophets.

Can such a perspective enrich our reading of the Crucifixion story? I believe that it must. Consider, for instance, the following application of the study of millennial movements to the earliest phases in Christian history, as proposed by two Christian seminarians:

> From any rational perspective, the New Testament church never should have happened. The church began with two crises of faith [the Crucifixion and the failure of the Second Coming to materialize], either of which alone could have destroyed the embryonic gathering of believers. But inspired by its counterculture foundations and its charismatic leaders, the early Jesus movement and later the young church were able to transform initial challenges to their faith into even stronger commitments to ministry and mission.

Our interest lies above all with the Crucifixion, and the way in which it evidently drove those who believed in Jesus as the messiah of Israel to the margins of the Jewish community.

At Jesus' death, his disciples found themselves faced with acute disappointment. The one whom they had expected would usher in the messianic "kingdom of God" had instead been executed as a criminal. When the crisis came[,] he had not even delivered himself, as was doubtless aptly pointed out by their enemies. Here we see a double threat to the community's perception of its own reality: internally their understanding of themselves was threatened by the disappearance of the one who embodied their expectations; externally they no longer could claim credibility from the public.[23]

The challenges confronting the first Christians in the wake of the Crucifixion appear monumental by any standard. For many, they would have remained insurmountable but for the resourcefulness and the commitment of Christianity's founders and apostles. The modern authors quoted above relate to cognitive dissonance as a valuable tool, one that could be used to sustain evangelical enthusiasm in Christian churches even today, just as Christian leaders channeled it creatively in the first century.

How, then, did cognitive dissonance and the struggle with it leave a mark on the first generations of Christians? John Gager and those who have adopted his approach point above all to the enthusiastic surge of missionary activity with which the first Christian believers reacted to the disappointment and embarrassment of the Crucifixion. Precisely when we might have expected Jesus' disciples to maintain a low profile and remove themselves from the public eye, we remember them as having sought to win converts, disseminating their beliefs as widely as possible.

No doubt some of Christianity's essential foundation myths took shape in this context as well. (Remember, the term *myth* here means a story or belief that conveys a centrally important religious truth, a truth that does not depend on historical or factual accuracy.) When "the real world" considered Jesus dead, his disciples proclaimed that he had risen from his grave, had ascended to heaven, and had taken his rightful place beside his heavenly father. Whereas Jesus' miserable end convinced others that he could not have been the messiah, his followers found confirmation in Hebrew Scripture that such events should have befallen the savior of Israel. Whereas the still unredeemed state of the world suggested to many that Jesus did not bring the redemption that Jews traditionally expected of the messiah, the first Christians looked forward to the Second Coming in their lifetime, when Jesus would complete the work of salvation that he had begun. At the same time, membership in the new community depended on a confession of faith that Jesus evidently had never demanded of his followers during his lifetime. Thus does the Gospel of Matthew recount a well-known exchange between Jesus and his closest disciples, attributing a declaration to Jesus that appears in none of the other Gospels:

> He said to them, "But who do you say that I am?" Simon Peter replied, "You are the Christ, the Son of the living God." And Jesus answered him, "Blessed are you, Simon Bar-Jona! For flesh and blood has not revealed this to you, but my Father who is in heaven. And I tell you, you are Peter, and on this rock I will build my church, and the powers of death shall not prevail against it." (Matthew 16:15–18)

This belief in Jesus now served as the rock on whose foundation the Christian church developed. It assured salvation to those who would espouse it. It set a new line of demarcation between those within the community of the elect and the others who remained outside.

Who were those who resisted, refusing to accept the reality of the crucified, resurrected, and ascended Christ and of the heavenly kingdom he had inaugurated? The Jesus movement still resided within the Jewish community and the world of Judaism. Besides the belief in Jesus, all that distinguished Jews from pagans also distinguished the first Christians from the pagans of the Greco-Roman world. In defining what gave them their exclusive title to salvation, therefore, Christian teachers had to differentiate between themselves and the Jews. The Jew who obstinately refused to recognize Jesus as Christ rapidly became Christianity's primary "other." The majority of Jews expressed and exemplified the worldview that the disciples' cognitive dissonance and creativity propelled them to refute. As the first century progressed and the mission of Paul offered full-fledged membership in Christian communities to non-Jews who would not convert to Judaism, the distinction between the followers of Jesus and mainstream Jews slowly sharpened, and power struggles within the Jewish community at large easily led from distinction to animosity. The Jews' rejection of the new faith despite its foundation in Judaism cast them as the enemies of Christ par excellence. In Christian eyes, although they should have accepted Jesus before all others, the Jews betrayed God's offer of salvation. The psychological and social reality of first-century Christianity easily facilitated the branding of Jews, either their leaders or the people as a whole, as responsible for Jesus' demise.

## THE PARTING OF THE WAYS

Let us look more closely at two examples of how the early stages in this gradual parting of the ways between Judaism and Christianity helped spawn the notion of the Jew as Christ killer.

## THE GOSPEL ACCORDING TO MATTHEW

First, I turn to the passage from Matthew, which has proven more controversial in this regard than any other in the Passion narratives.

> Pilate said to them, "Then what shall I do with Jesus who is called Christ?" They all said, "Let him be crucified." And he said, "Why, what evil has he done?" But they shouted all the more, "Let him be crucified." So when Pilate saw that he was gaining nothing, but rather that a riot was beginning, he took water and washed his hands before the crowd, saying, "I am innocent of this man's blood; see to it yourselves." And all the people answered, "His blood be on us and on our children!" Then he released for them Barabbas, and having scourged Jesus, delivered him to be crucified. (Matthew 27:22–26)

*His blood be on us and on our children!* Matthew portrays the Jewish crowd as demanding the execution of Jesus, over and against the desire of Pilate to release him. Though the synoptic Gospels generally focus on Jesus' conflict with the Jewish leadership of his day—Pharisees, chief priests, and scribes—and actually tend to cast the crowds of people as supportive of Jesus, here the masses viciously clamor for his blood. The people accept full responsibility for his death, not only on themselves but on their descendants. Contrasted so starkly with Pilate, they demonstrate ever so clearly who are the friends of Christ, and who are his foes.

What sense should one make of this passage? Recall that the Gospel of Matthew dates from the late 70s or early 80s of the first century. In the wake of the Jewish rebellion against Rome (66–70) and the destruction of Jerusalem and the temple (70), social boundaries within the Jewish community were being redrawn, and various groups struggled for power against the background of catastrophic change. Insofar as the loss of Jerusalem and its temple cult shattered the foundations of traditional Jewish life, it also marked a critical turning point in the self-consciousness of early Christianity. Most Jews probably assumed that the disaster expressed the will of God, who had punished his people for forsaking their covenant with him. They sought new leadership and a new understanding of God's purpose that would enable them to cope with their tragedy. As the smoke gradually cleared, the heirs of the Pharisees, soon to become the rabbis of the Talmud, began their rise to power in the Jewish community. But in Christian circles, especially as non-Jewish voices gained prominence in their midst, many concluded that the Jewish refusal to embrace the new belief in the crucified messiah lay at the heart of the matter. As foretold of the messiah by the biblical prophets, Jesus' self-sacrifice on the cross offered salvation to all who would believe in him. The last and greatest of all sin offerings, the Crucifixion rendered the temple and its sacrificial cult essentially pointless.

The destruction of the temple and the rise of the Pharisees-rabbis who rejected belief in Jesus undoubtedly weighed heavily on Jewish Christians in particular, and Matthew spoke most directly to them. On the one hand, they had continued to identify with the Jewish people, its history, its culture, and its national destiny, much as Jesus himself did. On the other hand, developments in Christian beliefs and in Jewish society now challenged such a Jewish self-definition, making it increasingly difficult to bridge the gap between the two communities. Which way were they to turn? From start to finish, Matthew's Gospel addresses their dilemma. It opens by tracing Jesus' ancestry back to the Jewish patriarch Abraham, and not, as Luke's Gospel did, to Adam, the father of all humanity. Its Jesus speaks, prays, reasons, and teaches much like a Jew, even a Pharisee. And yet, having reassured Jewish Christians of their legitimacy in the church, it ends with a clear-cut, emphatic response to their dilemma. As the gospel draws to a close, Jesus revisits and reassures his disciples after his death (Matthew 28:19–20). "Go therefore and make disciples of all nations, baptizing them in the name of the Father and of the Son and of the Holy Spirit, teaching them to observe all that I have commanded you; and lo, I am with you always, to the close of the age." Thus did Matthew instruct Jewish Christians: Jesus himself insisted that they choose between the Jewish community and the increasingly non-Jewish church, opting decisively for the church.

Progressing from Jesus' distinctly Jewish past to the universal aspirations of his church, the Gospel of Matthew thus laid the groundwork for the collective betrayal of Jesus by the nameless crowd of Jews in Jerusalem. In so doing, it hardly testifies to the events of the Jesus' last days, but it portrays those events in expressing its own Christian reality some fifty years later. In Matthew's version of the Beatitudes, Jesus says: "Blessed are you when men revile you and persecute you and utter all kinds of evil against you falsely on my account. Rejoice and be glad, for your reward is great in heaven, for so men persecuted the prophets who were before you" (5:11–12). Like many others, this passage offers a double insight into the nature of the Gospels. First, it blends the contemporary Christian experience of the evangelist with the experience of Jesus himself—in this case the rejection (cast as persecution) of Christianity by the majority of Jews in Matthew's day. As the New Testament scholars of the acclaimed Jesus Seminar concluded some years ago, it is highly unlikely that Jesus himself would have uttered these words.[24] As such, this passage fits well with the indictment of the Jews in the "parable of the vineyard," similarly unsuited to the historical Jesus, when the tenant farmers confront their landlord's son. "When the tenants saw the son, they said to themselves, 'This is the heir; come, let us kill him and have his inheritance.'

And they took him and cast him out of the vineyard, and killed him" (Matthew 21:38–39).[25] Second, Matthew's condemnation of the Jews casts his Christian experience as validated by the ancient biblical tradition that it fulfills—the Israelite people's persecution of its righteous prophets—to which Matthew's Jesus soon returns in his scathing indictment of the Pharisees and scribes.

> You serpents, you brood of vipers, how are you to escape being sentenced to hell? Therefore I send you prophets and wise men and scribes, some of whom you will kill and crucify, and some you will scourge in your synagogues and persecute from town to town, that upon you may come all the righteous blood shed on earth, from the blood of innocent Abel to the blood of Zechariah the son of Barachiah, whom you murdered between the sanctuary and the altar. Truly, I say to you, all this will come upon this generation. O Jerusalem, Jerusalem, killing the prophets and stoning those who are sent to you! How often would I have gathered your children together as a hen gathers her brood under her wings, and you would not! Behold, your house is forsaken and desolate. (Matthew 23:33–38)[26]

Here, too, the desolation of Jerusalem betrays Matthew's historical context, not Jesus'. And the apostles of Jesus that suffer at the hands of the Jews follow in a long line of God's chosen, righteous and prophetic types, who have experienced similar abuse, from Abel to Zechariah to Jesus himself.[27] Though Luke's version of the same speech depicts the Wisdom of God as dispatching prophets and apostles whom the Jews will persecute, Matthew casts the dispatcher as Jesus himself, accentuating his rejection by the Jews further still.

As for the cry of Matthew's Jews, "His blood be on us and on our children," it too teaches nothing about what transpired on the fateful day of Jesus' execution and much about how the Crucifixion became meaningful for the evangelist in his late-first-century Jewish (and Jewish-Christian) context. The Jewish people en masse, much more than Pilate and his Roman subordinates, bore responsibility for killing that very savior whom God had sent to redeem them. These Jews had disowned Jesus, and, inasmuch as their descendants would inherit their guilt, they had effectively disowned themselves of God's favor and their status as his chosen people. Jewish Christians should respond accordingly, transferring their loyalties and their affiliation from the Jewish community to the church. Furthermore, just as the evangelists depicted the Jews' responsibility for the Crucifixion as predicted in Jesus' parable of the vineyard, so was the cry of "His blood be on us and on our children" steeped in the traditions and symbols of Hebrew Scripture. As various scholars have shown, one must recognize Matthew's debt to the biblical notion of "blood-guilt" (for example, in Genesis 9), popular participation in the execution of a blasphemer (Leviticus 24), the acceptance of God's curse of mortal sinners by "the whole people" (Deuteronomy 27), and the ritual of hand washing as an assertion of innocence in the slaying of a guiltless person (Deuteronomy 21). Washing his hands, Pilate declared himself innocent of the shedding of Jesus' blood. The "whole people" refused to follow suit and willfully assumed that bloodguilt themselves.

Matthew's Gospel does not yet reflect a definite and lasting line of demarcation between Jewish and Christian communities. It does not write off the crowd entirely, arriving at the conclusion reached by various Christian theologians in the next century that the entire Jewish people, now and for all time, shared in the guilt for the Crucifixion. Nonetheless, it did sow the seeds for such an understanding, and the greatest of church fathers typically understood Matthew 27:25 as such. At the beginning of the third century, for instance, the North African Tertullian cited "His blood be on us and on our children" as proof of the truth of God's declaration in the Ten Commandments: "I the Lord your God am a jealous God, visiting the iniquity of the fathers upon the children . . . of those who hate me" (Exodus 20:5).[28] Commenting on Matthew in Roman Palestine, Tertullian's contemporary Origen interpreted the verse unequivocally. The Jews had persecuted and killed the prophets, and so, too, did they bear out Isaiah's prophecy: "When you spread forth your hands, I will hide my eyes from you; even though you make many prayers, I will not listen; your hands are full of blood" (Isaiah 1:15). Consequently, Origen concluded, "Guilt for the blood of Jesus fell not only on those who lived then, but also on all subsequent generations of Jews, until the end of the world."[29] Two centuries later, St. Jerome formulated the consensus of the church fathers on this verse and its bearing on the Jews. "The curse has been fulfilled in their eternal damnation: 'His blood be on us and on our children!'"[30]

Finally, the Jewish-Christian context and target of Matthew's message reminds us that precisely the intimacy of the social ties between late-first-century Jews and Christians intensified the anti-Jewish hostility of the Passion narratives. Along these lines, one should take note that the condemnation of the Jews for killing their prophets and even the cry of "His blood be on us and on our children" find echoes in the teachings of the classical rabbis, contemporaries of the evangelists and the church fathers, and not merely in the Hebrew Scriptures to which all Jews and Christians laid claim.[31] As this book progresses, such interdependence of Jewish and Christian traditions will emerge as a noteworthy and recurring theme in the career of the Christ-killer myth.

## THE GOSPEL ACCORDING TO JOHN

Turning from the synoptic Gospels to John, we find that the anti-Judaism evident in the Gospels in general and their Passion narratives in particular intensifies in the Fourth Gospel. Though Mark, Matthew, and Luke portray Jesus in conflict with groups of Jewish leaders (Pharisees, scribes, priests), John portrays an antagonism between Jesus and his followers on one hand and the collective of "the Jews" on the other. This phrase appears more than sixty times in John alone, and only fifteen times in the synoptic Gospels altogether. Of the sixty-two instances in John, twenty-five make reference to the people at large with overtones of hostility; of these, at least six occur in the Passion narrative. More significantly, John repeatedly depicts Jesus, his disciples, and his subsequent followers as distinct from the Jews, contrasting, as it were, between "us" and "them." Twice does the gospel mention "the Passover of the Jews" (2:13, 11:55), as if to suggest that its audience did not consider this Jewish national festival its own. Addressing the Jews directly, just as they seek to stone him for blasphemy, John's Jesus declares:

> Is it not written in your law (Psalm 82:6), "I said, you are gods"? If he called them gods to whom the word of God came (and scripture cannot be broken), do you say of him whom the Father consecrated and sent into the world, "You are blaspheming," because I said, "I am the Son of God"? (10:34–36)

Jesus' distancing of himself from Jewish tradition—*your* law—contrasts sharply with the adamant protest of Jesus in Matthew's Gospel (5:17), "Think not that I have come to abolish the law and the prophets; I have come not to abolish them but to fulfill them." Likewise, John's Jesus warns his disciples that the Jews will persecute them, too, as he condemns the Jews and justifies himself in terms of *their* law:

> If I had not come and spoken to them, they would not have sin; but now they have no excuse for their sin. He who hates me hates my Father also. If I had not done among them the works which no one else did, they would not have sin; but now they have seen and hated both me and my Father. It is to fulfill the word that is written in their law, "They hated me without a cause." (15:22–25)

Indeed, the thread of Jewish hostility toward Jesus runs ominously throughout the Gospel of John. "The Jews persecuted Jesus" (5:16) for desecrating the Sabbath. Soon thereafter, "the Jews sought to kill him" (7:1), and they agreed that "if anyone should confess him to be Christ, he was to be put out of the synagogue" (9:22). Reading on, we find that "the Jews took up stones *again* to stone him" for blasphemy (10:31).

John's Passion narrative follows suit, highlighting the Jewish insistence that Jesus die more than any other Gospel. Having questioned Jesus, after "the Jews" first insisted that "it is not lawful for us to put any man to death" (18:31), Pilate went out to the Jews again, and told them, "I find no crime in him. But you have a custom that I should release one man for you at the Passover; will you have me release for you the King of the Jews?" They cried out again, "Not this man, but Barabbas!" Now Barabbas was a robber. Then Pilate took Jesus and scourged him. And the soldiers plaited a crown of thorns, and put it on his head, and arrayed him in a purple robe; they came up to him, saying, "Hail, King of the Jews!" and struck him with their hands. Pilate went out again, and said to them, "See, I am bringing him out to you, that you may know that I find no crime in him." So Jesus came out, wearing the crown of thorns and the purple robe. Pilate said to them, "Behold the man!" When the chief priests and the officers saw him, they cried out, "Crucify him, crucify him!" Pilate said to them, "Take him yourselves and crucify him, for I find no crime in him." The Jews answered him, "We have a law, and by that law he ought to die, because he has made himself the Son of God." When Pilate heard these words, he was the more afraid; he entered the praetorium again and [questioned Jesus again]. . . . Upon this Pilate sought to release him, but the Jews cried out, "If you release this man, you are not Caesar's friend; every one who makes himself a king sets himself against Caesar." When Pilate heard these words, he brought Jesus out and sat down on the judgment seat at a place called The Pavement, and in Hebrew, Gabbatha. Now it was the day of Preparation of the Passover; it was about the sixth hour. He said to the Jews, "Behold your King!" They cried out, "Away with him, away with him, crucify him!" Pilate said to them, "Shall I crucify your King?" The chief priests answered, "We have no king but Caesar." Then he handed him over to them to be crucified. (John 18:38–19:16)

In John, Pilate protests Jesus' innocence to his Jewish accusers not once (as in the synoptic Gospels) but three times. In each case, they adamantly insist upon his crucifixion. Whereas the synoptic Gospels attribute this murderous insistence to the chief priests, the elders, and "the crowd" (and once, as in Matthew, "all the people"), John repeatedly specifies "the Jews": five times in the verses quoted in this paragraph alone.

The Jews of John's Crucifixion story, cutthroat and unyielding, pose an unusually thorny problem for modern Christian theologians and interpreters of Scripture, especially in our post-Holocaust era. John's can well be termed the most theologically refined, even the most sublime, of the four Gospels. Its Passion narrative constitutes the most powerful presentation of the story underlying the essential beliefs of Christianity. And yet its rendition of that story appears to place the blame for the Crucifixion squarely on the shoulders of "the Jews," whom it characterizes as bloodthirsty, hateful, and determined. No wonder that the question of John's ostensive anti-Judaism or anti-Semitism has engaged New Testament scholars incessantly over the past several decades.

Much discussion has focused on "the Jews" of John's Gospel. Perhaps the evangelist did not use the term to denote the entire Jewish people but rather the people of a particular geographical region. Perhaps he meant some elements within the Jewish community at large considered especially antagonistic by "Johannine" Christians, not yet removed completely from that Jewish community. John's references to Jewish believers in Jesus "being put out of the synagogue"—perhaps an allusion to the curse of heretics (*Birkat ha-Minim*) that found a permanent place in the daily Jewish worship service—certainly support an impression of conflict between opposing Jewish interest groups who vied for power after the Romans' destruction of Jerusalem. Coupled with John's repeated mention of division between Jews who opposed Jesus and other Jews more sympathetic, including some in positions of authority, these references (7:40, 9:16, 10:19, 11:45, 12:42) demonstrate that the process of separation between Christianity and Judaism had hardly finished running its course. Modern readers of John have indeed recognized that accounts of hostility between Jesus and his opponents in their day testify no less—and perhaps much more—directly to the experience of Johannine Christians in theirs. Even then, the conflict between Christians and their Jewish opponents was still very much a conflict that transpired *within* the Jewish community.

These modern insights into John can perhaps allow us to understand how its author harbored such intense animosity toward Jesus' fellow Jews, those whom Jesus had ostensibly come to save. Nevertheless, no efforts to put John's negative portrayal of the Jews into its proper historical context can undo the intensity of the anti-Jewish message that it transmitted to posterity. Once he circulated his gospel, the evangelist surrendered control over its meaning to his readers, and they, interpreting the gospel as they did over the course of many centuries, only sharpened its anti-Jewish implications. The Catholic editors of one very helpful recent collection entitled *Anti-Judaism and the Fourth Gospel*—which contains a broad spectrum of over two dozen scholarly perspectives, and which offers a "select" bibliography of recent scholarly literature on the subject with no less than four hundred entries—formulate the enduring problem with noteworthy candor. They acknowledge that "(a) the Fourth Gospel contains anti-Jewish elements, (b) the anti-Jewish elements are unacceptable from a Christian point of view, and (c) there is no convincing way to simply neutralize or remove the anti-Jewish dimensions of these passages to save the healthy core of the message itself."[32]

The authors of these words acknowledge the need to grapple with John and its anti-Judaism on theological terms, which move off in a direction different from mine in this book. I remain interested in the Christ-killer myth and the course of its historical "career," as Christians and Jews continued to part company, and then thereafter. How did the idea of the Jew as the killer of Christ continue to develop? How did it continue to give expression to the needs and aspirations of Christians as they progressively lost a sense of affiliation with the Jewish people? Yet before one can consider the subsequent history of the Christ-killer myth, it is important to appreciate its precedents in Hebrew Scripture, which Christian teachers appropriated to voice their own particular messages.

## 2

# "IN YOUR BLOOD, LIVE!"

The image of Jesus hanging on the cross highlights much of the divide separating Jews and Christians. Throughout the ages, Jews have typically reacted to the cross with horror, hostility, even disgust. For their part, Christians see in the cross both the foundation and vindication of their faith—defined in opposition to that of the Jews. The Crucifixion sealed the replacement of the old law (Judaism) with the new (Christianity). It substituted faith in Christ for the observance of the biblical commandments. And owing to the Jews' presumed responsibility for the death of Jesus, it led God to disown them as his chosen people, replacing them with a new, spiritual, Christian people of Israel. Asked to explain the difference between Judaism and Christianity, most would probably explain that Christians accept the crucified Jesus as their messiah or Christ, whereas Jews do not.

In the eyes of Jews and Christians, the cross may symbolize a world of difference between them. Yet for those who subscribe neither to Christianity nor to Judaism—and especially for non-Jews and non-Christians during the first Christian century—the two faiths may appear more alike than different. Jesus himself lived and died as a Jew, without ever forsaking his ancestral faith. Those of his followers who laid the foundation stones of Christianity in the aftermath of his death continued to observe the teachings of Judaism and identify with the Jewish people, despite their failure to woo most other Jews to their belief in Jesus as the messiah. Even the apostle Paul, who provided the theological justification for Christianity's departure from the Jewish community, intended to write off the Jews and Judaism much less than many subsequent Christians supposed.

From Jesus to Paul to the writers of Gospels (whether Jewish or not) and even beyond, Christianity came to life in a markedly Jewish setting. We ought not to marvel that when the first Christians gave expression to their deepest feelings and beliefs—even those that eventually differentiated them from Jews—they did so as most first-century Jews would have done: by turning to the Hebrew Scripture to justify and explain them. Christian belief concerning the death of the messiah, the very crux of the Jewish-Christian divide, is charged with earlier language, symbols, and ideas from the Hebrew Bible, which Christians call the Old Testament. The roots of the Christ-killer story, which has extended for two thousand years after Jesus, actually date from long before him. Though the Passion narrative may have roots in other ancient Near Eastern mythologies as well, its precedents in the Hebrew Bible nourish its contents and meaning much more directly, and these precedents deserve our attention above all else.

## THE FATHER'S SACRIFICE OF THE SON

In Christian eyes, the crucifixion of Jesus amounted to God's sacrifice of his beloved son. Although the Hebrew Bible condemns child sacrifice, investigators of biblical religion have debated vigorously over the extent to which such practice may have held sway in ancient Israel. Whether or not Israelites ever did slay their children as offerings to the biblical God or some pagan deity, the theme of "the death and resurrection of the beloved son," as one writer has termed it, figures significantly in Hebrew Scripture and in the biblical civilization that it spawned. One certainly finds the idea in the story of Jephtha and his sacrifice of his own daughter. But above all else, the story of the Akedah, the binding of Isaac, has dominated the biblical religious imagination from ancient to modern times, with countless echoes in works of philosophy, art (fig. 2.1), and literature, among Jews, Christians, and Muslims.

The Bible relates that after many years of childlessness, Sarah, wife of the Hebrew patriarch Abraham, finally bore him a son, Isaac. Sarah was then ninety years old, and Abraham was one hundred. At long last, Abraham had an heir through whom God's lavish promises of a glorious destiny could extend to future generations. Soon thereafter, we read of Abraham's last major trial.

> After these things God tested Abraham, and said to him, "Abraham!" And he said, "Here am I." He said, "Take your son, your only son Isaac, whom you love, and go to the land of Moriah, and offer him there as a burnt offering upon one of the mountains of which I shall tell you." (Genesis 22:1–2)

Abraham set off in compliance with God's command and three days later prepared to sacrifice his son.

> When they came to the place of which God had told him, Abraham built an altar there, and laid the wood in order, and bound Isaac his son, and laid him on the altar, upon the wood. Then Abraham put forth his hand, and took the knife to slay his son. But the angel of the Lord called to him from heaven, and said, "Abraham, Abraham!" And he said, "Here am I." He said, "Do not lay your hand on the lad or do anything to him; for now I know that you fear God, seeing you have not withheld your son, your only son, from me." (Genesis 22:9–12)

**FIGURE 2.1.** Peter Paul Rubens (1577–1640), *The Sacrifice of Isaac*. The Nelson Atkins Museum of Art, Kansas City, Missouri (Purchase: Nelson Trust) 66–3. Photo by Jamison Miller.

Abraham then found a ram to sacrifice in place of Isaac, after which God's angel called out to him a second time:

> By myself I have sworn, says the Lord, because you have done this, and have not withheld your son, your only son, I will indeed bless you, and I will multiply your descendants as the stars of heaven and

as the sand which is on the seashore. And your descendants shall
possess the gate of their enemies, and by your descendants shall all
the nations of the earth bless themselves, because you have obeyed
my voice." (Genesis 22:16–18)

Can we relate Abraham's near sacrifice of Isaac in the Hebrew Bible to
the death of Jesus in the New Testament? Here we must proceed very cautiously. On the one hand, the Genesis story resounds with ideas essential to
Christian understanding of the Crucifixion: it highlights the dynamic of the
relationship between father and beloved son, underscoring the enormity of
the sacrifice. It emphasizes the divine purpose underlying the call to sacrifice.
It presents the offering of the son as a cultic ritual, complete with altar, wood,
fire, and sacrificial knife, thus suggesting that the ram that died in Isaac's place
somehow substituted for the son. It depicts the sacrifice of the son as the ultimate expression of faith and devotion. And it establishes that the merit of
this act of faith will allow for the ultimate victory and vindication of the
father's descendants.

On the other hand, all this does not prove that the Crucifixion story
*consciously* draws on the Akedah. Despite allusions to Isaac as an exemplary
martyr in several other first-century Jewish texts—the Fourth Book of the
Maccabees and Josephus's *Jewish Antiquities,* for instance—they hardly suffice to explain how some first-century Jews could conceive of their God as
having sacrificed his son and messiah. Although quotations from Hebrew
Scripture abound in the New Testament, allusions to the Akedah are few, far
between, and questionable. And crucial elements of the Passion narratives have
no echo in the binding of Isaac.

Still, we can move ahead with care. Just as this book will seek not to
reconstruct the actual events of Jesus' last days but rather to track the story
of the Crucifixion over the course of centuries, so, too, can we appreciate that
the Akedah contributed to that story even after the accounts of Jesus' death
had taken shape. New Testament writers may have avoided reference to the
binding of Isaac, but, beginning in the second century, the fathers of the church
interpreted the story of Genesis 22 as an unmistakable, very meaningful forecast of the Passion. Among the earliest surviving Christian texts outside the
canon of the New Testament, the *Epistle of Barnabas* declares that God re-
solved "to offer the vessel of the spirit as a sacrifice for our sins, in order that
the type established in Isaac, who was offered upon the altar, might be fulfilled."[1] For the fathers of the church, this correspondence between the Crucifixion and Akedah extended both to him who offered the sacrifice (the father)
and to the sacrificial victim (the son). Later in the second century, Irenaeus of
Lyon wrote that "Abraham, according to his faith, followed the command
of the word of God, and with a ready mind delivered up, as a sacrifice to

God, his only-begotten and beloved son, in order that God also might be pleased to offer up for all his seed his own beloved and only-begotten son, as a sacrifice for our redemption."[2] And the North African church father Tertullian, reflecting on the selflessness of Jesus' martyrdom, concluded that "Isaac, when led by his father as a victim, and himself bearing his own wood, was even at that early period pointing to Christ's death; offered, as he was, as a victim by the father; carrying, as he did, the wood of his own passion."[3]

At the same time as they presented the bound Isaac as a historical *type* or precedent for the crucified Jesus, however, early Christian writers argued no less emphatically that just as the New Testament replaces and surpasses the Old, so did the excellence of Jesus outstrip that of Isaac. The biblical Isaac never died on the altar. Neither Abraham the father nor Isaac his son in fact made the ultimate sacrifice, whereas God the father and his son Jesus did. As Clement of Alexandria elaborated, Isaac "is a *type* of the Lord, a child as a son; for he was the son of Abraham, as Christ the son of God, and a sacrifice as the Lord. *But he was not immolated as the Lord. Isaac only bore the wood of the sacrifice, as the Lord the wood of the cross....* Isaac did everything but suffer, as was right, yielding the precedence in suffering to the Word."[4] Melito of Sardis vigorously concurred: "Christ suffered, whereas Isaac did not suffer; for he was a model of the Christ who was going to suffer."[5] Curiously, in their interest to reserve this status of the sacrificed son exclusively for Jesus, some of the later church fathers moved on to protest the correspondence between Isaac and the Christ altogether. The great fourth-century theologian Athanasius of Alexandria found an entirely different biblical *type* for God's crucified son: not Isaac "was sacrificed, but He who was pointed out in Isaiah; 'He shall be led as a lamb to the slaughter.'"[6] (We shall return below to this alternative precedent for the Crucifixion in Hebrew Scripture.)

During these first Christian centuries, at the same time as the church fathers linked the Akedah and the Passion story, Jewish scholars reread the binding of Isaac in a strikingly similar fashion. As the rabbis of the Talmud pondered the biblical tale, they too stressed the sacrifice of Isaac the son no less, at times even more, than that of Abraham the father. They construed Isaac as the religious martyr par excellence. In him they found the prototype of the lamb of God that for centuries had been sacrificed daily at the temple in Jerusalem until the Romans destroyed it some forty years after Jesus' Crucifixion. As one of the Targums (the Jewish translations of the Bible into Aramaic) considered a list of newborn animals that the book of Leviticus deemed acceptable for sacrifice (oxen, sheep, and goats), it explained that "the lamb was chosen to recall the merit of the lamb of Abraham, who bound himself upon the altar and stretched out his neck for your name's sake."[7] Like the offerings at the temple, Abraham's sacrifice of his son atoned for the sins of his Israelite descendants. Understandably, the "merit of the fathers" generated by the Akedah has figured prominently in the prayers for Rosh Hashanah and Yom Kippur, the Jewish high holy days or "days of awe," when worshipers seek vindication and forgiveness for their sins in the face of divine judgment. To this day, the traditional liturgy implores God, "May you on this day mercifully remember the binding of Isaac in favor of his descendants."[8]

More important still, postbiblical Jewish traditions about the Akedah relate the sacrifice of Isaac to the Jewish Passover festival, which commemorates God's redemption of the biblical Israelites from slavery in Egypt and looks forward to the final messianic redemption on the same model. Some early rabbinic sources teach that Isaac was both born and bound during the Hebrew month of Nissan, the month of the Passover. The Targum of the Land of Israel offers a fascinating homily on the biblical verse that recounts the miraculous salvation of the Israelites on the night of the Passover: "It was a night of watching by the Lord, to bring them out of the land of Egypt; so this same night is a night of watching kept to the Lord by all the people of Israel throughout their generations" (Exodus 12:42).

> Four nights are there written in the Book of Memorial. The first night, when the Word of the Lord was revealed upon the world as it was created. . . . The second night, when the Word of the Lord was revealed unto Abraham. . . . Was not our father Isaac thirty-seven years old at the time he was offered upon the altar? The heavens were (then) bowed down and brought low, and Isaac saw their perfections, and his eyes were blinded at the sight, and he called it the second night. The third night, when the Word of the Lord was revealed upon the Egyptians . . . ; His right hand slew the firstborn of the Egyptians, and His right hand spared the firstborn of Israel. . . . The fourth night, when the end of the age will be accomplished, that it might be dissolved, the bands of wickedness destroyed, and the iron yoke broken.[9]

According to this midrash, four major historical events chart God's plan for the history and salvation of the world: the Creation, the Akedah, the Exodus, and the final messianic redemption. The significance of Isaac's sacrifice was cosmic indeed, ranking alongside the major instances of divinely wrought salvation in human history, both past and future.

Contrary to the simple meaning of the Bible, rabbinic tradition dared to suggest that Abraham actually completed the sacrifice of his son, slaying Isaac upon the altar on Mount Moriah. According to the biblical story, God commanded Moses and the Israelites to sacrifice a lamb on the night of their liberation from Egypt, and to smear the lamb's blood on their doorposts. When God would set out to slay all of the firstborn in Egypt, the sight of blood in the doorways of the Israelites would lead him to spare their children. What would God see in the blood that would induce him to save them? The *Mekhilta of Rabbi Ishmael*, a third-century collection of rabbinic homilies on the Book of Exodus, understood God to mean that he would spare the Israelites when "I see the blood of the sacrifice of Isaac."[10] As we have seen, the merit of the Akedah served Abraham's children well, but was Isaac's blood in fact shed? Some creative rabbinic preachers might well have understood "the blood of the sacrifice of Isaac" to mean the blood of the ram that substituted for the bound Isaac, or perhaps that Abraham had drawn blood from his son before the angel of God had intervened to save him. Yet other rabbinic voices soon chimed in more boldly, referring to the ashes of Isaac that remained on the altar. For these rabbis, little doubt remained that Isaac had suffered and had been slaughtered.[11]

Can we make sense of these Christian and Jewish interpretations of the Akedah, which date from the same period of the first four or five centuries? On the one hand, they proceed in parallel directions: Focusing on the sacrificed son no less than the sacrificing father, they portray Isaac as the exemplary victim, the sacrificial lamb of God, a martyr whose truly pious and selfless self-sacrifice enables God's faithful to receive forgiveness and salvation. On the other hand, they also seem to reflect an ancient Jewish-Christian rivalry over who has "title" to the genuine, ultimate Akedah. Christians viewed the crucifixion of Jesus as a refined, more perfect sacrifice of the son by his father, inasmuch as Jesus suffered and died, whereas Isaac did not. It was the gift of Jesus' sacrifice that brought forgiveness, expiation, and salvation for those who would acknowledge the power of the cross. For their part, Jews reread the Akedah as a perfect sin offering, complete with the blood and ashes of the victim, a sacrifice that yielded merit and atonement for the children of Abraham. Modern scholars at times appear to resurrect this rivalry, hotly debating the origin of the distinctive spirituality and theology of the Akedah: Was it Christianity in response to the Crucifixion, or Judaism independently of the Crucifixion, perhaps even prior to it? Did the death of Jesus bequeath its fascination with the binding of Isaac to Western civilization, a fascination that has exercised the minds of modern thinkers no less than those of the church fathers and classical rabbis? Or did Christianity's Jewish roots include a model of a holy father sacrificing his guiltless son that underlies the belief in the crucified messiah? In a word, who had it first?

The answer to this question need not preoccupy us. Rather, the interpretation of the Akedah among the church fathers and the rabbis of the Talmud suggests a pattern that will manifest itself at numerous points throughout this book. Judaism and Christianity have always had a great deal in common. Precisely for that reason, the parting of their ways generated friction, competition, and outright animosity. It is ironic but sadly true that although both faiths treasured beliefs concerning the father's sacrifice of the son, these very traditions gave expression to the deepest hostilities between them.

## THE LAMB OF GOD

The connections between the Akedah and Passover lead us to another, perhaps even more significant building block for the Crucifixion story in Hebrew Scripture: the paschal lamb, which, as we have noted, God instructed Moses and his fellow Israelites in Egypt to sacrifice in preparation for their redemption from slavery.

> They shall take every man a lamb according to their fathers' houses, a lamb for a household. . . . Your lamb shall be without blemish . . . , and you shall keep it until the fourteenth day of this month, when the whole assembly of the congregation of Israel shall kill their lambs in the evening. Then they shall take some of the blood, and put it on the two doorposts and the lintel of the houses in which they eat them. They shall eat the flesh that night, roasted; with unleavened bread and bitter herbs they shall eat it. . . . For I will pass through the land of Egypt that night, and I will smite all the first-born in the land of Egypt, both man and beast; and on all the gods of Egypt I will execute judgments: I am the Lord. The blood shall be a sign for you, upon the houses where you are; and when I see the blood, I will pass over you, and no plague shall fall upon you to destroy you, when I smite the land of Egypt. This day shall be for you a memorial day, and you shall keep it as a feast to the Lord; throughout your generations you shall observe it as an ordinance forever. (Exodus 12:5–14)

Moses proceeded to relay God's instructions to his people.

> Select lambs for yourselves according to your families, and kill the paschal lamb. Take a bunch of hyssop and dip it in the blood which is in the basin, and touch the lintel and the two doorposts with the blood which is in the basin; and none of you shall go out of the door of his house until the morning. For the Lord will pass through to slay the Egyptians; and when he sees the blood on the lintel and on the two doorposts, the Lord will pass over the door, and will not allow the destroyer to enter your houses to slay you. You shall observe this rite as an ordinance for you and for your sons for ever. (Exodus 12:21–23)

Finally, God prescribed for the continued observance of this ritual in generations to come:

This is the ordinance of the paschal lamb: no foreigner shall eat of it; but every slave that is bought for money may eat of it after you have circumcised him. No sojourner or hired servant may eat of it. In one house shall it be eaten; you shall not carry forth any of the flesh outside the house; and you shall not break a bone of it. (Exodus 12:43–46)

This chapter in Exodus constitutes the biblical foundation for the seder night, when Jews to this day open the Passover festival with a highly ritualized banquet commemorating their ancestors' redemption from slavery. Much has changed since the days of animal sacrifice in the temple, and the recitation of the Passover Haggadah, relating the story of the Exodus, has since replaced the sacrifice of the paschal lamb which the biblical Israelites reportedly revived once they entered the Promised Land. And yet, the significance of the Passover night has remained largely intact. The Bible considered participation in the paschal sacrifice a fundamental requirement for membership in the Israelite community. We can see in the passage above that, as a rule, extended families offered and ate the paschal lamb as a group, not individuals on their own. Even today, perhaps more Jewish families, from the ultra-orthodox to the most avowedly secular, participate in a Passover seder than in any other religious observance (with the possible exception of ritual circumcision). Many do not even understand why it is so important to them. Furthermore, the Passover celebration—whether that of the sacrifice or that of seder with its reading of the Haggadah—serves not only to remember past events but also to instill a sense of inclusion and participation in them. The talmudic teaching that "in every generation a person must see himself as if he himself left Egypt" rings loud and clear for those at the seder table,[12] whose elaborate rituals re-create the experience of the Exodus. The Passover extends salvation not only to Israelites of old, but to all who come to relive these past events by symbolically participating in them and internalizing their meaning.

Christians often refer to Jesus as Agnus Dei, the Lamb of God, because the founders of Christianity understood the Crucifixion as their messiah's fulfillment of the ancient Passover sacrifice. Adapting the imagery of the matzah, the unleavened bread of the Passover holiday, the apostle Paul preached to his flock of new Christian believers (1 Corinthians 5:7), "Cleanse out the old leaven that you may be a new lump, as you really are unleavened. For Christ, our paschal lamb, has been sacrificed." In the Gospels of Matthew, Mark, and Luke (the synoptic Gospels), Jesus was crucified on the first day of the Passover, in the Gospel of John on the previous day, when the Jews prepared and then sacrificed the paschal lamb in the temple. All four Gospels depict the Last Supper with mention of the Passover. In the opening chapter of John's Gospel, John the Baptist calls Jesus the Lamb of God, and the comparison makes its mark on the entire book, through the description of the Crucifixion when Jesus' bones, unlike those of the two thieves crucified beside him, were not broken. "For these things took place that the scripture might be fulfilled, 'Not a bone of him shall be broken'" (John 19:36).

The New Testament clearly portrays Jesus as a paschal lamb, but why? Why does the Passover figure so prominently in Christians' understanding of the crucified Christ? On a historical level, perhaps because the physical process of crucifixion resembled that of sacrificing the paschal lamb. Discussing the Old Testament practices that found fulfillment in Christianity, the second-century church father Justin Martyr related how

> that lamb which was commanded to be wholly roasted was a symbol of the suffering of the cross which Christ would undergo. For the lamb, which is roasted, is roasted and dressed up in the form of the cross. For one spit is transfixed right through from the lower parts up to the head, and one across the back, to which are attached the legs of the lamb.[13]

The Samaritans living in Israel sacrifice a paschal lamb to this day, and twentieth-century photographs of their ritual suggest a striking similarity to crucifixion (fig. 2.2).

Yet the comparison between the Passover and the Crucifixion extends far, far deeper. Just as the paschal lamb substituted for the children of Israel, such that the lamb's blood ensured their salvation and liberation when God wrought destruction upon the Egyptians of old, so did the crucified Jesus redeem those who numbered among Christianity's new Israel of the spirit. "You know that you were ransomed from the futile ways inherited from your fathers, not with perishable things such as silver or gold, but with the precious blood of Christ, like that of a lamb without blemish or spot" (1 Peter 1:18–19). The Israelites freed from their Egyptian slavery experienced a rebirth of sorts, making their way out of the amniotic-like waters of the Red Sea, through the reeds that surrounded it, and into a new, pristine life of service to God alone. So, too, did the cross liberate the Christian from enslavement to the law and to sin, allowing for rebirth into a life of genuine freedom. Just as the rabbis of the Talmud called upon Jews of all generations to reexperience the Passover and participate in its redemption themselves, so did Paul encourage others to follow his example, to participate in Jesus' self-sacrifice, and thus to die to and be born again.

> For I through the law died to the law, that I might live to God. I have been crucified with Christ; it is no longer I who live, but Christ who lives in me; and the life I now live in the flesh I live by faith in the Son of God, who loved me and gave himself for me. (Galatians 2:19–20)

FIGURE 2.2. The Samaritan Passover Sacrifice, reprinted from Joachim Jeremias, *Die Passahfeier der Samaritaner*. Beiheft 54 of *Zeitschrift fur die alttestamentliche Wissenschaft* (1932), pl. 33. Courtesy of Walter de Gruyter GMBH & Co.

And just as Jews from biblical antiquity to the present have deemed observance of the Passover a critically important sign of identification with the Jewish people, so does Christian commemoration of the Crucifixion celebrate "a redemption that is not only remembered, but appropriated afresh by all who celebrate the feast, from generation to generation."[14] Or, in Paul's words, faith in the crucified Christ and the power of the cross is the litmus test for membership in the new covenant as opposed to the old.

> For the word of the cross is folly to those who are perishing, but to us who are being saved it is the power of God. . . . Jews demand signs and Greeks seek wisdom, but we preach Christ crucified, a stumbling block to Jews and folly to Gentiles. (1 Corinthians 1:18–23)

The stark contrast between old covenant and new in Christian teaching, together with the role of the cross in marking the transition from one to the other, contributed to the Christian "typecasting" of the Jew as killers to Christ. But let us focus for the moment on one particular dimension to the Passover that figures in both Judaism and Christianity and that must therefore figure in our reading of the Crucifixion story. Laying the groundwork for the Exodus, the Bible describes the episode of the burning bush, in which

God prevailed upon Moses to represent him before Pharaoh and to lead the Israelites out of Egypt. Acceding to the divine command and bidding farewell to his father-in-law, Jethro, in Midian,

> Moses took his wife and his sons and set them on an ass, and went back to the land of Egypt; and in his hand Moses took the rod of God. And the Lord said to Moses, "When you go back to Egypt, see that you do before Pharaoh all the miracles which I have put in your power; but I will harden his heart, so that he will not let the people go. And you shall say to Pharaoh, 'Thus says the Lord, Israel is my first-born son, and I say to you, Let my son go that he may serve me; if you refuse to let him go, behold, I will slay your first-born son.'" At a lodging place on the way the Lord met him and sought to kill him. Then Zipporah took a flint and cut off her son's foreskin, and touched his legs with it, and said, "Surely you are a bridegroom of blood to me!" So he let him alone. (Exodus 4:20–26)

For thousands of years, readers of Scripture have struggled to make sense of this baffling biblical scene. As for the plain meaning of the tale, many have wondered what really happened at this unnamed lodging place. Whom did God seek to kill, and why? Whose legs did Zipporah, Moses' wife, touch with the bloody foreskin, Moses' or those of her circumcised son? In either case, what did she do, throw the foreskin at his feet or, as many have suggested, smear the blood on his genitals? And, on a deeper level, why does the Bible relate this occurrence precisely at this point in the narrative of the Exodus? These questions and others have yielded nearly endless possibilities for understanding this text, and, as is so often the case, such a wide range of interpretations suggests that the text in question defies any simple explanation. Furthermore, one need not marvel if a story like this one intrigues different sorts of readers, and not simply the usual community of biblical scholars. As one scholar has proposed, a Freudian psychoanalyst would hardly be amazed were a patient to have an Oedipal dream of God trying to kill his father, such that his mother cut off the end of his penis to save his father's life and announced to father and son alike, "You are my bridegroom."[15] Among all these issues, our chief concern lies with the connection between this strange episode of circumcision and the developing account of the Exodus. This tale of circumcision and the wondrous effect of its blood (in Exodus 4) comes on the heels of God's prediction to Moses that he will slay the sons of Egypt. It clearly anticipates the passage concerning the Passover sacrifice (in Exodus 12) with which we opened this section. In each case, God undertakes to smite male children, and in each case a ritual that results in the letting of blood—circumcision or the sacrifice of the paschal lamb— serves to save its participants from destruction. Both passages refer to the application of the blood: that of the foreskin to the legs of him who was endangered, that of the paschal lamb to the doorways of the Israelites in Egypt. In either case, the same Hebrew verb root defines the act of smearing the blood. Moses' wife "touched (*va-taga‘*) his legs" with the foreskin, sealing a covenant of blood, while the Israelites in Egypt were to "touch (*ve-higa‘tem*) the lintel and the two doorposts with the blood" of the lamb, ensuring their salvation at the hands of God. Although I have seen this mentioned in no biblical commentary, I believe that on a symbolic level the doorposts and lintels of the Israelites may also correspond directly to the legs and genitals of Moses (and/or his son), especially in view of the phallic/genital significance of the doorway in Freudian dream symbolism.

The correspondence between circumcision and the Passover sacrifice and the centrally important role of blood in either case were not lost on those who molded Jewish and Christian traditions. Hebrew Scripture itself links the two explicitly. The initial instructions for the Passover sacrifice that we encountered above specified that "no foreigner shall eat of it," where the word for foreign (*‘arel*) literally means uncircumcised. Scripture recounts that when the Israelites finally completed their forty years of wandering in the wilderness and entered the Promised Land, Joshua supervised the circumcision of all the males born in the wilderness, and only then could they reinstitute the celebration of the Passover. Just as circumcision and sacrificing the paschal lamb both entailed the letting of blood, both signified membership in the community of the divine covenant, in God's chosen people. The Bible imposes the identical punishment on those who fail to fulfill these two essential religious obligations. When God first instructed Abraham to circumcise himself and his offspring, he concluded (Genesis 17:14), "Any uncircumcised male who is not circumcised in the flesh of his foreskin *shall be cut off from his people*; he has broken my covenant." And not only must the uncircumcised not participate in the offering of the paschal lamb, but an Israelite otherwise capable of celebrating the Passover who fails to do so likewise "shall be cut off from his people" (Numbers 9:13). Curiously, among all of its "positive" ("thou shalt"), ritual commandments, biblical law imposes this severe punishment of *karet*, of being "cut off" from the community, for failure to observe these two precepts alone.

Rabbinic tradition develops the connection between the blood of circumcision and the blood of the paschal lamb further still. We have already quoted the midrashic compendium of the *Mekhilta*, in which the rabbis suggested that the blood of the paschal lamb in Egypt evoked memories the blood of the Akedah and salvation that it ensured for Abraham's descendants. The same anthology offers an alternative explanation of the merit that allowed for the redemption of the Israelites from Egypt.

> The time had arrived for the fulfillment of the oath which the holy one, blessed be he, had sworn to Abraham, to deliver his children. But as yet they had no religious duties to perform by which to merit redemption. . . . Therefore the holy one, blessed be he, assigned them two duties, the duty of the paschal sacrifice and the duty of circumcision.[16]

The midrash then supports its proposition by quoting the biblical prophet Ezekiel (16:6), who compared God's ultimate redemption of Israel to a marriage with a young maiden, first rescued in her infancy, and still covered with the blood of her own childbirth. "And when I passed by you, and saw you wallowing in your blood, I said to you: In your blood, live; indeed, I said to you: In your blood, live."[17] Since the Hebrew word for "your blood" is actually in the plural (*damayikh*, literally "your bloods"), the midrash could reason that when God saw the blood on the Israelite doorways in Egypt, he saw both bloods: that of circumcision and that of the paschal lamb. Both allowed for the salvation of Israel.

But the rabbis did not stop there. For Ezekiel's prophecy repeated the phrase "in your blood, live," and the Bible, they believed, never repeated itself without a reason. Why mention these two bloods *twice*? As a later midrash posed the question,

> What could Scripture have intended when it wrote, "in your blood, live," two times? It must be that God said, "By the merit of the blood of the covenant of circumcision and the blood of the paschal lamb I will redeem you from Egypt. On account of their merit you will be saved at the end of days." That is why it says, "in your blood, live," twice.[18]

Not only did the blood of circumcision and the blood of the Passover lamb enable the Exodus of old, but they would also facilitate the messianic redemption yet to come. To this day, traditional Jews recite this verse from Ezekiel at the ritual circumcision ceremony and at the Passover seder. Recalling God's salvation of their ancestors, they look forward to their own salvation yet to come.

*In your blood, live.* Just as the Hebrew Bible considered circumcision and participation in the Passover essential requirements for membership in the Israelite community, so did early Christianity emphasize that the crucified Christ had somehow embodied and replaced them both. As we have seen, Paul wrote in Galatians that "if you receive circumcision, Christ will be of no advantage to you," for the new covenant had replaced the old; and in Corinthians that "Christ, our paschal lamb, has been sacrificed." Moreover, just as Jews have consistently found the rituals of circumcision and the Passover essential and uplifting in ways they find difficult to rationalize, so has

Christianity institutionalized the celebration of Jesus' Crucifixion. For Catholics at least, the wine and Host of the sacrament *become* the blood and body of the sacrificed Christ at Eucharist, and those who partake of the sacrament experience the saving power of the cross.

For Jews and Christians alike, at the deepest levels of biblical religion, the key to salvation somehow lies rooted in the mysteries of the sacrifice of blood. In this sense, too, biblical Judaism had laid the groundwork for Christianity's Crucifixion story long before the birth and death of Jesus.

## THE SUFFERING SERVANT OF THE LORD

Beyond the father's sacrifice of his son and the slaughter of the lamb of God, whose blood has the power to save, the Crucifixion story depicts the suffering and death of God's trusted servant—afflicted, abused, and tortured by his compatriots so as to atone for the sins of others. Here, too, Hebrew Scripture laid the groundwork for the Passion narratives of the New Testament, and we turn briefly to two of its most telling contributions.

### THE SERVANT POEMS OF SECOND ISAIAH

Four passages in the second part of the book of Isaiah (42:1–4, 49:1–6, 50:4–11, 52:13–53:12) sing the praises of God's servant and stand out from the other prophecies around them. The fourth and best known is most important for us.

> Behold, my servant shall prosper, he shall be exalted and lifted up, and shall be very high. . . . Surely he has borne our griefs and carried our sorrows; yet we esteemed him stricken, smitten by God, and afflicted. But he was wounded for our transgressions, he was bruised for our iniquities; upon him was the chastisement that made us whole, and with his stripes we are healed. All we like sheep have gone astray; we have turned every one to his own way; and the Lord has laid on him the iniquity of us all. He was oppressed, and he was afflicted, yet he opened not his mouth; like a lamb that is led to the slaughter, and like a sheep that before its shearers is dumb, so he opened not his mouth. By oppression and judgment he was taken away; and as for his generation, who considered that he was cut off out of the land of the living, stricken for the transgression of my people? And they made his grave with the wicked and with a rich man in his death, although he had done no violence, and there was no deceit in his mouth. Yet it was the will of the Lord to bruise him; he has put him to grief; when he makes himself an offering for sin, he shall see his offspring, he shall prolong his days; the will of the Lord shall prosper

in his hand; he shall see the fruit of the travail of his soul and be satisfied; by his knowledge shall the righteous one, my servant, make many to be accounted righteous; and he shall bear their iniquities. Therefore I will divide him a portion with the great, and he shall divide the spoil with the strong; because he poured out his soul to death, and was numbered with the transgressors; yet he bore the sin of many, and made intercession for the transgressors.

Once again, many of the questions that this passage has raised for biblical commentators need not concern us at the moment: the identity of the servant (perhaps the prophet, the people of Israel, or some messianic figure), the precise functions of the servant, and the place of these four poems in Isaiah. More urgent is whether this passage laid the groundwork for Christian understanding of Jesus' death.

The correspondence between Isaiah's servant and Christianity's crucified messiah is striking. Exalted destiny notwithstanding, the servant suffers and dies a miserable death and, bearing their guilt, makes many others "to be accounted righteous." He is maltreated, pierced, wounded, arrested, sentenced, led away like a sheep to the slaughter, and stricken to death among felons. The description fits so neatly that this passage served Christian disputants well throughout centuries of debates with Jews. Clearly, they argued, the Hebrew Bible forecasts the Crucifixion, and, in this particular case, Jews often felt hard-pressed to respond.

Not a few New Testament passages echo these verses of Isaiah 53. Among Jesus' miracles reported in Matthew (8:17), for instance, was that he freed many souls of the demons possessing them "to fulfill what was spoken by the prophet Isaiah, 'He took our infirmities and bore our diseases.'" Luke (22:37) depicts Jesus himself as instructing his disciples, "For I tell you that this scripture must be fulfilled in me, 'And he was reckoned with transgressors.'" And in Acts (8:26–33), God directed the disciple Philip to meet an Ethiopian eunuch, who, as Philip arrived, was reading Isaiah's description of the servant "as a sheep led to the slaughter." Philip then instructed him as to the verses' real meaning.

Did Jews construe Isaiah's suffering servant as a prototype of their messiah before the birth of Christianity? Very possibly. Scholars have recently found evidence in the Dead Sea Scrolls for such messianic expectations during the century before Jesus, and even for individuals believed to be the messiah along these same lines. Some investigators have weighed the influence of the suffering servant on the appreciation of the Akedah in rabbinic sources, arguing that it nourished the notion of Isaac's martyrdom and its power of atonement. Whether or not this occurred, the fact remains that the first Christians looked back at Jesus through the prism of the servant, whose miserable death cast pallor on Jewish-Christian relations for many centuries thereafter.

## The Psalm of "The Hind of the Dawn"

This chapter cannot draw to a close without quoting the following verses from Psalm 22 (1–18):

> My God, my God, why hast thou forsaken me? Why art thou so far from helping me, from the words of my groaning? O my God, I cry by day, but thou dost not answer; and by night, but find no rest. But I am a worm, and no man; scorned by men, and despised by the people. All who see me mock at me, they make mouths at me, they wag their heads; "He committed his cause to the Lord; let him deliver him, let him rescue him, for he delights in him . . . !" Many bulls encompass me, strong bulls of Bashan surround me; they open wide their mouths at me, like a ravening and roaring lion. I am poured out like water, and all my bones are out of joint; my heart is like wax, it is melted within my breast; my strength is dried up like a potsherd, and my tongue cleaves to my jaws; thou dost lay me in the dust of death. Yea, dogs are round about me; a company of evildoers encircle me; they have pierced my hands and feet—I can count all my bones—they stare and gloat over me; they divide my garments among them, and for my raiment they cast lots.

Here, too, God's servant suffers a miserable death at the hands of his enemies. They encircle him like dogs, mock him viciously, refuse to quench his unbearable thirst, pierce his hands and legs, and cast lots for his clothing. The similarities between this scene and that of Jesus' Passion are unmistakable. No wonder that this psalm provided Jesus' renowned lament from the cross (Mark 15:34), "My God, my God, why hast thou forsaken me?"

How ought the modern reader to appreciate the debt of the Crucifixion story to these various precedents from within Hebrew Scripture? On the one hand, such precedents anchor the Crucifixion story firmly in Jewish tradition—not only in its symbolism and literary devices but also in its conscious theological appeal to the religion of Israel. On the other hand, the Passion's debt to Hebrew Scripture speaks to its character as a myth—that is, a *story* imbued with cosmic significance and religious meaning rather than a factually accurate or journalistic reporting of historical events. The Akedah, the Passover sacrifice, the suffering servant, and psalm of "the hind of the dawn" all bear on the question posed by John Dominic Crossan in his reading of the Crucifixion story: Does it constitute *history remembered* or *prophecy historicized*? As we follow the career of the Jewish Christ killer from the Gospels up until our own day, this question and its implications must remain uppermost in our minds.

# 3

# "YOU KILLED YOUR LORD"

Even before the Gospels appeared, the apostle Paul (or, more probably, one of his disciples) portrayed the Jews as Christ's killers and as foes of the true faith. Commiserating with his Christian followers in Thessalonia, he compared their suffering in their own country with the suffering that Christians in Judea had endured "from the Jews, who killed both the Lord Jesus and the prophets" (1 Thessalonians 2:14–15). In a similar vein, the Acts of the Apostles, written by the author of Luke's Gospel, repeatedly turned to the Jews and reproached them for having "crucified and killed" Jesus, their Lord and messiah (Acts 2:23, 2:36, 4:10, 4:27, 5:30, 10:39, 13:27–28). But though the New Testament clearly looks to the Jews as responsible for the death of Jesus, Paul and the evangelists did not yet condemn all Jews, by the very fact of their Jewishness, as murderers of God and his messiah. That condemnation, however, was soon to come.

Our story thus moves on from the first century to the second. Christian and Jewish communities continued to separate and distinguish themselves from one other. Simultaneously, the four Gospels with their Passion narratives gradually came to enjoy the official, "canonical" status of Holy Scripture in most Christian churches. They now provided the prism through which Christians viewed their relationship with Jesus Christ, molding a belief in the saving power of the cross on which he died. And they bequeathed to the next generations of Christians an image of the Jew as the murderous enemy of their savior, which helped to explain how and why they had come to replace the Jews as God's beloved, chosen people.

Although the parting of the ways was not yet complete, by the middle of the second century, it was clear that Gentile Christianity was here to stay, situated often *alongside* but no longer *within* the Jewish community. Now that the newly born religion had proven viable, the apostolic phase in the history of Christianity gave way to that of the church fathers, the patristic period, usually understood as extending from the second to the seventh centuries. The apostles of Christianity had already proclaimed the "good news" of salvation in Christ. As they continued to preach that message and win new souls for the faith, Christian leaders now sought to systematize their theology, to provide organization and lasting structure to their churches, to regulate the behavior and religious practice of believers and clergy, and to struggle against the empire of Rome—a struggle in which Christianity ultimately triumphed. How did the fathers of the church contribute to the role of the Jew in the Crucifixion story? Conversely, what did the image of the Jews as Christ killer do for them?

Having canonized the gospel accounts of Jewish responsibility for the Crucifixion, church fathers labeled the Jew—any and every Jew—as killer of Christ and hence as deicide. Intent upon defining Christianity with greater precision, they identified Christians and their New Testament by contrasting them with the Jewish people and their Old Testament. Christians found life in Christ and his cross; the Jews had perpetrated his death upon the cross and had lost their holy city, their temple, and their homeland as a result. The two categories became polar opposites and helped Christian teachers clarify the character and boundaries of their churches. The second-century Justin Martyr, one of the first church fathers, declared rhetorically to the Jews at large: "He was pierced by you."[1] And John Chrysostom (literally, the golden-mouthed), a popular preacher in late-fourth-century Antioch who later became patriarch of Constantinople, used the Christ-killer label to proclaim that Christianity and Judaism were mutually exclusive. "Where Christ-killers gather, the cross is ridiculed, God blasphemed, the Father unacknowledged, the Son insulted, the grace of the Spirit rejected. . . . In a word, if you admire the Jewish way of life, what do you have in common with us? If the Jewish rites are holy and venerable, our way of life must be false. But if our way is true, as indeed it is, theirs is fraudulent."[2]

Yet perhaps the most fascinating development of the Christ-killer myth during the patristic period appears in Melito's *On the Pascha* (a word meaning Easter, the Passover on which Easter is based, and, by extension, the Passion), a fascinating work that demands our attention. Generally identified with the bishop of Sardis (in Asia Minor, modern-day Turkey) early in the second half of the second century, Melito evidently prepared his work for inclusion in the Easter liturgy of his church. Although Easter, the holiest day in the Christian calendar, now commemorates the resurrection of Jesus from the grave, for many in Melito's day it still commemorated the Crucifixion. Much as Passover does for the Jews, Easter functioned (and still functions) for Christians as a sacred time of redemption, celebrating the liberation from enslavement to sin that Jesus' self-sacrifice on the cross offered the faithful. As explained in the last chapter, the Gospels date the Crucifixion to the Passover festival itself (Matthew, Mark, Luke) or to the previous day (John), when the Passover sacrifice was brought to the temple, and Melito makes the most of this connection. He retells the biblical story of the Passover and Exodus, announcing their fulfillment in the Passion of Jesus, the true paschal lamb of God. Jesus' Passion has rendered ancient Jewish observance, and that of the Passover in particular, obsolete and ineffectual.

*Once, the slaying of the sheep was precious,*
   *but it is worthless now because of the life of the Lord;*
*the death of the sheep was precious,*
   *but it is worthless now because of the salvation of the Lord;*
*the blood of the sheep was precious,*
   *but it is worthless now because of the Spirit of the Lord;*
*a speechless lamb was precious,*
   *but it is worthless now because of the spotless Son;*
*the temple below was precious,*
   *but it is worthless now because of the Christ above;*
*the Jerusalem below was precious,*
   *but it is worthless now because of the Jerusalem above. (44–45)*

Melito's review of biblical history reveals that Jesus, the true pascha, had already appeared repeatedly in the guise of many biblical characters, suffering in order to save, and that God had always intended to replace the preliminary covenant of the law with the permanent, perfect covenant of the cross.

*He is the Pascha of our salvation.*
*It is he who in many endured many things:*
*it is he that was in Abel murdered,*
   *and in Isaac bound,*
   *and in Jacob exiled,*
   *and in Joseph sold,*
   *and in Moses exposed,*
   *and in the lamb slain,*
   *and in David persecuted,*
   *and in the prophets dishonored.*
*It is he that was enfleshed in a virgin,*
   *that was hanged on a tree,*
   *that was buried in the earth,*
   *that was raised from the dead,*
   *that was taken up to the heights of the heavens.*
*He is the lamb being slain. (69–71)*

In the wake of the Crucifixion and the replacement of the Old Testament by the New, Christ now offers to all people what the Law once offered directly to Israel alone.

*Come then, all you families of men who are compounded with sins,*
   *and get forgiveness of sins.*
*For I am your forgiveness,*
   *I am the Pascha of salvation,*

> *I am the lamb slain for you;*
> *I am your ransom,*
> *I am your life,*
> *I am your light,*
> *I am your salvation,*
> *I am your resurrection,*
> *I am your king.*
> *I will raise you up by my right hand;*
> *I am leading you up to the heights of heaven;*
> *  There I will show you the Father from ages past. (103)*

What, however, became of Jews? Bewailing the fact that "God has been murdered" (96), Melito finds the Jews collectively guilty of the crime.

> *It is he that has been murdered.*
> *And where has he been murdered? In the middle of Jerusalem.*
> *By whom? By Israel. (72)*

The crime exemplifies Israel's treacherous and ungrateful nature.

> *What strange crime, Israel, have you committed?*
> *  You dishonored him that honored you;*
> *  you disgraced him that glorified you;*
> *  you denied him that acknowledged you;*
> *  you disclaimed him that proclaimed you;*
> *  you killed him that made you live. (73)*

Most important, the evil of Israel explains their rejection and replacement by God.

> *But you did not turn out to be "Israel";*
> *  you did not "see God,"*
> *  you did not recognize the Lord. (82)*

As a result, Israel continues to endure the divine wrath.

> *Therefore, O Israel,*
> *  you did not quake in the presence of the Lord,*
> *    so you quaked at the assault of foes . . . ;*
> *  you did not accept the Lord,*
> *    you were not pitied by him;*
> *  you dashed down the Lord,*
> *    you were dashed to the ground.*
> *And you lie dead,*
> *  But he has risen from the dead*
> *    and gone up to the heights of heaven. (99)*

Some writers have labeled Melito "the first poet of deicide."[3] Whether or not he was the first, I draw extensively on *On the Pascha* because it condemns the Jews collectively as Christ killers with extraordinary hostility and passion. Though their own law and ritual—those of the Passover above all—embodied the truth of the gospel, the Jewish people murdered Jesus, their own God who had come to redeem them. They conspired and moved against him with cunning, hatred, and treacherous guile. Though the gospel stories of the Crucifixion allot important roles to Pilate and his Roman soldiers, Melito gives them no mention. He condemns Israel and Israel alone. To him, the equation of Israel and deicide appears axiomatic. And, owing to their crime, Melito's Jews have forfeited their favored status in God's plan for the salvation of the world. *Israel*, as some other writers before Melito had already suggested, denotes those who *see God*. Confronted with Jesus, the ultimate lamb of God, however, the Jews failed to see. God, therefore, no longer reckons them as Israel. They lie vanquished in punishment for their deicide, and the nations of the world who have replaced them (superseded them, as theologians might say) as God's chosen have ascended with the crucified and resurrected Christ to the lofty heights of heavenly salvation.

Why did Melito lash out at Israel as he did? Can we appreciate Melito and *On the Pascha* in their own proper context? Two ways of understanding his broadside attack on Israel present themselves, and we can learn from them both. As one writer recently suggested, we can conceive of two notably different Melitos.[4]

## MELITO AND THE CITY OF SARDIS

First, we can situate Melito in the context of a bustling, cosmopolitan, second-century Mediterranean city. To do so, we must rely on a letter attributed to Polycrates, Christian bishop of Ephesus (also in Asia Minor), preserved in the *Ecclesiastical History* of the renowned church father Eusebius (263–339). Defending the Eastern, "Quartodeciman" celebration of Easter on Passover eve, the fourteenth day of the Hebrew lunar month Nissan, the letter lists a distinguished group of Christian luminaries who maintained this practice, from the apostle Philip to "Melito the eunuch whose whole career was in the Holy Spirit, who lies at Sardis awaiting the visitation from heaven when he shall rise from the dead." The writer reports that "these all kept the fourteenth day of the Pascha in accordance with the Gospel, in no way deviating, but following the rule of faith."[5] Eusebius also lists various writings of Melito of Sardis, including two books "on the Pascha." Some of these works were known to other church fathers like Clement of Alexandria, Origen, and Gennadius of Marseilles. And in one fragment preserved by Eusebius, Melito speaks of his visit to the land of the Bible, perhaps establishing him as the first known Christian pilgrim to the Holy Land after the apostle Paul.

If we accept the identification of Melito, author of *On the Pascha*, as Eusebius's Melito of Sardis, we gain considerably more insight into the work and its author. We can place Melito in Sardis, known for its communities of Jews, Christians, and pagans living side by side. Using yet another detail from Eusebius's book, we can date Melito to the reign of the Roman emperor Marcus Aurelius (161–180) and perhaps even more precisely to the 170s. We learn that Melito was a noteworthy Quartodeciman, timing his celebration of the Pascha, Easter, according to the Crucifixion story in the Gospel of John. His Easter fell on the very evening (of the 14th of Nissan) when the Jews of Sardis prepared and then conducted their Passover seder. In all, we emerge with an impression of Melito as a learned and influential, though perhaps somewhat controversial, Christian leader.

Archeology helps round out this picture of Melito and his urban home—in this case a joint Harvard-Cornell archeological expedition conducted at Sardis between the late 1950s and the mid-1970s. There archeologists excavated and reconstructed one of the largest ancient synagogues ever unearthed (fig. 3.1), part of an impressive Roman bath and gymnasium complex evidently ceded to a large, thriving, and powerful local Jewish community during the third century. This third-century synagogue, whose hall approached sixty meters in length, loomed nine meters high, and held as many as a thousand people, contained elaborate marble decoration, artwork (including mosaics), furniture, religious ornaments, and inscriptions. The same excavations recovered seventy-nine texts that named more than thirty donors who contributed to the elaborate synagogue complex; they included at least nine city councilors of Sardis. Though Jews had lived in Sardis for centuries—perhaps as early as the biblical prophet Obadiah (v. 20) mentioned "the exiles of Jerusalem who are in Sepharad [= Sardis?]"—and continued to do so until the seventh century, the construction of the synagogue clearly signaled a high point in the annals of the community. The synagogue led one of the senior archeologists to conclude:

> With a directness which written evidence alone cannot convey, the Sardis building and its contents illuminate a Judaism almost unknown before. And because these Jews lived as they did in a city so important to the Greco-Roman world, they have a claim on our attention unmatched by remote Qumran with its Dead Sea Scrolls, or by the border village of Dura [Europas], despite its spectacular art. This must be the single most important building left to us by the Jews of the ancient world.[6]

The synagogue and the vibrant Jewish community that built this "single most important building" invite us to reconsider Melito's *On the Pascha*. They

FIGURE 3.1. The Synagogue of Sardis: main hall, looking east. © Archaeological
Exploration of Sardis/Harvard University.

beckon us to anchor Melito's condemnation of the Jews as Christ killers in
the realities of an urban society in which Jews and Christians lived side-by-side,
intermingled freely, and yet competed avidly for the loyalties of prospective
converts. Many have argued that Melito perceived the prominent, prestigious
Jewish community of Sardis as a clear and present danger to his church. Particularly at festival times, many Christians were attracted to Jewish communities and their synagogues, lured, perhaps, by participatory rituals that they
found to be fun, fulfilling, and unusually authentic. Attracted to the mono-
theism of the Bible, many pagan converts to Christianity viewed their new
faith as a sort of Judaism for Gentiles. These Jewish ceremonies, which Jesus
and his disciples had maintained in their day, invariably struck them as the
"real thing," drawing them closer to their newly adopted spiritual roots and
the lifestyle practiced by their savior. When John Chrysostom railed against
the Christ killers and their synagogues in late-fourth-century Antioch, precisely this sort of Christian interest in the autumn holidays that John labeled
"Trumpets, Fasts, and Booths" (Rosh Hashanah, Yom Kippur, and Sukkot)
aroused his wrath.

Chrysostom delivered his sermons collected under the title "Against the
Jews" during the mid-380s, several years after Emperor Theodosius I had made
Christianity the official religion of the Roman Empire. If Jewish ritual attracted
Christians even then, how much more might Melito have perceived it as a
threat two centuries earlier, when Christianity was younger, still illegal, and

often subject to imperial persecution? And, of all the Jewish holidays, Passover in particular highlighted the dangers a bishop might have understood them to pose to his flock. The elaborate rituals of the Passover seder call explicitly for all to participate actively, young and old alike. They include a sumptuous feast, singing, perhaps dancing and costumes, stage directions, and props. Aimed especially at children, they seek to impart a spiritual message through a fun-filled, meaningful experience. For a Christian layperson convinced that nationality distinguished between Jews and Christians much more than did religious beliefs, why not celebrate the holiest day of the Christian calendar just as Jesus himself did: by commemorating Israel's exodus from Egypt? The Quartodeciman rite made the Jewish Pesach/Passover and Christian Pascha/Easter more indistinguishable, only nourishing (or aggravating) this tendency further. For when the Jews of Sardis relived the Exodus at their Passover seder on the very night that the Quartodeciman Melito conducted the Easter vigil in his church, they implicitly declared that Christianity's New Testament had not replaced the Old. When some Christians then ventured across the street into the Jewish neighborhood and joined in the Passover celebration, they suggested that the rites of ancient Judaism had not found fulfillment in those of the church. On the contrary, their understanding (for Melito: their misunderstanding) of Christianity led them in the opposite direction, from the church to the synagogue.

Worst of all, this night of Passover and Easter brought the struggle between Christianity and Judaism to a head. On this night, the Jews had laid their hands on the Christian savior. Throughout the Middle Ages, Christian authorities restricted Jewish movement around Easter, especially on Good Friday (the day of the Crucifixion), fearing that Jews would mock the crucified Jesus before the eyes of those who revered him. And if medieval Christians feared Jewish insults in established Christian societies where Jews constituted a small, second-class minority, how much more would Melito have had good reason for worry? Within a competitive urban environment such as Sardis, one could easily perceive the Jewish triumph over Jesus as a more recent reaffirmation of the Jewish victory over the ancient Egyptians.

*On the Pascha* sought to meet this hostile Jewish challenge. Just as the writers of the Gospels formulated the Christ-killer myth as an expression of their own historical context and their own Christian experience, so too did Melito of Sardis. How, exactly, did Melito adapt this aspect of the Crucifixion story to his own circumstances, needs, and outlook? To understand how, we must appreciate how Melito read the Hebrew Bible that Christians had inherited from Judaism: with a method of interpretation called *typology*, from the Greek word *typos*, meaning model. Though similar to the Christian allegory that enabled many of the church fathers to demonstrate that Hebrew Scripture revealed the truth of Christianity, typology and allegory differed in several key respects.

When Melito understood the stories and commandments in Christianity's Old Testament as *typoi*, models of the New Testament that Jesus' Crucifixion had inaugurated, this meant several things: (1) he affirmed their literal, historical truth in their own time, as well as their value as a model of greater, Christian things to come; (2) now that the events and observances that they prefigured had materialized, he considered them displaced, obsolete, and worthless in and of themselves; and (3) because the truth underlying these *typoi* expressed itself differently over time, and because typology invariably caused a reader to look forward in history from the model to its greater fulfillment, he could understand them as having yet additional fulfillment as time wore on. In other words, just as one could extrapolate from the ancient past to understand the more recent past, so could one extrapolate from the past to shed light on the present (and future). What did this entail for his sense of Passover, Easter, and their confrontation in second-century Sardis? I will refer to *On the Pascha* point by point.

(1) Melito recounted the biblical story of the Exodus and the Passover as historical fact, linking the sacrifice of the paschal lamb as to God's redemption of the Israelites from slavery. But he proceeded immediately to elaborate the *typological* importance of the lamb and its blood:

> O strange and inexpressible mystery!
>   The slaughter of the sheep was found to be Israel's salvation,
>   and the death of the sheep became the people's life,
>     and the blood won the angel's respect.
> Tell me angel, what did you respect?
>   The slaughter of the sheep or the life of the Lord?
>   The death of the sheep or the model (typos) of the Lord?
>   The blood of the sheep or the Spirit of the Lord?
> It is clear that your respect was won
>   when you saw the mystery of the Lord occurring in the sheep,
>     the life of the Lord in the slaughter of the lamb,
>     the model (typos) of the Lord in the death of the sheep. (31–33)

Melito's typological reading of Hebrew Scripture confirmed the literal truth of the Exodus story and, at the same time, "unpacked" its far greater significance as a model of the salvation-bearing sacrifice of Jesus on the cross yet to come.

(2) Nevertheless, now that the Crucifixion has occurred, its ancient precedent loses its typological value. Why bother to keep the inferior model once its perfect fulfillment has materialized?

> This is just what happens in the case of a preliminary structure:
>   it does not arise as a finished work,

*but because of what is going to be visible through its image. . . .*
*But when that of which it is the model arises,*
*That which once bore the image of the future thing*
        *is itself destroyed as growing useless*
*having yielded that image of the future to what is truly real;*
*and what once was precious becomes worthless*
        *when what is truly precious has been revealed. (36–37)*

As Melito explained in no uncertain terms, the sacrifice of Jesus on the cross had drained the Law of Moses of its value. The Jewish Passover was now worthless.

(3) Melito's typological reading of the Passover story, however, did not stop with its fulfillment in Jesus' crucifixion. It extended to the celebration of Easter in Melito's own day. For typology not only allowed for the reenactment of a past event, but it also could entail the reassignment of roles as that historical drama recurred. When the crucified Jesus became the true paschal lamb, and when those who believed in him became the new Israel, the Jews forfeited their status as Israel. Instead, they assumed the role of Pharaoh and the Egyptians who had persecuted God's chosen people long ago. Just as God had once killed the firstborn of Egypt, punishing the Egyptians for slaughtering the sons of the Israelites, dashing them to the ground (26) and causing them to wail bitterly over the loss of their children (27–29), he has since brought death and suffering to the Jewish people, punishing them for slaying his son, causing them to lament the deaths of their own firstborn, dashing them to the ground (99).

How did this bear on the players in the Passover-Pascha drama in Melito's Sardis? *On the Pascha* explains how, as it berates the Jews for killing the Lord at their Passover feast.

*And you were making merry*
        *while he was starving;*
    *you had wine to drink and bread to eat,*
        *he had vinegar and gall;*
    *your face was bright,*
        *his was downcast;*
    *you were triumphant,*
        *he was afflicted;*
    *you were making music,*
        *he was being judged;*
    *you were giving the beat,*
        *he was being nailed up;*
    *you were dancing,*
        *he was being buried;*

> you were reclining on a soft couch,
>     he in grave and coffin. (80)

Melito here offers eight striking contrasts between the Jewish killers of Christ and the crucified Jesus himself. The second line of each couplet refers to Jesus with details drawn directly from the Passion narratives of the Gospels: Jesus' thirst, his being given vinegar and gall, his affliction, his judgment, his actual crucifixion, his burial, and so on. Yet the first line of each couplet describes Jesus' killers with particulars that the Gospels do not mention: their rejoicing, their music, their dancing, their eating bread and wine, and their reclining on a soft couch.

If Melito did not glean this information from the traditional Passion narratives at his disposal, what was the source of his description? None other than the Passover seder itself—not that of the Jews of Jesus' day early in the first century, when the temple still stood, but that of the Jews of mid-second-century Sardis celebrating their Passover at exactly the same moment as Melito celebrated his Easter. By his time, the Passover seder had begun to assume the traditional form that it still has today, complete with wine, unleavened bread, joyous singing, perhaps even dance, reclining on a soft couch, and, perhaps most important, some version of the Haggadah, a Jewish typological explication of the Exodus story. As we saw in chapter 2, Jews have celebrated the Passover (first by offering its sacrifice and then by telling its story) so as to internalize its experience, to share in the salvation that it brought the people of Israel. When casting his own Jewish neighbors as the slayers of Christ, Melito testified that the Pesach/Passover narrative recited by Jews at their seder and the Pascha/Easter narrative of his Christian church encapsulated the conflict between Judaism and Christianity. Every time Jews made merry at their Passover, they denied the salvation in Christ that the Christian observance of Easter affirmed. For Melito, that amounted to nothing less than killing Christ on the cross, again and again and again.

## MELITO AND THE RHETORIC OF CHRISTIAN THEOLOGY

In contrast with this impression of Melito and *On the Pascha*, a strikingly different picture of the author and his work bears consideration. Much as we might like to anchor Melito and his anti-Jewish hostility in the dynamic urban life of second-century Sardis, these connections might not work as well as we would hope. For there are good grounds to challenge the identification of *On the Pascha*'s author with Eusebius's Melito of Sardis. Apart from the name Melito and a book on the same centrally important Christian subject, nothing substantiates it, whereas a careful comparison of Eusebius's reporting with *On the Pascha* may actually militate against it. Consequently, one can also question the logic and significance of Melito's label as a Quartodeciman. Moreover, a careful review of the archeological evidence dates the impressive Sardis synagogue to the mid- to late third century, approximately one hundred years after Melito. How can it thereby explain the threat that Melito supposedly perceived in a well-developed Jewish community a century earlier?

Here, then, emerges a different way of reading Melito and his Easter homily. *On the Pascha* never lashes out at the Jews, only at Israel, and one can conclude that the author hardly intended it as an attack on the Jews of his own day or his own immediate surroundings. Rather, Melito used his typological interpretation of the Bible to explain how—and why—the Passion of Christ had inaugurated a new era in the history of salvation, the once-binding old law had given way to the new, and the Christian faithful had replaced the now faithless people of Israel. Comparing the crucifixion of Jesus with the Akedah story in a different homily, Melito noted that Jesus "carried the wood on his shoulders as he was led up to be slain like Isaac by his father." Yet he quickly added that one story was superior to the other. "But Christ suffered, whereas Isaac did not suffer; for he was a model of the Christ who was going to suffer."[7] Accordingly, as one historian has written, when one reads *On the Pascha* from such a perspective, "Israel loses any sense of a historical reality" and becomes instead an exemplar of a people unfaithful to God.[8] The Jews and the local synagogue (in Sardis or anywhere else) figure but minimally, if at all. Rather than read *On the Pascha* as an attack on contemporary Jews, one can understand it as a Christian defense of Hebrew Scripture and its once valid divine authority. For in demonstrating the Christian truth of the Old Testament, Melito resists the challenge of Marcionites and other Christians heretics (who debunked the Old Testament as the teaching of an inferior, materialistic cosmic power) no less than he denounces the Jews. I will try to unravel the strands of this alternative reading of Melito.

(1) *The Bible contains a single story of salvation.* As I indicated above, Melito's typology allows him to conclude that both the Old and New Testaments proclaim the identical message of salvation in Christ. The events and the narrative of Israel's exodus from Egypt *typify* and find perfection in the crucifixion of Jesus. Passover/Pesach and Easter/Pascha are truly one and the same, such that when the gospel of Christ replaced the Law of Moses, it upheld and fulfilled its essential truths.

Not only does *On the Pascha* identify with the biblical Passover by elucidating its eternal Christian meaning, but it celebrates Easter just as contemporary Jews may have celebrated their Passover. Indeed, Melito's poem displays some striking similarities to the traditional Passover Haggadah.

- The Talmud instructs the Jews assembled at their Passover seder to retell the story of their redemption as the transition from disgrace to glory; and the rabbis beheld this transition both in their ancestors' liberation from physical slavery in Egypt and in the biblical patriarchs' replacement of pagan idolatry with a belief in the true God. As it explains Jesus' liberation of humanity from the bondage of sin, *On the Pascha* belabors this spiritual dimension of the Passover at great length.

- The feast at the Seder table concludes with the eating of the *afikoman*, a slice of unleavened bread (*matzah*) that symbolically represents both the paschal sacrifice that brought salvation to Israel of old *and* the messiah who will bring lasting redemption to Israel in the future. *Afikoman* derives from the Greek *aphikomenos*, meaning *he who is coming*; and Melito uses this term twice, referring to Jesus, the true paschal lamb of God (66, 86). Like the Haggadah, Melito acknowledges the biblical instruction to consume the paschal lamb with unleavened bread, *matzah*, and bitter herbs, *maror* (93).

- As the traditional seder liturgy reaches its climax, Jews toast God their savior, proclaiming: "He brought us out of slavery into freedom, out of grief into joy, out of mourning into festivity, out of darkness into great light, out of subjection into redemption."[9] So, too, does Melito declare:

> *It is he that delivered us from slavery to liberty,*
> *from darkness to light,*
> *from death to life,*
> *from tyranny to eternal royalty. (68)*

- Perhaps most striking of all, Melito enumerates the wonders that the savior performed for his people, guiding them from Adam to Noah, Noah to Abraham, Abraham to Isaac, Jacob, and his sons, all the way down into Egypt, where he watched over them and protected them.

> *It was he who lit your way with a pillar*
>   *and sheltered you with a cloud,*
>   *who cut the Red Sea and led through*
>   *and destroyed your enemy.*
> *It is he who gave you manna from heaven,*
>   *who gave you drink from a rock,*
>   *who legislated for you at Horeb,*
>   *who gave you inheritance in the land,*
>   *who sent out to you the prophets,*
>   *who raised up your kings. (84–85)*

Anyone familiar with the Passover seder should immediately note the resemblance between this passage and the popular song of *Dayyenu*, which lists the many miracles associated with the exodus from Egypt:

He brought us out of Egypt, and punished the Egyptians; he smote their gods, and slew their firstborn; he gave us their wealth, and split the Red Sea for us; he led us through it on dry land, and engulfed our foes in it; he sustained us in the desert for forty years, and fed us with the manna; He gave us the Sabbath, brought us to at Mount Sinai; he gave us the Torah, and brought us to Israel; he built the Temple for us to atone for all our sins.[10]

Whether or not one considers *On the Pascha* a sort of Christian Haggadah for Easter, symbols and traditions centrally important in the Jewish celebration of Passover found an equally important place in Melito's celebration of the Passion. In the case of the *Dayyenu*, Melito's list of divine miracles precedes the earliest surviving version of this popular Haggadah poem by at least six hundred years. Did Christians actually have it first? The answer to this question matters less than the reality of a common ground shared by Jews and Christians throughout much more of their history than many of us have recognized.

(2) *Israel did not see God* (82). As the drama of Passover replays itself on a new cosmic level, the mighty hand of God distinguishes between those who believe and those who do not. Just as in ancient Egypt, some acknowledge the power of God, and others do not. The miracle of Passover and Pascha entails God's rejection of the faithless no less than it does his salvation of the elect. In the words of the Haggadah, "He split the sea for us . . . and sank our oppressors in its depths." And thus Melito:

> But while the sheep is being slain
>     and the Pascha is being eaten
>     and the mystery is being performed
>     and the people is making merry
>     and Israel is being marked,
> then came the angel to strike Egypt,
>     the uninitiated in the mystery,
>     the non-participating in the Pascha,
>     the unmarked with the blood,
>     the unguarded by the Spirit,
>     the hostile,
>     the faithless. *(16)*

The Easter narrative of Jesus' Passion hinges on this same kind of contrast between elect and damned, on reversal, upheaval, and a turning of the tables in their respective destinies. In the story of the Exodus, the lords of Egypt meet their physical destruction as God redeems Israel from slavery. Now, in the drama of Easter, God dooms the formerly privileged people of Israel to oblivion, as the Passion of Christ offers spiritual life to those who previously had none.

(3) *The Mark of the Blood of the Lamb.* We can now appreciate Melito's concern with the Crucifixion, and, above all, with Israel's role in the Crucifixion. For at center stage in this miracle-drama of Passover and Easter stands the lamb of God. Both in Egypt at the time of the Exodus and in Jerusalem at the time of Jesus, the sacrifice of the lamb expresses the unity and the devotion of the faithful. Its blood saves the faithful, just as it ensures the defeat of their enemies. As the words of Melito above make clear, the triumphant heroes of Passover and Easter are those who partake of the Pascha, those who reenact the mystery, those marked as God's people: Israel. Those doomed to defeat are the uninitiated, the nonparticipating, those unmarked with the blood of the lamb, the hostile, the faithless. As noted in the last chapter, the Law of Moses makes participation in the Passover sacrifice a prerequisite for membership in the community of Israel; one who fails to participate "shall be cut off from his people." So, too, did the apostle Paul make life in Christ contingent upon participation in his sacrifice on the cross.

Nothing better connects the various strands in this reading of Melito than his portrayal of Israel as a people of Christ killers, a nation of deicides. On the one hand, their crucifixion of Jesus at the time for offering the paschal sacrifice identifies him as precisely that: the Lamb of God, the mark of whose blood brings salvation to the faithful and disgrace to the faithless. By killing Jesus, they bring their own biblical story of the Passover to perfection: the model gives way to that which it prefigured, the blood of the sheep to the blood of the savior, Old Testament to New. On the other hand, the murderous act of Israel explains the role reversal in its recent history that itself is so prominent in the paschal narrative. Just as the Egyptian oppressors of God's chosen people—"my first-born son, Israel" as the Book of Exodus puts it—forfeit their power and status, so do the killers of God's firstborn son Jesus fall from election to disgrace.

Casting the Jews stereotypically as Christ killers enables Melito the theologian to explain why Christianity has now replaced Judaism in the drama of salvation history. At the same time, it enables Melito, against the wishes of his Christian rivals who disavowed the Old Testament, to cling to the Scriptures of Israel, even as he rejects the Jewish people. For they "did not turn out to be 'Israel.'" They did not see God, as the true Israel must; they did not recognize the Lord (82). Casting the Jew as killer of Christ proves essential to Melito's status and self-concept as a Christian.

Which Melito, then, wrote *On the Pascha*? Does the work arise from the tensions of Jews and Christians living side by side in a bustling second-century Mediterranean city and from danger that the rituals of Passover might lure Christians from the church to the synagogue? Or must we understand the work as a theological statement, as a church father's definition of what belief in Christianity entails, formulated for the most sacred day in the Christian calendar? Though one must not rush too quickly toward identifying the author as the bishop of second-century Sardis or overestimating the influence of Sardis's Jewish community, I believe that both possibilities remain open. More important, neither one precludes the other. Both ways of reading *On the Pascha* can add to our understanding of the text and its implications.

Whichever route one follows, the work illuminates how the identification of the Jew as Christ killer affected the ways that Christian leaders positioned themselves and their communities vis-à-vis Jews and Judaism during the first Christian centuries. Perhaps most important, the extent to which Melito sought to strike out directly against the Jews of his own time and place bears little on the potential power of his Christ-killer imagery. Even if Melito used the term "Israel" as a stereotype, to epitomize the faithless, disbelieving, non-Christian "other," his choice of stereotype was hardly accidental. Moreover, his manner of expression had critical consequences for the way that Christians conceived of Jews for centuries to come. The collective identification of the Jews as killers of Christ had begun. Its career would prove long and perilous.

# PART
# II

# THE MYTH IN HISTORY

# 4

# IGNORANCE AND INTENTION

D id they or didn't they? During the centuries following Melito of Sardis and his *On the Pascha*, few Christian teachers questioned the role of the Jews in perpetrating the murder of Jesus. Instead, the church fathers of Roman times and their successors during the Middle Ages wrestled with a different, no less fascinating question: Did the Jews know that Jesus was their savior and their God when they pressed for his death? The image of the Jew as Christ killer depends greatly on how one understands the mind of the Jew to work and to have worked on that fateful day of the Crucifixion in first-century Jerusalem. As he condemned the Jewish people collectively for deicide, Melito of Sardis seems to have considered this question, too.

> *"I did," says Israel, "kill the Lord.*
> *Why? Because he had to die." (74)*

And we know that Melito subsequently concluded, adapting an earlier pun on the Hebrew word *Yisra'el*, or Israel:

> *But you did not turn out to be "Israel";*
> *you did not "see God,"*
> *you did not recognize the Lord. (82)*

As we shall see in chapter 7, Jews may well have responded to the accusation that they had killed God precisely as Melito maintained, albeit with good cause. But Melito evidently presumed that the Jews did not recognize Jesus for who he really was. Thus they crucified him and forfeited their status as Israel, God's chosen people.

Throughout the Middle Ages, Christians in monasteries, schools, and universities continued to wonder how the Jews of Jesus' day perceived him. But the question had implications that extended far beyond the walls of the medieval cloister or the ivory tower of the academy. It bore directly on the status and destiny of the Jewish minority in Christian society. In the first part of this chapter, I show how Christian answers to this question developed during the Middle Ages; in the second part, I consider how these answers may have affected the lives of Jewish men and women over the course of history.

## THE CHRIST-KILLING MENTALITY

When Christian scholars asked whether the Jews recognized Jesus as the messiah and Son of God, they naturally looked for answers in Scripture. Yet the New Testament passages that they marshaled on either side of the question may not be those that we would think of immediately. Curiously, the Gospels' graphic descriptions of Jesus' death, the insistence of the Jewish crowds that Pilate crucify Jesus, or even the mob's acceptance of responsibility for the execution—"his blood be upon us" (Matthew 27:25)—received little mention in their discussions. What passages did they consider relevant?

On the one hand, three texts suggested to many medieval readers that those responsible for the Crucifixion did not know what they were doing:

1. Luke's description of Jesus on the cross: "And Jesus said, 'Father, forgive them; for they know not what they do'" (23:34);
2. Peter's address to the Jews of Jerusalem in the wake of Jesus' death: "And now, brethren, I know that you acted in ignorance, as did also your rulers" (Acts 3:17); and
3. Paul's reflection on the saving power of the cross: "None of the rulers of this age understood this; for if they had, they would not have crucified the Lord of glory" (1 Corinthians 2:8).

On the other hand, three different passages suggested that the Jews, or at least their leaders, knew exactly who Jesus was:

4. Jesus' parable of the vineyard, addressed to the chief priests and elders in the temple: "There was a householder who planted a vineyard, and set a hedge around it, and dug a wine press in it, and built a tower, and let it out to tenants, and went into another country. When the season of fruit drew near, he sent his servants to the tenants, to get his fruit; and the tenants took his servants and beat one, killed another, and stoned another. Again he sent other servants, more than the first; and they did the same to them. Afterward he sent his son to them, saying, 'They will respect my son.' But when the tenants saw the son, they said to themselves, 'This is the heir; come, let us kill him and have his inheritance.' And they took him and cast him out of the vineyard, and killed him" (Matthew 21:33–39).
5. Jesus' rebuke of the Pharisees: "Jesus said, 'For judgment I came into this world, that those who do not see may see, and that those who see may become blind.' Some of the Pharisees near him heard this, and they said to him, 'Are we also blind?' Jesus said to them, 'If you were blind, you would have no guilt; but now that you say, "We see," your guilt remains'" (John 9:39–41).

6. Jesus' final instructions to his disciples: "If I had not come and spoken to them, they would not have sin; but now they have no excuse for their sin. He who hates me hates my Father also. If I had not done among them the works which no one else did, they would not have sin; but now they have seen and hated both me and my Father. It is to fulfill the word that is written in their law, 'They hated me without a cause'" (John 15:22–25).

Did the Jews kill Christ intentionally? One could conceivably add many other passages to our list and find compelling evidence for whichever verdict one preferred. Those who argued the case on one side therefore developed various strategies for overcoming the evidence on the other side. Some, for example, questioned the identity of groups of people mentioned in the texts: the "the rulers of this age," who would never have done what they did had they known, in passage 3, or those who hate Jesus and God in passage 6. Others distinguished between Jesus as Christ and as God; those who killed Jesus, they reasoned, could have sooner recognized that he was the messiah than that he was divine. Still others differentiated between the guilt of the leaders of the Jews and that of the people at large; the leaders, they reasoned, were much better equipped than the laity to understand. In all, the consensus of Christian opinion evolved in an interesting fashion, and it is helpful to focus on three stages in its development.

## St. Augustine

The most influential voice in the Christian theology of medieval Europe was Augustine of Hippo (354–430), who left his mark on virtually every aspect of Western culture. Augustine affirmed repeatedly that the Jews slew Jesus, even though the Romans actually put him to death. It was to these Jewish Christ killers, Augustine maintained, that the biblical poet referred when he wrote, "Their teeth are spears and arrows, their tongues sharp swords" (Psalm 57:4), and when he described "evildoers, who whet their tongues like swords, who aim bitter words like arrows" (Psalm 64:3). Augustine explained: "Let not the Jews say, we have not killed Christ. For to this end they gave Him to Pilate the judge, in order that they themselves might seem, as it were, guiltless of His death." Pilate wanted to free Jesus, and scourging him with the genuine intention of sparing his life, he ultimately gave in to the insistence of the Jews that Jesus die. They, in turn, have tried to shirk their responsibility when they claim that Roman hands, not their own, did the horrible deed. "But if he [Pilate] is guilty because he did it, though unwillingly, are they innocent who compelled him to do it? By no means." How, precisely, did the Jews kill Jesus? Augustine addressed his reply directly to the Jews: "With the sword of the tongue: for you did whet your tongues. And when did you smite, if not when you cried out, 'Crucify, crucify'?"[1] To emphasize the Jews' guilt, Augustine referred frequently to their self-incriminating cry, "His blood be on us and on our children!"[2]

Nevertheless, when Augustine asked if the Jews recognized Jesus as the messiah and God, he responded emphatically that they did not. Why, then, did they kill him? Upon hearing Jesus claim to be the Son of God, they actually understood his meaning even better than some Christian heretics did, even though the Jews remained blind to its truth. "The very blind, the very slayers of Christ, still understood the words of Christ. They did not understand Him to be Christ, nor did they understand Him to be the Son of God; but they did understand these words to refer to a Son of God that was equal with God"— which many Christian "heretics" did not concede that Jesus taught.[3] Yet the Jews found Jesus' claims intolerable and blasphemous. "Despising this form of a servant, they could not understand the Lord Christ equal to the Father, although they had not the least doubt that He affirmed this of Himself, and therefore were they enraged." In other words, the Jews genuinely believed that Jesus had blasphemed, claiming that he was divine, and for that reason they pressed for his crucifixion. To that extent, Augustine dared to admit, they acted with genuine conviction, although in the final analysis they acted unjustly, "because they did not comprehend God in the man."[4]

## THE AGE OF THE CRUSADES

For hundreds of years, with very few exceptions, Christian scholars followed Augustine's lead. One after another reiterated, in some cases almost by rote, that the Jews who killed Christ had failed to understand who he was. Only in the last years of the eleventh century and early in the twelfth, some seven hundred years after Augustine expressed himself on this issue, do we find that it began to awaken any new or interesting discussion.

At the outset, churchmen of the period of the Crusades generally accepted Augustine's view that the Jews killed Christ owing to their blind ignorance, but they explored its logic and its implications in greater depth. Anselm of Canterbury (1033–1109) in many ways set the intellectual reawakening or "renaissance" of the twelfth century on its course. Truly the genius of early Scholasticism, Anselm explored the rational basis for Christian religious belief, and among his most influential works numbers *Why God Became Human*, a philosophical defense of Christianity. In brief, Anselm argued that justice requires the human race to compensate God for its original sin against him, but that sin left human beings so spiritually crippled that they lack the ability to do so. Any repentance or offering they might make to God would not suffice to compensate God for the specific evil acts that sin causes them to commit; it therefore cannot begin to settle accounts, as it were, for Original Sin itself. Only God, not tainted by human sin, had the capability to make amends for that sin, while justice dictated that humans must compensate God for their rebellion against him. Only someone both human and divine—and therefore not born into Original Sin, as all other humans are—could offer the necessary restitution. Wanting human beings to enjoy salvation rather than suffer eternal punishment, God himself became truly human, and he sacrificed himself to atone for the sins of all men and women.

Anselm's argument bears upon an understanding of the Christ killers' mentality both implicitly and explicitly. Implicitly, because *Why God Became Human* insists upon the rational necessity of the Incarnation and the Crucifixion: only thus could a just, rational God have ensured human salvation. And if, in fact, there was no other way, then perhaps one should not hastily dismiss the Jewish retort caricatured by Melito of Sardis: "He had to die." Explicitly, because Anselm remains convinced of basic human rationality. Early in the treatise, when he identifies the enemies of Jesus responsible for the Crucifixion, he inquires: "Why did the Jews persecute him even unto death?"[5] And subsequently he quotes New Testament passage 3 on our list above to the effect that had the Jews comprehended the true nature of their deed, "they would not have crucified the Lord of glory." Anselm explained emphatically that "no person could ever desire, at least knowingly, to kill God." Committed in ignorance, then, this crime of the Jews did not qualify even as mortal sin—a sin that, unless atoned for, damns the soul of the perpetrator forever.

Anselm set the tone for much of the discussion that followed him over the next several decades. Even when others appeared to strike a different note in their appraisal of the killers of Christ, the Anselmian influence remained apparent. One such disciple of Anselm was Peter Alfonsi, a Spanish Jew who converted to Christianity in 1106 and then traveled to England, where he taught astronomy and Arabic and may even have served as court physician to King Henry I. Peter's *Dialogues of Peter and Moses the Jew* survives today in some eighty medieval manuscripts. By medieval standards, it was a best-seller—for reasons one can well understand. Peter bore the name Moses before his baptism, and the book presents itself as a log of the spiritual and intellectual voyage that brought him from the synagogue to the church. The Jews who had once respected his learning and wisdom now suspected that ulterior motives had induced him to convert, and Peter composed his work to set the record straight. Denouncing the beliefs of traditional Judaism, especially the teachings of the rabbis of the Talmud that struck him as absurd, he first explained his departure from Judaism. Attacking Islam, he next elaborated why he chose not to become a Muslim. Defending the beliefs of the church, he finally justified his embrace of Christianity. Throughout, Peter amassed his evidence both from the books of the Bible and from the logic of rational argument.

The tenth of the twelve "dialogues" or discussions between Peter and his alter ego Moses sets out to prove that "Christ was crucified and killed by the Jews by their free will."[6] As the conversation gets under way, Peter offers a rather Anselmian explanation for the Crucifixion: Only the sacrifice of God incarnate in a human being could liberate humanity from the clutches of the devil and Original Sin. Moses then asks Peter the obvious question: If Jesus had to die to provide for the salvation of humankind, "why do you condemn his killers and why do you assert that they are guilty of sin when they only fulfilled his will?" Peter replies that had they acted to fulfill God's will, they would be blameless, but because "they denied him and slew him from envy," they remain guilty as charged. Peter then illustrates his argument with an analogy.

> Once a certain man had a boat, and it was his intention to burn it, in order to harvest the nails from it and to make charcoal from its planks. However, while he was deliberating over this, an enemy of his came to the boat at night, and not knowing his intention, he burned it from hatred. When the morning came, however, the aforementioned man found the nails of his ship on one side, and the charcoal on another, just as he wanted. And another example: There was a certain stone house that belonged to a man, which he wanted to dismantle so that he could make for himself another building from its stones. By chance, an enemy of his tore it down one day so that not one stone remained standing, and he did this not to fulfill his will—of which he was ignorant—but from hatred. However, when the already mentioned man came to his house on the next day, he found that what he had thought to do and wanted to do had already been accomplished. . . . For the same reason, they are guilty and subject to judgment who slew Christ—not in order to fulfill his will but from the poison of hatred and envy.

Peter's argument reminds us of Melito's response to Israel, when it claimed that Jesus had to die: "He had to suffer, but not by you." The good that derives from a criminal act does not excuse the criminal who committed the crime for the wrong reasons. And what were these reasons? Peter notes that the Jews denied Jesus, slaying him out of envy and hatred.

Peter's assessment of the Jewish mentality sounds far less sympathetic than Augustine's or Anselm's. Nonetheless, despite the Jews' denial, envy, and hatred of Jesus, Peter does not state that they recognized him as messiah and Son of God, slaying him in any event. On the contrary, the analogies of the burning of the boat and the destruction of the house specify that the evildoers acted out of hatred and out of ignorance of the owners' intentions. They did not understand the consequences of their crimes, because they understood neither the nature of that which they destroyed nor the intentions of its owner. Only thus could Peter still lavish praise on the Jewish sages at the time of Jesus, deeming them righteous, men who should have been prophets. Only thus could Peter include the Jewish killers of Christ among the objects of Jesus' mercy and love. "We perceive this from his words while hanging on the cross, saying: 'Father, forgive them for they know not what they do' (Luke 23:24). This shows that he loved them beyond measure, even though they acted wickedly against him."

A third illustrious churchman of the early twelfth century developed the notion of Jewish ignorance further still. Famed lover, writer, teacher, and monk, Peter Abelard (1079–1142) displayed more understanding for the Jews than most Christians of his age. Abelard loved to defy convention, and he also ventured further than his predecessors, his contemporaries, and his successors in insisting that merit and sin are to be found in human intention, not in human actions. Arguing that only the informed consent of the mind makes an act good or bad, Abelard's book *Know Thyself*, commonly known as his *Ethics*, assured him a lasting place in the history of moral philosophy.

Now, if evil intention, and only evil intention, makes an action sinful, then one must reevaluate the most heinous of crimes committed without such intention: crimes such as adultery, murder, and even the most notorious murders of all.

> If one asks whether those persecutors of the [ancient Christian] martyrs or of Christ sinned in what they believed to be pleasing to God . . . , we cannot say that they have sinned in this, nor is anyone's ignorance—not even the disbelief with which no one can be saved—a sin. For those who do not know Christ and therefore reject the Christian faith because they believe it to be contrary to God, what contempt have they in what they do for God's sake?[7]

What has Abelard told us? Sin lies in the human will. Those who crucified Jesus and persecuted him and his disciples did so in ignorance of the extent of their crime. No ignorance can ever be sinful, not even the ignorance of God that stands in the way of one's salvation. The Jews' failure to believe in God as they should is not sinful, nor was their responsibility for Jesus' death. Precisely the opposite is the case. Because they persecuted Jesus and his apostles with the intention of serving God, "they would have sinned more gravely" had they spared them against the dictates of their own conscience.[8]

Anselm had minimized the guilt of the Jewish Christ killers, concluding that a sin committed in ignorance was only a venial or relatively minor sin, not a mortal sin. Abelard now pursued that logic without much regard for traditional Catholic sensitivities. Owing to their good intentions, not only did these Jews not sin, but they would have sinned had they failed to crucify Jesus.

True, this good intention did not assure the Jews a place in heaven. Though Abelard may have exonerated the Jews from guilt, he emphasized that unbelievers like them were destined to hell. "It is sufficient for damnation not to believe in the Gospel, to be ignorant of Christ, [and] not to receive the sacraments of the Church," even though the cause of such failure is ignorance, not wickedness.[9] But this disclaimer did not allay the opposition to Abelard's defense of those who killed Jesus. When his opponents condemned him for heresy in 1140, they included his exoneration of Jesus' crucifiers among the charges that they leveled against him.

## THE MASTERS OF PARIS

As the twelfth century wore on, the new interest in the Christ-killing mentality gradually led to a departure from Augustine's view of Jewish ignorance. We can see this process at work in the teachings of the professors, or masters, of Christian theology at the great medieval university of Paris. Yet, at the same time as we prepare to grapple with their often difficult academic language, we should remind ourselves that human nature has not changed much between the thirteenth and twenty-first centuries. Medieval universities may have been thoroughly religious institutions populated, administered, and controlled by churchmen. The very medieval word for student, *clerk*, means nothing but *cleric*, or member of the clergy. But students then had much the same needs and concerns as students do today, as we see in the serenade that a student at Paris wrote to woo his girlfriend to his home.

> *Enter my little room, which is*
> *Adorned with quaintest rarities:*
> *There are the seats with cushions spread,*
> *The roof with curtains overhead:*
> *The house with flowers of sweetest scent*
> *And scattered herbs is redolent:*
> *A table there is deftly dight*
> *With meats and drinks of rare delight;*
> *There too the wine flows, sparkling, free;*
> *And all, my love, to pleasure thee.*[10]

Scholastic masters and students may in fact have debated how many angels can stand on the head of a pin, but they and their discussions remained rooted in the realities of the world that we know.

That said, we must appreciate the new appraisal of Jesus' crucifiers that crystallized in the schools of twelfth- and thirteenth-century Paris, a bastion of the intellectual elite of the period. A thirteenth-century papal bull dubbed Paris and her schools the "mother of the sciences," and in medieval eyes theology ranked as the most important science. No doubt the blossoming of the great university of Paris, the desire of the schoolmen to iron out all inconsistency in Catholic doctrine, and the established, at times even outspoken, Jewish community of Paris all stimulated interest in the Jews and in their attitudes toward Christ and Christianity. And although the influence of Augustine remained unrivaled, a new trend slowly emerged. Among others, the twelfth-century Peter Lombard, bishop of Paris and author of the *Sentences* (the most widely used theology textbook in the Middle Ages), asserted that the leaders of the Jews in Jesus' day recognized him as messiah, even if they failed to understand that he was the Son of God. Along with some other writers, the Lombard also began to appreciate the *ignorance* of some Jews involved in Jesus' death as inherently incompatible with the *envy* and *malice* of others: one could not have killed Jesus out of envy *and* in ignorance of who he really was, as some earlier teachers (Peter Alfonsi among them) had contended. In the thirteenth century, various masters—notably those who belonged to the newly founded orders of Dominican and Franciscan friars—built upon this conclusion, arguing that even the ignorant masses of Jews sinned grievously. Though they did not know Jesus for what he was, they could and should have known. Some of them, perhaps, willfully brought their own ignorance upon themselves.

Greatest of all the masters of Paris was St. Thomas Aquinas (1225–1274), the Dominican friar whose magnum opus, the multivolume *Theological Summa,* has been compared to a gothic cathedral for the majesty of its structure and the art of its presentation. Much as the church of the Middle Ages hallowed the teachings of Augustine, the Catholic Church of modern times proclaims its allegiance to the theology of Aquinas. And in the matter of the Crucifixion, Thomas appears to have taken issue with Augustine. In formal scholastic fashion, he inquired "whether the persecutors of Christ recognized him," carefully reviewed the evidence on either side of the question, and based his conclusion on a distinction between educated and uneducated Jews at the time of Jesus:[11] "Among the Jews were those of higher and lesser standing." The uneducated remained unaware of Jesus' true nature. But the educated, "those of higher standing who were called their princes, knew ... that he [Jesus] was the messiah promised in the law; for they recognized in him those things which the prophets had predicted for the future. Yet they were ignorant of the mystery of his divinity."

Thus far, Aquinas appears to have adopted the viewpoint of Peter Lombard and others before him: The elders of the Jews knew that Jesus was Christ, but not God. Yet this conclusion that the Jewish leaders did not comprehend that Jesus was divine did not sit well with Thomas, and he pressed his point further in a radically new fashion.

Even so, one must understand that their ignorance did not excuse them from their crime, since it was, in a sense, *voluntary* [or *affected*] *ignorance.* For they beheld the blatant signs of his divinity, but they corrupted them out of hatred and jealousy of Christ; and they wished not to believe his words, by which he proclaimed himself to be the son of God.

Although, at first glance, Thomas acknowledged that the Jewish leaders, too, somehow did not know what they were doing, he whittled away at the essential difference between ignorance and intention as he analyzed their sin. Unlike Anselm, who held that the ignorance of the Jewish Christ killers rendered their crime a relatively minor, venial sin, and unlike Abelard, who doubted if they sinned at all, Aquinas ruled otherwise, using this puzzling idea of *voluntary ignorance.* "When someone expressly desires to be ignorant," so that knowledge might not restrain him from committing a sin, "such ignorance excuses sin neither completely nor partially, *but rather increases it.*" And this ignorance went hand in hand with what Thomas elsewhere called the Jews' "willful malice" toward the Holy Spirit. It, too, only added to their guilt. To the extent that the Jews did not know who Jesus was, they did not wish to know, preferring to let their malice govern their will and their action. In the eyes of Aquinas, the Jews killed Christ with the worst intention possible. In all but the most limited, technical sense, they acted deliberately.

Aquinas thus broke new ground, and other Parisian masters quickly proceeded in the same direction, eliminating any distinction between the ways in which the Jews knew that Jesus was messiah and God. The Franciscan friar John Duns Scotus (1265–1308) maintained that "the rulers of this age" who, according to the apostle Paul, crucified Jesus in ignorance of who he was (passage 3 on our list above) were not the Jews, but kings, princes, or even demons. As for Anselm's argument that no one would knowingly kill God, Duns Scotus simply stated: *non credo*, "I do not believe" that.[12] The Jews truly intended to crucify the Lord. In a similar vein, Scotus's fellow Franciscan Nicholas of Lyra (1270–1349) rejected the argument that recognizing Jesus as Christ came more easily than knowing him to be God. The Jewish leaders knew the Bible well enough to see the whole picture. If their knowledge was at all deficient, it was owing to their murderous hatred and envy of Jesus.

Within a century and a half, professors at the University of Paris, and Dominican and Franciscan friars in particular, had, in effect, overturned the Augustinian tradition of Jewish ignorance. Their treatment of the issue with care and precision, in their lectures on theology as well as in their biblical commentaries, testifies to the extensive importance that it had for the church and for medieval Christian society. How, precisely, was the issue relevant?

## BETWEEN THEORY AND PRACTICE

Though theoretical, discussion of what motivated the killers of Christ bore directly on the way in which Christians perceived and treated the Jews during the Middle Ages. From the fourth century, when the emperors of Rome first tolerated Christianity and then adopted it as the official religion of the empire, the question of the Jews and their place in a properly ordered Christian society remained a pressing one for churchmen and statesmen alike. No longer did the church risk persecution at the hands of the state. It now expected the state to serve the needs of the church, that it translate theology into political policy and practice, and that it regulate the affairs of state and society as befitted a Christian state and society. When medieval Christians wrestled with the question of where the Jews belonged in such a Christian world, the general conviction that the Jews killed Christ and the particular understanding of their motivations proved most relevant. A revealing pattern of development emerges along a route very similar to that which we followed in the first half of this chapter.

### AUGUSTINE AND HIS LEGACY

Even when the emperors of Rome embraced Christianity and worked to ban the various pagan cults in the empire, they reaffirmed the long-standing rights of the Jews to practice their Judaism freely. Theodosius I (ca. 346–395), the very emperor who proclaimed Christianity the religion of the state, declared that "the sect of the Jews is prohibited by no law."[13] Though Christian emperors limited the various privileges that Jews had enjoyed for some time, their protection of both Jews and Jewish rituals should impress us no less. Whether or not churchmen agreed with this policy, they had no choice but to make their peace with it. And of all the church fathers, it was, once again, St. Augustine who understood it as part of God's plan for human history.

Augustine dedicated some fifteen years to writing his magnum opus, *On the City of God*, which explains how political or worldly history (the history of Rome in particular) fits into God's scheme for spiritual or salvation history. Within this context, Augustine briefly describes the life of Jesus and his death at the hands of the Jews, "who killed him and would not believe in him," and he then explains why God did not slay the Jews in punishment for their crime of deicide. On their own merits, the Jews hardly deserved to survive in a Christian world. But God preserved them for the sake of his church. For by preserving the books of the Old Testament and actually embodying them in their everyday lives, the Jews serve as witnesses to the truth of Christianity. They demonstrate to the rest of the world that Christianity is not a recent invention but has an ancient past, inasmuch as it grows out of God's covenant with Israel and fulfills it. The Old Testament foreshadows the New. It implicitly teaches the truth of the new covenant between Christ and his faithful, and by their very survival the Jews testify unwittingly to the roots and the truth of that covenant. Augustine found support for his position in Psalm 59:12, where God gives instructions for dealing with his enemies: (in Augustine's Old Latin translation) "Slay them not, lest at any time they forget your law; scatter them by your might." The church has a license—even an obligation—to scatter, subjugate, and enslave the Jews to advance toward its own objectives, but not to kill them, either literally or figuratively. The Jews and Judaism have a proper place in Christendom. They still have a role to play in God's plan for the salvation of his world.

Though one could discuss Augustine's contribution to the history of Jewish-Christian relations at great length, I limit myself here to several key observations. At the outset, one must note the importance that the Jewish role in the Crucifixion has in Augustine's train of thought: the Jews' slaying of Christ justified their elimination, but God has shown them his goodness and his mercy, sparing them because they still serve a purpose.

Equally important, the Jews' capacity for realizing that purpose depends directly on their blindness—that is, on their testifying to the truth of Christianity *unknowingly*. Referring to the Psalm I have quoted, as well as to other biblical prophecies of Jewish infidelity toward God, Augustine explained in the *City of God*:

> When they do not believe our scriptures, their own, which they read blindly, are thus fulfilled in them. . . . For we realize that on account of this testimony, which they unwillingly provide for us by having and by preserving these books, they are scattered among all the nations, wherever the church of Christ extends itself.[14]

Elsewhere, Augustine captured the complex relationship between the Jew and his Bible in a fascinating, though somewhat baffling metaphor. Reading the books of Holy Scripture that they preserve so faithfully, the Jews appear "as the face of a blind man appears in a mirror—by others it is seen, but by himself it is not seen."[15] A blind man in a mirror: what logic could there possibly be in such an image? Why should a blind man stand in front of a mirror in the first place?

Perhaps we can make sense of Augustine's metaphor by rephrasing our question: How does the face of the blind man appear in the mirror? How can we know what it looks like? Only by standing behind or beside the blind man and looking into the same mirror along with him. What do we then see? We see the blind man seeing nothing; we see ourselves seeing the blind man seeing nothing; and we see ourselves seeing. Only thus can we truly appreciate the difference between blindness and sight. So, too, Augustine proposes, only when Christians encounter the Jew reading the Bible and read it along with him can they fully comprehend its truth. Only then can they understand how the Jew reads blindly and what the meaning of Scripture truly entails. The Christian requires the blind biblical Jew beside him to differentiate between blindness and sight, darkness and light, body and soul, falsehood and truth, infidelity and faith.

The blind ignorance of Augustine's Jewish Christ killers thus goes hand in hand with his understanding of how the Jews have survived—and must survive—in a properly ordered Christian world. And Augustine's instruction on how the Jews must survive in turn conditioned medieval Christian attitudes toward the Jews for centuries to come. Granted, the church demanded that the rights of Jews in Christian society be carefully restricted. Jews might not own Christian slaves; they should not hold positions of authority over Christians; Christian princes should not favor Jews over Christians in any way; and, owing to their role in the Crucifixion, Jews should remain in their own homes and neighborhoods during the days leading up to Easter. Underlying all these decrees, however, lay the assumption that the Jews *belonged* in Christian society. The rule of "Slay them not" provided the theoretical bedrock for Jewish survival in medieval Europe, as long as it enjoyed a place in the policy of the church. Surprising as it may sound, medieval Jews confidently reminded princes and even popes of this Augustinian doctrine at times when their lives or religious practice were endangered. Responding to one such Jewish plea, one pope acknowledged his responsibility to the Jews, "bound as we are by the divine command to tolerate them in their law."[16]

## THE TWELFTH CENTURY

Western Europe eventually emerged from the "dark ages" of the ninth, tenth, and early eleventh centuries into the heyday of medieval Christian civilization. The ongoing reconquest of Spain from its Muslim rulers, the Crusades, and the continuing conversion of central and northern Europe all expanded the borders of Christendom. As commercial activity began to flourish once again in European cities, the idea that wealth derived from financial profit and not merely from the land revitalized the European economy. For its part, a stronger Catholic Church now sought to translate its vision of an ideally ordered Christian society into practice, subordinating everyone and everything to its goals. At the same time, kings and princes worked to consolidate their own power, defending their own interests against those of the church and those of powerful noblemen. Geographic, political, and economic development affected cultural life, too. Europe imported new books, grappled with new ideas, and encountered new worlds of thought; respect for the classics, the sciences, and the arts grew accordingly. In a word, the age of the Crusades heralded new worlds of opportunity. As different interest groups scrambled to capitalize on this opportunity, they reassessed their own standing vis-à-vis the others living around them. It should hardly surprise us that in twelfth-century Europe, Christian attitudes toward the Jews began to show signs of change.

How so? In general, Christian thinkers were virtually obsessed with classifying people and practices around them. As novelty blossomed, they needed to determine how everything fit into the ideal Christian vision, and this surely led them to consider Jews and other "others" with a new sense of urgency. Conquest and international trade encouraged Christians to compete with other religions that they encountered. Curiously, twelfth-century Europe produced more works of anti-Jewish polemic than all of the earlier Christian centuries combined. More than ever, the medieval church conscientiously promoted missionary campaigns among various non-Christian groups, and these efforts extended eventually to the Jews. Alongside these efforts to subdue the enemies of Christ outside Christian society, new concern arose for dissent and deviation within the ranks. The church now discovered heretics in unprecedented numbers, both because change encouraged religious experimentation and because the church now looked for heretics more diligently than before. Hypersensitivity to dissent from within similarly nourished concern with the Jews. Infidels like pagans and Muslims, Jews nonetheless lived together with believing Christians just as heretics did, exposing them to their damnable error.

Against this background, various factors helped to put the issue of the Christ killers' intentions back on the table. First, with the rebirth of cities and their distinctly urban societies and cultures, Europeans began to "rediscover" the individual, expressing new concern for what motivated a particular human being to act in a particular fashion. Human intention now engaged Christian thinkers and teachers to an extent unknown since Augustine, and, as we have seen, philosophers like Anselm and Abelard came to understand merit or sin as residing primarily in the human will. The role of the Jews in the Crucifixion offered a wonderful case in point. Second, as growing cities and towns became home to schools and, soon thereafter, to universities, Christian learning developed outside the monastery. Urban life injected new rigor and sophistication into the traditional study of Christianity, generating a critical spirit and a yearning for consistency, thoroughness, and academic honesty in all intellectual matters, sensitive theological issues included. One could no longer sidestep the contradictions in the teachings of Scripture and the church fathers as easily as in the past. Simply put, churchmen pressed to know: given the conflicting biblical evidence, on the one hand, and the weight of logic and reason, on the other, what did the Jews *really* understand and intend when they killed Jesus? Third, the holy wars waged by the church beginning in the middle of the eleventh century, and the First Crusade of 1096 above all, generated new interest in the Jews' intentions. The crusaders typically "took up the cross," wearing it as an identifying sign on their clothing. They set out to avenge the suffering that the infidels had inflicted on Jesus and the church. As we shall see below in chapter 6, when crusaders attacked Jews in Spain, in France, in Germany, and in the Holy Land, the Jews' role in the Crucifixion invariably fueled their passion. Unprecedented in early medieval Europe, the anti-Jewish violence accompanying the Crusades reawakened Christian thinkers to the problem of the Jews and their status, and that, too, stimulated discussion of what it meant to kill Christ.

As twelfth-century Europe questioned the place of the Jews in Christian society in general, it therefore renewed interest in the mentality of the Jewish Christ killers in particular. With an urgency unknown in earlier centuries, some now aired their doubts concerning the Augustinian view that the Jews crucified Jesus in ignorance. Yet most twelfth-century churchmen ultimately reaffirmed the right of the Jews to live as Jews in Christendom. So, too, they did not yet disavow the tradition of Jewish ignorance in any concerted fashion. In the opening years of the thirteenth century, Pope Innocent III (1198–1216) followed Augustine's lead when he declared that "Christian piety accepts the Jews who, by their own guilt, are consigned to perpetual slavery because they crucified the Lord." Ironically, Innocent claimed, Christians suffer the rebuke of Muslims for tolerating the Jews by whom "our redeemer was condemned to the suffering of the cross."[17]

## THIRTEENTH-CENTURY FRIARS AND JEWS

Together with appraisals of the Jews' intentions in crucifying Jesus, Christian ideas of the Jews and their place in a properly ordered Christian world soon advanced in a new direction, especially among friars of the newly founded Dominican and Franciscan orders, upon whom the church relied to combat its enemies and impose its will on European society. Despite earlier indications of change on the horizon, it was only in the thirteenth century that we find forceful expression of the view that contemporary Jews and Judaism no longer deserved the protection of the church, no matter what Augustine had instructed. Some now took steps against the preservation of Jewish life and religious practice, as if the Augustinian maxim of "Slay them not" no longer applied to the Jews of their day.

How and why did this development come about? I have written at length about this and here can offer only the briefest of summaries. In 1232, as a dispute over the books and rational philosophy of Moses Maimonides (1138–1204) raged among the Jews of Spain and southern France, some avid Jewish opponents of Maimonides' blend of philosophy and religion appealed to the Dominican and Franciscan inquisitors combating heresy in southern France. If you are committed to persecuting heresy, they insisted, then rid us of these books that lure our people away from their age-old religious beliefs. Acting on these complaints, the inquisitors apparently burned some of Maimonides' works—most probably *The Guide of the Perplexed* and *The Book of Knowledge*—in the Provencal town of Montpellier, wreaking emotional havoc among the Jews of the area.

Looking back, we can sense that the ice had broken. For the first time, Christian authorities had intervened in the internal religious affairs of the Jewish communities, ruling on what Jews should and should not believe, what books they may or may not read. This particular intervention did not signal a premeditated attack on contemporary Judaism, but simply a knee-jerk reaction to the charges of heresy aired by the Jews themselves. Yet the time appeared ripe for this sort of intervention, and, as the 1230s wore on, the church began to express a concerted interest in the Talmud and in contemporary rabbinic Judaism, contrasting them with the fossilized biblical religion of antiquity that Augustine had imagined Judaism to be. The attack on the Talmud quickly gained momentum. In 1236, Pope Gregory IX granted an audience to Nicholas Donin, a vengeful Jewish convert to Christianity who presented the pope with a thirty-five-count indictment against the Talmud. In 1239, the pope issued orders for the confiscation of the Talmud from the Jews of Christian Europe during the following spring. Later in 1240, King Louis IX (Saint Louis) of France and a panel of church officials put the Talmud on trial, condemned it as a Jewish heresy, a perversion of the Judaism of the Bible, and ordered its destruction. In 1242, thousands of manuscript volumes of the Talmud perished in a public bonfire in Paris, the first in a series of hostile measures against talmudic Judaism over the course of the later Middle Ages.

What had happened, virtually all of a sudden? In a program of scrupulous regimentation that struck out at deviation of every sort in Christian Europe, the church had awakened to the reality that Judaism did not cease to develop on the day of Jesus' crucifixion, on that day when the New Testament presumably replaced the Old. If this New Testament charted the only legitimate direction in which the religion of biblical Israel could develop, and if the Jews had survived solely to testify to that Old Testament which had given birth to Christianity, then a *postbiblical* or talmudic Judaism was an impossibility. Augustine had defined the Jew and Judaism as biblical; yet contemporary Judaism was grounded in the teachings of the Talmud, which was composed during the five or six centuries following the Crucifixion. By definition, contemporary Judaism could not be genuine. It was heresy, a distortion of the truth, even as far as Judaism was concerned. By extension, the medieval Jews who practiced it no longer filled the role that God had given their ancestors. Why should they continue to enjoy the toleration of "Slay them not," if they no longer served the purpose of "lest at any time they forget your law"? Accordingly, as the church continued to wage war on Jewish books, it also struck out at the Jews themselves, subjecting them to unprecedented missionary campaigns and other forms of harassment. And as the rulers of late medieval England, France, Spain, Sicily, Portugal, and much of Italy and Germany progressively expelled the Jews from their lands, one does not hear the voices of churchmen protesting that Christians still need the Jews in their midst.

How did this relate to the Crucifixion? Augustine, we recall, construed the Jews as performing their appointed task in Christendom precisely because they resembled "the blind man in the mirror." The value of the Jews in a Christian world depended on their blindness, their ignorance of Christian truth, their testifying to that very truth unknowingly, despite themselves. But if the Jews had forsaken the religion of the Bible, replacing it with a religion of the Talmud that God had never ordained, how could one still consider them blind? Quite the opposite. Understanding that it found fulfillment in Jesus, the rabbis of the Talmud—and their medieval followers—deliberately abandoned the Judaism of the Bible. They replaced it with a fabrication of their own, fearful that they might lose recognition as the chosen people. They knew very well who Jesus was, but they refused to believe in him and crucified him.

The Jew who consciously chose not to believe gradually began to overshadow the blind, ignorant Jew as imagined by Augustine, Anselm, Abelard, and others. This Jew willfully chose to kill his savior and his God, a proposition that is in itself astounding. What kind of rational creature would will to reject the truth? What truly human being would wish to kill God? The way in which one poses such a question leaves little room for doubt as to the answer: one who is not a rational creature at all, not a truly human being, but is rather an irrational, essentially inhuman agent of Satan, God's eternal foe. When Thomas Aquinas concluded that the leaders of the Jews willed to kill Christ and God, he expressed this new Christian way of imagining the Jew in his own academic fashion. But the idea of the contemporary, talmudic Jew as a deliberate unbeliever, one who consciously preferred heresy to truth, had implications far beyond the theoretical academic discussion of a university classroom, as we shall soon see in the next chapter.

For the moment, we should briefly mention that a more damning notion of the Jew as Christ killer soon echoed in the circles and even in the streets of Paris that Thomas Aquinas traveled. One of thirteenth-century Jewry's most feared opponents was the Dominican friar Paul Christian, a Jewish convert to Christianity who spent his life as a Christian debating and missionizing among his former coreligionists. In 1263, he debated against Rabbi Moses Nachmanides at the acclaimed Disputation of Barcelona, and soon thereafter he made his way north into France, arriving in Paris late in the decade. There he prevailed on King Louis IX to force the Jews of Paris to confront him in a very similar public disputation, held in 1269 or 1270, just as Thomas Aquinas was lecturing in theology at the University of Paris. But curiously, although the friar had made no issue of the Crucifixion in Barcelona, he appears to have highlighted it in Paris. More curiously still, although Jews had encountered and parried charges of deicide for centuries, the issue appears to have aroused local Christians and Jews alike, inciting hostile anger on the one hand and instilling fear on the other. A contemporary Hebrew account of the disputation describes the event rather passionately.

> On one occasion, all the communities of Paris assembled in the building of the Dominicans' residence, and all of Israel gathered there, men, women, and children. All the uncircumcised of Paris also assembled there and all of the Parisian clergy—a vast number, many more than twenty thousand people. For the heretic [Friar Paul Christian], planning to destroy them in one fell swoop and to excite the teeth of the lions against them, wished to speak of the torture and execution of Jesus.

Word evidently spread that on this particular day, the disputation would depart from the learned discussion of ancient texts to focus on matters that everyone took to heart. All assembled, Christians moved by curiosity and/or religious zeal, the Jews, no doubt, under duress. The issue of the Jews' crime against Jesus had assumed a new currency, and Friar Paul knew that he could exploit it to undermine the security of the Jews of Paris. The eyewitness report quotes him directly:

> Listen, all you peoples, to the shame and the disgrace which these Jews committed on our savior Jesus, in that, for no crime of his, they afflicted him and killed him and hanged him and tortured him in grave and exotic ways, one worse than the next. All his wonders are certain, but they still do not confess their sin. They deserve to be killed, and woe to those creatures that tolerate them.

We then read that Rabbi Abraham, the Jew assigned to respond to Friar Paul, "was very much afraid to speak of the slaying of Jesus, because this revealed [Friar Paul's] intention to exterminate all the Jews." Only the intervention of the royal police seems to have saved the Jews from a violent end at the hands of the mob. "Praise be to God that we left there in peace."[18]

As this Jewish informant testifies, the charge of deicide now had teeth and a burning urgency. Friar Paul spoke not of blind, ignorant Jews who long ago killed Jesus in error, such that if they sinned at all, their sin was merely venial, not mortal. He stridently indicted *these Jews*, the Jews of Paris standing before him, who themselves inflicted shame and disgrace on Jesus. He argued not that the Jews fail to understand but that they refuse to confess their sin. One senses that these Jews could fully understand the extent of that sin. Unlike the blind Jews whom, according to Augustine, God wished to preserve and protect on account of their blindness, these contemporary Jews deserve to be killed. "Slay them not" could not apply to them. *Woe to those creatures that tolerate them.*

Yet another Dominican who worked to undermine Jewish survival in thirteenth-century Christian Europe was Paul Christian's colleague Friar Raymond Martin. Like Paul, Raymond sought to draw Jews into the church. But unlike Paul, who excelled at preaching, both to Jews and to Christians, Raymond made his mark in the study of Hebrew and rabbinic literature. Though born a Christian, Raymond acquired a truly masterful knowledge of the Hebrew Bible, the Talmud, and other classical rabbinic texts. His magnum opus, *The Dagger of the Faith* (*Pugio fidei*), spans more than one thousand pages in its printed edition. A comprehensive guidebook for Christian missionaries and disputants, it first cites biblical and rabbinic texts that support Christian teaching in their original Hebrew and Aramaic, then translates them into Latin, and then offers detailed instructions for using these arguments effectively.

Friar Raymond's commitment to converting the Jews of his day stemmed from his conviction, in which he, too, differed with Augustine, that the Jews had not remained faithful to their biblical heritage. One can, in fact, distinguish three distinct stages in the history of the Jews and Judaism as Raymond understood it. First, Raymond identified the law and prophecies of the Old Testament, which, if read correctly, establish the truth of Christianity. Second, he focused on the Talmud and other works of the ancient rabbis following the crucifixion of Jesus, works which the rabbis falsely claimed preserved the instruction that God had first revealed to Moses at Mt. Sinai. To believe this, Friar Raymond contended, is "nothing other than the insanity of a ruined mind."[19] And third, Martin demonized the "modern" Jews of his own day. He condemned them for following maliciously in the errors of the rabbis of the Talmud, abandoning the beliefs and practices which, though not correct in a Christian sense, were still authentically Jewish.

In denying that Christianity fulfills the promises of their Bible, in fabricating a new talmudic religion to take its place, and in deliberately corrupting the text of Scripture to justify their claims, the rabbis of the Talmud struck Friar Raymond as having thoroughly deserted the Law that God once gave their ancestors. With regard to the practice of circumcision, for instance, he railed furiously in his earlier work, *The Muzzle of the Jews*:

> But do not the Jews, who take the sexual organ of everyone who is circumcised, adult or child, into their most defiled of mouths, mouths

with which they blaspheme Christ, and then suck for as long as the
blood flows—do they not eat just like the pig who soils his snout
with abundant filth? Abraham did not do this. Moses did not order
it. God did not command it.[20]

None other than the devil stands at the heart of the Judaism of the Talmud.
Responsible for its teachings, he has been the object of Jewish worship and
devotion ever since.

Friar Raymond's image of bloodthirsty—literally blood-sucking—Jews
blaspheming against Jesus Christ hardly conjures up an image of well-
intentioned folk who crucified Jesus in ignorance of his real identity. Referring to John 15:24 (passage 6 on our list at the beginning of this chapter),
Raymond underscored that the Jews knew and saw all the miraculous evidence
necessary to verify Jesus' credentials. Their depravity led them to reject such
proof. And their "fox-like guile" sustains them in their blasphemy. These are
hardly good candidates for toleration by the church, and Raymond never cited
Augustine's refrain of "Slay them not" with regard to them. Friar Raymond's
convictions may have led him to try and save Jewish souls. But when his "take"
on the Jews of his day filtered down to the less educated masses of Christianity, they frequently feared more for their own lives, even at the expense of the
Jews.

# 5

# FABLE AND FANTASY

The Christ-killer myth influenced more than the thoughts and theories of Christians about the Jews. Appraisals of the Jews' guilt in the murder of Christianity's God and savior had direct effects on the status of the Jewish minority in a Christian world. As the Middle Ages wore on, especially as Christians came to view the Jew as a deliberate unbeliever, an agent of Satan, and a heretic vis-à-vis his own biblical Judaism, the Christ-killer myth entered a new stage in its development, fueling Christian fantasy in a way that it never had before.

Beginning in the twelfth and thirteenth centuries, the church's preoccupation with issues of Jewish status and survival filtered down to lower echelons of the Catholic hierarchy. Parish priests, monks, and laypersons joined popes, bishops, and theologians in wondering how the Jew properly fit into their European Christian society that was changing so rapidly. Among the many results of this obsession, charges of horrific crimes were leveled against Jews, and these libels often overflowed into anti-Jewish violence, taking a considerable toll in Jewish life, property, and morale. In this chapter, I shall examine three types of such libels: (1) the *ritual murder* accusation, charging that Jews vented their hostility toward Christ and Christianity by regularly killing innocent Christians, usually boys and usually in the spring; (2) the *Host-desecration* accusation, charging that Jews defiled and attacked the consecrated Host of the Eucharist; and (3) the *blood libel*, a libel of *ritual cannibalism*, charging that Jews slaughtered innocent Christians in order to partake of their blood in their perverse rituals, typically as an ingredient in baking unleavened bread (*matzah*) for Passover or concocting potions for curing leprosy.

Fantasies like these had a long, deplorable history. Accusations of ritual murder and ritual cannibalism targeted Jews in the ancient Greek world, before the birth of Christianity, and one still encounters them in the twenty-first century, especially in the Arab world. Other out groups have suffered from such libels, too: witches, heretics, gypsies, and even Christians during the first centuries in the history of the church. Yet medieval Europe witnessed a striking resurgence of such anti-Jewish slander, and a great many historians have struggled to figure out why. Some investigators even point to these medieval fantasies as the first expressions of a genuine, irrational European

93

anti-Semitism—as opposed to a theologically based anti-Judaism—that ultimately laid the groundwork for the Holocaust.

A book like this one cannot begin to offer a thorough treatment of these anti-Jewish libels. Yet looking closely at examples of the three accusations imparts a better appreciation of the popularity and potency of the Christ-killer myth in Western culture, beginning in the later Middle Ages. I shall touch only briefly and selectively on explanations for why the libels flourished when they did. Rather, focusing on the prominence of the Crucifixion story in these charges, I shall highlight how, as in the case of the Crucifixion itself, one finds that stories assumed a life of their own, wielding tremendous influence, irrespective of their factual accuracy or historical "truth."

## WILLIAM OF NORWICH, THOMAS OF MONMOUTH, AND THE RITUAL MURDER ACCUSATION

William of Norwich was twelve years old in 1144. Apprenticed to a skinner, William occasionally visited with the Jews of his town and even worked for them, although during Lent of that year two of his kinsmen forbade him from consorting with the Jews anymore. On the Monday before Easter, a man appeared at William's home, claimed to work for the local archdeacon, gave William's mother some money, and departed together with the boy. William dropped in briefly at the home of his aunt a day later and then disappeared. On the Saturday before Easter, a local nun and a forester found William's slain and abused body in the woods at the edge of the town.

These seem to be the rudimentary "facts" of the case as reported by Thomas of Monmouth, a Benedictine monk who first came to Norwich some five years later, in his *Life and Miracles of St. William of Norwich*, written during the early 1150s. Thomas's book falls into the category of *hagiography*: records of the good deeds, miracles, and piety of holy men and women, accounts intent upon establishing their qualifications for sainthood. Upon his arrival in Norwich, Thomas dedicated himself to reconstructing the "truth" of William's death: that he died a true Christian martyr, much like Jesus himself; that, in the wake of his martyrdom, his bodily remnants and his soul worked many miracles; and that the key to appreciating his death lay in the murderous guilt of the Jews. As will become clear, much more than the memory of a young lad, son of illiterate and not quite exemplary peasants, was at stake in Thomas's efforts.

In the opening book of the *Life and Miracles*, Thomas retells William's story on two interwoven levels. On one level, having interviewed William's relatives and neighbors, he presents "evidence" to prove that the Jews abducted William for their own demonic ritual purposes, brutally subjecting him to the cruelest of tortures and a slow, agonizing death. On another level, much as a painter often shows what transpires inside the walls of a house, while those figures standing outside the house (in the painting) have no idea what is happening inside, Thomas exposes the deeper, hidden meaning of the story—nothing less than the hand of God at work—from the very beginning: William was "by divine goodness conceived."[1] This child's attraction to the bright light of candles established his purity beyond any doubt. He prayed devotedly, often subsisted on bread and water, gave zealously to the poor, and learned "his letters and the Psalms and prayers" with extraordinary dedication. Propelled by God's grace, William "strove with earnest effort, by kindness to all, to gain the love of all and to be burdensome to none."[2]

Thomas wanted his readers to appreciate that all that happens to William was ordained by God. And the two levels on which the author presents William's story, both the visible evidence of the "facts" and the hidden workings of divine providence, converge in his reconstruction of the "events" of William's death. The Jews hired William, Thomas reports, because they admired his work, or, more probably, because they had conspired against him from the start.

> They esteemed him to be especially fit for their work, either because they had learnt that he was guileless and skillful or because, attracted to him by their avarice, they thought they could bargain with him for a lower price. Or, as I rather believe, because by the ordering of divine providence he had been predestined to martyrdom from the beginning of time, and, as one of little prudence and so the more fit for them, was drawn on gradually, step by step, and chosen to be mocked and to be put to death by the Jews in scorn of the Lord's passion. For I have learnt from certain Jews, later converted to the Christian faith, how they then planned to do this very thing with some Christian; and, in order to carry out their malignant purpose, at the beginning of Lent they chose the boy William, being twelve years of age and a boy of unusual innocence.[3]

Thomas thus plays his cards. What might otherwise appear to be happenstance here reflects the will of God. When William disappeared during Holy Week of 1144, all was already in place. When readers then encounter the "factual" evidence of what occurred, they have no choice but to see what the townspeople of Norwich could not see in 1144 and needed Thomas to reveal to them as he retold the story some five to ten years later.

So the story proceeds. The mysterious man who took William away from his mother only pretended to be the cook of the archdeacon and in fact worked for the Jews. This person—"I am not sure," Thomas writes, "whether he was a Christian or a Jew"—overcame the protests of William's fearful mother with money:

He begs; she refuses. He begs, but only that he may make away with the boy. She refuses, afraid lest she should lose him. He asserts that he is the archdeacon's cook, but she does not at all believe him. So between her and the other you might have seen a struggle as between a sheep and a wolf (who seemed at first glance far the strongest) in defense of a third. The lamb was between them. Here stood the sheep and there the wolf. The wolf stands to it that he may rend and devour; the sheep holds her ground that she may rescue and save.[4]

Money induced the mother to give up her child, and Thomas continues to interweave both superficial and deeper meanings of what takes place.

So the traitor took three shillings from his purse with intent to get the better of the mother's fancy and to bend the fickle stubbornness of a fickle woman, seduced by the glitter of money to the love of gain. Thus the money was offered as the price of an innocent's service, or rather in truth as the price of his blood. . . . The wrangling still went on: on one side with prayers, and on the other with the pieces of silver.[5]

In the end, the mother yielded. "The lamb was handed over to the wolf, and the boy William was given up to the betrayer." This betrayer, "the imitator in almost everything of the traitor Judas," proceeded to deliver William to the Jews of Norwich.[6]

With William in the clutches of the Jews, Thomas's storytelling strategy of blending the visible and the hidden proves critical. For one thing, what in his mind *must have happened* to William becomes what *in fact did happen*, since one has no better way of knowing. Granted, Thomas reproduces the secondhand testimony of William's aunt, who claimed to have heard the story from her daughter, who claimed to have watched Jews torture William. But this evidence, highly doubtful if not totally unreliable, convinces far less than the expectations already instilled by the author in the reader. Moreover, these expectations add credibility not only to Thomas's revelation of *who* murdered William but also to his lengthy, graphic description of *what* they did to the boy's body. William's qualification as a saint depends on his death as a genuine Christian martyr. Since this basically nondescript twelve-year-old lad does not otherwise radiate a willingness to sacrifice himself on behalf of Christ and his church, Thomas must go to great lengths to portray his suffering and death as comparable to those of Christianity's foremost martyr, Jesus'. It is not easy to determine just how much Thomas "created" the ritual murder libel of the twelfth century, and how much he played on existing expectations.

Yet in either case, Thomas lays the groundwork for William's murder accordingly. Like Jesus, William is the lamb. A Judas-like traitor brings about his demise, and the money that he pays William's mother—three silver shillings—recalls the thirty pieces of silver paid to Judas. "Thus the money was offered as the price of an innocent's service," Thomas first reflects, but he then prefers an alternative explanation: "or rather in truth as the price of his blood." Likewise, one cannot fail to note the timing of the whole affair. The Jews begin to plot against William at the beginning of Lent, as Christians prepared themselves to commemorate the Passion during Easter week. Because the crucifixion of Jesus occurred on the first day of Passover (according to the synoptic Gospels), Thomas takes pains to establish that the Jews scourged and killed William on the first day of Passover—so much so that Thomas may have fallen prey to his own subterfuge.[7] As Thomas meticulously reconstructs the events of Easter week in 1144, he establishes that William's Judas-like betrayer abducted him "on the Monday after Palm Sunday." On Tuesday morning, William and his betrayer stop briefly at the home of the boy's aunt in Norwich. The torture and execution took place the next day, "which in that year was the Passover for them"; this would have been Wednesday, which in fact was the second day of Passover. William's body was discovered over the Easter weekend itself, whereupon it set out along the path that led to the boy's sanctification as a martyr and saint. Yet ever since the days of the Talmud, perhaps for as much as a thousand years prior to William's death, the Jewish calendar never allowed the first day of Passover to fall on Wednesday. (If it were to fall on Wednesday, Yom Kippur would fall on Sunday, immediately following the Sabbath, which the rabbis would not permit.)

Exactly what did the Jews do to William? Thomas obliges the curious reader with a lengthy description:

> Then the boy, like an innocent lamb, was led to the slaughter. . . .
> After the singing of the hymns appointed for the day in the synagogue,
> the chiefs of the Jews . . . suddenly seized hold of the boy William as
> he was having his dinner and in no fear of any treachery, and ill-
> treated him in various horrible ways. For while some of them held
> him behind, others opened his mouth and introduced an instrument
> of torture which is called a teazle, and, fixing it by straps through
> both jaws to the back of his neck, they fastened it with a knot as tightly
> as it could be drawn.
>
> After that, taking a short piece of rope of about the thickness of
> one's little finger and tying three knots in it at certain distances marked
> out, they bound round that innocent head with it from the forehead
> to the back, forcing the middle knot into his forehead and the two
> others into his temples, the two ends of the rope being most tightly
> stretched at the back of his head and fastened in a very tight knot.

The ends of the rope were then passed round his neck and carried round his throat under his chin, and there they finished off this dreadful engine of torture in a fifth knot.

But not even yet could the cruelty of the torturers be satisfied without adding even more severe pains. Having shaved his head, they stabbed it with countless thorn-points, and made the blood come horribly from the wounds they made. And so cruel were they and so eager to inflict pain that it was difficult to say whether they were crueler or more ingenious in their tortures. For their skill in torturing kept up the strength of their cruelty and commanded the use of their weapons.

And thus, while these enemies of the Christian name were rioting in the spirit of malignity around the boy, some of those present adjudged him to be fixed to a cross in mockery of the Lord's Passion, as though they would say: "Even as we condemned the Christ to a shameful death, so let us also condemn the Christian, so that, uniting the lord and his servant in a like punishment, we may retort upon themselves the pain of that reproach which they impute to us."

Conspiring, therefore, to accomplish the crime of this great and detestable malice, they next laid their bloodstained hands upon the innocent victim, and, having lifted him from the ground and fastened him upon the cross, they vied with one another in their efforts to make an end of him.[8]

In a word, the Jews of Norwich scourged and crucified William, just as the Jews of Judea had scourged and crucified Jesus.

Why did the Jews behave in this way? Thomas responded to this question as well, suggesting that the Jews regularly perpetrated such crimes. Thomas claimed that he heard as much from Jewish converts to Christianity, and he tells about one such convert later on in his work.

As a proof of the truth and credibility of the matter we now adduce something that we have heard from the lips of Theobald, who was once a Jew, and afterwards a monk. He verily told us that in the ancient writings of his fathers it was written that the Jews, without the shedding of human blood, could neither obtain their freedom, nor could they ever return to their fatherland.

Hence it was laid down by them in ancient times that every year they must sacrifice a Christian in some part of the world to the Most High God in scorn and contempt of Christ, that so they might avenge their sufferings on Him; inasmuch as it was because of Christ's death that they had been shut out from their own country, and were in exile as slaves in a foreign land.

Wherefore the chief men and Rabbis of the Jews who dwell in Spain assemble together at Narbonne, where the Royal seed [resides], and where they are held in the highest estimation, and they cast lots for all the countries which the Jews inhabit; and whatever country the lot falls upon, its metropolis has to carry out the same method with the other towns and cities, and the place whose lot is drawn has to fulfill the duty imposed by authority.

Now in that year in which we know that William, God's glorious martyr, was slain, it happened that the lot fell upon the Norwich Jews, and all the synagogues in England signified, by letter or by message, their consent that the wickedness should be carried out at Norwich.[9]

The leaders of world Jewry, we read, hold an annual convention in Narbonne to determine which Jewish community must undertake the ritual murder of a Christian in any given year. Thomas here provides us with an early rendition of the myth of the international Jewish conspiracy, which one noted historian of the Middle Ages has aptly called a "warrant for genocide."[10] We shall return to the conspiracy myth in the next chapter. For the time being, we should note how it enables Thomas of Monmouth to explain why the Jews killed William: because that is what Jews do, owing to their membership in the Jewish people. The Jews killed Christ, and they have suffered as a result. To avenge that suffering, they continue to reenact their crime in scorn and contempt of Christ, hoping thus to regain their freedom and their homeland.

Simply put, the nature of the Jew as Christ killer enables Thomas to know everything that the Jews of Norwich did to William and why they did it. Indeed, Thomas presents the violence inflicted on William's body as bearing the inimitable signature of the Jews: no one else could conceivably have perpetrated so brutal a crime. The Jews of Norwich, he charges, realized this themselves. As they bound William's hands and feet, they craftily deviated from the details of Jesus' crucifixion, hoping that "it might not be supposed that he had been killed by Jews."[11] And immediately after the murder, one of the Jewish leaders, inspired by a "divine impulse" as Thomas relates, warned his partners in crime of the likelihood of their discovery. "If the body be found the deed will surely not be attributed to Christians, but the guilt of the whole business will be laid upon us beyond a doubt, for it will not seem probable that Christians would have wished to do this kind of thing to a Christian, or Jews to do it to a Jew."[12] Yet for all of their efforts, the Jews could not avoid detection, and the Jewish leader's prophecy fulfilled itself.

One Henry of Sprowston, the woodsman who discovered William's body, quickly determined from what he saw "that it was no Christian but in very truth a Jew who had ventured to slaughter an innocent child like him with such horrible barbarity."[13] Subsequently, as Thomas argues vehemently that William did qualify as a genuine Christian martyr, he deplores those skeptics "who admit that he was cruelly killed but who are uncertain by whom and why he was eliminated and therefore do not presume to affirm that he was either a saint or a martyr." To them he replies with confidence:

> We hold of a certainty that he was slain by the Jews, because it is proven both by their custom on the day of the Passover and by the character of the tortures inflicted and the sure marks of the wounds. . . . Because we know that these Jews truly perpetrated this crime in scorn of the Lord's Passion and Christian law, so can we prove the truth of the deed with many arguments.[14]

Only the killers of Christ could have murdered William at the time and in the manner that they did.

Most historians continue to view the Norwich ritual murder libel of 1144 as the first of its kind in medieval Europe, a model for many similar accusations that would come in its wake. Thomas of Monmouth's book makes William's "ritual murder" a particularly well documented one, and one can rightly wonder how the historian ought to treat reports of such Jewish atrocities. Yet how one *should* confront such a story and how investigators *have* approached it have sometimes been far from the same.

One level on which to study the Norwich affair is, of course, the level of what in fact happened to William and the nature of the Jews' involvement. Yet ulterior motives propelled Thomas of Monmouth to tell William's story. He began with the assumption that only the Jews could ever perpetrate such a crime. How, then, can one determine from his book what actually occurred or use it to weigh the guilt or innocence of the Jews? But the extent to which even presumably "critical" modern scholars have studied William's murder in these terms is truly astounding. Various non-Jewish writers, as much as they may have rejected Thomas's report of an international Jewish conspiracy, have maintained the possibility that some Jew or Jews of Norwich did the deed. The *Catholic Encyclopedia* decries the slander of the Jews for committing ritual murder, but maintains the possibility of a factual basis for the story. "It seems, however, quite possible that in some cases at least the deaths of these victims were due to rough usage or even deliberate murder on the part of Jews and that some may actually have been slain in *odium fidei*"—that is, in hatred of *the* faith.[15] In his *The Anguish of the Jews*, a bitter critique of Christian anti-Judaism written in the mid-1960s, Father Edward Flannery raises the same possibility.[16] In 1964, M. D. Anderson's *A Saint at Stake* seriously weighs the likelihood that Jews of Norwich committed the crime, and the book received encouraging reviews by representatives of various academic fields, including medicine, history, and the social sciences.[17] Jewish historians, for their part, have repeatedly succumbed to the temptation to "prove" the innocence of their fellow Jews, and they too have felt compelled to offer alternative explanations for what transpired in 1144. Perhaps the malicious Jewish apostate Theobald, whom Thomas of Monmouth credited with his report of the international Jewish conspiracy, himself concocted the rumor that the Jews committed ritual murder. Perhaps the Jewish celebrations of Purim, which sometimes included the hanging of a Haman-like figure in effigy, underlay the Christian notion that the Jews repeatedly reenacted the Crucifixion. By directly engaging those who have condemned the Jews, their vindicators appear to acknowledge, at least tacitly, the validity of the presupposition that Jews may well have been involved.

Stanford University historian Gavin Langmuir aptly labeled the treatment of William's murder by historians a "historiographic crucifixion," one in which the Jews, not Jesus, suffered torture and death for crimes they never committed. As Langmuir explained, an "intellectual trick" underlies this sort of historical interpretation, an argument grounded in the silence of the sources and the ignorance of the historian. The reasoning, he says, is this: "We do not know that Jews killed any of these alleged victims, but we cannot be absolutely certain that they did not; therefore it possible that some of the children were indeed killed by Jews, and therefore the accusation of ritual murder so long supported by Christians may not be baseless."[18] Precisely here lies the crux of the problem, just as we saw in chapter 1 concerning Raymond Brown's presumptions of "verisimilitude" or plausibility for the Passion narrative. Why the tendency to assume that Jews may, after all, have committed ritual murder? Why not assume just as plausibly that the charge results from an age-old tradition of Christian anti-Judaism in general, and the myth of the Christ killer in particular? In other words, why not begin with an entirely contrary premise: that there exists no good reason to suppose that Thomas of Monmouth's hagiography, teeming with visions, miracles, demons, and expressions of divine providence as it is, accurately records the events of 1144?

The answer lies in the power of the Christ-killer myth itself, the extent to which it has permeated the Western way of thinking about Jews, not only in the Middle Ages among churchmen but even in modern times among historians. This brings us to the second, alternative level on which to approach the "ritual murder" of William of Norwich, an approach treating the *narrative* of ritual murder as the historical *event* worthy of study, not what the story relates that its characters did or had done to them. As with the Gospels' accounts of the Crucifixion, historians can much more fruitfully document the career of the story than they can establish its factual accuracy. In the case of the Passion narrative, I followed John Dominic Crossan in arguing that one cannot allow oneself—neither on critical nor on ethical grounds—to assume probability from plausibility, or plausibility simply from the lack of impossibility. In the case of Norwich, it is additionally important to consider why Thomas told his story and the effect that the story had on generations to follow. This line of inquiry has gained momentum only recently, as investigators have begun to realize its value. Was Thomas the first to report on Jewish ritual murder in Norwich, or had the story begun to travel before he arrived in town? Did rumors that Jews had killed a Christian in the German town of Würzberg in 1147 in fact precede—and perhaps influence—the emergence of the story in Norwich? How, in turn, did Thomas's story circulate? To what extent did it underwrite ritual murder accusations against other twelfth-century Jewish communities, both in England and the continent?

The answers to these important questions lie beyond our concern at the moment, but we can adopt the basic premise that underlies them. Let us return to Thomas himself, who evidently had much to gain from promoting his story. The fame of a local martyr and saint would enhance the reputation of Norwich and its cathedral, just as a stream of pilgrims to William's relics would bring tourism and good business to town. The passion with which Thomas argues his case and lashes out at those who doubted it suggests that sainthood for William could result in considerable personal gain for Thomas, too, perhaps in his standing among the local clergy. Writing less than a century after the Norman duke William the Conqueror invaded Anglo-Saxon England, perhaps Thomas believed that attacking the Jews could serve to unite Christian England on a new basis, healing the lingering soreness in relations between the rulers and the conquered. Whatever his personal stake entailed, his tactics should not be confused with his goals. Thomas's ultimate objective was not to convict the Jews of ritual murder. Rather, condemning the Jews as ritual murderers and crucifiers allowed him to establish their victim's status as a Christlike martyr and saint. The same malice that had led the Jews to kill Jesus in the first century still fueled them in the twelfth, as the timing and graphic description of William's murder made so clear.

As for the Jews of Norwich, it appears that they had the good fortune to escape this ritual murder libel unscathed. But the charge became fashionable, reappearing in England, France, Germany, and Spain before the end of the twelfth century, and Jews in many medieval towns were not as lucky as those in Norwich. The rumors gained credence and acceptability, as an Austrian poet confirms for us early in the thirteenth century.

> In every year it happens still
> the Jews Christ's passion offer,
> when a Christian boy they kill.[19]

As the Middle Ages wore on, not only did the accusations spread throughout Europe, recurring with greater frequency, but they yielded additional varieties of anti-Jewish slander, in which the Christ-killer myth continued to play a central role.

## THE BODY OF CHRIST AND THE HOST-DESECRATION ACCUSATION

Late medieval sources relate that during Holy Week of the year 1290—perhaps on Easter Sunday itself—a Christian woman in Paris, who had pawned her clothing in order to borrow thirty silver coins from a Jewish moneylender, redeemed her pledge in exchange for a consecrated wafer of the Eucharist that she received at mass. Mocking the Host, the Jew stabbed it ruthlessly with a penknife, failing to dismember it but causing it to bleed profusely. He then hammered nails into it, but it still refused to be disfigured. When the Jew threw it whole into the fire, the Host leapt up and flew around the Jew's house, and the Jew, piercing it with a lance, sought to force the Host into the outhouse. Submerged in a pot of boiling water, the Host again arose of its own accord and appeared to the Jew in the form of the crucified Christ. "Armed with the sign of the cross," another Christian woman rescued the Host from the house of the Jew and delivered it to her parish priest. The intransigent Jew himself was burned at the stake, and his wife and children, astonished by the miracles they had witnessed, converted to Christianity.

This was the first of the many Host-desecration stories of the later Middle Ages. The libel quickly spread throughout the Christian West, contributing to the death of many thousands of German Jews in the Rintfleisch massacres of 1298 and the Armleder massacres of the late 1330s, and it reappeared in dozens of European communities as the Middle Ages wore on. The story exerted its influence even in the absence of Jews—in "historical" chronicles, in sermons and stories, in holy sites attracting pilgrims, in theater and religious art. To cite but one example: King Edward I of England expelled the Jews from his kingdom in 1290, and they would not reappear in Britain until the late 1650s. Yet the fourteenth and fifteenth centuries saw the proliferation of the Host-desecration story in England: in collections of miracle stories, many of them dedicated to the miracles of the Virgin Mary; in the art of illuminated manuscripts used for Christian prayer and meditation; and on stage, as in the popular Croxton *Play of the Sacrament*, which itself evoked memories of an alleged ritual murder committed by Jews in East Anglia in 1191.

These stories of Jewish evil typically had several key elements:[20]

- the acquisition of the consecrated Host by a Jew or by Jews from a Christian—in many instances a woman, who might well have borrowed money from the Jew or worked as a servant in his home;
- the physical abuse of the Host and the resulting miracles—as accounts of the 1290 episode in Paris would have it, the Host was

stabbed, pierced, scourged, thrown into the fire, lanced, dissected, and submerged in boiling water;

- the discovery of the bleeding Host and the miracles it had produced, leading to the conversion or punishment of the treacherous Jews;
- the emergence of a cult around the Host, the vessels containing it, and the site—often the house of the Jewish perpetrator or the synagogue—on which the desecration and miracles had occurred.

As the list suggests, these tales could have either a violent or a "happy" end, or sometimes a blend of the two.

Did Jews ever desecrate the Host? Some historians have suggested that they may occasionally have done so. Given the mutual hostility that colored Jewish-Christian relations in medieval Europe, this should hardly be surprising. How else might Jews have treated a consecrated Host that came their way—a Host that members of the hostile Christian majority venerated as the body and blood of their God? Without discounting this possibility, one must still wonder as to the extent to which Jews would have risked their lives to procure a consecrated Host simply to abuse it. However attractive the prospect of reviling it may have been, at least in theory the Eucharist was for them nothing more than a wafer. Moreover, whatever individual Jews may or may have done in these isolated instances hardly explains the anti-Jewish story at the heart of the Host-desecration libel. Rather, the story derives from associations between Jews, the Eucharist, and the body of Christ that the Eucharist represents, associations deeply rooted in the foundations of Christianity.

Several historical developments preceding the Host desecration libel of 1290 may explicate its "logic." First, as we saw in earlier chapters of this book, Christians imagined that the Jewish hatred of Jesus extended far beyond his Crucifixion in the first century. Not only did Jews of future generations share in their ancestors' responsibility for Jesus' death, but they also expressed their hostility in distinctively Jewish forms of intolerable behavior. Justin Martyr, one of the first of the church fathers, accused the Jews of slandering and cursing Jesus in their synagogues on a daily basis, and many other spokesmen for Christianity echoed his accusations. Second, because Christianity commemorated the Crucifixion and Resurrection at Easter time, Jewish contempt for Jesus and the cross, both as Christians perceived it and as Jews may have actually have expressed it, naturally intensified during Holy Week. In a letter to the king of France in 1205, Pope Innocent III complained that on Good Friday the Jews "publicly run to and fro throughout the towns and streets and, *in accordance with their custom,* everywhere laugh at the Christians because they adore the crucified [Christ] on the cross."[21] From the sixth century, various popes and councils of the Catholic Church therefore demanded that Jews not appear in public among Christians from Holy Thursday until after Easter Sunday. Though these measures may at times have aimed to prevent the Christian mob from attacking Jews no less than to prevent the Jews from reviling the Christian savior, especially during public processions bearing the Host, they shed light on our concerns nonetheless. For they establish that the church's rituals for commemorating Jesus' death reinforced the perception of present-day Jews as the killers of Christ—whether in the eyes of the clergy, the laity, or both.

Third, around the time of the first decrees against the public appearance of Jews, a Christian folktale, often called simply "The Jewish Boy," began to circulate in medieval Europe. Gregory of Tours, a sixth-century monk, recorded the story in his work titled *The Glory of the Martyrs*.[22]

> The son of a Jewish glass-worker was studying and learning the alphabet with Christian boys. One day while the ritual of the mass was being celebrated in the church of the blessed Mary, this Jewish boy approached with the other young boys to partake of the glorious body and blood of the Lord. After receiving the holy Eucharist, he happily returned to his father's house . . . and between embraces and kisses mentioned what he had so happily received.

The father, however, hardly shared in his son's delight. After denouncing him for betraying his family's faith, the father "seized the boy and threw him into the mouth of a raging furnace." Yet the same divine mercy that saved the biblical Daniel's friends Hananiah, Mishael, and Azariah from the furnace saved this Jewish boy, too. Upon leaving the furnace, the lad related that the Virgin Mary, "the woman who was sitting on the throne in that church where I received the bread from the table and who was cradling a boy in her lap, covered me with her cloak, so the fire did not devour me." The tale of "The Jewish Boy" illustrates the connections that the Christian mind drew between the sacrifice of an innocent youngster, the ruthless violence of the Jews, Christian martyrdom, the Eucharist, and the Christ child himself. Long before the Host-desecration libel of 1290, Christian folklore concluded that the hostility of the Jews toward Christ naturally extended to the Eucharist that embodied him—and to any innocent youngster who would somehow resemble Jesus, in this case by receiving *his* flesh into his own. Indeed, the ritual-murder libels were in large measure libels of ritual crucifixion. Jews allegedly committed such acts as an expression of their Christ-killing identity. They, their victims, and all the details of their terrible crimes confirmed that Jewish hostility toward Christ constituted a very clear, constant, and present danger to the contemporary Christian world.

Fourth, the centuries leading up to the Paris Host-desecration libel of 1290 had generated new and increased concern with the sacrament of Holy

Communion, whereby the priest consecrates the Eucharist and sacramental wine and miraculously transforms—in theological language, *transubstantiates*—them into the body and blood of Christ. This mystery of the mass lies at the bedrock of Catholic ritual. Here the duly ordained priest re-creates the Passion of Christ on the altar, allowing believers literally to partake of the sacrifice that brings them salvation, to receive Christ's flesh and blood into their own, and to enter the kingdom of heaven. A present-day historian of the period has put it very well: "To eat God was to take into one's self the suffering flesh on the cross. To eat God was *imitatio crucis* [imitation of the cross]," emulation of Jesus' crucifixion.[23] Or as a modern manual for Catholics explains the link between the Eucharist and the Passion narrative: "In the Mass, Christ continues to make that offering of Himself to His Father, by the hands of the priest."[24]

The connection between the crucified Christ and the bread and wine consumed by Christians in church has a firm basis in the New Testament. Paul wrote to the Corinthians (1 Corinthians 10:16–17): "The cup of blessing which we bless, is it not a participation in the blood of Christ? The bread which we break, is it not a participation in the body of Christ? Because there is one bread, we who are many are one body, for we all partake of the one bread." Recall, too, the Gospel's account of the Last Supper (Mark 14:22–24):

> And as they were eating, he took bread, and blessed, and broke it, and gave it to them, and said, "Take; this is my body." And he took a cup, and when he had given thanks he gave it to them, and they all drank of it. And he said to them, "This is my blood of the covenant, which is poured out for many."

Nevertheless, beginning in the eleventh century, as Christian intellectuals thought critically about Holy Communion, they often found it confounding, as mysteries tend to be. Some questioned the real presence of Christ in the Eucharist, while defenders of what became the normative, orthodox point of view rushed to assert it and explain it. The church sought to resolve the dispute at the ecumenical Fourth Lateran Council in 1215, the first of whose decrees proclaims the mystery of the sacrament. Without communion, no one can be saved, and only the Catholic Church can administer it.

> There is indeed one universal church of the faithful, outside of which nobody at all is saved, in which Jesus Christ is both priest and sacrifice. His body and blood are truly contained in the sacrament of the altar under the forms of bread and wine, the bread and wine having been changed in substance, by God's power, into his body and blood, so that in order to achieve this mystery of unity we receive from God what he received from us. Nobody can effect this sacrament except a

priest who has been properly ordained according to the church's keys, which Jesus Christ himself gave to the apostles and their successors.[25]

How significant was the Fourth Lateran Council's decree? On the one hand, it introduced nothing new, for, as I have shown, the essential belief that the wine and wafer consecrated in the mass *were* the blood and body of Christ extended back to the earliest phases in Christian history. On the other hand, the Fourth Lateran Council formalized this belief as Christian *dogma*, and in so doing obligated every Catholic to believe it. As the *Catholic Encyclopedia* explains, when revealed truths "are proposed or defined by the Church, and thus become dogmas, we are bound to believe them in order to maintain the bond of faith."[26] The Fourth Lateran decree thus placed greater emphasis on the truth of transubstantiation, sensitizing Christians to its importance and underscoring their obligation to accept it. In the wake of the council's decree, preoccupation with the Eucharist extended beyond bishops and theologians to the Christian laity at large. It spawned popular fraternities, public processions, dramas, music, artwork, rituals, and, of course, superstitions—all surrounding the Eucharist and its worship. Among these, the June feast of *Corpus Christi* (that is, the feast of the body of Christ) deserves special mention. This new Christian festival was sparked by the visions of a Belgian nun early in the thirteenth century, sanctioned by a church council in 1246, and adopted by the pope in 1264. By the end of the century, Eucharist consciousness and culture were everywhere, challenging Christians to focus on the mysteries of transubstantiation in their daily lives and thoughts. Everyone shared in this involvement with the Eucharist. And because the Eucharist embodied the physical body of Christ, the *corpus mysticum Christi* or "mystical body of Christ" now came to symbolize the church, the community of Christian faithful, in all of its integrity and sanctity. Among the many marks that this way of thinking made on Christian society, it defined and accentuated the distinction between Catholic and heretic, who denied the real presence of God in the Host, and between Christian and Jew, who had rejected and slain the God of the Eucharist himself.

A hint of the Host-desecration libels yet to come appears in a letter of Pope Innocent III, who eventually presided over the Fourth Lateran Council, to two French bishops in 1205.[27] Denouncing the Jews for their malice and their insolence, Innocent notes that "even the Saracens, who persecute the Catholic faith and do not believe in the Christ whom the Jews crucified, cannot tolerate" them. The letter then elaborates the worst of their reported abominations: "Whenever it happens that on the day of the Lord's resurrection (Easter) the Christian women who are nurses for the children of Jews receive the body and blood of Jesus Christ, the Jews make these women pour their milk into the latrine for three days before they nurse them again."

I have found no confirmation of Innocent's charges in any Jewish source, and one wonders if such behavior occurred. Again, the possibility that it did is not far-fetched; one simply cannot know for sure. Yet the pope's conviction that the Jews *would have* acted in this fashion returns us to the logic of the Host-desecration accusation. Medieval Jews, by their own self-definition, rejected Christian belief in Jesus as false. For them, the consecrated Host amounted to nothing more than a wafer. And although the rabbis forbade feeding Jewish children the food of a sacrifice that they considered taboo, such a prohibition did not extend to the milk of a Gentile wet nurse, who they did not insist eat only kosher food.[28] Why incur the wrath of Christians by insulting the Eucharist in this way? Why risk one's life in desecrating the sacrament?

Although they never addressed this question directly, by the time of the Host-desecration libel of 1290, Thomas Aquinas and some of his academic colleagues had provided an answer. As we saw in the previous chapter, Aquinas now taught that the Jews who engineered Jesus' crucifixion understood who he really was and killed him anyway. To put it more accurately, they killed him not in spite of their understanding but precisely because they understood who he was. The Host-desecration libel simply carried the logical implications of this outlook one step further: whereas Jews of all generations share in the responsibility for the Crucifixion and whereas they killed Jesus because they understood his gospel to be true, they now know for a fact that he is present in the Eucharist, which they blaspheme and attack relentlessly, over and over again. They might refuse to believe in Jesus Christ or to worship, but they unquestionably understand that he is present in the consecrated wafer.

Some historians have proposed a psychological explanation for the anti-Jewish libels in late medieval Europe. These libels allowed Christians to project onto the Jew their own deep-seated pangs of guilt concerning violence in their society in general, the abuse of their children in particular, their skepticism about the Eucharist, and perhaps even their doubts about God. On the surface, the Host-desecration libel accused Jews of torturing the Christian savior, causing him to suffer no less than he had when they crucified him. But on a deeper level, one investigator suggests, we must imagine Jesus' cry of "My God, my God, why hast thou forsaken me?" resonating in the mind of the doubter.

> Since the fantasy made the host cry out that God had forsaken it, people who believed the fantasy could use it to express—in a socially acceptable way—their fear that God was not in the host, while at the same time they suppressed the fear on a conscious level by attributing the cry to the host itself and killing Jews.[29]

Moreover, fantasies about the suffering of Christ, truly present in a bleeding or desecrated Host, could help Christians overcome more profound fears that God may have abandoned them altogether.

Some readers may find such psychological reasoning helpful in understanding why the Host-desecration libel flourished in Christian society; others not. In either case, however, the linkage between this story and the Christ-killer mythology should not be overlooked. The ritual murder/ritual crucifixion libel builds on the conviction that all Jews, at any time and place, crucified Jesus. Jews supposedly reenact their crime at particular times and places. Host desecration goes one step further. "As often as you eat this bread and drink the cup," Paul wrote to the Corinthians, "you proclaim the Lord's death until he comes." In the Christian imagination of the Middle Ages, the real presence of Christ at each and every mass meant that his sacrifice recurs constantly, simultaneously, in a limitless number of contexts. As one study of anti-Jewish libels has recently noted, "each vicious action against Christians is at once a present, past, and future Crucifixion," and so, too, the mass. Ironically, Jews and Eucharist together served to make the reality of the cross universal and eternal.[30]

## MURDER, MATZAH, AND BLOOD: ACCUSATIONS OF RITUAL CANNIBALISM

Christian fantasies about Jews readily assumed yet another demonic twist. As shown above, ritual-murder libels stressed the connection between the Jews' crucifixion of Jesus at Easter time and their celebration of Passover. The doctrine of transubstantiation underscored that every time a Christian receives the sacrament, he or she eats of the real body of Christ, the ultimate paschal lamb. And soon after the church gave this doctrine the status of dogma, Catholic ritual began to limit the consumption of the sacramental wine. Although laypersons had previously received communion "under both kinds," both bread and wine, from the thirteenth century on, they received it "under one kind" only: the consecrated bread, transubstantiated into Christ's flesh. The wine remained for the priest who administered the sacrament, undoubtedly nourishing the awe, fascination, and fear concerning the blood of Christ that the consecrated wine had become. Hand in hand with these developments went a new preoccupation with the humanity of the crucified Christ, humanity that revealed itself in his body, his agony, and his blood, a humanity that had extensive effect on Christian religious piety, as we shall see in the next chapter.

Ritual murder, the Crucifixion and its brutality, the celebration of Passover, the bread of the Eucharist (like matzah, it too unleavened), partaking of Christ's body that this bread became, the mystery and power of the blood of Christ—all these converged in anti-Jewish libels of ritual cannibalism, often called simply "the blood libel." According to these accusations, not only did Jews commit ritual murder, but they also used the blood of their victims for ritual purposes, often as an ingredient in the unleavened bread for Passover, the Passover wine, or various medicines. The first documented medieval blood libel occurred in the German town of Fulda around Christmas in 1235 and, evidently, did not involve charges of ritual crucifixion. But the two types of accusations soon did intersect and reinforce one another, as a Flemish poet of the thirteenth century seemed to intimate in his verse.

> And when they had stripped off his clothes,
> The dirty Jews, the stinking dogs,
> They inflicted many wounds on him
> With daggers and knives
> And then, still in the same place, caused
> All of the blood to flow from his body
> And collected this blood in a vessel.
> They did this
> Because with this blood, I know,
> They wished to celebrate their sacrament;
> For it was their custom, and this is no lie,
> To obtain a Christian child every year
> Young, healthy, and rosy,
> This child they put to death
> In order to have his blood.[31]

Yet the convergence of the ritual murder and blood libels is most explicit in what may have been the most celebrated blood libel of all, which emerged in the death of Simon of Trent in 1475.

On Easter Sunday of that year, the mutilated corpse of young Simon was discovered in the underground water cistern at the home of a Jew named Samuel in Trent, in northern Italy, not far from the border with Germany (present-day Austria). The investigation of the local authorities led to the arrest, imprisonment, extensive interrogation, torture, trial, and eradication of the local Jewish community, which numbered three households and several out-of-town guests. By the time the proceedings ran their full course in 1476, all but one of the men had been executed, and the women and remaining man had been baptized. They stood convicted of kidnapping, torturing, and murdering Simon in imitation of Jesus' crucifixion, then collecting, distributing, and using his blood in observance of the Passover. In the magistrates' own words, the Jew was "bloodeater and drinker, and blasphemer of the holiest passion of Jesus Christ his godly majesty and the most praised Virgin Mary."[32]

What happened to the Jews of Trent may seem tragic, horrific, even startling, but this was neither the first such blood libel nor the last. A brilliant reconstruction of the affair by historian Ronnie Po-Chia Hsia examines why the Trent libel had the extensive effect that it did, and one can use it to explore the depth of the blood accusation itself. First, the context of these events is important. The Jewish presence in western Europe was declining rapidly. Already expelled from England (1290), France (first in 1306, more permanently in 1394), and much of Germany, the Jews would be soon be banished from Spain (1492), Sicily (1492), Portugal (1497), and southern Italy (1541). Where they remained—in portions of Germany, in the papal states, and in northern Italian cities—their treatment worsened steadily. Fifteenth-century Italy served as the setting for inflammatory sermons on the part of Franciscan preachers who lashed out at the Jews for their hostility toward Christ, his Christian church, and Christians—hostility, alleged the preachers, that led them to exploit Christians by lending them money at exorbitant rates of interest. Earlier in the century, Friar Bernadino of Siena, himself a bitter opponent of the Jews, had accused suspected heretics of brutally murdering a Christian child every year, pulverizing his body, and drinking the potion made from the powder. Friar Bernadino da Feltre preached in Trent during Lent of 1475, rebuking Christians for tolerating the Jews and warning them of impending disaster. Trent itself lay midway between the papal curia in Rome to the south and the German capital of the Holy Roman Empire to the north. Its ruler was at once a prince subject to the German emperor and a bishop under the authority of the pope, and its politics illuminated the tensions in the difficult relationship between Catholic Church and secular state. Over the course of 1475 and 1476, various interested parties sought to steer the course of the proceedings one way or the other, exerting their political influence overtly and covertly. In fifteenth-century Trent, as in twelfth-century Norwich and elsewhere, anti-Jewish libels blended the peculiar circumstances of a given setting with complex issues at the bedrock of Jewish-Christian relationships—and at the very foundations of Christianity.

Second, word of what happened in Trent spread like wildfire, and the affair became a cause célèbre in the contemporary Christian world. The invention of the printing press allowed for the rapid incorporation of Simon's story—and the interpretation of that story—into the prevailing Christian mentality. Printing transformed Simon of Trent into a martyr and saint with amazing speed. Prose, poetry, and artwork elaborate how sketchy, inconclusive "factual" information testified to the certain "truth" embedded in the story, a "truth" that fanned the flames of popular piety and religious zeal.

Third, and most important, is that mythic "truth" itself. According to the story that emerged from the torture chambers of Trent, the Jews needed the body and blood of a Christian to sacrifice in their Passover rituals. They kidnapped the toddler Simon, subjected him to the most gruesome and agonizing tortures and death—restraining and gagging him, piercing his body and tearing apart his flesh with pincers, collecting his blood for their ritual use, killing him, disposing of the corpse in a ditch—and proclaimed their hatred for Christ and Christianity.

On the one hand, then, the authorities fabricated what Ronnie Hsia has called an "ethnography of blood," interrogating the Jews endlessly about the symbolism and significance of blood in their religion, its use and abuse, and its propulsion of the Jews to commit ritual murder, especially at Passover and Easter time. Although the Jews at first protested their innocence and ignorance and then, when tortured until ready to cooperate, were at a loss to provide the answers desired of them, the persistence and ruthlessness of their torturers eventually produced the results that they sought. Most ironically, the Jews of Trent ended up suffering much of the very agony that they had purportedly inflicted on little Simon. If popular piety resulted in the ritual murder of any innocent victims in Trent on Easter weekend of 1475, those victims were the Jews. On the other hand, the motifs of Passover, Easter, the sacrifice of an innocent young boy, and the need for his blood all pointed clearly in yet another direction: the Passion of Christ. The libel of Trent entailed not only ritual murder and ritual cannibalism, but ritual crucifixion as well. Recounting the crimes of the Jews in what became the most influential pamphlet printed in the wake of the affair, Giovanni Tiberino,[33] a physician who examined Simon's dead body on that Easter Sunday, emphasized repeatedly how the Jews had suspended their victim as if on a crucifix. "Behold, O faithful Christian, Jesus has again been crucified between thieves. Behold what the Jews have done, so that they might rule over Christians. Glorious Simon, innocent, virgin martyr scarcely weaned, who could not yet even speak in human fashion, was extended on the cross by the Jews in contempt of our faith."

Indeed, Simon's crucifixion-like death testified to the same international Jewish conspiracy alleged by Thomas of Monmouth in the Norwich libel of the mid-twelfth century. The Jews beheld the bleeding Simon and declared, Tiberino reports, "Just as we slaughter him like Jesus, god of the Christians who is nothing, so may our enemies be confounded forever." Not surprisingly, Tiberino did not rest his pen without condemning the heresy and anti-Christian blasphemy of the Talmud and reproving the Jews for regularly cursing Christians in their synagogue worship. Along with many other anti-Jewish libels of the later Middle Ages, that of Trent expressed a Christian perception of Jews as so hostile toward Christ and his church that they could no longer be tolerated. As one of the condemned Jews was made to "confess" at his trial, "now that the news is out [that] Jews kill Christians for blood and to scorn Jesus, the whole world will hate Jews."[34] And Tiberino demanded of his reader, "Listen, you who tolerate so cruel a breed of humans in your own towns." Only in October 1965, upon the promulgation of the Second Vatican Council's landmark declaration concerning the Jews (see chapter 8), did the Catholic Church withdraw the status of martyr from Simon of Trent and declare the Jews executed for his murder innocent of that crime.

## MEDIEVAL LIBELS AND THEIR LEGACIES

The libels against the Jews rarely found enthusiastic support among the highest authorities in medieval Christendom. Although Pope Innocent III (1198–1216) complained that the Jews "secretly take advantage of every opportunity to kill their Christian hosts,"[35] he never accused the Jews of *ritually* murdering Christians. In the wake of the first blood libel at Fulda, the Holy Roman Emperor Frederick II established a commission to investigate the horrifying charges against the Jews. The commission summoned numerous experts, interviewed Jews who had converted to Christianity, and reported to the emperor without hesitation:

> Neither the Old nor the New Testament states that the Jews lust for human blood; on the other hand, it is expressly stated in the Bible, in the laws of Moses, and in the Jewish ordinances designated in Hebrew as the "Talmud," that they should not defile themselves with blood. Those to whom even the taste of animal blood is prohibited surely cannot thirst for that of human beings, (1) because of the horror of the thing; (2) because it is forbidden by nature; (3) because of the human tie that also binds the Jews to Christians; and (4) because they would not willfully imperil their lives and property.[36]

Though no friend of Emperor Frederick and himself one of the first to condemn the Jews' Talmud to the flames, Pope Innocent IV (1243–1254) similarly denounced the persecution of Jews on charges of ritual murder and cannibalism.

> Despite the fact that, among other things, Holy Scripture pronounces the law, "Thou shalt not kill," and despite the fact that it prohibits the Jews, while celebrating the Passover, to touch any dead body, people nonetheless accuse them of sharing the heart of a murdered boy during this festival. It is believed that their law mandates this, although it is blatantly contrary to their law. No matter where a dead body is found, their persecutors wickedly throw it up to them.[37]

And, referring to the first European blood libels, Innocent reiterated, "Nor shall anyone accuse them of using human blood in their religious rites."[38]

Though a long, impressive series of popes, statesmen, theologians, and scholars have since joined Frederick and Innocent in denouncing such libels, the need for them to do so should impress us no less than their denunciation itself. For all that Christian leaders protested against the ritual murder and blood libels, the accusations only spread, penetrating deeper and deeper into the mind and culture of Christian Europe.

In June 1490, as the story of Simon of Trent continued to fuel the anti-Jewish fantasies of European Christians and as the ruthless activities of the

Spanish Inquisition gained momentum almost daily, a Spanish Christian named Benito Garcia, who had converted from Judaism to Christianity several decades earlier, made his way home from a pilgrimage to Compostella. At an inn in the town of Astorga, he had the misfortune of spending the night in rowdy, rather drunken company. Rifling through his belongings, his companions allegedly discovered an allegedly consecrated Host. With their suspicions aroused, they conveyed Garcia to the local clergy. Arrested, interrogated, and subjected to excruciatingly painful torture, he "confessed" that he, together with several other *conversos* (Jewish converts to Christianity) and unbaptized Jews, had used the consecrated Host and a human heart in a demonic conspiracy against Christianity and Christian society.

The Inquisition quickly entered the picture and arrested those whom Garcia had named as his accomplices. Subterfuge and torture characterized their interrogations, too, which extended for months. The inquisitors did not know exactly what they were looking for or where they were headed when they began. But by the end of the judicial proceedings late in 1491, their fantasies and instruments of torture had created a story of ritual murder, crucifixion, Host desecration, and blood sorcery all in one. The Jews confessed that they kidnapped a Christian boy from La Guardia, tortured him mercilessly, crucified him, tore out his heart, collected his blood, and used heart, blood, and Host in a magical rite that promised insanity to any inquisitor who would threaten them. Once the inquisitors had constructed and "authenticated" the conspiracy, the story assumed an active life of its own. Spanish writers freely embellished the story, adding graphic detail to the agony inflicted upon the body in memory of Jesus' Passion. Every spot along the road traveled by the Holy Child of La Guardia to his miserable end became holy, fit for a church, a chapel, or the performance of miracles. Learned scholars continued to defend the "truth" of the inquisitors' story well into the nineteenth and twentieth centuries. To this very day, the legend of *el santo niño* (the Holy Child) still flourishes. He is still the patron saint of La Guardia, and the church still supports and benefits from his cult. Presented with such an amazing story, one might well forget the most astonishing fact of all: There was no child reported missing or murdered in La Guardia in 1490, no body ever discovered, and no accoutrements of torture or magic were ever unearthed among the belongings of the convicted parties.

The same mythology that created the Holy Child of La Guardia underwrote many other anti-Jewish libels during the centuries to come. After the Middle Ages, when few Jews remained in western Europe, the accusations spread into central and eastern Europe, where they reappeared in the seventeenth, eighteenth, nineteenth, and twentieth centuries. With the return of the Jews to western Europe, the libels returned as well. Between 1887 and 1911, dozens of ritual murder accusations were leveled against Jews in France,

Germany, Moravia, Bulgaria, Austria-Hungary, Russia, and elsewhere. According to one recent calculation, the years 1870–1940 gave rise to more
accusations of ritual murder, crucifixion, and cannibalism that all previous
centuries combined! Accusations of Jewish ritual murder surfaced even in
Massena, New York, in 1928. In 1840, the ritual murder–blood libel made
its debut in the Arab world when Jews in Damascus were tortured after having allegedly killed a Christian cleric, one Father Thomas, and used his blood
in their rituals. The Arab-Israeli conflict continues to nurture such anti-Jewish
slanders (fig. 5.1). And, in 2002, the Saudi newspaper *Ar-Riyadh* published
the following article on the Jewish holiday of Purim by a lecturer at King Faysal
University:

> During this holiday, the Jew must prepare very special pastries, the
> filling of which is not only costly and rare—it cannot be found at all
> on the local and international markets.
>
> Unfortunately, this filling cannot be left out, or substituted with
> any alternative serving the same purpose. For this holiday, the Jew-
> ish people must obtain human blood so that their clerics can prepare
> the holiday pastries. In other words, the practice cannot be carried
> out as required if human blood is not spilled!!
>
> Before I go into the details, I would like to clarify that the Jews'
> spilling human blood to prepare pastry for their holidays is a well-
> established fact, historically and legally, all throughout history. This

FIGURE 5.1. Saudi Arabian Blood Libel, 2002. http://www.adl.org/anti_semitism/
arab/saudi_blood_l.asp. Courtesy of the Anti-Defamation League of B'nai B'rith.

was one of the main reasons for the persecution and exile that were their lot in Europe and Asia at various times.

This holiday [Purim] begins with a fast, on March 13, like the Jewess Esther who vowed to fast. The holiday continues on March 14; during the holiday, the Jews wear carnival-style masks and costumes and overindulge in drinking alcohol, prostitution, and adultery. This holiday has become known among Muslim historians as the "Holiday of Masks."

Who was Esther, and why the Jews sanctify her and act as she did, I will clarify in my article next Tuesday, Allah willing. Today, I would like to tell you how human blood is spilled so it can be used for their holiday pastries. The blood is spilled in a special way. How is it done?

For this holiday, the victim must be a mature adolescent who is, of course, a non-Jew—that is, a Christian or a Muslim. His blood is taken and dried into granules. The cleric blends these granules into the pastry dough; they can also be saved for the next holiday. In contrast, for the Passover slaughtering, about which I intend to write one of these days, the blood of Christian and Muslim children under the age of 10 must be used, and the cleric can mix the blood [into the dough] before or after dehydration.

Let us now examine how the victims' blood is spilled. For this, a needle-studded barrel is used; this is a kind of barrel, about the size of the human body, with extremely sharp needles set in it on all sides. [These needles] pierce the victim's body, from the moment he is placed in the barrel.

These needles do the job, and the victim's blood drips from him very slowly. Thus, the victim suffers dreadful torment—torment that affords the Jewish vampires great delight as they carefully monitor every detail of the blood-shedding with pleasure and love that are difficult to comprehend.

After this barbaric display, the Jews take the spilled blood, in the bottle set in the bottom [of the needle-studded barrel], and the Jewish cleric makes his coreligionists completely happy on their holiday when he serves them the pastries in which human blood is mixed.

There is another way to spill the blood: The victim can be slaughtered as a sheep is slaughtered, and his blood collected in a container. Or, the victim's veins can be slit in several places, letting his blood drain from his body.

This blood is very carefully collected—as I have already noted—by the "rabbi," the Jewish cleric, the chef who specializes in preparing these kinds of pastries.

The human race refuses even to look at the Jewish pastries, let alone prepare them or consume them![39]

Curiously, for all its inaccuracy—Purim falls on the fourteenth day of the Hebrew month Adar, *not* March 14—the Saudi column's accusations focus on Purim, not Passover. Yet there does remain a connection with Passover, Easter, and the Crucifixion nonetheless. Purim usually falls at the beginning of Lent, Passover at the end; Holy Week is prominent in either case. Jewish revelry at Purim time has included the hanging in effigy of the biblical villain Haman, which, according to the accusations of Christian writers, at times resulted in the crucifixion-like slaughter of an innocent Gentile. The Saudi column's mention of a slaughtered sheep itself recalls the Passover sacrifice; the dough recalls the matzah and Eucharist; and the barrel perhaps recalls the tortures that Jesus endured before his crucifixion. The exploitation of Christian mythology about Jews in the Muslim world reveals just how portable it is and has been. The image of the Jew as Christ killer has appeared in innumerable contexts, in variable guises, serving multiple purposes in Christian (and even non-Christian) societies and cultures.

# 6

# A MYTH OF MANY FACES

The previous chapter ended with a leap from the Middle Ages to the twenty-first century. The anti-Jewish libels that translated the Christ-killer myth into a regimen of demonic rituals in which Jews regularly engaged—a regimen that teaches much more about Christian beliefs and doubts than it does about Jewish behavior—have withstood the passage of time. Reason, science, enlightenment, progress, and all the other bywords of modern civilization that we believe distinguish us from our medieval predecessors have not succeeded in overcoming a way of thinking about Jews that extends back to the first Christian centuries. Though this book can hardly touch upon every appearance of the Christ-killer myth between then and now, I shall discuss selected categories of its appearances, important aspects of Western civilization's social and cultural life in which it has made its mark. In this chapter, I turn to three such categories, testifying to the wide-ranging impact that the myth has had over time.

## HOLY WAR

September 11, 2001, added immeasurably to the importance of terms like "holy war," "jihad," and "crusades" in our daily vocabulary. Although more than nine centuries have elapsed since the Catholic Church launched the first of *the* Crusades against its (chiefly Muslim) enemies in the Middle East, many of the wounds inflicted by those holy wars have yet to heal. In the eyes of some, perhaps many, the Crusades have not yet ended, and the final score has yet to be settled.

Today, however, we often forget at least one aspect of the Crusades that motivated Christians of old—churchmen, princes, knights, and common folk—to set out on their campaigns against the infidel. The very word *crusade* derives from *crux*, the Latin word for cross. The Crusades were wars waged by believers against unbelievers, in the name of and for the sake of the crucified Christ. The cross was ever present in the minds and on the bodies of the crusaders. Pope Urban II, when rallying Christians to join in the First Crusade of 1096, reportedly instructed the crusaders to "take up the cross," to emblaze it on their clothing, as a sign of their commitment and special status.

In so doing, one historian has suggested, he invented "one of the most successful instances of the 'logo' in history."[1] As preachers presented it and as crusaders perceived it, the cross served to inspire, to excite, to motivate. It roused Christians to take up arms against the infidels, to retaliate for the evil done to Jesus, to avenge the pollution of the land and of the sites that his life and death had made holy. No less important, it set an example. It appealed to Christians to emulate the experience of the cross: to sacrifice themselves to the struggle against evil; to undergo pain, trial, and suffering as Jesus had himself undergone; to prepare eagerly to die a martyr's death so that they could join Jesus in heaven as well. Consider the charge reportedly given to the knights of the First Crusade as they besieged Jerusalem in 1099:

> Rouse yourselves, members of Christ's household! Rouse yourselves, knights and foot soldiers and firmly seize that city, our commonwealth! Give heed to Christ, who today is banished from that city and is crucified . . . and forcefully take Christ away from these impious crucifiers. For every time those bad judges, those confederates of Herod and Pilate, make sport of and enslave your brothers they crucify Christ. Every time they torment them and kill them they lance Christ's side.[2]

These words make no explicit mention of the Jews, but their spirit could not help but point the crusaders in the Jews' direction.

Given this basic role played by the cross in the appeal, the ideology, and the actual waging of the Crusades, crusading naturally incited Christians to seek vengeance for the Crucifixion from those whom they deemed responsible for it. Indeed, as the cross motivated crusaders to make their way towards the land where Jesus had lived, to Calvary where he had died, and, ultimately, to the Holy Sepulcher where he had been buried (and from which he had been resurrected), Christian memories of the Passion brought Jews into ever sharper relief as the killers of Christ.

Although the church and the papacy never instructed the crusaders to attack the Jews—canon law, in fact, forbade the slaughter of Jews—enthusiastic Christian warriors could easily forget that Jews, at least in theory, had a rightful place in a properly ordered Christian society. During the spring and summer of 1096, as the First Crusade got under way, bands of armed crusaders attacked Jewish communities in western and central Germany. The crusaders converted those Jews whom they could, while others who fell in their path they killed. Jewish communities of the Rhine valley—in Speyer, Worms, Mainz, Cologne and its suburbs, Metz, and Trier—and others, including Regensburg and Prague to the east, suffered serious losses in life and property. This marked the first outbreak of widespread anti-Jewish violence in medieval Christian Europe.

Why did the massacres occur? Perhaps economically grounded jealousies soured relations between German Jews and their neighbors. Perhaps the tensions of the ongoing Investiture Controversy between the popes and the emperors of Germany made the Jews their victims. Yet the evidence makes clear that religious zeal motivated the attackers above all else. Consider the reasoning which a Jewish chronicle of these persecutions of 1096, written in Hebrew within several decades of the events, places in the mouths of the crusaders:

> They said to each other: "Look now, we are going to a distant land to make war against mighty kings and are endangering our lives to conquer the kingdoms which do not believe in the crucified one, when it is actually the Jews who crucified him." They stirred up hatred against us in all quarters and declared that either we should accept their abominable faith or else they would annihilate us all, even infants and sucklings. The noblemen and common people placed an evil symbol—*a vertical line over a horizontal one*—on their garments.[3]

In his own memoirs, the contemporary French abbot Guibert of Nogent confirmed that this very reasoning inspired attacks upon the Jews, as he described events in Rouen in 1096.

> The people who had undertaken to go on that expedition under the badge of the cross began to complain to one another. "After traversing great distances, we desire to attack the enemies of God in the East, although the Jews, of all races the worst foes of God, are before our eyes. That's doing our work backward!"[4]

The logic was both simple and compelling: Although the pope had called upon Christians to fight the Muslims, crusading aimed ultimately to avenge the wrongs committed against Christ. Who should rightfully suffer this revenge more than the Jew? In this spirit, Rabbi Jacob Tam of Rameru (in northeastern France), one of the greatest rabbinic scholars of the Middle Ages, was nearly murdered Passion-style during the Second Crusade, half a century after the First. A Jewish writer of his day recounted:

> On the second festival day of Pentecost (*Shavu'ot*), the errant ones from the land gathered at Rameru, and they came to the house of our master Rabbi Jacob, may he live, and took all that was in his house. They ripped up a Torah scroll before his face and took him out to a field. There they argued with him about his religion and started assaulting him viciously. They inflicted five wounds upon his head, saying: "You are the leader of the Jews. So we shall take vengeance upon you for the crucified one and wound you the way you inflicted five wounds on our god."

At the very last possible moment, Rabbi Jacob bribed a Christian knight to intervene and save his life.[5]

The wrongful crucifixion of Jesus figured so centrally in the motivations and rallying cries of the crusaders that the symbolism of the Passion story appears even in Jewish martyrologies of the Crusades—that is, in stories told and written by Jews who survived the violence about Jews who died on behalf of their faith. Outnumbered and easily overpowered by their enemies, the only way that Jews could claim to have defeated their attackers lay in claiming that *their* martyrs were genuine, while those of the church, from the crusaders to Jesus himself, were not. The crusaders venerated Jesus as the ultimate self-sacrificing martyr. Seeking to avenge his death, they lashed out at the Jews: "You are the descendants of those who killed our God and hanged him on a tree. He himself said, 'The day will come when my children will come and will avenge my blood.'"[6] To which Jews who glorified their own martyrs responded,

> For naught they have thrown our corpses to the ground, for the sake of an illusion they have killed our saints, for the sake of a vile corpse they have spilled the blood of righteous women, and for the sake of the words of a subversive idolater they have shed the blood of children and nursing infants.[7]

For both Christian attacker and Jewish victim, the crucified Jesus clearly lay at the heart of the contention between them.

Owing to the Jews' role as Christ killers, the Crusades boded ill for them from the outset. Popular—or at least unofficial—piety motivated bands of crusaders to take revenge on Jews for Jesus' crucifixion, and, although leading Christian clergymen did not openly call for such violence, their preaching on behalf of holy war reinforced the perception of the deicidal Jew as the mortal enemy of Christ and his church.

One key churchman to do so was the famed Peter the Venerable, abbot of the powerful French monastery of Cluny during the first half of the twelfth century. When the pope sought to organize the Second Crusade in 1146, Peter turned to King Louis VII of France and vehemently urged him to take part.[8] Again, although the Muslims of the Middle East, not the Jews, were the declared enemies of the Crusade, Peter harped on the Jews in his appeal to the king, even more than he discussed the Saracens. Echoing the cries of the crusaders who had attacked the Jews in 1096, Peter wondered why Christian leaders should bother

> to pursue and to persecute the enemies of the Christian faith in far and distant lands if the Jews, vile blasphemers and far worse than Saracens, not far away from us but right in our midst, blaspheme,

abuse, and trample on Christ and the Christian sacraments so freely and insolently and with impunity. How can zeal for God nourish God's children if the Jews, the greatest enemies of Christ and of the Christians, remain totally unpunished?

Although God does not wish "the damned and damnable Jews" to be killed by Christians, he does wish them "a life worse than death, like Cain the fratricide." They too have killed their brother, and such is their just desert from the time of the Passion until the end of the world. Nonetheless, the Jews continue to insult Christ and Christianity, and Peter warns the French king of some of the ways in which they do so, such as their traffic in holy objects stolen from churches. (If one wishes to understand Peter's animosity, perhaps it is significant that his monastery borrowed considerable sums from Jewish moneylenders.) Many a Christian thief, Peter complained, "sells those goods which he has robbed from holy churches to the synagogues of Satan. He sells the vessels of the body and blood of Christ to the killers of Christ's body and the spillers of Christ's blood." The Jews abused Christ with insults and injuries during his lifetime, and they still blaspheme him daily.

The connection between crusading, the death of Jesus, and the Jews becomes clearer in a sermon that Peter delivered in the presence of the pope soon after he had written to King Louis, a sermon "In Praise of the Lord's Grave."[9] Peter extols the virtues of the Holy Sepulcher at great length, but one can summarize his message rather succinctly: the death of Jesus brought salvation to the world and therefore outweighs his birth in importance. Much as the womb of the Virgin Mary carried Jesus before his birth, the Holy Sepulcher received him after his death. Still standing (unlike the cross), the Sepulcher exemplifies the Christian hope for the ultimate salvation, and it charts the proper course for achieving it. Forsaking the pleasures of this world, a Christian must dedicate himself to the holiness, memories, and miracles enshrined in the grave of his savior, joining the mass of faithful souls that it has attracted and liberating it from the infidels.

Peter links the Holy Sepulcher to the cross. Referring to themes discussed in chapter 1, he reminds his audience that Jesus was placed in the grave after being killed "impiously" by the Jews, who followed in the footsteps of their ancestors who had killed God's prophets. And Peter places the Jews in the same category as "the pagan," his term for the Muslim "infidel," who again threatens the Holy Land with armed violence. God confirms his election of the believers in Christ and his rejection of the Jewish and Muslim infidels with a heavenly sign, a fire that spontaneously and miraculously kindles the lamps in the Holy Sepulcher every Easter. Peter thanks God for setting the hearts of Christians ablaze with love for him, for enlightening them with its splendor. But this miracle of light has a darker side as well.

And since the perfidious enemies of your Christ disparage his death more than his other acts of humility, in adorning the monument of his death with a miracle of such light you demonstrate how great is the darkness of error in which they are confined. While they despise his death above all, you honor the monument of his death above all. What they consider especially shameful you prove especially glorious with so wonderful a sign. You reject the Jews like the hateful Cain, the pagans like the worshippers of Baal.

The land in which Jesus lived and died, the cross on which he was killed, the grave in which he was buried—all these became standard features in Crusade propaganda. But it was the cross that appealed to the crusader above all else, forging a special bond between him and his savior, motivating him to share, to participate somehow, in the ordeal of the Passion. In so doing, the cross invariably moved Christians to focus on those immediately responsible for the agony that Jesus endured. Consider, for example, the "model sermons" composed by the thirteenth-century Franciscan friar Gilbert of Tournai for preaching the Crusade. In one of them, Gilbert addresses his listener, charging him to internalize the shame that the infidels cast on Jesus and his cross. "Thus, if you are a friend of God, remember the disgrace, which the enemies of the cross of Christ caused Christ, when they put their sacrilegious hands on the holy city of Jerusalem." Although Gilbert proceeds to identify these enemies as the Saracens of the present, his words could not help but direct the Christian to consider those guilty of Jesus' disgraceful end in his own day. Moreover, these words moved that Christian to action. *If* he qualifies as a true *friend of God*, then he will remember that disgrace, and he will, presumably, respond as he should.[10]

In another sermon, Gilbert appeals to the conscience of his listener with graphic details of Jesus' suffering on the cross, conveyed in a litany of barbed comparisons that recall Melito's condemnation of the Jews in chapter 3 ("you were making merry while he was starving, you had wine to drink and bread to eat, he had vinegar and gall," etc.).

Christ was naked on the cross, you dress in stately dresses. . . . Christ had his hand transfixed, you wear stitched sleeves, gloves and rings; Christ had his foot transfixed, you wear pointed, laced, turned up and pierced shoes; Christ wore a crown of thorns, you wear hairpins, hats, bands, ribbons, and garlands; Christ drank vinegar, you get drunk on wine. . . . Christ had his side pierced by a lance, and you gird yourselves with a gold or silver belt; Christ redeemed your soul with his precious blood, you sell it to the devil for a cheap price; he was crucified once by the Jews, you again and again crucify him in his limbs and increase the pain of his wounds.[11]

Where does Gilbert seek to lead the Christian whose guilty conscience he hopes to awaken? One need not look hard for the answer, which Gilbert links to an appropriate biblical phrase. "Rouse your fury with regard to those who are the rebels of the cross and crucify Christ in his limbs. Because of this Christ will come with the cross, so that those who crucified him feel the blindness of their damnation."[12]

## RELIGIOUS DEVOTION

In the wake of the Crusades, from the end of the eleventh century onward, Catholic Christianity focused with increasing intensity on the humanity of Christ. And the humanity of Christ found its most profound expression in the very real pain and suffering of Jesus' Passion. From the ivory tower of theological seminaries to the sermons of bishops and priests to the prayers and reflections of monks, nuns, and laypersons, the Christ that now dominated the Christian religious mind and spirit was less a majestic creator-king than a human savior, whose crucifixion offered redemption to those who would have faith.

The depth and extent of this phenomenon defy any simple explanation, but several developments that I have already discussed testify to it in one way or another. Anselm of Canterbury's highly influential late eleventh-century book *Why God Became Human* emphasized the compelling necessity for the Incarnation, for God to become human, to live, and to sacrifice himself in order to bring salvation to the world. The Crusades began just as Anselm finished writing his book, mobilizing the laity of Christian Europe to walk in the footsteps of the earthly Jesus, to visit and conquer the places where he lived and died, to avenge the wrongs he had endured. And during the eleventh, twelfth, and thirteenth centuries, the dogma of transubstantiation obligated Christians to recognize the human body of Christ in the Eucharist. One found that real presence of Christ's body not only on the altar of every church during the mass, but also in the arts, the society, and the hearts and minds of late medieval Europe.

All of these expressions of Christ's humanity directed attention to the death of Jesus as the climax of his life. In late medieval piety, Passion devotion was everywhere. Many scholars have established that "the humiliated, tortured, whipped, nailed-down, pierced, dying but life-giving body of Christ, the very body literally present in the Eucharist—this body became the dominant icon of the late medieval church and the devotion it cultivated and authorized." Or, in a word, Jesus' bleeding, dying body had come to be identified as "the essence of Christ's humanity."[13] I noted earlier how professors of theology, concerned with the intentions of the Jews who crucified Jesus, fueled a new, more horrific conception of the Jewish Christ killer. Intensifying concern with the Eucharist helped to precipitate anti-Jewish libels of Host desecration, ritual murder, and ritual cannibalism. Crusading unleashed Christian hostility toward those believed responsible for the death of the savior. And in the coming pages, we shall see how Christian religious devotion enshrined the Passion of the human Christ in the minds and hearts of the faithful. As clerics and laypersons alike forged their relationships with God through the experience of the Passion, they internalized a demonic stereotype of the Jew who had caused Jesus his suffering. This image lingered on in Western consciousness long after the medieval preoccupation with the crucified Christ had subsided.

Writing during the second half of the twelfth century, the German abbot Ekbert of Schönau was a pivotal figure in the new trend of Passion devotion. Ekbert's *Stimulus amoris* (*Prick of Love*) pondered the events of Jesus' life and death, emphasizing the spiritual and moral lessons to be gleaned from Jesus' biography. He condemned the Jews as Christ killers in highly emotional language, emphasizing their gratuitous violence, their "insatiable hostility," their blasphemy, and their bonds with Beelzebub, "prince of the demons." Yet beyond simply translating these commonplace motifs of Christian anti-Judaism into an inspirational tone, Ekbert's rather brief work demonstrates some of the strategies that countless other authors have since used to develop the theme of the Jews' deicide. Thomas Bestul brings an instructive example in his important study *Texts of the Passion*. The Gospel of Matthew (26:48–50) describes Judas's betrayal of Jesus as follows:

> Now the betrayer had given them a sign, saying, "The one I shall kiss is the man; seize him." And he came up to Jesus at once and said, "Hail, Master!" And he kissed him. Jesus said to him, "Friend, why are you here?" Then they came up and laid hands on Jesus and seized him.

Ekbert presents the scene somewhat differently:

> How willing your spirit was for the Passion, good Jesus, you showed clearly when you met of your own accord those bloody men coming with your betrayer, seeking your soul in the night with lanterns and axes and arms, and you revealed yourself at a sign which they received from the leader of the shameful act. For you did not turn away from the bloodthirsty beast approaching for a kiss of your mouth, but the mouth in which no deceit was found you applied sweetly to the mouth which abounded in malice. O innocent lamb of God, why you and that wolf? What linking of God to Belial?[14]

This passage exemplifies two noteworthy characteristics of Ekbert's meditation. First, it does not adhere to the story of the Passion as related by any one gospel. Rather, it conflates details gleaned from different Gospels, "harmonizing" them, as many might have put it. But conflation and harmonization invariably yielded a picture that went further than anything before it. As time wore on, devotional works such as Ekbert's took more and more freedom in embellishing the gospel story to achieve a desired effect. Meditation and devotion gave freedom to the imaginations of the preacher and those whom he addressed, sometimes allowing the imagination to run wild.

Second, Ekbert's description of the betrayal of Jesus aims to generate emotions much more than it aims merely to impart knowledge. Every Christian knew that Judas had betrayed Jesus on the night of the Last Supper and that Jesus offered no physical resistance to his arrest. But Ekbert retells this well-known story so as to generate admiration for Jesus on the one hand, anger and disgust toward his betrayers on the other. As many medieval Christian writers did, Ekbert dehumanizes Judas, calling him a *bloodthirsty beast*. Those who come to arrest Jesus are, likewise, *bloody men*. And the mouth-to-mouth kiss joining Jesus' pure, deceit-free mouth to a mouth *which abounded in malice*, a base act of defilement and pollution, cannot but awaken feelings of revulsion among those who imagine it. So, too, Ekbert's description of the Jews' torture of Jesus following his arrest. "Most beloved Lord, how great were the indignities you bore there at the hands of your own people! Your honorable face . . . they befouled with the spittle of defiled lips, struck with impious hands, covered with a veil in derision, and they beat you, Lord of all creatures, as though you were a contemptible servant."[15] As Bestul notes with insight, stark pictures of bodily contact and the emission of bodily fluids fanned the flames of anti-Jewish hatred, inculcating the notion that the Jewish killers of Christ, now as then, violated sacred boundaries in a manner both horrendous and intolerable.

Ekbert's meditation reached the hands of Bonaventure, one of the leading Franciscan friars of the thirteenth century and the Catholic theologian best remembered for his cultivation of Passion devotion. Bonaventure taught and wrote in Paris not long after the church had condemned the Talmud as having no place in a properly ordered Christian society, and at the same time that Thomas Aquinas, who wrote that the Jews had killed their savior intentionally, lectured there. Yet if the Dominican friar Thomas excelled as the systematic, scientific theologian, we remember the Franciscan Bonaventure no less as an inspirational and impassioned mystic. Bonaventure transformed meditation on Jesus' life and death into a regimen for Christian piety, highlighting the need to visualize all that Jesus underwent. He classified the various stages of Jesus' suffering, numbering them—for easier remembrance and better appreciation—and prescribing specific steps on the path that the meditating Christian must travel in order to digest the lessons of the Passion.

In so doing, Bonaventure followed Ekbert's lead in harmonizing and thereby embellishing the Gospels. When it came to the Jews, he, too, highlighted and expanded on their defilement of Jesus' body and blood with their own bodies and bodily fluids. Bonaventure's *The Tree of Life* reviews Jesus' career, from incarnation to resurrection. Upon reaching the account of Jesus' last days, the work straightforwardly identifies the proper point of departure for effective meditation. "The first thing that occurs to the mind of anyone who would contemplate devoutly the passion of Christ is the perfidy of the traitor."[16] Hauled before the council of the Jews after his arrest, Jesus "endured much shameless infamy"—whereupon Bonaventure reproduces Ekbert's description almost verbatim: "His face . . . was defiled by spittle from impure lips, struck by impious and sacrilegious hands, and covered in derision with a veil. The Lord of all creation suffered blows as if he were a lowly slave."[17] Bonaventure pressed the point at every available opportunity, as in another meditative work on Jesus, *The Mystical Vine*, where he reviewed the seven bonds that held this symbolic vine together.

> The fifth bond was the rope by which Jesus was tied to the scourging post; although the very lashes of the scourge that were repeatedly wrapped around his body could also properly be called bonds. Cruel, harsh, and unjust as they were, I love the thongs of those infamous whips to which it was given to touch your most holy body and to become steeped in your most pure blood. O sweet Jesus, if your blood ran so freely in the scourging that, according to legend, the post bespattered with it retains to this day some marks of red, how much more of your blood must have soaked the scourges that actually cut into your flesh . . . !
>
> The sixth bond was the crown of thorns that so cruelly pressed the beloved head of Christ, and left upon it the traces of its many spikes, drawing from every wound a trickle of blood that ran down, we may suppose, his sacred face where the spittle of the Jews had hardly dried.[18]

Subsequently in the same work, Bonaventure enumerates the seven instances at which Jesus' blood was shed, and he returns to his abuse, suffering, and death, at the hands of the Jews. One passage in particular demonstrates well how Bonaventure moves from his (embellished) interpretation of the New Testament Passion story to instructions for visualizing the scene in one's imagination.[19] First, he establishes what he believes occurred.

> The third shedding of blood occurred when they plucked his cheeks. . . . Some interpret this to mean that the wicked Jews tore his face with their fingernails; others, that they plucked his beard. Neither could have been done without the shedding of blood.

Then he reflects on the scene in his imagination.

I see the sacrilegious hands of this most impious mob, who are not content with striking, slapping, and covering with spittle the adorable face of Jesus all-good, but no, in their burning rage, also pluck His cheeks and draw from that most sweet face the blood that reddens our rose.

By far the most influential of these manuals for meditation on the Passion was an illustrated, late-thirteenth-century work composed expressly for the instruction of Franciscan nuns. The *Meditations on the Life of Christ* was incorrectly attributed to Bonaventure because it proceeded along the same course charted in his own meditations, and this link with the acclaimed "Seraphic Doctor" of the Franciscans, as Bonaventure was called, no doubt enhanced the work's popularity. The *Meditations* far exceeds the devotional treatises of Ekbert and Bonaventure in its length. It prescribes contemplation on the life and death of Jesus for every day of the week, offering highly detailed instructions for what the devoted penitent should think, feel, and imagine. Appropriately, the day for meditating on the Passion was Friday, itself divided into appropriate hours for meditation: the previous night for the Last Supper, Jesus' agony, and the arrest in Gethsemane; the morning for tearful reflection on the trial; early afternoon for the Crucifixion itself; and the end of the day for the burial.

The *Meditations* conveys an inspirational message based on stark contrasts and vivid visual imagery. "Just as the Lord Jesus strove in many ways to bring about the salvation of the Jews, so, in the opposite way, did they try with all their might to defame and confound him."[20] The author instructs his reader to "watch carefully, with strong sorrow, how the Lord of all things was so despised by those most evil servants," how "those rapacious wolves surrounded him with great anger, gnashing their teeth," how "he spoke to them meekly, but they rioted with the fury of barking dogs, surrounding him on all sides."[21] As the time of the Passion approached, "the devil armed his followers and sharpened their hearts against him [Jesus] to cause his death."[22] The author directs the reader to meditate properly over every detail of the Passion narrative, which spans over fifty pages in the modern edition of the *Meditations*; for every detail has significance.

What should we think [but] that our Lord, blessed God above all things, from the hour of his capture at night until the sixth hour of his crucifixion, was in a continuous battle, in great pain, injury, scorn, and torment, that he was not given a little rest! But in what battle is he tormented? You will hear and see. One of them seizes him (this sweet, mild, and pious Jesus), another binds him, another attacks him, another scolds him, another pushes him, another blasphemes him, another spits on him, another beats him, another walks around him, another questions him, another looks for false witnesses against him, another accompanies the one that searches, another gives false testimony against him, another accuses him, another mocks him, another blindfolds him, another strikes his face, another goads him, another leads him to the column, another strips him, another beats him while he is being led, another screams, another begins furiously to torment him, another binds him to the column, another assaults him, another scourges him, another robes him in purple to abuse him, another places the crown of thorns, another gives him the reed to hold, another madly takes it away to strike his thorn-covered head, another kneels mockingly, another salutes him as king. . . . He is led back and forth, scorned and reproved, turned and shaken here and there like a fool and an imbecile.[23]

The litany goes on and on, but the quotation is long enough. This passage demonstrates well how the *Meditations* appeals to its readers on an emotional, inspirational level. The work does not aim to convey presumably historical information as such. Instead, it uses visual images of what presumably happened to Jesus to drive its readers into a frenzy, galvanizing their emotions which can then be directed toward particular objectives. Indeed, factual accuracy matters little to the author. At the beginning of his book, he declares outright that one may present the biblical story of Jesus as one sees fit, so as "not to contradict the truth of life and justice and not to oppose faith and morality."[24] The "truth" of one's rendition of the Passion story depends above all on where it leads, not on the exact correspondence of its details with ancient authoritative sources.

More than two hundred manuscripts of the *Meditations* survive today; many undoubtedly were lost. Beginning in the fourteenth century, the work was translated, abridged, and adapted in various European languages, and it has continued to inspire other works of a similar nature. A thorough review of this literature would serve little purpose here, but I will make brief mention of *The Dolorous Passion of Our Lord Jesus Christ*, by the German nun Anne Catherine Emmerich (1774–1824). Soon after taking her nun's vows as a teenager, Emmerich developed stigmata on her hands; images of the cross appeared on her chest, and she had ecstatic visions of Jesus and the Virgin Mary. Though they subjected her to prolonged investigation and examination, the ecclesiastical authorities could find no sin (of heresy, witchcraft, or the like) in Emmerich, and her fame only spread. The German poet Clemens Brentano sat with Emmerich at length and recorded her visions, which he proceeded to publish after her death. Her work, too, has enjoyed considerable popularity. It has been translated into multiple languages, and it has recently reentered the limelight, owing to its influence on the screenplay for Mel Gibson's film, *The Passion of the Christ.*

After reading *The Dolorous Passion*, one can well understand its usefulness for the screen. Though based on the Gospels' accounts of Jesus' last days, Emmerich's work moves from the terse narrative style of Scripture to the rich, colorful, highly detailed, verbosity of an epic. Her visions and meditations dwell much less on the moral, inspirational lessons of the Passion than those of her medieval predecessors, yet much more on filling in the "gaps" in the gospel stories. Her visions offer less a harmonization of those stories than an exhaustive, highly imaginative reconstruction of the events that the gospel reports. She spares no detail in describing the violence inflicted on Jesus. She dwells on the scenery and topography of the Holy Land, the architecture, the physical characteristics of the actors in her drama. As Gibson would do in his film, she repeatedly spots the devil working the crowd among Jesus' enemies. A broad array of additional details not found in the Gospels—from secret agents dispatched by the Jewish leaders who feed disinformation to the mob to a blow-by-blow description of Jesus' placement on the cross—reveal the full freedom that she has given to her imagination. The reader is left to visualize, to contemplate, to imagine further, if that is at all possible.

As she does with every detail of the Passion story, Emmerich expands upon earlier descriptions of the bloodthirstiness and evil of the Jews, their leaders above all. As in medieval works such as the *Meditations on the Life of Christ*, the Jews abuse Jesus, cruelly and gratuitously, at every possible opportunity. Thus does Emmerich picture the violence that Jesus suffered at the court of Caiphas.

> A crowd of miscreants—the very scum of the people—surrounded Jesus like a swarm of infuriated wasps, and began to heap every imaginable insult upon him. Even during the trial, whilst the witnesses were speaking, the archers and some others could not restrain their cruel inclinations, but pulled out handfuls of his hair and beard, spat upon him, struck him with their fists, wounded him with sharp-pointed sticks, and even ran needles into his body; but when Caiphas left the hall they set no bounds to their barbarity. They first placed a crown, made of straw and the bark of trees, upon his head, and then took it off, saluting him at the same time with insulting expressions . . . and whilst repeating these scoffing words, they continued to strike him with their fists and sticks, and to spit in his face. Next they put a crown of reeds upon his head, took off his robe and scapular, and then threw an old torn mantle, which scarcely reached his knees, over his shoulders; around his neck they hung a long iron chain, with an

iron ring at each end, studded with sharp points, which bruised and tore his knees as be walked. They again pinioned his arms, put a reed into his hand, and covered his Divine countenance with spittle. They had already thrown all sorts of filth over his hair, as well as over his chest, and upon the old mantle. They bound his eyes with a dirty rag, and struck him.[25]

Emmerich does focus on the Jews in one regard that Bonaventure and the *Meditations* conspicuously ignored: their acceptance of collective responsibility for the Crucifixion as related in Matthew, "His blood be on us and on our children!" Here she turns aside from her straightforward description of the events to confide, one might say, in her readers.

> Whenever, during my meditations on the Passion of our Lord, I imagine I hear that frightful cry of the Jews, *His blood be on us, and on our children*, visions of a wonderful and terrible description display before my eyes at the same moment the effect of that solemn curse. I fancy I see a gloomy sky covered with clouds, of the color of blood, from which issue fiery swords and darts, lowering over the vociferating multitude; and this curse, which they have entailed upon themselves, appears to me to penetrate even to the very marrow of their bones—even to the unborn infants. They appear to me encompassed on all sides by darkness; the words they utter take, in my eyes, the form of black flames, which recoil upon them, penetrating the bodies of some, and only playing around others.[26]

Though Emmerich preached to her readers much less than her medieval predecessors did to theirs, her selection of the Jews for such special reflection is impressive. Her work, like the work of those who have relied on her, points to the lasting contribution of the medieval traditions considered here: to Christian piety and religious devotion, to popular perceptions of the Passion, and to the history of anti-Judaism.

Clearly, the image of the demonic Jewish Christ killer propounded by such works of meditation and religious devotion somehow served the needs of the pious Christian. How so? What did the picture of the bloodthirsty deicide "do" for the faithful? The Christ-killing Jew of the meditations actually served a number of valuable purposes, none of them mutually exclusive. Paradoxically, in so doing, he may well have reinforced the need to conceive of him in such terms.

First, much like the rituals of the Jewish Passover and the Christian *Pascha* or Easter already discussed, Passion-centered devotion and meditation strove not only to instruct Christians concerning the Passion but also to involve them in it. The texts and rituals in this tradition, as investigators have noted, offered tools and techniques for relocating the believer to another time and place, the time and place of the utmost importance, so that he or she could experience the miracle of the Crucifixion firsthand. Bonaventure opened *The Tree of Life* with the following charge to his readers:

> With Christ I am nailed to the cross, says St. Paul. . . . The true worshiper of God, the true disciple of Christ, wanting to conform perfectly to the savior of all who was crucified for his sake, should try in the first place, with earnest intent, always to carry about, in soul and in body, the cross of Jesus Christ, until he can feel in himself the truth of the apostle's words.[27]

And at the beginning of *The Mystical Vine* he wrote: "Let us be bound with the bonds of the passion of the good and most loving Jesus, so that we may also share with him the bonds of love."[28] The author of the *Meditations on the Life of Christ* put it more simply still: "If you wish to profit you must be present at the same things that it is related that Christ did and said . . . leaving behind all other cares and anxieties."[29] Experiencing the Crucifixion properly depended on capturing Jesus' own experience in one's heart, one's imagination, and one's soul. In precisely this spirit, one must understand the flagellants of late medieval Europe, who scourged themselves to suffer what Jesus had suffered and who banded together in religious associations, confraternities, for the purpose of perpetuating "the memory of the passion of Christ."[30] And thus did St. Catherine of Siena (1347–1380) declare:

> Pour out your being by burning desire with the lamb who was slain and poured his life out for us. Rest in the cross—with Christ crucified. Delight—in Christ crucified; delight in suffering. Be a glutton for abuse—for Christ crucified. Let your heart and soul be grafted into the tree of the most holy cross—with Christ crucified.[31]

In a word, Catherine concluded, "make his wounds your home." The gruesome imagery of Jewish brutality surely helped in doing that, especially when the descendants of Jesus' murderers, of the same nature and equally guilty as their ancestors, were still to be found in the present age.

Second, focusing on the Jews' deicide in all its horror and detail helped the Christian reap other benefits from his or her meditation. As Catherine of Siena's words make very clear, devotional "participation" in the Crucifixion led the Christian in the path of *imitatio Christi*, the imitation of Christ, in his or her external behavior. And this, in turn, produced a spiritual and moral transformation within his or her soul. Again the author of the *Meditations* addressed the Franciscan sister, for whom he wrote: "Not only that penal and mortal crucifixion of the Lord, but also that suffering that went before, is cause for strong compassion, bitterness, and stupor."[32] Passion-centered devotion cultivated essential moral characteristics: love, compassion, mercy—most immediately for Jesus himself, but then, by his own example, for others, one's enemies included, as well. The Jews who killed Jesus reinforced that example with their own counterexample. The fourteenth-century Ludolph of Saxony concluded the lengthy and vivid description of the Passion in his *Life of Christ* with a series of prayers. Contemplating Jesus' betrayal by Judas, he implored God: "Let me imitate your example of unruffled patience and humility. Help me with your grace and advice to bear reproaches and everything I encounter with patience. May I never basely exchange you for anything of transitory value. And for the glory of your name may I suffer grief and humiliation with equanimity."[33] So, too, in considering the charges fabricated against Jesus before the Sanhedrin, Pilate, and Herod, Ludolph prayed: "Make me, I ask, bear injuries and insults patiently and gladly for the glory of your name."[34]

Third, visualizing violence can be titillating for some, while it allows others to achieve a profound sense of release, what many would call catharsis. Violence has throughout history assumed an important role in the religious rituals of various cultures: pagan, Jewish, Christian, and others. In many instances, cultic sacrifice—that is, rituals of shedding blood, whether actual or symbolic—allows a community to resolve divisive tension and conflict. It allows for atonement, forgiveness, a sense of cleansing, the conviction that its participants have been saved from impending disaster or utter destruction. Similarly, graphic descriptions of violence contribute much to the power of memories of the past, especially in stories of the lives and deaths of saintly martyrs. These tales typically bring the conflict between forces of evil and good to a head: tyrant and subject, oppressor and oppressed, infidel and believer, the enemy of God and his saint. Paradoxically, in the most powerful of these stories both sides to this cosmic battle contribute roundly to the violence. The violence, one might say, unites them and thereby makes their story a coherent one. The villain inflicts violence with malicious pleasure, relishing the suffering of the innocent. The victim desires to suffer and to die a violent death with no less passion than his tormentor's. Without the visual imagery of brutal violence, the story does not "work." The common ground where the villain's lust to kill meets the victim's passion to die a sacrifice generates an experience that some writers have labeled nothing less than sublime.

This perspective certainly sheds light on devotion to the Passion. As one scholar of Christian literature has aptly observed, "the greater the violence, the better and more enduring the truth, and the greater our obligation to believe in it."[35] For Christians, Jesus is the ultimate sacrificial victim, the martyr par excellence. His crucifixion entails violence and murder that are truly gratuitous, and that therefore yield atonement, rebirth, and salvation to all that would acknowledge its power. For his part in the pictures of the

Passion that the writers of the devotion texts projected, the Jewish Christ killer assumes a critical importance, too. Inflamed by malice, in league with the devil, inured to any sense of compassion, the Jew contributes to the effectiveness of the Passion no less than Christ himself. Catherine of Siena wrote enthusiastically to Christians to "lock yourselves into the wounds of Christ crucified."[36] She, like every other preacher and visionary, knew that the Jews had opened those wounds for her. Along with many others before and after her, Catherine attests to Father Gerard Sloyan's observations that the Crucifixion story has, over the centuries, nurtured a "Christian piety of pain" and that the principal victims of that Crucifixion have, in fact, been the Jews.[37]

## POLITICAL PROPAGANDA

Identification with the suffering endured by Jesus at the hands of the Jews became so deeply rooted in the minds and feelings of European Christians that it found expression in countless dimensions of Western social and cultural life. Some of these have already been discussed in this book, and Part 3 will dwell on the fine arts, drama, and film. The remaining pages of this chapter focus on some instructive examples of the Christ-killer myth's applications in the subsequent history of anti-Semitism, and political propaganda in particular. These examples are often pointedly anti-Jewish, but at times they may appear far removed from the conflict between Judaism and Christianity. In either case, they help us to appreciate the extent to which the Western mentality had internalized the Christ-killer myth. The "fact" of the Jew's guilt in the Passion story did not require a second thought, and attention could be shifted to a different question: If the true Christian shared in the agony of the Crucifixion along with Jesus, and if, as everyone knew, the Jews of every generation conspired to destroy Jesus, who "qualified" as the Jewish crucifiers' latest victim? That role seemed to confer a great deal of status, and preachers and propagandists clamored to show how it rightly belonged to their respective causes.

Martin Luther, the great Protestant reformer of the sixteenth century, repeatedly grouped the enemies of Christ under the same umbrella, blaming most of the ills of contemporary society on "Jews, Papists (Catholics), and Turks." In his preaching, it often served his purposes to transfer the characteristics of one of these hated groups to another, as he did rather notably in his "Sermons on the Passion." Luther gives the New Testament Passion narratives a rationale that goes hand in hand with the Passion-centered devotion that had come to dominate European Christianity.

> The history of Christ's wrongs is given us especially to the end that
> we may not be offended when similar wrongs are inflicted upon us

also, but that we may always refer to it for consolation and learn to be patient. For if God's son, our master and our head, was falsely accused, delivered to Pilate by the high priests, scribes and elders, and surrendered to the Gentiles to be crucified, is it to be wondered at if we receive similar treatment . . . ? We should rejoice when our experience is such that we can truthfully boast: This was the experience of my Lord Jesus also. For if we are like him in suffering, we are warranted in the hope of being like him in glory too.[38]

Not only ought the believer to participate in the Passion with Jesus and thereby become a better Christian, but the experience of the Passion confirms that one is truly like him, destined for salvation and glory. At present, Luther argues, "the pope . . . has the very bag of Judas hanging from his neck." He takes money and property "in exchange for the gospel, which he betrays and sells . . . as the Jews dealt with the Lord Jesus before Caiaphas and Pilate."[39] Luther claims that the pope and his bishops fabricate charges against him and his followers, twisting their words to mean what they never intended, persecuting them without cause. In all, the pope desires "to treat us and the gospel as the Jews here treated Christ."[40] One should hardly conclude from this that the Jews do not bear collective responsibility for Jesus' death. Luther's words do not suggest, as some medieval preachers did suggest, that all sinners, Christian and otherwise, share in that guilt. Rather, he conveys a more partisan message. Leaders of the Catholic Church share in the Jews' role as killers of Christ in the way that true Christians now relive his Passion. Just as the Jews incurred everlasting guilt for their murder of Jesus, so the pope and company should expect a similar fate. "For it is impossible that God should look on such deeds in silence; innocent blood cries so mightily into his ears that he must rise and inflict punishment."[41] If Luther's Protestant church and doctrine are divine, Catholics, like the Jews, are their deicides.

Luther's sermons testify to the versatility of the Christ-killer motif. Even as most European kingdoms expelled their Jews during the later Middle Ages, the Jewish Christ killer retained his importance in Western culture, continuing to appear in literature, drama, and art in the absence of the Jews themselves. From Chaucer to Margery Kempe, from the cycles of Corpus Christi Day miracle plays to the poetry of the seventeenth century, European literature retained its picture of the Jewish Christ killer, who inflicted violence on that which was most sacred to the culture and society of Western Christianuty.[42]

But the Jews returned to modern Europe, and, over the course of the eighteenth and nineteenth centuries, they gained "emancipation," full-fledged citizenship, in major Western countries, including England, France, Germany, Italy, and the United States. Paradoxically, these changes for the benefit of the Jews heralded a new wave of anti-Judaism, both in its essentially medieval Christian version and in the guise of a newer breed of European anti-Semitism. Though some philosophers called for Jewish emancipation on the eve of the French Revolution, for instance, more traditional voices could still proclaim that "a Jew is a born and sworn enemy of all Christians" and that Christians properly "regard Jews as the God-killing executioners of Jesus Christ."[43] Within a century, Europe had given birth to modern anti-Semitism (a term first made fashionable by a German journalist in the 1870s), a political, religiously charged, often racist ideology that climaxed with the Holocaust. Though different in many respects from Christian anti-Judaism of ancient and medieval times, one hardly replaced the other. Anti-Semitism found eager allies among traditional Christian detractors of the Jews, and it borrowed many terms and ideas from the long history of the Jewish-Christian conflict.

Modern anti-Semitism infused new life and meaning into many of these, long after the power of the medieval papacy had waned. Perhaps with the exception of the Holocaust itself, no chapter in modern history illustrates this better than the Dreyfus Affair, which dropped like a bombshell on France at the end of the nineteenth century, exploding French politics, society, and culture, and their long-standing bonds between church and state. In 1894, Alfred Dreyfus, a Jewish artillery officer on the French general staff, was falsely charged with having sold state secrets to Germany. Forged evidence and foul play quickly resulted in his court-martial, conviction, public degradation, and sentence of life imprisonment on Devil's Island (off French Guyana). As Dreyfus's supporters protested his innocence, opponents of the Jews embarked on a massive campaign of anti-Semitic propaganda, bewailing the Jews' subversion of the French military, the French nation, and the essence of France herself. People talked about little else. Dreyfusards and anti-Dreyfusards, as Dreyfus's supporters and opponents were dubbed, railed against each other in the media, in the courts, and in every available political forum. Anti-Jewish riots broke out in French-ruled Algeria. Some French Jews went into hiding. After the original forgery had been exposed and the forger had committed suicide in jail, Dreyfus was returned to France from Devil's Island only to be retried and reconvicted, and opposition to the Jews did not abate. Dreyfus received a presidential pardon in 1899, but not until 1906 did the high court of France exonerate him and did he regain his military commission.

I have made a long, complicated story very short. The Dreyfus Affair marks a critical turning point in the history of modern France, and it has also been credited with awakening Theodore Herzl, the father of modern Zionism, to the critical need for a Jewish national home as an antidote to anti-Semitism. The story has been told and analyzed at great length, and my concern here lies exclusively with one aspect of the anti-Semitic rhetoric that resounded in France toward the turn of the century. Though surely an episode in the history of the new, distinctively modern and political anti-Semitism, the Dreyfus Affair demonstrates well that one cannot differentiate neatly between that anti-Semitism and the older, Christian anti-Judaism. For the anti-Semites enthusiastically exploited the traditional charges of that anti-Judaism. The Jews were in league with the devil. They thirsted for Christian blood, whether that of the individuals who had engineered Dreyfus's conviction or that of the French people as a whole. They formed an international conspiracy, aimed at bringing the French nation to its ruin, intent on ruling the world with its global wealth. Owing to the negligence and complicity of sympathetic leaders, the Jews had infiltrated the ranks of the French military and state bureaucracy, polluting and defiling the purity that had once been the hallmark of French society and culture. And, almost needless to say, the Jews were deicides, ready to betray and crucify their redeemers, now just as then. There are countless examples, and I mention only a few.

As Dreyfus was led to his degradation ceremony, an angry crowd expressed itself unabashedly. "Death to the Jews!" "Death to the traitor!" "Death to Judas!"[44] The identification of Dreyfus with Judas (fig. 6.1) seemed obvious: both Jews, both intent on betraying, even crucifying, the master whom he claimed to serve (in Dreyfus's case, France). A poem that appeared in the anti-Semitic press between Dreyfus's conviction and degradation depicted God as condemning the Jews, lamenting that the blood of his son is rising up and crying out against them; "an errant, proscribed race," these "descendants of Judas," driven by their lust for money, should not be made soldiers.[45] So deeply did this image take hold in the French collective mentality that a French diplomat who had come to recognize Dreyfus's innocence could remark to a colleague, "This time Judas is innocent!"[46] On the eve of the Dreyfus Affair, a prominent Catholic bishop who linked the Jews and the Freemasons as partners in a conspiratorial "Synagogue of Satan" had written: "How strange this people of Israel is, compared with the rest of humanity! How great and majestic in its history, so long as it remained obedient to the Lord! How great also, and above all terrible in its hatred of the messiah, whom it refused to recognize and whom it killed on the cross!"[47]

Judas, in other words, was not Dreyfus but was the entire Jewish people, and the anti-Dreyfusards railed repeatedly against the Jewish "syndicate of betrayal."[48] When Major Joseph Henry confessed to forging the evidence that had incriminated Dreyfus and then killed himself, the anti-Dreyfusards pronounced him and his actions heroic. His blood was like that of Jesus, sacrificed to the malice of the Jews on behalf of his countrymen. Some twenty-five thousand contributed to a fund to support Henry's widow. Many subscribers enclosed supportive notes with their donations, and a goodly number of these clamored for relief from the menace of the Jews. For instance: "Sacred heart of Jesus, hasten the promised miracle which will proclaim the triumph

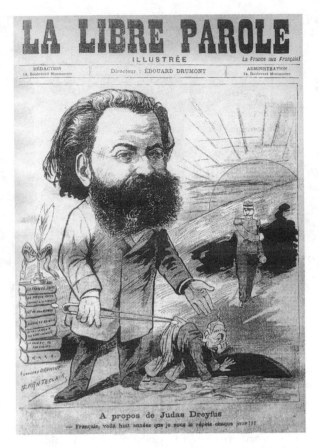

FIGURE 6.1. Judas-Dreyfus, *La libre parole*, no. 70,
November 10, 1894, p. 1.

of your church and deliver the Catholic nations from the shameful yoke of those who crucified you."[49] In a similar vein, the conservative Catholic newspaper *La Croix* (*The Cross*) chastised France for its infidelity that explained its present woes. Until those sins are forgiven, "Christ must inflict on the eldest daughter of the church a punishment reminiscent of his own passion. That is why he allowed her to be betrayed, sold, jeered at, beaten, covered with spittle, and crucified by the Jews."[50]

Politics motivated others to exploit the saga of the Crucifixion in their own behalf. Although historians disagree as to whether he had the Jews in mind, the American statesman William Jennings Bryan lashed out at big business and capitalism at the Democratic Party's national convention in 1896 (while Dreyfus himself remained incarcerated on Devil's Island), and anti-Semitism reared its head elsewhere during the 1896 presidential campaign as well (fig. 6.2). "You shall not press down this crown of thorns on labor's

HISTORY REPEATS ITSELF.

FIGURE 6.2. "History Repeats Itself." Political cartoon from the 1896 presidential election campaign that appeared in *Sound Money* on April 15, 1896. http:// projects.vassar.edu/1896/0415csm.html. Courtesy of Rebecca Edwards.

brow; you shall not crucify mankind upon a cross of gold."[51] Yet the myth of an international conspiracy of thoroughly Jewish financiers bent on ruling the world reached its most elaborate exposition in the infamous forgery of the *Protocols of the Elders of Zion*. The *Protocols* first appeared early in the twentieth century, was endorsed by the American industrial magnate Henry Ford, and still enjoys great popularity in the Arab world today. Though reprinted hundreds of times in many languages, the *Protocols* is actually a rather sloppy adaptation of a pamphlet first titled "In the Jewish Cemetery in Prague" and later published as "The Rabbi's Speech," itself a reworking of a German novel written in 1868. "The Rabbi's Speech" portrays the leader of world Jewry plotting the overthrow of Christendom. "For eighteen centuries Israel has been at war with that power which was first promised to Abraham but which was taken from him by the cross." As a result, the rabbi declares, "for eighteen centuries our wise men have been fighting the cross courageously," and now, at last, the time of their victory fast approaches.[52] Though the *Protocols* does not mention the Crucifixion, it states that the Jewish domination of the world seeks "the complete crash of the Christian religion" and the

SABIOS DE SION
PROTOCOLOS

PLAN:
Destruir la Cristiandad
Esclavizar la Humanidad

FIGURE 6.3. Cover of the 1963 Spanish edition of the
*Protocols of the Elders of Zion.* Courtesy of Simon
Wiesenthal Center Archives.

reinstatement of the true heirs of King David to the throne that the church, with its false Davidic messiah, usurped from them.[53] The unstated connection between this and the myth of the Jewish Christ killer is made explicit in the cover of a Spanish edition of the *Protocolos de los Sabios de Sion*, published in Madrid in 1963 (fig. 6.3).

Much as in the case of the blood libel, the preposterousness of the *Protocols* has not driven the myth of the international Jewish conspiracy underground, even in the wake of the Holocaust. The book and its ideas still thrive in different parts of the world, especially in Arab lands (fig. 6.4) and in under-

**FIGURE 6.4.** Cover of the 2002 Arab edition of the *Protocols of the Elders of Zion*. Achbaar Allyum Press, Egypt. Courtesy of Ha-Merkaz le-Moreshet Modi'in, Ramat ha-Sharon, Israel.

developed countries, some of them Christian, some not. Egyptian television recently developed the book into a forty-part series of television programs, and Syrian officials still quote from it publicly. They certainly make one wonder about the continued successes of ancient mythology, the deadly potential of the story.

# MYTH AND COUNTERMYTH

N ews of Mel Gibson's film *The Passion* triggered vociferous responses
from all quarters of the Jewish community. Just as Christians did, Jews
debated the contents of the film, its wisdom, its fairness, and its legitimacy as
an artist's expression of his love for God. Among the most resounding cries
were those of the film's opponents, those who railed against its traditional
understanding of the Jews' role in the crucifixion of Jesus. After a private
screening of the movie months before its general release, Abraham Foxman,
director of the Anti-Defamation League of B'nai B'rith, stated to the press:
"The film unambiguously portrays Jewish authorities and the Jewish mob as
the ones responsible for the decision to crucify Jesus. . . . We are deeply concerned that the film, if released in its present form, could fuel the hatred, big-
otry and anti-Semitism that many churches have worked hard to repudiate."[1]

Nearly two thousand years after his death, Jesus' Passion continues to
exercise the passions of Christians and Jews alike. For many Jews nowadays,
it still exemplifies the darkest side of Christian anti-Semitism and the perception of Jews that allowed the Holocaust to occur in the heart of Christian
Europe. The story awakens the most deep-seated Jewish fears and insecuri-
ties. It obsesses Jewish intellectuals and communal leaders, especially those
involved in interfaith relations.

This sense of mortal danger is nothing new. As we saw in chapter 4,
when the Dominican friar Paul Christian confronted the Jews of Paris in a
public disputation in 1270, the accusation of deicide terrified the Jewish community more than any other. Whereas the rabbi representing the Jews did not
hesitate to respond freely, at times even impudently, to his rival's other arguments, the Christ-killer label stymied him. He "was very much afraid to speak
of the slaying of Jesus, because this revealed his [Paul's] intention to exterminate all of the Jews."[2] Rabbi Abraham meekly referred to Jesus' prayer that
his killers be forgiven and then sought to deflect the conversation to other
matters. He evidently sensed that in public debate over the Crucifixion, the
stakes were too high. Just as Abraham Foxman sensed in the case of *The
Passion*, the Jews had much, perhaps too much, to lose.

In view of the fear and hypersensitivity that the charge of deicide awakens among Jews, we would do well to consider their responses to the Christ-

killer myth at this midpoint in our story. How did they counter the basic Christian teaching that they had killed their God and messiah and that they still bore guilt for those actions? Did their reactions to the Passion narrative, powerful and engaging as it is, extend beyond an attempt to exonerate themselves? What effect might "the greatest story ever told" have had upon them, too? As will become clear, even as Jews struggled to refute the Christ-killer myth, they found themselves attracted by the Crucifixion, which somehow they tried to appropriate for themselves. Moreover, as one reviews Jewish responses to the Crucifixion story from ancient to medieval to modern times, one notes a striking degree of continuity. Less than one might have expected has changed.

## EXPLAINING THE DEED

The cross itself has evoked fright, discomfort, revulsion, and hostility among Jews who confront it. It was in the name of the cross that Jews typically suffered in Christian lands, and Jews, too, have long recognized that the cross and its story lie at the heart of the antagonism between Judaism and Christianity. For most Jews of the Middle Ages, the crucifix and other icons in Christian churches and Christian homes—not to mention on the persons of Christians themselves—tainted Christianity with idolatry. Along with Jewish objections to the doctrine of the Trinity, the Christian veneration of icons led many rabbinic authorities to rule that Jews could under no circumstances enter a church—as opposed to a Muslim mosque, which could be considered a place acceptable for Jewish worship. Numerous Jewish texts refer to the crucifix simply as "the abomination" (*to'evah*) or "the detestable idol" (*shikkutz*). And, as an incident related by the thirteenth-century British monk-historian Matthew Paris demonstrates well, the conflict over the cross could prove a matter of life and death, in both physical and spiritual senses.

> An English deacon loved a Jewess with unlawful love, and ardently desired her embraces. "I will do what you ask," said she, "if you will turn apostate, be circumcised and hold fast to the Jewish faith." When he had done what she bade him he gained her unlawful love. But this could not long be concealed, and was reported to [Archbishop] Stephen of Canterbury. Before him the deacon was accused; the evidence was consistent and weighty; he was convicted and then confessed all these matters, and that he had taken open part in a sacrifice which the Jews made of a crucified boy. And when it was seen that the deacon was circumcised, and that no argument would bring him to his senses, he solemnly apostatized before the archbishop and the assembled prelates in this manner: A cross with the Crucified was brought before him and he urinated on the cross, saying, "I renounce the new-fangled law

and the comments of Jesus the false prophet," and he reviled and slandered Mary the mother of Jesus, and made a charge against her not to be repeated. Thereupon the archbishop, weeping bitterly at hearing such blasphemies, deprived him of his orders. And when he had been cast out of the church, [an English Baron named] Fawkes . . . dragged him away to a secret spot and cut off his head.[3]

Still, neither did incidents like this one occur every day, nor could Jews make do simply with their own revulsion as they combated the stigma of Christ killer that Christianity had imposed upon them. Although the third-century bishop Melito of Sardis had addressed *On the Pascha* to his Christian parishioners, not to the Jews whom he condemned for crucifying Jesus, his poem reveals that Christians confronted Jews directly with their accusations and that Jews responded in their own defense.

> *What have you done, Israel? Or is it not written for you,*
>   *"You shall not shed innocent blood,"*
>     *so that you may not die an evil death?*
> *"I did," says Israel, "kill the Lord.*
>   *Why? Because he had to die."*

The Jewish retort to the bishop appears too well conceived to be contrived. In fact, it numbers among at least six different strategies for refuting the deicide charge that appear in classical and medieval Jewish sources and that deserve some explanation.

    1. *Jesus deserved his punishment.* The Talmud forbids the entrapment of criminal suspects into confessing their crimes, except in the case of one who has secretly tempted other Jews to leave the faith, such that the lack of eyewitness testimony to his wiles would otherwise make a conviction impossible. Several passages indicate that this procedure allowed for the conviction of one Ben Stada in the Israeli town of Lod, and then for his execution, by stoning or hanging, on the day before the Passover holiday. Numerous scholars, though hardly all, accept the identification of Ben Stada with Jesus, both in these passages and in others. Yet at one point the Talmud appears to refer unmistakably to Jesus' crucifixion, despite some discrepancy between its own account and that of the Gospels.

> On the eve of the Passover they hanged Jesus the Nazarene. Forty days earlier the herald preceded him, crying: Jesus the Nazarene is to be stoned for having bewitched, deceived, and led Israel astray.[4]

The reliability or unreliability of this rabbinic tradition need not concern us. The issue at hand is its explanation for the Crucifixion: Jesus deserved what he received. He deceitfully sowed the seeds of religious dissent and discord in the Jewish community, threatening its faith with his subversive witchcraft. According to biblical law (Deuteronomy 13) one who commits these crimes must suffer capital punishment, and Jesus died as he did with good reason.

In all fairness, this rabbinic report probably teaches us next to nothing concerning Jesus and his last days but reflects the historical context in which it was related and transmitted—just as was the case of the New Testament Passion narratives. Indeed, the rabbis would have perceived Jesus' teaching as treacherous—and his entrapment as legitimate—only after the sect of the earliest Christians had begun to emerge within the Jewish community and before most of that sect left the community's mainstream. Several generations after the Crucifixion, in other words, the rabbis effectively condemn Jesus for having generated the friction *in their day* between Jews who accepted rabbinic authority and Jewish believers in Jesus. For this reason did he deserve his miserable end.

Striking confirmation of this rabbinic attitude toward Jesus and the early Jewish Christians can be found in an infamous collection of Jewish stories about Jesus—most of them extremely uncomplimentary—titled *Toledot Yeshu* (*The Life Story of Jesus*). Though this collection evolved in various versions that reached their final form only during the Middle Ages, much of its material stems from centuries earlier and from the traditions of the rabbis of the Talmud. The *Toledot Yeshu* portrays Jesus' birth as being a result of an adulterous union. Upon reaching adulthood, Jesus stole into the innermost sanctuary of the temple in Jerusalem and made off with the closely guarded secret of God's holy name. This gave him the magical powers to perform the miracles that won him the support of several hundred followers. The sages of Israel lodged a complaint with the Roman Queen Heleni, and they enlisted the aid of Judas Iscariot, who, armed with the same secret knowledge of God's name, polluted Jesus in an airborne duel. As a widely circulating version of the *Toledot Yeshu* reports, the queen delivered Jesus to the Jewish sages after his defeat, and they bound him to the pillar of the Holy Ark in the synagogue in Tiberias. The mob of "fools and apostates who believed his words" tried in vain to set him free.

> They were there until the eve of Passover, which that year fell on the Sabbath. Jesus came with his disciples to Jerusalem on the eve of Passover, this being Friday, and he rode on a donkey. He said to his disciples: "It was said about me, 'Rejoice greatly, O daughter of Zion . . . your king comes to you . . . riding on an ass.'" At this time everyone cried and bowed down to him and he entered the house of study with his three hundred and ten disciples. One of them whose name was Gisa came and said to the sages, "Do you want the Wicked One . . . ? We, the three hundred and ten disciples have already sworn

by the Ten Commandments not to say who he is, but, when you come in the morning, greet us and I will go and bow to him, and the one to whom I render obeisance is the Wicked One. . . . " The sages entered the house of study where those who came from Antioch were, and the very same Wicked One was with them. Gisa entered with them. He left the congregation and bowed to Yeshu the Wicked. Immediately the sages understood; they rose against him and grabbed him. . . . The evil men began to cry but were not able to save him. At that same time he was killed. It was on Friday, and the eve of Passover.[5]

The story successfully strives to ridicule Jesus and his followers. More precisely, it ridicules the Christian account of the Crucifixion, without which many details in its own ensuing narrative make little sense (the crown of thorns, the vinegar given Jesus to drink, the coincidence of the eve of the Passover and the eve of the Sabbath, rumors of the Resurrection, etc.). Yet the *Toledot Yeshu* does more than simply ridicule and malign. It depicts Jesus and his followers as fomenting rebellion in the Jewish community and as undermining its religious law, order, and unity. In a word, it justifies his execution. Ironically, the *Toledot Yeshu* lavishes praise on Peter and Paul for expediting the departure of the new Christian sect from the Jewish community in the wake of Jesus' execution, and it says this was accomplished at the beckoning and with the assistance of the rabbis. Though historians today appreciate that Jesus lived and died as a well-intentioned Jew and that the legacy of Paul underlay the transformation of Christianity into a rival religion, the *Toledot Yeshu* saw things otherwise: Jesus was a villain, and Peter and Paul were heroes. Jesus fractured the divinely ordained religious unity of the Jewish people from within, and for this he deserved to die. Peter and Paul minimized the danger of the new sect by removing it from the fold, and for that they were praiseworthy.

   2. *The Jews facilitated salvation.* According to Melito of Sardis, the Jews explained that they killed Jesus "because he had to die." This argument struck at the core of the church's Christology, its theological understanding of Jesus, his role, and his accomplishments. Was the Crucifixion necessary to bring salvation to humankind? If so, how can one indict the Jews for implementing the divine purpose? Early in the fourteenth century, *Sefer Nitzaḥon* (*The Book of Victory*), a Jewish guidebook for resisting Christian preachers and missionaries, proposed a similar response to the charge of deicide. The Jew should retort to the Christian:

> You say that he came to die at the hands of man. If so, those who killed him fulfilled his will, and it was through them that his counsel and decree to redeem the souls from hell were carried out, while nothing at all was accomplished through those who did not touch him. Indeed, if the former had also refrained from harming him like

the latter, then his entire advent would have been useless and in vain. Consequently, you should reverse your words and say that those who fulfilled his will and through whom his counsel was carried out are the righteous men, while those who did not touch him are wicked because they did not hasten to carry out his counsel so that he might redeem people from hell. Indeed, it is amazing that you call those who hanged him evil men and sinners.[6]

Put more simply, Christians should thank the Jews profusely for having crucified Jesus, without which they would never have been saved.

3. *The Crucifixion represents the will of God.* Jews could and did use this line of argument to focus not only on their own praiseworthiness, but also on the theological implications of the Passion narrative. Did God will the Crucifixion? If not, how could it have occurred? If so, why blame the Jews? One encounters this challenge to Christians in a twelfth-century book titled *The Polemic of Nestor the Priest*, perhaps the earliest handbook of Jewish anti-Christian polemic that has survived.

Tell me now concerning your God whom you worship: Does he or does he not have power? If you say that he does have power . . . , inform me about that which the Jews did to him. Did they do it to him according to his will or against his will? If you say according to his will . . . everything which the Jews did to him was good and just according to your word, since they did his will. If you say they did to him that which he did not want, can someone who cannot save himself from the hands of the Jews, the Greeks, and the infidels possibly be a God?[7]

4. *Jesus himself said, "Father, forgive them . . . "* The Gospel of Luke recounts that while on the cross, Jesus begged God to pardon those who were executing him. Did God heed his prayer or not? As we have seen (chapter 4), medieval churchmen wrestled with this question, but Jews raised it, too. One thirteenth-century text, now included in Joseph Kimhi's *Sefer ha-Berit (The Book of the Covenant)*, asked as follows:

It is written in the Gospel that when they afflicted Jesus, Jesus cried out to his father and said, "My father, forgive this people for they know not what they do." If it is so that he prayed for his father to forgive us, either his prayer was sincere [or it was not]. If his prayer and supplication were sincere, his death and the sufferings he underwent are forgiven us. It is not right that we undergo any punishment for his death since he forgave us and prayed for us. If his prayer is not sincere and he said one thing with his mouth and another in his heart, then the rest of his words are insincere.[8]

*5. ". . . for they know not what they do."* Even if their ancestors did kill Jesus, Jews could argue, they hardly intended to murder their messiah or the Son of God himself, and they should be judged according to their intentions. God would never have condemned the Jews to their ongoing exile for such a well-intentioned deed. The same thirteenth-century author elaborated:

> It was not their intention to kill the son of God but . . . to kill a human being, the son of a man and a woman. No sin is [to be imputed] to them because [all] things [are considered] with respect to the intention of the heart. Therefore, they are not justified in saying that by trying Jesus, our exile has been protracted for many years.[9]

*6. The Jews did not crucify Jesus.* Although ancient and medieval Jews rarely rejected the Christian contention that their ancestors were responsible for the Crucifixion—as modern Jews (and Christians) often do—some premodern Jewish voices did begin to hint in such a direction. Recalling the biblical teaching (Deuteronomy 21:23) that "a hanged man is accursed by God," *The Polemic of Nestor the Priest* rebukes the Christian for adoring the cross: "If he was crucified, you have rendered his body accursed." The key word here, of course, is *if*. Echoing, perhaps, the early heresy of Docetism that denied the humanity of Christ altogether, or perhaps under the influence of the Koran's teaching (Sura 4:157) that Jesus was never crucified,[10] did the author intend to deny the truth of the Passion narrative altogether? In a similar vein, the fourteenth-century *Sefer Nitzahon* challenged the common Christian interpretation of Psalm 22 as a biblical forecast of the Crucifixion. Afflicted and in danger, the psalmist exclaims in clearly symbolic language (v. 12): "Many bulls encompass me." Noting that according to the Christian interpretation, "these are the Jews that judged" Jesus, the author responds: "Where do we find that the people of Israel are called bulls? The Romans and other nations are called that," and he offers supporting evidence from other books of the Bible.[11] Although the Jewish author intended chiefly to discredit the Christian interpretation of this very suggestive Psalm, his comments certainly hint at the argument that the Romans, not the Jews, bear the responsibility for Jesus' demise.

Denial of responsibility for Jesus' death has certainly been the dominant theme in modern Jews' consideration of the Crucifixion story. The generally acclaimed father of Jewish historical studies, the nineteenth-century German scholar Heinrich Graetz, reappraised the New Testament characters of the Jewish priests and the Roman Pilate in his highly influential *History of the Jews.*

> That Pilate on the contrary found Jesus innocent and wished to save him, while the Judaeans had determined upon putting him to death, is unhistorical and merely legendary. . . . After the verdict of death was pronounced by the Roman authorities, the condemned prisoner belonged no more to his own nation, but to the Roman state. It was

not the Synhedrion but Pilate that gave the order for the execution of one who was regarded as a state criminal and a cause of disturbance and agitation.[12]

The Romans, not the Jews, argued Graetz, bore primary responsibility for Jesus' execution, and most prominent Jewish historians since have accepted that verdict. When, in the aftermath of World War I, the Israeli historian Joseph Klausner published the first modern Jewish biography of Jesus, he praised Jesus and his ethical teaching, a stance that incurred the wrath of other Zionist intellectuals. But when it came to the Crucifixion, Klausner followed squarely in Graetz's footsteps.

> Through fear of the Roman tyrant, those who were then the chief men among the Jews delivered up Jesus to this tyrant. No Jews took any further part in the actual trial and crucifixion. Pilate, the "man of blood," was responsible for the rest. The Jews, *as a nation*, were far less guilty of the death of Jesus than the Greeks, as a nation, were guilty of the death of Socrates; but who now would think of avenging the blood of Socrates the Greek upon his countrymen, the present Greek race? Yet these nineteen hundred years past the world has gone on avenging the blood of Jesus the Jew upon his countrymen, the Jews, who have already paid the penalty, and still go on paying the penalty in rivers and torrents of blood.[13]

First published during World War II, Solomon Zeitlin's *Who Crucified Jesus?* went further still in limiting the role of the Jews. Alluding to the treacherous villain of the Nazi occupation of Norway in 1940, Zeitlin characterized those priests who handed Jesus over to Pilate as Quislings "who proved ready to sell out Judea to the Romans for personal gain."[14] They hardly represented the mainstream of the Jewish people or the Jewish religion. Some forty years later, Zeitlin's student Ellis Rivkin reworked his mentor's title in his own book on understanding the Crucifixion. Rivkin asked not who crucified Jesus but *What Crucified Jesus?* Reflecting on the events of Jesus' last days in their historical context, and clearly with an eye toward fostering ecumenical goodwill, Rivkin proposes that our focus "shift from casting blame on persons to casting blame on the time, the place, and the situation." He concludes that "it was the Roman imperial system that was at fault, not the system of Judaism."[15]

   Though by far the most popular, denial of responsibility is not the only strategy of response to the deicide charge that modern Jewish scholars inherited from their predecessors. In the earliest editions of his *History of the Jews*, before he had begun to argue the innocence of the Jews, Graetz stressed that they did play an instrumental role in Jesus' demise and, given his crimes, rightly so. Graetz thus joined Abraham Geiger and other Jewish intellectuals in concluding that Jesus deserved his punishment. Several decades later, the prominent American Reform rabbi Emil Hirsch offered the same argument against the "Christ-killer" indictment that Melito of Sardis had caricatured seventeen centuries earlier—albeit in a much more conciliatory tone.

> It is far from my mind to treat irreverently a dogma which bodies truth for many of the best of men who now draw breath under the sun. But if that dogma is true . . . , had Jesus not died, would man be cleansed of his guilt, washed by the blood of Golgotha? If such redemption is the consummation of the divine scheme of salvation . . . , far from hating the Jews for thus helping along as they had to . . . , those who rejoice that the death of Jesus has taken from them the taint of guilt, should turn with gratitude to the Jews, but for whom such salvation would not have been wrought.[16]

And, at the beginning of the twentieth century, British writer Paul Goodman referred those Christians who would condemn the Jews to Jesus' own prayer for their forgiveness: "Father, forgive them, for they know not what they do."

> There are but two alternatives as to the effect of this prayer. If the Jews, from the Christian standpoint, are to be held liable for the alleged crucifixion of Jesus by some of their forefathers, then his prayer to God was not heard—a supposition which will hardly be admitted by his followers; but if his prayer was granted by God—as every Christian must unreservedly concede—then there can be no question but that the Jews were absolved both by Jesus, as well as by God Himself, from the punishment of their admittedly unconscious guilt.[17]

All in all, even as ancient and medieval times recede far into the background, little has changed in the Jewish arsenal of self-defense against their collective condemnation for Jesus' murder.

## APPROPRIATING THE MYTH

Most strikingly, Jewish concern with the cross and the Crucifixion story has far exceeded the limits of denial and self-defense. Judaism and Christianity have maintained an intense, complicated relationship characterized by mutual influence, cultural exchange, and shared traditions and symbols—not by hostility and rejection alone. But although such ambivalence regarding the rival religion has long been recognized in the case of Christian attitudes toward Jews and Judaism, we have only recently begun to appreciate the involvement of Jews in the issues, beliefs, and religious symbolism of Christianity. Jewish interest in the Passion narrative affords us a fascinating case in point.

One should note at the outset that Jews have continuously acknowledged the importance of the Gospels and their accounts of the Crucifixion for a proper understanding of Jesus and his death. Jewish tradition offered no alternative, independent account of his life and death. Many teachings of the rabbis of the Talmud that have been thought to refer to Jesus—such as the references to Ben Stada mentioned above—may not refer to him at all. Those that do generally date from at least two or three centuries after Jesus; and, of these, many developed far away from Jesus' native land. In all, the rabbis appear to have had no knowledge of what happened to Jesus that does not reflect the influence of Christian tradition in general, and that of the Gospels in particular. This hardly establishes that ancient Jews read and studied the New Testament. To the contrary, the discrepancies between what the classical rabbis have to say about Jesus and what one reads in the Gospels—quite apart from the imaginative, often cynical parody of his story in the *Toledot Yeshu*—suggest that the story of Jesus and his execution were "in the air" in the Mediterranean world, so that most Jews gained their knowledge indirectly, very likely by word of mouth. Yet Christian tradition remained their ultimate source. As we have seen, ancient and medieval Jews rarely disavowed the responsibility for the Crucifixion that the Gospels attributed to them. They defended their actions as the Gospels described them, but they did not deny them. One might say that as "the people of the book," the Jews' respect for Scripture extended to scriptures other than their own. When condemned as Christ killers, they affirmed their description as killers, though not of Christ, not of their savior and God's son.

Modern Jews, of course, typically deny the "killer" charge most emphatically. Curiously, however, this denial has itself resulted from a more serious engagement with the Gospels—and with new, critical methods for analyzing the biblical text developed by Christian scholars of the New Testament. There exists no documented Passion narrative prior to those of the Gospels, and certainly no independent Jewish source against which to evaluate the Gospels' story. Each and every one of the modern Jewish writers whom I have cited begins and ends his reckoning of Jesus' death with the same gospel texts that underlie both the teaching of Christian churches and that of Christian biblical scholarship. Understandably, the perspective and presuppositions that Jews take with them into any discussion of the Crucifixion differ greatly from those of Christian writers on the subject. But the basic story line remains the same. Indeed, the exclamations of the great nineteenth-century American rabbi Isaac Mayer Wise—that "the Christian story, as the Gospels narrate it, is a big babble," that "the trials of Jesus are positively not true" but rather are "pure inventions," that "the crucifixion story as narrated is certainly not true," and that "it is extremely difficult to save the bare fact that Jesus was crucified"[18]—are truly the exception that proves the rule.

Even before modern Jewish scholars employed the tools and theories of Christian New Testament scholarship, Jewish writers of the Middle Ages displayed an impressive familiarity with the currently pressing issues of Christian theology. *The Polemic of Nestor the Priest*, for example, was well versed in the subtleties and nuances of Christian doctrine on the Trinity and the Incarnation, knowledge that the author pressed to his advantage in challenging the entire rationale for the Crucifixion. Both *Nestor* and the *Sefer Nitzaḥon* that followed it questioned why a truly omnipotent God would have to suffer at all in order to bring salvation to his creatures. In so doing, they voiced precisely the challenge—raised by skeptical Christians as well—that led the great Christian thinker Anselm of Canterbury to rationalize the Incarnation in his influential book *Why God Became Human*. And the Jewish author who argued that the good, innocent intentions of his ancestors who killed Jesus rendered them innocent of deicide entered into a debate over human will and intentionality that raged among medieval Christian theologians—including Anselm at the end of the eleventh century, Peter Abelard in the twelfth, and Thomas Aquinas in the thirteenth. As we saw in chapter 4, Abelard himself maintained that sin lies in the will alone. Ignorant of Jesus' identity, not only were the Jews who killed him innocent of their crime, but they would have sinned grievously had they set him free, since they believed him rightly deserving of capital punishment.

Jewish interest in the Crucifixion led further still. Most interesting of all are the attempts of various Jews, from antiquity to the present, somehow to participate in the power of the cross and the Crucifixion, perhaps even to appropriate that power for themselves. Rather than subscribing to belief in Jesus Christ, these Jews asserted that the glory, the prestige, and the good that resulted from the Crucifixion actually belonged to them, not to Christians. As such, they offer us a wonderful example of Jewish ambivalence concerning Christianity. On the one hand, Jews generally feared and despised both Christ and his church. On the other hand, they assimilated much from the Christian culture surrounding them, so that they exploited their Christian rival's most cherished symbols to express their thoroughly Jewish, at times openly anti-Christian ideals and aspirations. In what follows, I draw examples from different genres of sources and from a range of historical periods. Considered together, they testify to a recurring, profoundly meaningful, but commonly overlooked phenomenon in the history of Jewish-Christian relations.

## PESACH (PASSOVER) VERSUS PASCHA (EASTER)

Although it was long presumed—correctly so—that Christian conceptions of Jesus Christ as the Lamb of God derived from the Jewish Passover, some investigators have recently suggested that early Christianity, imbued with paschal imagery as it was, exerted a major influence on the Jewish Passover. Just as Melito of Sardis and other fathers of the church claimed that Christianity, not Judaism, fulfilled the biblical promises of both the Akedah and the Passover, so, too, did Jews vie for "title" to the salvation-bringing sacrifices of the son by the father and of the true paschal lamb by God's truly faithful. The traditional Jewish liturgy for the seder, these historians argue, reflects a marked sensitivity to Christian belief and practice, and it took shape as it did in reacting consciously against them. Why, for example, does the Haggadah mention Moses but once, and then merely in passing, such that he has no part in this celebration of the Exodus? Perhaps to downplay the Christian belief that God brought salvation to his people through a human intermediary. As it interprets the biblical verses concerning the liberation from Egypt, why does the Haggadah sidestep the foundational account of the story in Exodus and focus instead on a passing review of the events in Deuteronomy? Perhaps because the founders and fathers of the Christian church emphasized those very passages in Exodus that Melito did (see chapter 3). Why does the Haggadah's popular song of *Dayenu*, which lists the wonders performed by God for his people over the course of history, first appear early in the Middle Ages, rather late in the development of the service for the seder? Perhaps in response to strikingly similar poetry in early Christian celebrations of Easter, as in Melito's *On the Pascha*. And why does the body of the Haggadah approach its climax by insisting that "whoever has not mentioned the following three things on Passover"—namely, the *pesach* (paschal lamb), the *matzah* (unleavened bread), and the *maror* (bitter herbs)— *relating them explicitly to the Israelites' salvation from Egypt*, "has not fulfilled his religious obligation"? Perhaps to refute the Christian Easter's celebration of Jesus, the lamb of God, as the true Passover sacrifice; of Christ's flesh as embodied in the unleavened bread of the Last Supper and the mass; and of Christ's suffering on the cross as symbolized in the bitter herbs eaten with the lamb. Shared traditions at the heart and soul of Judaism and Christianity clearly fueled competition and ill will in either direction between them. Whose Passover—that of the seder or that of the cross—originally offered salvation to its participants? Who worked a more lasting influence on whom? The answer, of course, is that this was a two-way street.

## THE BLOOD OF THE MARTYRS

Chapter 2 detected a similar process of appropriation at work in the interpretation of the Akedah story. Some talmudic rabbis dared to suggest, with varying degrees of subtlety, that Abraham perhaps did shed Isaac's blood on the altar, thereby challenging the Christian notion that only the crucifixion of Jesus, the sacrifice of God's son by his father, realized the true promise and blessing of the Akedah. Some rabbis, in other words, wanted to demonstrate that the Christian Akedah had not outdone the Jewish one.

Medieval Jews took this contest to a new phase: Christianity taught that Jesus, especially in his role as the ultimate Akedah, represented the perfect self-sacrificing martyr, who willingly had his blood shed on behalf of God, the faith, and the faithful. The church, in turn, called upon Christians to follow Jesus' example, to risk their lives in the service of God, promising a choice reward to those who would, in fact, die as martyrs of Christ. During the Crusades, for example, the crusader who would suffer a martyr's death in fighting the infidel could anticipate easy entry into paradise. But what happened when, as we saw in the previous chapter, these holy wars in the name of Christ and his cross led to the religious martyrdom of Jews in Christian Europe, Jews who refused to abandon their own faith and submit to the crusaders' demand to convert to Christianity? Those Jews who survived to memorialize these martyrs repeatedly portrayed them as fulfilling the example of the bound Isaac, but they did not suffice with that. Remarkably, *they proceeded to cast their martyrs on the model of Jesus.* European Jews remembered their martyrs of the Crusades not only as the heirs to the biblical Isaac, but in matching and even in outperforming the suffering of the crucified Christ.

The Hebrew chronicles of the First Crusade, written in praise of those Jews who martyred themselves, offer us many glimpses of this tendency. Just as the Gospels report about Jesus on the cross, many of these Jewish martyrs had their clothes removed and stolen. Relating incidents of Jewish martyrdom, the Hebrew reports use imagery of the Passover sacrifice, suggesting that the Jewish martyr, just like Jesus, claimed to represent the genuine paschal lamb of God or *agnus Dei*. The hair-raising story of a young woman named Rachel who slaughtered her four children rather than risk their capture and forced conversion by the crusaders reveals how prominently the image of the cross loomed in the minds of medieval Jews:

> Who ever witnessed the like of this? Who ever heard of something like the deed of this righteous, pious woman, the young Mistress Rachel, daughter of Rabbi Isaac ben Rabbi Asher, wife of Rabbi Judah. She said to her companions, "I have four children. Even on them have no mercy, lest these uncircumcised ones come and take them alive and they be maintained in their error. . . . " One of her companions came and took the knife to slay her son, and when the children's mother saw the knife she burst into wild and bitter sobbing, and she struck her face and her breast, saying, "O Lord, where is your steadfast love. . . . " The woman took the lad, small and very pleasant as he was, and slaughtered him, and the mother stretched out her arms to receive their blood, and she received the blood in her sleeves instead of in the chalice of blood.[19]

The horrific tale goes on, but I stop to ask: Why does Rachel *stretch out her arms* in this way, as if holding a *chalice of blood*? On one level, the phrase, like many other elements of these stories of Jewish martyrs, recalls the gathering of the blood of sacrificed animals at the temple in ancient Jerusalem. On the other hand, as is clear in a contemporary work of ivory from northern Germany (fig. 7.1), the image recalls a well-known scene in Christian religious art: Christ on the cross, with Synagoga, personifying the Old Testament that the Crucifixion rendered obsolete, under his left arm, and Ecclesia, the newly established church of the New Testament, under his right arm. As she stretches out her arm to Jesus, Ecclesia appears to be collecting his blood in a chalice. For this blood of the martyred Christ on the cross offered salvation to the faithful. The Jews who told Rachel's story appropriated precisely the same symbols to argue the opposite: the blood of the true martyrs remained that of the Jews, not of Jesus and his followers. They and those who survived to benefit from their merits would enjoy the ultimate salvation.

Though the church fathers had claimed that the New Testament outdid the Old because Jesus died on the cross while Isaac lived through the Akedah, the Jews who remembered the First Crusade now imagined that their martyrs outstripped both Isaac and Jesus. They numbered in the hundreds; Jesus, like Isaac, was merely one. "Inquire and seek: Was there ever such an *akedah* since the time of Adam? Did it ever occur that were one thousand and one hundred *akedot* on one single day—all of them comparable to the *akedah* of Isaac?"[20] Unlike Isaac, these Jews in fact died. And, in several instances, they appear to suffer execution not once (as Jesus did) but, owing to the strength of their spirit, twice or even three times. A man named Shemariah of the town of Mehr convinced his captors to give him and his family one last night alone before they would submit to baptism. During the night, Shemariah arose, slew his wife and three children, and "afterward he slaughtered himself and fainted, but he still was not dead."[21] On the morrow, Shemariah's captors found him and, upon his refusal to convert, buried him alive. The next day they found that he still had not died, and they buried him alive once more—in all, his third execution. Similarly, after one group of Jews in the city of Mainz had been slain,

> the uncircumcised ones . . . hurled them naked, through the windows down onto the ground, mounds and mounds, piles and piles, until they were like a tall mountain. Many of them were still alive when they threw them . . . and they beckoned to them [their attackers] with their fingers, "Give us a little water so that we may drink." When the crusaders saw as much . . . , they asked: "So you wish to baptize yourselves, so that we will give you water to drink and you can still be saved?" They shook their heads and looked to their father in

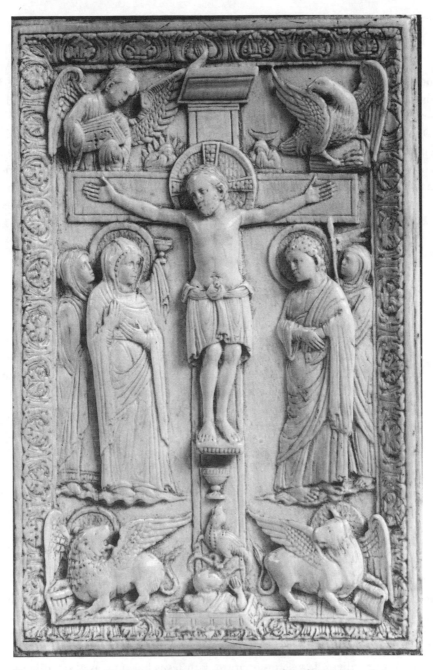

FIGURE 7.1. The Crucifixion of Jesus: Synagoga and Ecclessia. Ivory. Cologne region, mid-eleventh century. Hessisches Landesmuseum, Darmstadt, KG 54:210b. Reproduced with permission of the Hessisches Landesmuseum, Darmstadt.

heaven. . . . They [the enemy] continued to strike them, adding greatly to their blows, *until they slew them a second time*.[22]

As they bewailed their persecution in Christian lands, some Hebrew poets of the Middle Ages felt entitled to cast their fellow Jews as "crucified ones," and they looked forward to the revenge that God would ultimately grant them, a day on which "the crucified (Jews) will crucify their crucifiers."[23] One poet portrayed the Jewish martyrs of the Crusades as those who truly emulated the Akedah, since Abraham in fact slaughtered his son. Isaac then rose from the dead, and Abraham would have sacrificed him a second time had not God sent his angel to stay his hand.

> *With steady hands he slaughtered him according to the rite,*
> *Full right was the slaughter.*
> *Down upon him fell the resurrecting dew, and he revived.*
> *The father seized him then to slaughter him once more.*
> *Scripture, bear witness! Well grounded is the fact:*
> *"And the Lord called Abraham, even a second time from heaven."*[24]

With such cries, Jews of the Christian world hardly saved themselves from slaughter, but they sought at least in spirit to defeat their foes at their own game, challenging the basis of their enemies' faith: our martyrdom, they protested, the blood of our self-sacrifice, even our own crucifixion—and our salvation that these brought with them—were genuine. Yours are not. Our martyrs outstrip your martyrs, and even Jesus, your martyr par excellence. Our cross puts your cross to shame!

## FROM THE HASKALAH TO THE HOLOCAUST

If medieval Jews could subtly appropriate the power of the Crucifixion story for themselves, modern Jewish intellectuals of the last several centuries have done so unabashedly, with much greater determination and with considerably less reticence. The European Enlightenment of the eighteenth century, whose spokesmen proposed emancipation for Jews provided that they prove their acceptance of the liberal, naturalistic, and yet still Christian values of Enlightened philosophy, helped trigger what some have labeled the modern Jewish "reclamation" of Jesus. Historians, rabbis, and philosophers of the modern Jewish enlightenment, the *Haskalah*, have exerted themselves to identify with the teachings of Jesus, to recast his Judaism as "normal" rather than deviant, and thereby to forge a bond between themselves and the Christian world around them. Jewish fascination with Jesus has increased steadily over the course of the past two centuries, and virtually no aspect of Jewish culture fails to reflect it.

Understandably, nineteenth-century Jewish thinkers committed to building spiritual bridges between Jews and Christians typically identified with the more universalistic, moral, and ethical dimensions of Jesus' teaching, without accepting him as messiah and Son of God. As such, the Passion narrative was not prone to foster increased goodwill between synagogue and church, and it engaged liberal Jewish theologians considerably less. Yet as time passed, the physical suffering endured by Jews in Christendom in modern times—from the pogroms of the late nineteenth century, to the disasters wrought by World War I, to the destruction of millions of European Jews during the Nazi Holocaust—induced many Jewish intellectuals, writers, and artists to focus intensely on the crucified Jesus and his cross. Some simply viewed the renewed persecution of Jews as more of the same, yet another chapter in the long history of anti-Jewish acts committed by Christians in the name of the cross. Building upon the more ecumenical spirit of the *Haskalah* and the Jewish reclamation of Jesus that it nurtured, others openly identified with the crucified Christ and his Passion, claiming it for themselves and their violence-stricken nation. Many, of course, landed somewhere between these two poles, giving new, more modern expression to the ambivalence toward Jesus that had characterized Jewish culture since ancient times. Here I must suffice with several illuminating examples.

The Yiddish writer Shalom Asch (1880–1957) struck an especially ecumenical note in his portrayals of Jesus. Asch actually devoted a trilogy of novels to Jesus, Mary, and the apostle Paul during the later years of his life. But even in his early short story "In a Carnival Night" (1909), Asch depicts Jesus, the Jew of Nazareth, as descending from his cross in St. Peter's Cathedral in Rome to be flogged, half-naked, along with other Jews during the annual Roman carnival, in a brutal and humiliating public spectacle. Making his way through the byways of Rome to suffer with his fellow Jews, Jesus the "Man-God" recalls the Christian martyrs of old who had cried out to him as they died in the jaws of the lions. He then encounters the messiah by the gates of Rome, just as rabbinic legend had depicted him, awaiting God's call to redeem the world. And, in the presence of the messiah, Jesus bemoans the evil and destruction that many Christians have perpetrated in his name.

> They tore the sheet from my body and made themselves banners. They dipped the banners in my blood, and with these before them, and my name on their lips, they spread desolation among my brothers. My word of peace they have turned into a war cry; the forgiveness I proclaimed they have turned into vengeance. . . . See, they utter in my name words which I did not speak; they have not comforted the lowly; they have not wiped away the tears of those that suffer.

Frustrated and despondent, Jesus rebukes those who invoke his name but abuse his Passion in doing so. "O, ye strangers, who has given you the right to enter into judgment between brother and brother? You knew not and know not my pain, you understood not and understand not my sorrow." Instead, Jesus now identifies with the suffering of his Jewish brethren: "With my brothers and sisters I will bear all suffering and humiliation." As for their Christian persecutors, "my soul is weary of their songs of praise. For they bow down to my image, and have forgotten my word."[25]

Asch was not the only Jewish writer of the day who formulated his worldview as he contemplated the cross. The Yiddish and Hebrew poet Uri Zvi Greenberg (1896–1981) also struggled with the image of the crucified Jesus as he wrestled with the state of his fellow Jews and their common heritage during the decades that led from pogroms to world war to Hitler's Final Solution. In 1923, one year before he left Europe for the new Zionist home (*yishuv*) in the land of Israel, Greenberg published his "Uri Zvi farn Tzeylem" ("Uri Zvi in Front of the Cross"), a Yiddish poem printed in the form of a cross (fig. 7.2) over which appeared the capital letters typically found above the Christian crucifix: INRI, the Latin initials for "Jesus of Nazareth, King of the Jews." Like Shalom Asch, Greenberg claimed Jesus for the Jews. Yet unlike Asch, who casts Jesus as the man-god of Jewish and Christian martyrs alike, Greenberg rails against Jesus' own betrayal of his Jewish heritage. Centuries of Christian history have led Jesus to forget his Jewish origins, and with them he has lost any sense of kinship with his suffering brothers and sisters. Two thousand years of inactivity on the cross have inured Jesus to the suffering of Jews at his feet: a pile of severed Jewish heads, tattered prayer shawls, stabbed parchments, bloodstained shrouds. Though Greenberg the Jew identifies with Jesus—"each morning I am nailed up anew on the burning red crucifix"—Jesus pays him no attention.

> You've become inanimate, brother Jesus. For two thousand years you've been tranquil on the cross. All around you the world expires. Damn it, you've forgotten everything. Your petrified brain can't grasp: a Star of David at your head, over the star, hands in priestly blessing; under them, olive groves and ethrog (citron) gardens.[26]

Olive groves and citron gardens betray Greenberg's idyllic longings for the Promised Land, the only context in which one can appreciate Jesus as one should. Greenberg soon proclaimed in another poem, "Malkhes fun Tzeylem" ("Kingdom of the Cross"): "The dead man in the church is not my brother, but Jesus [*is*]; Bethlehem is Latin, not my ancestral village Beys-Lechem. . . . By the sun, it is a lie, the worship of millions! It's the Jewish village Beys-Lechem! He is Ben-Yoysef, son of the Jews!"[27]

At the same time as Uri Zvi Greenberg stood in front of his cross, Jesus and his Passion proved equally inspiring for the Hebrew poet Zalman Shneour (1887–1959). Shneour's ballad "The Last Words of Don Henriques" (1924) recounts the execution of a Marrano at the hands of the Spanish Inquisition,

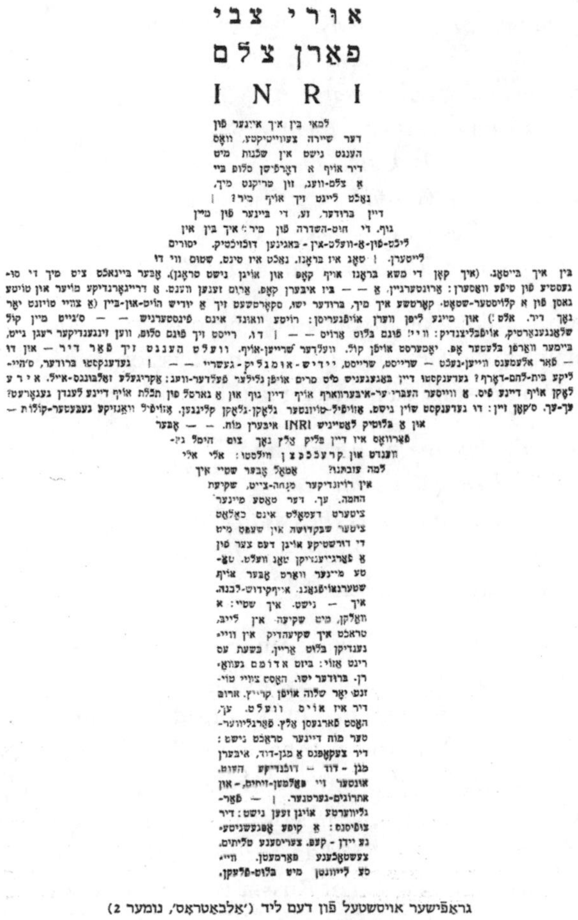

א ו ר י   צ ב י

פ א ר ן   צ ל ם

I   N   R   I

לאמאי בין איך אייגער פון
דער שײרה צעווייטיקטא. וואָס
העענטס ניטאָ אין שלגות מיט
דיר אויף א דערלויַז־ן בלוים בײ
א צלם־וועג, זון קרימגס מיך,
נאָלטע ליונט זיך אויף מיר !
דיין ברודער. זע, די בּיינער פון מיין
גוף. די חוס־חסדרה פון מיר : איך בין אין
ליכם־פון־א־ועלכ־אין־באנונגן דעלביזמם. יסורים
לייסטרן. │ סאָג אין בראנו. נאַלט אוז סינם, שטום ווי דו

בין איך ב"יסאָג. (איך קאן די משא בראַגנ אויף קאפ און אוין גיסאָ טראַגנ), אַכער ביינאָלס ציט מיך די סו-
גסטטיע פון טיפ וואזאָערן ; ארונטערנרינ. א — — בּיו איבצער זאַנטא. אָרום זאַנען הגעב. א דרײַנאָרנדיקע פיַער סטראַם טויסע
נאָסן פון א קלוסטער־שמאָם. קאָרטשעע איך מיך, ברודער ישו, סקעלעסטפם זיך א יורין הויס־און־בּיין (א צוזיי סוזונט יאָר
נאָך דיר. אלם (!) און מיגע ליזן ווערן אויפטוערזסן : ראָסם זואזנד אינס פינטסטערגיס — — סיניוס מיין קול
שלאָנעטנערטסיק, אויספלימינית : ה ו ד : פגם בלוס ארוום — — │ ד ל. רייסס זיך פגם סלום, ווען דינגזירזכער רעכנ נייס.
בּיימער הזלבן בלינטער אָפ. יאָמערטס אוין קול. וועלדער שרילסזן־אין. וו ע ל ם העגב זיך פ א ר דיר — אין די
— פאר אלססגען הינן־נעלט — שרייסס, שרייסס, ילרים־אימבּ ל יק ־ נעטטרי — — │ נעדנקסט ברודער, ס'חטי־
ליקע בית־לחם־דאָרן ? נעדענטטיו דין באַגנעגעניס ס'ס פרס אויף און גיליבער פעלדער־ווענ ; אָקריגעלב ז אלבואָם־א־אל. א י ר ע ע
לאקן אויף דינע פיס. א ווייטער הזעברי־יר־איבנצעראָארץ אויף דין גוף און א גארטל פון תּלת אויף דינע לענדן נטנגגרנ?
עד־עך. ס'קאַן וויין : דו נעדעגקעסם שיין גיסא. אַזוי פל-טמיזנסער בל'סקן־גלאַקן קליגנט. אַזוי יל ואַנויעע נעטעסטר־קולות ,
אוז צ בּלוסק לעשמיניע INRI איבערן מות. — — אָבער

פאַרווא־ס אין דיין מלין צלך נאָר צום היפל נו-
זענבגדס און קרעבבבבן חילסטו : אלי אלי
למה עזבתאני ! אָטאַל בּכבּר שטי איך
אין רוינודיקער מנחה־צייט. שקיעת
החמה. אך. דער סאָסא מינעער
ציסטערט דעסטלט אינם כאַלאַט
ציסער שפּקינעה אין שעפפ מיט
די דורדשטינ'אינען זצן וועלט. ואַ־
א פאריעזענ'ינ זצן וועלט. וצ־
סע מינער ווארם אַבער אויף
שטעראנאָ'פטאַגנ. איַיקירוים־לכנה.
אין — גיסט. איך שטי: א
חזלקן. מיט שקיעה אין לייב.
טראַלבט אין שקעתהינ אין ווי-
נעגדטו בלוט ארייַ. מטעטז עס
רינט אזוי : בּיום אדום גטחא־
רן. ברודער ישו. הטסס ז'ימיר טו־
נם־יאר שלהו אזיון קריַי. ארום
דיר אוז אויס ווטלם. עך.
הטסם מאַרגנסן אלף. פאַרגליװער—
סער מות דיינעך מאַרקט ניסא :
דיר צעקפסננס א כנן־דוד. איבערן
מגן − דוד − דולבנודיקע ה'־תזם.
אונטטר זוי אטלמסמזן־ויחזל.־און
אתרינגם־בטרטמגער. │ פאָ-
גליװטערטע אויגן ועען גיסא : דיר
צוסססונם : א קום פ אַנאגשוגסע.
גא יורן − קטם. צרויוסנגן סליחים.
צעשטטלבענע מטרכמטבן. ה יי-
סע לייװנטן מיט בּלוט־פלעקן.

גראָפּישער אויסשטעל פֿון דעם ליד (׳אלבאַטראָס׳, נומער 2)

FIGURE 7.2. "Uri Zvi in Front of the Cross." *Collected
Yiddish Works of Uri Zvi Grinberg*, Jerusalem 1975,
2:432. Reproduced with permission of Magnes Press.

and, in so doing, blends various aspects of Jesus' characterization by Asch
and Greenberg. In the heat of the blazing fire around him, Don Henriques
demands that Jesus not trust in the Gentiles who have sinned by converting
a Jew into God. He envisions Jesus at the head of a procession of Jewish
martyrs who have arisen from their graves in the Diaspora and now make their
way to the land of Israel. He calls out to Jesus to return home, where he will be
purified of the leprosy-like pollution in which the Gentiles have befouled him.

> And you, noble companion in pain,
> striding in front of them all,
> a new Sanhedrin bids you welcome,

*wrapped in new prayer shawls,*
*they'll lead you to the Jordan,*
*wash you clean in its holy water,*
*bathe your wounds and heal them,*
*to lighten your tear-darkened eyes,*
*to cleanse you from Gentile impurity,*
*from their sacrifices and incense,*
*and from the soot of the Torah rolls that they have burned.*

But perhaps most striking of all, Shneour's hero wrests Jesus' trial and verdict from the domain of the Gentile world. Jesus' Passion, his suffering, and the determination of his destiny truly belong to the Jewish people in their own land.

*No Pilate will have the power in Israel*
*to pass a bloody Roman sentence,*
*for the land is ours and ours the verdict of justice.*
*No stranger will then dare to sit in judgment*
*on a dispute between brothers.*[28]

Yet the twentieth century wore on, and anti-Jewish persecution and violence soon reached new heights. As it did, the image of the cross repeatedly served to horrify Jews who had once considered Christian Europe their home. Published in Tel Aviv toward the end of World War II, a short story entitled "In the Name of Rabbi Jesus of Nazareth," by the Hebrew writer Avigdor Hameiri (1887–1959), writes of the capture of several Austrian soldiers, three of them Jews, by Russian troops during the First World War. Hauled before a drunken platoon of Russians wildly celebrating their Christmas holiday in a room that reeked of liquor, cigarette smoke, and pork stew, the prisoners behold the severed head of a Jew decorating the banquet table. The Russian officer in charge discovers the Jews among them and proceeds to pass sentence upon them for their crimes against Jesus. Their military judges, he declares,

have deliberated and decided to punish you *quid pro quo*. That is to say, you drink Christian blood, and one of you must therefore drink Jewish blood. At long last you must savor the taste of Jewish blood. Second, you crucified the Son of God; one of you must therefore be crucified. And third, one of you will be buried alive, just as the Son of God was buried and then rose from the grave.

As the Russians proceed rather ineptly to exact punishment from the first two Jews, a non-Jew among the captive Austrians renounces his Christianity, in revulsion and horror over the acts now committed in its name. "Who is a Christian?!" he asks sarcastically. "I?! Together with these foul ones?!" Ironically, the story ends as Hungarian artillery bombards the Russian camp, and the Jewish narrator emerges alive from the very grave that his captors had dug for him—much as the resurrected Jesus of the Gospels did.[29]

The Jewish reclamation of Jesus evident in works of literature had no less profound a mark on modern Jewish art. Here, again, I can offer just a few examples from among very many. One of the first attempts to repossess the crucified Jesus as a Jewish martyr with whom all persecuted Jews might empathize is the statue *Ecce homo* (*Behold the Man*, 1873) of the Russian Jewish sculptor Mark Antokolsky (1843–1902).[30] Though Jesus' Jewish origins and identity may strike us as self-evident, Christian artists had ignored them for centuries, so that Antokolsky's Jewish Jesus, marked by traditional Jewish sidelocks, skullcap, and clothing cut a particularly innovative image. *Ecce homo* (John 19:5) invokes the words of Pontius Pilate in the gospel story, when Pilate finds no wrong in Jesus and crucifies him only to placate the Jews. In portraying Jesus on trial as a representative of his own people, Antokolsky attacked the Christ-killer myth that figures so importantly in the history of anti-Semitism. He reminded Christians of Jesus' Jewish character at the same time as he held Jesus up to the Jews as a model exemplifying the proper course that Judaism should take in its development. As the sculptor explained to a friend in 1874,

> Jews may have renounced and still renounce him, but I solemnly admit that he was [a Jew] and died as a Jew for truth and brotherhood. That is why I want to present him as a purely Jewish type . . . with a covered head. . . . I imagine to myself how Jews and Christians alike will rise against me. Jews will probably say, "How is it that he made Christ?" And Christians will say, "What kind of Christ did he make?"

Antokolsky's ambivalence toward Christianity and its cross resonates. On the one hand, Jesus died as a Jew on behalf of those very Jews who sought to kill him.

> He stood up for the people, for brotherhood and freedom, for that blind people who with such rage and ignorance shouted: "Crucify, crucify him!" I will represent him during that moment when he stands before the court of that people for whom he fell as a victim.

Antokolsky thus appears to have assimilated the age-old, traditional Christian notions of Jewish blindness, ignorance, and guilt in insisting upon Jesus' execution. On the other hand, his art reacts to the pogroms and other expressions of anti-Semitism that had already leveled a crippling blow on East European Jewry. Writing to the same friend, he berates Christians for having betrayed the teaching of Jesus, whose name they invoke to hide their evil. Soon after the crucified Jesus heralded a unique opportunity for genuine renewal in biblical religion, there appeared wise men, false interpreters who . . . began to exploit him. Popes . . . appeared, then luxury. . . . Then came the Crusades, burnings at the stake, and everyone worked in Christ's name against Christ. Why should one cover one's wish to harm one's neighbor instead of loving him with the name of such an idealist as Jesus . . . ? Who is a Christian nowadays? Isn't it strange and offensive that the genius for evil still exists?

One of the best-known works of art testifying to the modern Jewish fascination with the crucified Jesus is Marc Chagall's *White Crucifixion* (1938), completed just around the time of *Kristallnacht* (the anti-Jewish pogroms of November 9–10, 1938, in Nazi Germany) on the eve of World War II. This was neither Chagall's first Crucifixion nor his last. As early as 1912, his striking *Dedicated to Christ* or *Golgotha* blended images of Jews, Judaism, and the Crucifixion in a pealing reaction against the anti-Jewish pogroms and blood libels of the decades just passed. And the Crucifixion reappears in Chagall's painting throughout the later postwar decades of his life as well. *White Crucifixion* (fig. 7.3), however, will serve us well as a striking and final example of the complexity of the interest that a modern Jew could have in the cross.

Like much of Chagall's work, one finds *White Crucifixion* busy and crowded, such that an art historian's tally of what the painting portrays should prove helpful.

> This Christ is really crucified, stretched in all his immense pain above a world of horror. Men are hunted, persecuted, murdered; a fearful din fills the "vast ivory space" he dominates and permeates as if he wanted to bear it all and give it a meaning. But although Christ is the central figure, this is by no means a Christian picture. The scenes that frame the cross, twined round it like a crown of thorns—from the shattered village to the pillaged, burning synagogue—constitute an exemplary Jewish martyrology. On the left a hostile crowd presses forward and fugitives flee across the water in a boat. Below, white fire consumes the sacred books, and one of those taking flight to escape the horror wears a vest on which was formerly written in German: "I am a Jew"; high up in the sky, the elders wail. But Jewish is not solely this tale of woe: Christ himself is a Jew. Above his head Chagall has clearly written the Biblical "Jesus of Nazareth, King of the Jews," both in the traditional Latin abbreviation (INRI) and in Hebrew, thus providing Jewry's confirmation of Pilate's words. Round his loins Christ wears a loincloth with two black stripes resembling the Jewish tallith, and at his feet burns the seven-branched candlestick surrounded by a halo like that which frames his head. But, most important of all, this Christ's relation to the world differs

FIGURE 7.3. Marc Chagall, *White Crucifixion* (1938), oil on canvas, 154.3 x 139.7 cm. Gift of Alfred S. Alschuler to the Art Institute of Chicago. Copyright ©ADAGP, Paris, 2005. Photography © The Art Institute of Chicago.

entirely from that in all Christian representations of the Crucifixion. There it is not the world that suffers, except in grief for his death on the cross; all suffering is concentrated in Christ, transferred to him in order that he may overcome it by his sacrifice. Here instead, though all the suffering of the world is mirrored in the Crucifixion, suffering remains man's lasting fate and is not abolished by Christ's death. So Chagall's Christ figure lacks the Christian concept of salvation. For all his holiness he is by no means divine.[31]

In his own distinctive fashion, Chagall blends several different—and not entirely harmonious—approaches to the crucified Christ. To be sure, the artist identifies with him personally. At the same time, his Passion mirrors the suffering of the world at large, that of Jew and non-Jew alike. Most important, the artist has reclaimed the suffering of Jesus as an emblem of that of the Jews in the world of Christianity, just as the horrors of pogroms and blood libels will mushroom into those of the Nazi death camps.

Chagall continued to invoke the cross as World War II wore on. In a later version of *White Crucifixion* from 1940, Chagall added a yarmulke to Jesus' head and replaced the INRI initials above it with the tablets of the Ten Commandments, while the candle no longer burns at the bottom of the cross. Sketches of Jesus' *Way to Calvary* in 1941 depict the crucifixion of other Jews even before Jesus reaches the site of his execution, highlighting the perilous deportation of Jews to theirs. In *Yellow Christ*, a Jewish prayer shawl again serves as a loincloth for Jesus, who looks down sympathetically at Jewish refugees boarding a ship—alluding, no doubt, to Chagall's own passage to New York. (After Chagall reached North America, his *Descent from the Cross* substitutes his own name for the INRI sign, as an angel releases Christ/Chagall from bondage and returns his paint and brushes to him.) Following the Warsaw Ghetto uprising of 1943, *Obsession* portrays Jesus on his cross as having fallen, and in *The Crucified* of 1944, which followed the liquidation of Chagall's home town of Vitebsk, Jesus has been transformed into a Jew of the shtetl.

The list goes on, but Chagall's message is clear. "For me Christ was a great poet," the artist declared in 1944—yet one whose teaching the world has misunderstood and ignored. Decades after the war, he explained: "For me, Christ has always symbolized the true type of the Jewish martyr"—much as Chagall, in fact, viewed himself: "Like Christ I am crucified, fixed with nails to the easel."[32] Amazingly, even in the wake of the Holocaust, the most essential symbol of Christian civilization still offered the Jew a mirror in which to find and express himself. Just as he did in late ancient and medieval times, the crucified Jesus serves as the focus of the Jew's abhorrence for the Christian religion that has persecuted him over the course of centuries. And yet, the Jew belongs to that world, whose language and traditions nourish his definition of himself.

Recent history, perhaps the Holocaust above all else, has brought expressions of the Jewish stake in the Crucifixion story to the fore. With these in mind, our story resumes with a pressing question: How has the Christ-killer myth fared in Christian teaching since the Holocaust? Here one can certainly point to momentous change and development, as the following chapter will demonstrate.

# 8

# VATICAN II

- "Vatican Council Clears Jews of Sole Guilt in the Crucifixion" (*Washington Post*)
- "A Vote against Prejudice" (*Time*)
- "The Jews Absolved" (*Newsweek*)
- "Pope Paul Promulgates Five Council Documents, One Absolving Jews" (*New York Times*)

Headlines like these heralded the Second Vatican Council's promulgation of *Nostra Aetate*, a Roman Catholic "Declaration on the Relation of the Church to Non-Christian Religions," in October 1965. Although the declaration includes much else of theological importance for the Catholic Church, the most acclaimed and most controversial of its provisions reformulate the Catholic posture toward the Jewish people and their Jewish religion. One can summarize this reformulation as follows.[1]

1. The Catholic Church reaffirms its Jewish heritage and its debt to biblical Israel, its patriarchs, its prophets, and its covenant with God. Jesus and the apostles themselves sprang from the Jewish people.

2. Despite the Jews' failure to accept Jesus and his gospel, God still "holds the Jews most dear for the sake of their Fathers"; and, recognizing its kinship with the Jews, the Catholic Church eagerly "awaits that day, known to God alone, on which all peoples will address the Lord in a single voice."

3. Owing to these bonds, the Catholic Church calls for reciprocal respect, mutual understanding, joint biblical and the theological study, and "fraternal dialogues" between Christians and Jews.

4. The Catholic Church condemns the persecution and hatred of any people, including "displays of anti-Semitism, directed against Jews at any time and by anyone."

5. Most impressive of all, the Catholic Church renounces the age-old teaching that the Jews as a people collectively bear the guilt for Jesus' persecution.

> True, the Jewish authorities and those who followed their lead pressed for the death of Christ; still, what happened in His passion cannot be charged against all the Jews, without distinction, then alive, nor against the Jews of today. Although the Church is the new people of God, the Jews should not be presented as rejected or accursed by God, as if this followed from the Holy Scriptures.

6. The Catholic Church recognizes the "catechetical imperatives" of its reformulation: that is, the essential need to infuse the lessons of *Nostra Aetate* into the way that it teaches the catechism, the correct understanding of the faith, to its believers.

Despite its well-deserved reputation as a major breakthrough in Christian-Jewish relations, *Nostra Aetate* did not emerge in a vacuum, and to appreciate its importance, one must take note of its background and its long- and short-term precedents. Within some two decades after the Crucifixion, the apostle Paul himself (1 Corinthians 2:8) instructed that "none of the rulers of this age understood" the mystery of the Crucifixion, "for if they had, they would not have crucified the Lord of glory." Not only does this passage cast responsibility for Jesus' death on the rulers of the world, whom Paul does not identify as the Jews, but it also suggests that their actions stemmed from ignorance, not ill will. As shown in chapter 4, the author of Luke and Acts agreed with that perception. It is his Jesus who prays on the cross, "Father, forgive them; for they know not what they do" (Luke 23:34). And, in the wake of the Crucifixion, he presents Peter as informing the Jews of Jerusalem: "And now, brethren, I know that you acted in ignorance, as did also your rulers. But what God foretold by the mouth of all the prophets, that his Christ should suffer, he thus fulfilled" (Acts 3:17–18).

In his Epistle to the Romans, Paul works to counter the impression that God has cursed the Jews and rejected them forever. To the contrary, they were still his people, and they still had an essential role to play in his plan for the salvation of the world.

> Have they stumbled so as to fall? By no means! But through their trespass salvation has come to the Gentiles, so as to make Israel jealous. Now if their trespass means riches for the world, and if their failure means riches for the Gentiles, how much more will their full inclusion mean . . . ! If their rejection means the reconciliation of the world, what will their acceptance mean but life from the dead? (11:11–15)

Paul warns Gentile Christians not to boast that God has elected them at the expense of the Jews. For the Jews have retained their holiness. They, like natural olive branches, were indeed broken off from the tree so that the Gentiles might be grafted onto it. But if these wild, uncultivated Gentile branches could be so grafted, how much more easily could the natural Jewish branches be restored! And, in fact, God will restore them: "Lest you be wise in your own conceits, I want you to understand this mystery, brethren: a hardening has come upon part of Israel, until the full number of the Gentiles come in, and so all Israel will be saved" (Romans 11:25–26).[2]

Inasmuch as Christianity taught that Christ had died on the cross to atone for the sins of all men and women, some theologians of the Middle Ages concluded that all sinners must share in the guilt for the Crucifixion. Adopted by the Catholic Church in 1566, the Catechism of the Council of Trent gave this conclusion explicit and official approval.

> It was our sins which drove Christ the Lord to his death on the Cross: those, therefore, who wallow in sins and vices are in fact crucifying the Son of God anew, insofar as it depends on them, and holding him up to contempt. And this is a crime which would seem graver in our case than it was in that of the Jews; for the Jews, as the same Apostle says, "would never have crucified the Lord of glory if they had known him." We ourselves maintain that we do know him, and yet we lay, as it were, violent hands on him by disowning him in our actions.

The fathers of Trent thus transposed the issue of responsibility for the Crucifixion from a question of historical detail to one of universal cosmic truth: "Men of every estate and rank 'took counsel against the Lord and against his Christ.' Gentiles and Jews were the instigators, authors and executors of his sufferings. Judas betrayed him, Peter denied him, and all abandoned him."[3]

Statements like these notwithstanding, the myth of Jew as Christ killer held sway in the Christian consciousness from the first century until the twentieth. Textbooks used in Spanish, French, and Italian schools during the decades between World War II and the ratification of *Nostra Aetate* included frequent statements to the effect that "the Jewish people disowned and crucified Jesus," "the Jews stripped him, gave him gall and vinegar to drink, and nailed him to a cross," "Jesus, innocent, is put to death by the Jewish people," "the first great bearer of guilt for the deicide was Israel as a whole," and the like.[4] Even in a survey conducted in the United States as late as the first years of the Second Vatican Council itself, 61% of Catholics and 58% of Protestants still identified the Jews as the group "most responsible for crucifying Christ."[5]

What, then, precipitated what seems a sudden about-face that we find in *Nostra Aetate*? Unquestionably, the staggering, tragic blow that the Nazi Holocaust inflicted on the Jews of Christian Europe induced many prelates and theologians to take stock of what had gone wrong. Surely God had not sanctioned Hitler's Final Solution. How, then, could it have led to the slaughter of six million Jews in lands and among peoples that had faithfully worshiped the God of Christianity for so long a period of time? Had something malfunctioned within Christianity itself?

The American Catholic scholar John Pawlikowski boldly acknowledges this challenge. "It would be presumptuous for any Christian to delve into the overarching moral issues [raised by the Holocaust] without first having grappled with Christian culpability during the *Shoah* itself."[6] Or as the Protestant theologian Franklin Littell admonishes Christians concerned with the Holocaust: "Every discussion must begin with a painful, brute fact: The Holocaust, the planned and rationalized murder of *circa* 6,000,000 Jews, was a monstrous crime committed by baptized Christians in the heart of Christendom."[7] Littell blames the anti-Judaism of "Christian" civilization not only for Nazi genocide but for much of the suffering of other innocent people in our own day, including the "three million lovely and simple little Vietnamese slaughtered by ruthless machines controlled by men who think in abstractions." According to Littell, "there is a line connecting Auschwitz and Mylai" (where American servicemen massacred hundreds of Vietnamese civilians in 1968).

> It is defined by the truth that a "Christian" civilization's attitude to Jewish history and treatment of the Jewish people afford the litmus test as to how it will act on all critical decisions involving the resistance of helpless or weaker peoples.

Where did this "slide into damnation" begin? "With Christian lies about the Jewish people, with abandonment of the essential Jewishness of Christianity, with murder of those who could be identified as signal representatives of a counterculture the world hated and most of the baptized betrayed with enthusiasm." Alas, Littell concludes, Christianity's tragic betrayal of its Jewishness "did not end with the Holocaust."[8] The very title of Littell's book, *The Crucifixion of the Jews*, speaks to the extent that such myths as that of the Jewish Christ killer have wrought catastrophe over the course of Christian history.

Pawlikowski and Littell wrote as they did after Vatican II, but sentiments such as theirs, whether verbalized or not, had begun to make their mark even before the council. As the editor of the liberal Catholic magazine *Commonweal* asked in May 1961, "Could the Nazi horror have sprung full-blown out of nowhere, without centuries of anti-Semitism to nourish it and give it strength?"[9] Within several years after the Second World War, signs of change began to appear. In 1947, a group of concerned Catholics and Protestants meeting in Seelisberg, Switzerland, underscored the need "to present the Passion story in such a way as not to arouse animosity against the Jew, and to eliminate from Christian teaching and preaching the idea that the Jewish people are under a curse."[10] Held in Amsterdam in 1948, only months after the establishment of the State of Israel, the first assembly of the Protestant World Council of Churches expressed the problem in these words: "We cannot forget that we meet in a land from which 110,000 Jews were taken to be murdered. Nor can we forget that we meet only five years after the extermination of 6 million Jews." In their proclamation entitled "The Christian Approach to the Jews," the delegates went on to acknowledge their share of responsibility for the problem.

> Before our churches can hope to fulfill the commission laid upon us by our Lord there are high barriers to be overcome. We speak here particularly of the barriers which we have too often helped to build and which we alone can remove. We must acknowledge in all humility that too often we have failed to manifest Christian love towards our Jewish neighbours, or even a resolute will for common social justice. We have failed to fight with all our strength the age-old disorder of man which anti-semitism represents. The churches in the past have helped to foster an image of the Jews as the sole enemies of Christ, which has contributed to anti-semitism in the secular world.[11]

In 1961, the World Council's third assembly clearly alluded to the Crucifixion when it declared: "In Christian teaching the historic events which led to the Crucifixion should not be so presented as to fasten upon the Jewish people of today responsibilities which belong to our corporate humanity and not to one race or community. Jews were the first to accept Jesus and Jews are not the only ones who do not yet recognize him."[12]

In the Catholic Church, the guiding spirit of change that inspired the Second Vatican Council was Pope John XXIII (1958–1963). Born in 1881, Angelo Roncalli rose steadily through the ranks of the clergy, and, while serving as the pope's apostolic delegate to Turkey during World War II, he helped Balkan Jews flee persecution and death at the hands of the Nazis—not always to the pleasure of his superiors in the Vatican. During the first year of his papacy, Pope John removed references to Jewish "perfidy" and "perfidious" Jews from the Catholic liturgy for Good Friday, the day of Jesus' crucifixion. In June 1960, he granted an audience to Jules Isaac, a French Jewish historian who had devoted himself since World War II to documenting Christianity's "teaching of contempt" toward the Jews, which by perpetrating the Christ-killer myth had helped foster modern anti-Semitism. The pope assured Isaac of his hope to improve relations between Jews and Christians, an impression that he reaffirmed to a large group of American Jews visiting Rome several months later. Meanwhile, the pope also received petitions from institutions within the church, including the Pontifical Biblical

Institute in Rome and the Institute for Judaeo-Christian Studies at Seton Hall University in New Jersey, calling for a reformulation of the church's posture toward the Jewish people in general and their role in the Crucifixion in particular. Rabbis (among them the well-respected Abraham Joshua Heschel), Jewish organizations, and interfaith groups followed suit. As arrangments for the Second Vatican Council took shape, Pope John entrusted the task of preparing a declaration on the Jewish people to Augustin Cardinal Bea, the head of the Vatican's Secretariat for Christian Unity (later called the Commission for Christian Unity). John XXIII died in June 1963, but Cardinal Bea saw his papal charge through to fulfillment within the framework of *Nostra Aetate.*

Despite the wide range of voices that called for such a declaration, the path leading to its formal acceptance in October 1965 proved long and arduous. Pope John's death between the second and third of the council's four sessions did not make matters easier. Though support for the declaration was widespread, it did have outspoken opponents. Conservatives within the Catholic clergy itself insisted vehemently that the Jewish people did, in fact, bear collective responsibility for Jesus' death. An article appearing in the semiofficial Vatican newspaper *Osservatore Romano* in March 1961, only months before the council convened, asserted unabashedly that the "Jewish people had stained themselves with a horrible crime deserving of expiation."[13] The Arab world—and its delegates at the council—railed against the proposed declaration as a Zionist conspiracy to control global opinion and to woo Christian support for the state of Israel. A Syrian radio broadcast in 1964 proclaimed that "when the Jews dipped their hands into the innocent blood of Jesus Christ, they were in fact trying to assassinate Christ's principles and teachings."[14] The government of Jordan threatened sanctions against Catholic clergymen who would support the council's declaration. One influential prelate, the Jacobite Patriarch of Antioch, charged that, in declaring "the Jews to be innocent of the blood of Christ," the church of Rome would sin "against Holy Scripture, the apostolic tradition, the truth of history, and the teaching of the Fathers and Doctors."[15] Rolf Hochhuth's controversial play *The Deputy* (produced in 1963), which aggressively condemned Pope Pius XII and the Vatican hierarchy for failing to act to save European Jews during the Holocaust, nourished antagonism and defensiveness on all sides of the question. Throughout the four years of the council, some Jewish voices proved too outspoken for the taste of many within the church, and the delicate atmosphere was prone to turbulence as rumors emanated from various quarters.

Such was the volatile situation in which the Second Vatican Council crafted its declaration on the Jews.[16] Four draft versions of the text reached the floor of the council between 1963 and 1965. The first, presented on November 18, 1963, cited the same passages in Romans, 1 Corinthians, Luke, and Acts mentioned above in determining that it is theologically wrong to consider the Jews an "accursed people" or "a deicidal nation." Jesus died for the sins of all, and the Jewish people "remains most dear to God on account of the patriarchs and the gifts given to them." Yet the council never had an opportunity to approve this draft. The opposition, from Arab and other quarters, proved too vociferous, and, as the newly elected Pope Paul VI planned his pilgrimage to the Holy Land for the following year, the Vatican, fearing divisiveness, postponed the debate and the vote. By the time the council reconvened in 1964, Cardinal Bea's commission had drafted a new document, "On Jews and Non-Christians." This version devoted considerably more attention to non-Jewish non-Christians than its predecessor, and it addressed the issue of the Jews and the Crucifixion in more moderate terms. Specifically, it made no mention of the charge of deicide or the status of a "deicidal nation," not even to refute them. Rather, it sufficed with rejecting the notion of the Jews as "a despised nation," and it warned against imputing guilt for the Crucifixion "to the Jews of our own times." It also decried hatred and violence against the Jews, just as it disapproved "of injustices committed against human beings everywhere." By the end of the 1964 session, renewed debate, coupled with disappointment over the dilution of the original's emphatic rejection of the deicide charge, led to yet another revision of the declaration on the Jews. This third version, incorporated within a decree "On the Posture of the Church toward non-Christian Religions" now titled *Nostra Aetate*, gained the preliminary approval of the council's delegates on November 20, 1964, by a vote of 1,651 to 91. Once again, attention to the Christ-killer motif was more focused and decisive. "All that happened to Christ in His passion cannot be attributed to the whole people then alive, much less to those of today." Christian preachers and teachers, for their part, should "never present the Jewish people as one rejected, cursed, or guilty of deicide." But even the overwhelming support of the council delegates for this language did not put matters to rest. Again did conservative Catholics, including the Italian bishop Luigi Carli, insist that Jews today still "participate objectively in the responsibility for deicide." Again did the Arab world protest belligerently, speaking repeatedly of "Jewish crimes against Palestinian Arabs."[17] And again did the Vatican leadership waver. Rumors circulated that the fate of the declaration lay in the balance, and by the spring of 1965, these rumors became breaking headlines in newspapers worldwide. At last, the Vatican released the fourth and final rendition of *Nostra Aetate*, summarized at the beginning of this chapter, on September 30. Although it makes no reference to the "deicide" charge and reminds its readers that the Jewish authorities of Jesus' day and their followers did press for his execution, it otherwise maintains the substance and spirit of the version that preceded it. The Second Vatican Council formally ratified *Nostra Aetate* on October 15, 1965. Pope Paul VI promulgated it as the official doctrine of the Roman Catholic Church on October 28.

Yet the story of *Nostra Aetate* does not end here. One must also consider the manner in which the church has understood and implemented its teaching. In October 1974, the Vatican established a Commission for Religious Relations with the Jews, which at the beginning of 1975 issued "Guidelines and Suggestions for Implementing the Conciliar Declaration *Nostra Aetate*" and reiterated the council's ruling that "what happened in his passion cannot be blamed upon all the Jews then living, without distinction, nor upon the Jews of today."[18] Catholic dioceses seeking to translate this guideline into practice soon followed with their own sets of instructions. Interpreting the guidelines, for instance, the Diocese of Cleveland declared that "blaming the Jewish people for the suffering and the death of Jesus is both a theological and historical error. The Church clearly teaches that the sins of all are the reason for Christ's passion and death."[19] The Archdiocese of Galveston-Houston elaborated further:

> Catholics should avoid all language or impressions which would imply that we hold all Jewish people collectively, whether past or present, responsible for the death of Jesus. . . . We ask forgiveness of our Jewish brothers and sisters if in the past or present we have consciously or unconsciously contributed to anti-Semitism in the world by attributing to them the guilt for the crucifixion of Jesus. . . . Catholics must be ever alert for references to the Jewish people which would hold them responsible as a people for the death of Christ.[20]

Perhaps to regulate and standardize the application of its guidelines, the Commission for Religious Relations with the Jews issued in 1985 a document entitled "Notes on the Correct Way to Present the Jews and Judaism in Preaching and Catechesis in the Roman Catholic Church." The "Notes" offered detailed instructions to Catholic teachers and preachers for conveying the spirit of *Nostra Aetate*, which bore on present-day Catholic-Jewish relations no less than on matters of ancient history.

> There is no putting the Jews who knew Jesus and did not believe in him, or those who opposed the preaching of the apostles, on the same plane with Jews who came after or those of today. If the responsibility of the former remains a mystery hidden with God (cf. *Rom* 11:25), the latter are in an entirely different situation.

The "Notes" go on to explain that "the delicate question of responsibility for the death of Christ must be looked at from the standpoint of" *Nostra Aetate,* the "Guidelines and Suggestions," and the Catechism of the Council of Trent, which it quotes or paraphrases.[21] And when Pope John Paul II made a historic visit to the Great Synagogue of Rome in 1986, he too warned against "indiscriminately" imputing any "ancestral or collective blame" for the Crucifixion to the Jews of Jesus' own day or to those who have lived since then.[22]

How have those on either side of the Jewish-Christian divide understood *Nostra Aetate* and its implications? As one might expect, liberal Catholics, Americans especially and those who represent the Catholic Church above all, hail the Vatican II declaration as a turning point of fundamental importance in the history of Jewish-Christian relations. Rather optimistically, the Catholic weekly *America* labeled it "a revolutionary departure in attitudes and practices that have deep and gnarled roots in world history."[23] One American bishop has since concluded that "the declaration ended forever all speculation of collective Jewish guilt for the death of Jesus."[24] Most illuminating are the comments of Eugene Fisher, associate director of the United States Conference of Catholic Bishops' Secretariat for Ecumenical and Interreligious Affairs and consultor to the Holy See's Commission for Religious Relations with the Jews. He describes the step-by-step process that has led the church from *Nostra Aetate* to its more elaborate "Notes on the Correct Way to Present the Jews and Judaism" as an effort "to clean its own house of the rubble of centuries of misunderstanding."[25]

With regard to the Christ-killer myth, Fisher's use of the term "misunderstanding" is doubly meaningful. He refers not merely to the misunderstanding of what *first-century Jews did or did not do to Jesus*. More important, Fisher means that *Nostra Aetate* and the "Notes" that explained it rectified the age-old Christian misunderstanding of what *genuine Christianity had always taught* about Jesus' last days. In other words, one cannot assert that Vatican II corrected the earlier errors of the Catholic Church, because the Catholic Church, as God's church, cannot possibly err! Rather, in ruling as it did, "the Second Vatican Council restated this ancient but obscured tenet of our faith in unambiguous fashion, stating that one cannot blame all the Jews of Jesus' time 'nor Jews today' for Jesus' death." From the official doctrinal perspective of the Catholic Church, the Christ-killer myth never figured in truly Christian teaching; yet it flourished owing to centuries of misinterpretation of Scripture by Christians. Once and for all, *Nostra Aetate* explained what the Passion narratives in the Gospels meant—or, more precisely, what they did not mean.[26]

Although this represents the official view of the Church, not all Catholics have agreed with it. Studies of sermons, textbooks, and other educational materials conducted over the last decades show that old myths do indeed die hard, and that much work remains in order to rid Christians of the mentality that nourishes the image of the Jewish Christ killer. Traditionalist Catholic groups have themselves lashed out at Vatican II—and not at *Nostra Aetate* alone—as a betrayal of the genuine ideals of their church. Some have hinted that the council's declaration on the Jews marked yet another victory for the international Jewish conspiracy, a sign that it had exerted its control over the church itself.[27] Listing errors in the new *Catechism of the Catholic Church* adopted in 1992, some thirty years after *Nostra Aetate* began to take shape, another Traditionalist document cites the instruction that "the Jews are not collectively responsible for Jesus' death" and responds: "One is dumbfounded by this torrent of shameless lies, concluded by an incredible declaration of the disastrous Second Vatican Council." Just as St. Bernard of Clairvaux and other twelfth-century Catholic prelates condemned Peter Abelard's teaching that the Jews had not sinned grievously in crucifying Jesus as heresy, so, too, does this present-day author of the *Book of Accusation for Heresy against . . . the Supposed Catechism of the Catholic Church* list the following among the heresies of the church of today: "Error on the innocence of the Jews and the culpability of Christians in the passion and death of Jesus crucified."[28] One archconservative Catholic group goes so far as to depict the Second Vatican Council as the betrayal and execution of the savior all over again.

> Pilate started out with no intention to kill Christ. . . . Likewise, the bishops, prelates, and pope who gathered at the Vatican for a council in October of 1962 had no plan to destroy the Church or turn it into something else, but they did give the order to scourge the Church with an aggiornamento of "updates" to the Church to bring it in line with current worldly thought. . . . That council also generated the permission given to the enemies of the Church to crucify it; when Vatican II opened the windows of the establishment ruled from Vatican City, not only did the some of the smoke of Satan leak in, but some of the Church leaked out.[29]

Who, one wonders, might these crucifiers of the Church actually be?

At the opposite end of the spectrum, *Nostra Aetate* disenchanted some modern Catholics with what they perceived as its evasion of the burning questions. Had not the Gospels themselves generated the Christ-killer myth, rather than those who *mis*interpreted the Gospels as Eugene Fisher maintained? Had not the church itself incorporated the Christ-killer myth into its theology, sustaining it and fueling many of its dire consequences? One encounters such questions among Catholic writers like James Carroll, an ordained Catholic priest who explains that he left the priesthood because of the shortcomings of Vatican II and the papal leadership that followed in its wake. When *Nostra Aetate* was promulgated in 1965, Carroll was a seminarian who was studying for the priesthood. He recalls the perplexity with which he and his fellow students greeted the declaration and what it had to say about the Jews and the Crucifixion.

> I say perplexity because, while *Nostra Aetate* was put forward as if it were rebutting a marginal slander of gutter anti-Semitism, we young

students of the New Testament knew that the sacred texts of the Church placed just such blame on the Jews then living and "on their children." We knew that . . . the Church had defined itself as the replacement of Judaism, and that because Judaism had refused to yield to that claim, the Church had further defined itself as the enemy of Judaism. *Nostra Aetate* took up none of this, but by defining as a lie an affirmation at the Center of the Gospel, it clearly put such basic questions on the Church's near-term agenda. Indeed, *Nostra Aetate* implicitly raised the issue of whether, in its first generation, the Church had already betrayed its master.[30]

How have voices from within the church reacted to Carroll's indictment? Eugene Fisher reviewed Carroll's *Constantine's Sword* (together with a previous book of my own) for the *Catholic Historical Review*.[31] There he reproves Carroll for his faulty reading of Scripture, stating that Carroll should have followed the line of interpretation advanced by Raymond Brown "and others in the Catholic Biblical Association," who "point the way in this field." We encountered Raymond Brown's ideas in chapter 1 and shall return to him presently.

Non-Catholic reaction to *Nostra Aetate* has been similarly mixed. Though Protestants generally had much more to say about other sections of the decree than about guilt for the Crucifixion, an article appearing in the Protestant *Christian Century* denounced even this provision as condescending, self-aggrandizing, and altogether inappropriate. "What monstrous arrogance is this which assumes that Christians have the right and power to forgive Jews for a crime of which they are not guilty . . . ! They should be on their knees in contrition begging forgiveness."[32] As for the Jews themselves, some applauded the Vatican declaration as a giant step forward along the road to fruitful Christian-Jewish dialogue and reconciliation, even as a "symbolic watershed" in the emancipation of modern Jewry.[33] Some responded warmly to the new Catholic openness to ecumenical dialogue fostered by *Nostra Aetate* and the documents that followed it. Other Jews have still perceived that the ultimate goal of the church remains the conversion of the Jews, and they have approached the subject of dialogue with varied blends of fear, suspicion, skepticism, and cynicism. Again, the deicide issue has appeared to interest many Jews less than other, more pressing concerns, such as the prospects and value of ecumenical dialogue, and the relationship between the Hebrew Bible and Christian Scripture, which includes both Old and New Testaments. Yet some Jewish leaders have dismissed the renunciation of collective guilt for the Crucifixion as amounting to too little, too late, given the long history of Jewish suffering that the presumption of that guilt had triggered. Even Rabbi Leon Klenicki of the Anti-Defamation League, a pioneer in the advancement of

Catholic-Jewish relations during and after the Second Vatican Council, questioned the declaration's distinction between those Jews who "pressed for the death of Christ" and those blamed (unfairly) for his death, given the church's repeated insistence that the guilt of all human beings caused the Crucifixion. If this is so, asked Rabbi Klenicki, why attribute any blame at all to "the so-called Jewish authorities and continue a tradition that accuses Jews of deicide?"[34]

What importance do *Nostra Aetate* and Vatican II assume in our story? Simply put, what is the significance of the council's declaration? What does it say, and what does it not say? Even a hurried comparison of the declaration and earlier Catholic teaching reveals a world of difference in substance and tone. Whereas the Christ-killer myth once served as an excuse for Christian hostility toward the Jew, *Nostra Aetate* presents a strategy to disown the myth or at least to minimize its potency. With regard to the question of deicide, the bottom line rings loud and clear: one cannot hold the Jews, then or now, collectively guilty of that crime. Moreover, one certainly should not discount the far more extensive significance that *Nostra Aetate* has assumed for many modern Christians. Wendell Dietrich, professor of religion at Brown University, argues for the significance of the declaration on four grounds. First, insofar as it concerns the Jews, *Nostra Aetate* explicitly recognizes the errors in Christianity's age-old "teaching of contempt." Second, it stems from a refined modern social and ethical consciousness, including an imperative for respecting "the other" in one's own society. Third, it expresses a new, more positive attitude toward non-Christian religions in general. And fourth, it demonstrates the need for a new Christian theology of Judaism, a creative rereading of New Testament sources such as the Epistle to the Romans in order to reevaluate the role of Jews and Judaism in God's plan for human history.[35]

Does the history of the Christ-killer myth end here? Regrettably, I believe not. Consider the language of *Nostra Aetate:* "The Jewish authorities and those who followed their lead pressed for the death of Christ; still, what happened in His passion cannot be charged against all the Jews, without distinction." At the same time that the Vatican Council repudiated the notion of *collective* Jewish deicide, it upheld the belief in Jewish deicide on the part of "the Jewish authorities and those who followed their lead." Indeed, the assertion that *some Jews* bear the responsibility for the Crucifixion weighs no less in *Nostra Aetate* than the negation of the view that *all Jews* are guilty. And the Vatican commission's decision to remove the term "deicide" from that negation cannot but lead one to wonder if those very individuals who formulated the declaration could not extricate themselves from the mythology that this book has explored.

One example is Pope Paul VI, the very pope who in October 1965 formally promulgated the council's declaration on the Jews as the official teaching of the Roman Catholic Church. A mere eighteen months earlier, in April

1964, Pope Paul delivered a sermon for Passion Sunday in Rome, where he commented on the gospel reading for that day.

> It describes, in fact, the clash between Jesus and the Jewish people. That people, predestined to receive the Messiah, who awaited Him for thousands of years and was completely absorbed in this hope and in this certainty, at the right moment, when, that is, Christ came, spoke, and presented Himself, not only did not recognize Him, but fought Him, slandered and injured Him; and, in the end, killed Him.[36]

*That people . . . killed him.* He who presided over most of Vatican II seems himself very much immersed in the Christ-killer myth of old, its classic conception of collective guilt.

Even Augustin Cardinal Bea, by all accounts the most instrumental figure behind *Nostra Aetate*, expressed hesitation over matters at the heart of the deicide question. Within a year after the council's closing session, Bea published his own personal statement on what had transpired: *The Church and the Jewish People: A Commentary on the Second Vatican Council's Declaration on the Relation of the Church to Non-Christian Religions.* In a chapter on "The Jewish People and the Actual Events of the Passion," Bea focused on two problems in particular: "firstly, the precise part played by the Jewish people as a whole in the actual sad events of the passion of Jesus; and secondly, the issue raised by the lack of faith in Christ displayed by the large majority of that people."[37]

Bea's first problem bears most directly on our subject. Here the cardinal contends (1) that the guilt of deicide applies to those who have killed God knowing full well what they were doing; (2) that such New Testament passages as Jesus' prayer "Father, forgive them, for they know not what they do" (Luke 23:34) can in no way be regarded "as completely exonerating" those responsible for the Crucifixion; (3) that although "there was a certain ignorance [concerning Jesus' divinity] on the part of those who were responsible," it was hardly complete, because had it been so, they would not have needed God's forgiveness; and (4) that "the formal guilt of deicide" therefore "cannot be unequivocally attributed" to the Jewish leaders and those involved with them in Jesus' trial.[38] As for the second problem, Bea responded by reiterating Paul's teaching that God has not disowned the Jewish people forever. "The sons of Israel, who have not yet been incorporated into the new people of God, are still very dear to God for the sake of their fathers. . . . Their lack of faith is only for a time, until the day—known to God alone, as the Declaration says—when . . . all Israel will be saved."[39]

Viewed in historical hindsight, Cardinal Bea's attempt to walk a tightrope between classical Christian tradition and the moral and theological imperatives of a post-Holocaust age read much like the scholastic distinctions of thirteenth-century Thomas Aquinas in insisting on the ill will (and wicked intentions) of the first-century Jewish leadership.[40] The cardinal's conclusions appear much less forthcoming than the gist of *Nostra Aetate* preferred by many ecumenically minded Jews and Christians. For Bea, the fact remains that *some Jews*—not all, to be sure—were guilty of deicide to some extent, even if *not unequivocally* so. As Bea concluded an address before the fathers of the Vatican Council in November 1963, the most compelling reason for the declaration on the Jews was

> the example of burning charity of the Lord himself on the cross, pray-ing, "Father, forgive them, for they know not what they do." This is the example to be imitated by the Church, the Bride of Christ. This is the road to be followed by her. This is what the schema proposed by us intends to foster and promote.[41]

Bea's remarks cast *Nostra Aetate*'s words on the Jews of Jesus' day in a mark-edly different light. His call for charity and forgiveness rings loudest. He him-self rules out the possibility of complete exoneration. And, in no uncertain terms, he yearns for the day when Jews will see the light, convert to Chris-tianity, and be saved. Cardinal Bea appears to suggest that the church once again sits in judgment of the Jewish people. This time around, however, he charges the church to reach out to the Jews with more charitable understand-ing, love, and mercy than it showed them in the past.

Pope Paul and Cardinal Bea leave the door open to understanding the correction instituted by *Nostra Aetate* chiefly as a quantitative one: In the past, Christians held most Jews responsible for the death of Jesus. Now they should only hold some Jews so responsible, and they should relate to the Jews who have not accepted Christ in a spirit of forgiveness. From such a reading of the council's declaration, much of the Christ-killer myth remains intact: Jews did the deed, even if *the Jews* as a people did not. Perhaps most important of all, the church remains committed to the factual accuracy of the Gospels' Passion narratives rather simply construed. It accepts them as reliable testimony to the historical reality of Jesus' last days, instead of as myths testifying primarily to the historical context in which the evangelists composed their narratives. Committed to the divine revelation inherent in its Scriptures, the Catholic Church cannot but maintain its commitment to the essential "facticity" of the Crucifixion story, and this leaves little room for maneuvering to rid the story of its offensive implications. As em-phasized in the opening pages of this book, myths are not necessarily fac-tually inaccurate. But the truth that they impart is not the truth of events that occurred but the truth of the worldview of the storyteller. It is precisely this mythic quality of the Jewish Christ killer that Vatican II failed to acknowledge.

Perhaps I can better illustrate this point by referring to a particular interfaith gathering in November 1994, part of a series called the *Nostra Aetate* Dialogues, at which liberal Jewish and Christian scholars and theologians assembled to further mutual understanding in the positive spirit of Vatican II. On that particular evening, Raymond Brown, the Jesuit scholar whose work on the Passion narrative was discussed in chapter 1, and Michael Cook, a Reform rabbi and New Testament scholar at the Hebrew Union College in Cincinnati, presented their respective views on Jewish involvement in Jesus' crucifixion. As we saw, Father Brown's view conforms essentially to the official "party line" of the Catholic Church; in holding Jews, not Romans, primarily responsible for Jesus' death, he insists on the historical plausibility of the core of the Passion narrative—that is, that it reflects the events and context of Jesus' last days rather faithfully. After Brown presented his views on that November evening in 1994, Rabbi Cook proposed "an alternative stance": that "circumstances of the Gospel writers' own day" account for considerably more of the basic substance of their narratives than Brown would allow. Interestingly, this line of thought led Cook to an avowedly Jewish perspective on the matter of deicide.

> Since Jews today are respectfully aware that Roman Catholics consider Jesus *the* Son of God, they do fully enough comprehend that what happened to Jesus became and remains a matter of great consequence to Roman Catholics. But Jews would wish that Roman Catholics would reciprocate with *their* understanding that it is the Jewish view
>
> that (1) Jesus was *a* son of God in the same sense that we are all offspring of God;
>
> and thus that (2) *all* unjust killings of human beings (that of Jesus among them) may be *commensurate* one with another;
>
> that (3) these also include the unjust deaths of countless Jews over the centuries for the sole reason that they were vilified as "Christ-killers";
>
> and that (4) *their* deaths may have been even more unwarranted than that of Jesus given that *he* opted for a course that portended risk of arrest, even of execution, while these later Jews died only as an indirect consequence of *his* decision, not their own.

Cook declared that Father Brown's quest to trace and determine responsibility should extend to these matters, too.[42]

To what extent have *Nostra Aetate* and its legacy in the post–Vatican II Catholic Church risen to this challenge? The various voices heard in this chapter would offer a wide range of responses, and one cannot resolve the issue conclusively. One wonders, in fact, whether our post-Holocaust era can fairly expect the Catholic Church to extricate itself from positions and perspectives so basic to its beliefs. Can the church ever acknowledge that it, as an institution, bears responsibility for the wrongful mentality that *Nostra Aetate* condemns? Can Christian faith ever come to terms with a Passion narrative whose historical truth lies not in the events that it recalls, but rather in the meaning of those events for its narrators? At the very least, *Nostra Aetate* constitutes a wonderfully instructive case of a religious institution wrestling with its problematic past to confront the difficult challenges of the present and to define its direction for the future.

PART

# III

# THE MYTH AND THE ARTS

# 9

# THE PASSION IN RELIGIOUS ART

"What writing offers to those who read it, a picture offers to the ignorant who look at it." In these often quoted—and often misquoted—
words, Pope Gregory the Great (590–604) uttered one of the classic Western
judgments on the function of art in society. Sir Kenneth Clark has hailed
Gregory's statement as "one of the crucial events in the history of art."[1]
Though the meaning, intention, and implications of Gregory's statement might
not be as clear-cut as they first appear, its identification of the visual image
as an invaluable tool for promoting religious belief certainly underscores the
need to include the arts in our story. Art can prove most effective in educat-
ing the public, particularly when many are illiterate; it can win minds, hearts,
and souls. Gregory himself explained, "a picture is displayed in churches in
order that the unschooled may at least read by seeing on the walls what they
are unable to read in books."[2] As some have paraphrased, art served as "the
book of the illiterate," and it allowed the church to disseminate Christian
knowledge and belief among the masses, especially before the onset of printing, radio, television, and the Internet.

Yet as Pope Gregory himself pointed out, art served as more than a textbook for the uneducated. Religious art, or iconography, inspired at the same
time as it taught, appealing to the senses in order to awaken feelings of piety
and strengthen religious conviction. For Christianity, which charged its believers somehow to make the experience of Christ's Passion their own, be-
holding the Crucifixion in painting, sculpture, or even a dramatic spectacle
on stage could render the event much more accessible than could reading
Scripture or hearing a sermon. When one thinks of Western religious art, one
might well think first of the cross and the art of the Passion, whose messages
lie at the foundation of the Christian worldview.

Curiously, however, quite some time elapsed before crucifixion scenes
appeared in Christian iconography. The oldest surviving Christian iconography
dates from the second century, whereas the Crucifixion did not appear in art
until the fifth century, and even then appeared very infrequently. Only in the
seventh and eighth centuries, after the age of the church fathers and the later
Roman Empire gave way to that of the medieval monastery and the feudal
manor, does the crucified Christ become a common theme in religious art. And

not until the twelfth and thirteenth centuries did Passion iconography flourish in the medieval West. Although historians have debated the reasons why this did not occur earlier, we might rephrase the question in more positive terms: Why did the Crucifixion became a preferred subject for the Christian artist when it did, and what role did the Jews assume in this iconography of the Passion?

The twelfth and thirteenth centuries, the age of the Crusades, saw the rise of the medieval church to the peak of its power. It was then, more than at any other time in its history, that the Catholic Church imposed its discipline and its values on Western society, its institutions, and its rank and file alike. The image of the body of Christ, and that of the crucified Christ above all, found expression everywhere: from the cross emblazoned on the tunics of the crusaders, to the popes' descriptions of the unity of Christendom (with themselves as its "head"), to the "real presence" of Christ in the Eucharist, and to the art of the period. Furthermore, the same period witnessed a shift in the focus of Christian religious devotion from Christ the heavenly king to the very human, suffering Christ of the Crucifixion. Then, as we read, "the humiliated, tortured, whipped, nailed-down, pierced, dying but life-giving body of Christ, the very body literally present in the eucharist" came to dominate the popular piety cultivated by the late medieval church. (See chapter 6.) Such Passion-centered piety found a natural partner in Passion iconography. The cross gave way to the crucifix, as some would have it. Or as others have suggested, the earlier glance at images of the Crucifixion intensified into a prolonged, penetrating gaze. Piety and artistic expressiveness nourished and fed upon each other, and this mutual reinforcement bolstered the prominence of them both. Interestingly, once the Protestant Reformation and the Counter-Reformation of the Catholic Church put a damper on late medieval popular devotion, the intensity of the art of the Crucifixion waned as well.

The late eleventh through the mid-sixteenth centuries, then, were the heyday of Passion iconography in Western Christendom. How did the Jews and Judaism emerge in these presentations of the Crucifixion? Given the centrality of the Christ-killer myth in Christian doctrine on the one hand, and the educational and inspirational functions of religious art on the other hand, the concern for the Jews displayed in the art of the Passion demands our attention. Though highly selective, my discussion of the visual evidence will at times return us to matters considered earlier, corroborating earlier findings at some points and complicating them at others. I turn to three dimensions of the medieval Christian artist's linkage between the Jews and the crucifixion of Jesus.

## SYNAGOGA AND ECCLESIA

Christian art of the early Middle Ages depicts the Jews as Jesus' killers only rarely, but it frequently finds another role for them in scenes of the Crucifix-

ion. From the earliest days of Christianity, advocates of the new religion often contrasted their own beliefs with those of the Jews by symbolizing the
two religious communities and their respective testaments of Scripture with
the figures of two women. The apostle Paul saw these women portrayed in
the two wives of the biblical patriarch Abraham: Hagar and Sarah. Admon-
ishing the Galatians to liberate themselves from the bonds of the old biblical
law of Moses, he wrote:

> For it is written that Abraham had two sons, one by a slave and one
> by a free woman. But the son of the slave was born according to the
> flesh, the son of the free woman through promise. Now this is an
> allegory: these women are two covenants. One is from Mount Sinai,
> bearing children for slavery; she is Hagar. Now Hagar is Mount Sinai
> in Arabia; she corresponds to the present Jerusalem, for she is in sla-
> very with her children. But the Jerusalem above is free, and she is
> our mother. (Galatians 4:21–26)

Paul's strategy of validating his Christian beliefs by debunking those of the Jews
persisted in Christian theology, as did the representation of the two faiths in
the motherly figures of two women, who quickly assumed the names of
Synagoga and Ecclesia. Synagoga personified the Old Testament, Ecclesia the
New. Synagoga embodied the synagogue, the Jewish people, Israel of the flesh,
who had rejected Jesus and his offer of salvation. Ecclesia embodied the new
Israel of the spirit, Holy Mother Church, the community of Christian faithful.
By the fifth century, Christian preachers and teachers had begun to compose
imagined debates between Synagoga and Ecclesia, primarily as a means of edu-
cating Christians and fortifying their religious beliefs. The two women soon
found a place in the iconography of the early Middle Ages, where they typically appeared under the outstretched arms of the crucified Christ: Synagoga
under his left (*sinister* in Latin) arm, Ecclesia under his right arm (see fig. 7.1).

We find a wonderful example of this scene in an ivory tablet from early
medieval Metz (fig. 9.1). The crucified Jesus in the center of the tablet dominates the scene. Among others, we see figures of angels (and representations
of the sun and the moon) above Jesus; beside him, at the outer edges of the
tablet, Mary and John; beneath him, the Roman soldiers (whom Christian
tradition named Longinus and Stephaton) that lanced Jesus' side and gave
him vinegar and gall to drink; beside and beneath them, tombs which Jesus'
death miraculously opened, along with the gates of hell. Standing under Jesus'
left and right arms are, respectively, Synagoga and Ecclesia. As Synagoga
clutches the banner of her authority, Ecclesia attends to Jesus' wounds, capturing his blood, the key to human salvation, in her chalice.

What does Synagoga, who embodies the Jewish people, contribute to
this Crucifixion scene? Perhaps one can best respond by imagining the same

FIGURE 9.1. Synagoga and Ecclesia, ca. 1000, workshop in Metz. Courtesy of Musées de Metz.

scene without her. The ivory would then portray the most central tenet of
Christian belief: that Jesus died on the cross in order to save the world from
sin. Looking at such a tablet vertically, from top to bottom or from heaven
to hell, we would understand that the cosmic significance of this moment
exceeds that of any other. But that moment is all we would see. The scope of
the work would resemble that of a still photograph: a single event, isolated

in time, with no movement either backward or forward, out of the past or into the future.

When contrasted with Ecclesia as she is here, however, Synagoga adds precisely this sense of motion, of horizontal or historical dynamic, to the picture. She signifies the Old Testament background out of which Jesus and the miracle of his sacrificial death emerged; and, in so doing, she adds depth to the figure of Ecclesia, who, by contrast, now symbolizes the future history of the church that Christ's death established. Synagoga thereby transforms the effect of the scene from that of a still photo to that of a moving picture, or a video clip perhaps. Unlike all the other figures on the tablet, who gaze at Jesus and stand facing him, Synagoga has turned away from Jesus, and she looks up at him over her shoulder, almost reluctantly, perhaps reminding us of the backward-looking wife of the biblical Lot who was petrified as a result of her error. Significantly, Jesus looks down upon Ecclesia and returns her gaze, away from Synagoga. Synagoga is clearly on her way out, while Ecclesia has entered to take her place. (In some representations of Synagoga and Ecclesia, angels actually prod Synagoga away from the cross.) Yet she has an importance that goes well beyond herself. She allows the Christian viewer of the Crucifixion to understand where the church has come from and where it is going. She places the moment of Christ's death within the broader, more meaningful continuum of salvation history, extending from creation to Mount Sinai, to Calvary, and to doomsday.

Stubborn in her rejection of Jesus, displaced by God as a result, and yet testifying to the roots and purpose of Christianity, Synagoga thus reminds us of the blindly ignorant Jewish slayers of Jesus, the Jews who, as in the teaching of St. Augustine, "killed him and would not believe in him" yet retained an important role to play in the Christian world. As we saw in chapter 4, Augustine charged Christians not to slay the Jews or to put an end to their practice of Judaism. The Jews had killed Jesus without comprehending who he was. Though their crime justified their destruction, God had preserved them for a particular purpose. For they and their observance of the law, much like Synagoga in the ivory tablet, established that the salvation of the New Testament had arisen within the framework of the Old to perfect and fulfill its prophecies. Synagoga standing at the foot of the cross and Augustine's Jewish blind man standing before the mirror demonstrate to Christians the truth of Christianity by contrast. Precisely because they do not see the truth, they attest to the replacement of the old law of Moses by the new covenant of Christ's grace, the synagogue by the church.

Appreciating Synagoga and Ecclesia in these terms gives meaning to the relatively harmonious concord that art historians have correctly perceived in many of their early appearances. In the ivory tablet from Metz, they are of nearly the same height (if anything, Synagoga perhaps stands slightly taller).

More important, Synagoga displays no obvious signs of degradation or humiliation: no one prods her offstage, she and her banner stand erect, and she wears no blindfold. Yet as time wore on, concord and parity in the portrayal of Synagoga and Ecclesia gave way to discord and disparagement. Synagoga becomes visibly older, less attractive, and more poorly dressed than Ecclesia. In an early thirteenth-century German altarpiece from Soest (fig. 9.2), the force with which the angel removes Synagoga borders upon violence. Synagoga's crown has fallen from her head, and she wears a blindfold, whereas in other works of the period she carries a broken staff (or bannerpole), and the tablets of the Law seem to fall out of her hands (fig. 9.3, lower right). Just as the relative harmony in earlier portrayals of Synagoga and Ecclesia affirmed the rather tolerant approach of Augustine toward the Jews and Judaism, the newer, more belligerent portrayals signaled the growing acceptance of a different approach, one that did not bode well for the Jews of Christian Europe.

## JEWISH HOSTILITY

Hand in hand with their degradation of Synagoga, medieval Christian artists of the Passion eventually expressed a new interest in the Jews as Christ killers. The prominent role of the Jews in the New Testament Passion narrative and its interpretation in Christian theology left little doubt concerning their complicity in Jesus' death. The appearance of Jews in representations of the Crucifixion story was therefore commonplace; this should hardly surprise us, and it need not preoccupy us. But the representation of these Jews underwent several noteworthy developments during the later Middle Ages, and these changes confirm that a new, less tolerant, and more threatening Christian attitude toward the Jews of Western Europe had begun to emerge.

First, the Jews in scenes of the Passion narrative appear ever more consistently as contemporary Jews of the Middle Ages: in their dress, their beards, their headgear, their distinctive badges (that the church obliged them to wear from the early thirteenth century), and even in the caricatures of their faces. To be sure, medieval artists characteristically depicted biblical figures, from Old and New Testaments alike, in medieval dress and had few qualms about situating them in a physical setting that resembled the Europe of their day much more than the ancient Near East. Nonetheless, the stereotyping of the Jew was blatant, and it cast the contemporary Jew in an unquestionably hostile light. For example, various works identify Jesus' floggers as medieval European Jews by their conical hats and otherwise contemporary forms of dress. In a fifteenth-century French manuscript of Ludolph of Saxony's *Life of Christ*, a turban and lengthy beard identify Judas at the Last Supper as a medieval Jewish merchant, and Jesus and his other disciples, all bareheaded,

FIGURE 9.2. Synagoga and Ecclesia, ca. 1225, alterpiece from Soest, Staatliche Museen Berlin-Dahlem. Reproduced with permission of Bildarchiv Preussischer Kulturbesitz.

resemble contemporary Christian clergymen.[3] A fifteenth-century German painting of the Crucifixion (fig. 9.4) places round yellow badges on several figures in the angry, derisive mob, and others betray their Jewishness with their hats, their exaggerated facial characteristics, and their beards. The message of such portrayals is clear: contemporary Jews—that is, Jews of the medieval world—bear and express the same hostility toward Jesus that im-

FIGURE 9.3. Synagoga and Ecclesia, ca. 1260, Bonmont Psalter (Besançon Ms.54, f.15v.). Reproduced with permission of Bibliothèque Municipale de Besançon.

FIGURE 9.4. Kempton Master, Crucifixion, ca. 1460–1470. Reproduced with permission of Germanisches National Museum, Nuremberg.

pelled the Jews of first-century Jerusalem to kill him. The Jews of the present qualify as Christ killers no less than the Jews of the past.

Second, these and many, many other works expand the hostile role played by the Jews in the drama of Jesus' last days, having them inflict the physical violence upon Jesus that the Gospels attribute to the Romans. Recall the following report of the Gospel of Mark (15:15–15:23):

> So Pilate, wishing to satisfy the crowd, released for them Barabbas; and having scourged Jesus, he delivered him to be crucified. And the

soldiers led him away inside the palace (that is, the praetorium); and they called together the whole battalion. And they clothed him in a purple cloak, and plaiting a crown of thorns they put it on him. And they began to salute him, "Hail, King of the Jews!" And they struck his head with a reed, and spat upon him, and they knelt down in homage to him. And when they had mocked him, they stripped him of the purple cloak, and put his own clothes on him. And they led him out to crucify him. And they compelled a passer-by, Simon of Cyre'ne, who was coming in from the country, the father of Alexander and Rufus, to carry his cross. And they brought him to the place called Golgotha (which means the place of a skull). And they offered him wine mingled with myrrh; but he did not take it. And they crucified him.

Despite variations in several of the other Gospels' accounts—such as in the drink offered Jesus (wine, myrrh, vinegar, and/or gall), the point in the narrative at which Jesus was flogged, and the particulars of Jesus' passage to Golgotha with his cross in tow—those who inflict physical harm upon Jesus remain Pilate and his Roman soldiers. They scourge Jesus, they mock him, they spit at him, they place the crown of thorns upon his head, and they lead him off and crucify him.

Christian iconography of the Middle Ages, however, came to tell a different story. An illuminated German manuscript of the fourteenth century portrays Jesus crowned with thorns by rather malicious-looking Jews (fig. 9.5); in a German painting of the next century (fig. 9.6), the Jews who crown Jesus appear even more grotesque. Jesus' floggers themselves are often depicted as Jews—whether as otherwise Roman-like figures who simply have donned funnel-shaped Jewish hats (fig. 9.7) or as blatantly devilish characters adorned with Jewish beard, hat, and/or pointed nose.[4] (In a similar vein, some of the devotional works we encountered in chapter 6 transformed the Roman soldiers who spat at Jesus into Jews.) But perhaps most important of all, Christian iconography departed radically from the narrative of the Gospels by portraying the Jews as Jesus' actual crucifiers, as those who in fact nailed him to the cross, pierced him with a lance, and sponged his face with vinegar. This pattern spanned a lengthy period and can be found in works ranging from an eleventh-century Psalter to a twelfth-century stone relief, an illuminated manuscript from around 1300 (fig. 9.8), and an altarpiece from the end of the fourteenth century.[5]

Third, as the suffering of Jesus before and during his crucifixion became the central focus of Christian piety during the later Middle Ages, the Christian imagination expanded freely upon the Passion narrative itself and, in so doing, added further to the Jews' role in inflicting that suffering. Whereas,

**FIGURE 9.5.** Crowning with Thorns, 14th century. *Speculum humanae salvationis*, Cod. cremifanensis 243, f. 24v. Reproduced with permission of Stiftsbibliothek Kremsmünster.

for example, the Gospel of John (18:12–13) relates that, on the night of Jesus' arrest, "the band of soldiers and their captain and the officers of the Jews seized Jesus and bound him" and that they then "led him to Annas," a fourteenth-century German work on Jesus' suffering offers a much fuller description of what transpired:

> Then they seized Christ with raving violent devilish gesticulations, one grasped his hair, a second his clothes, a third his beard. These three were as foul hounds as ever might cling to him . . . and so he was pulled away, with violent wild raving abandon, with fierce blows of mailed hands and fists upon his neck and between his shoulders, on his back, on his head, across his cheeks, on his throat, on his breast. . . . They tore his hair from his head so that the locks lay strewn

**Figure 9.6.** Karlsruhe Passion Master, Crowning with Thorns, ca. 1450.
Reproduced with permission of Staatliche Kunsthalle Karlsruhe.

FIGURE 9.7. Flagellation of Christ, 13th century, Latin
Psalter Ms. Dresden A165, f. 8. Reproduced with
permission of Sächsische Landsbibliothek–Staats-und
Universitätsbibliothek, Dresden.

around on the ground; one pulled him one way by the hair, the other
pulled him back by the beard. . . . So they dragged him down from
the Mount. . . . And they hauled him to the gate of the town in such
a way that he never set foot properly on the ground . . . until they
brought him into Annas' house.[6]

Freely interpreting numerous passages from the prophecies of the Hebrew
Bible, late medieval artists and writers elaborated these and other scenes in
what some have termed the "Secret Passion" of Christ. The Secret Passion
entailed a series of tortures and humiliations never mentioned in the Gospels:
Jesus' arrest and violent conveyance to the chief priests, during which he was
led over a stony path, strewn with thorns and thistles, and dragged through

**FIGURE 9.8.** Unknown Master, Initial O with the Crucifixion, ca. 1300, Lüttich manuscript. Reproduced with permission of Westfälisches Landsmuseum für Kunst und Kulturgeschichte/permanent loan: Westfälischer Kunstverein.

the Kidron stream outside Jerusalem or some other foul water; the tortures that Jesus then endured during that first night of captivity; the physical abuse that Jesus suffered before his judges, Annas, Caiaphas, Herod, and Pilate; the details of the mocking, flagellation and "crowning" of Jesus following his judgment; the suffering he endured as he carried his cross to Calvary; and the gruesome process of nailing him on the cross.[7]

Condemned as those responsible for the Crucifixion and for the violence against Jesus that the Gospels attributed to the Romans, the Jews now figured prominently in the Secret Passion. Christian writers (see chapter 6) and Christian artists alike allotted them new, virtually limitless outlets for expressing their hatred of Christ and his church. Some of the works cited earlier illustrate this tendency, and, from among virtually countless works of art, we can turn only to several more. A fifteenth-century Italian illumination of the betrayal and arrest of Jesus attests well to the visual effects of thus embellishing the biblical narrative.[8] Later in the same century, an Umbrian artist then represented the suffering Jesus together with the *Arma Christi* (fig. 9.9), instruments of torture used against him that receive no mention in the Gospels, and a European Jew spitting upon him. But the phenomenon was hardly limited to Italy. Identified above all by their headwear and monstrous faces, the Jews maltreat Jesus in numerous unattested ways in renditions of the "Mocking of Christ" by Northern European artists such as Matthias Grünewald (fig. 9.10) and Sigmund Holbein (fig. 9.11).

The list of examples goes on and on, but even these few suffice to illustrate the contrast between the relatively peaceful portrayal of Synagoga at the foot of the cross in early medieval art and the violent representation of the Jewish Christ killer in the iconography of the later Middle Ages. How can

FIGURE **9.9.** Man of Sorrows with *Arma Christi*, late 15th century, Umbrian. Reproduced with permission of Rheinisches Bildarchiv, Cologne.

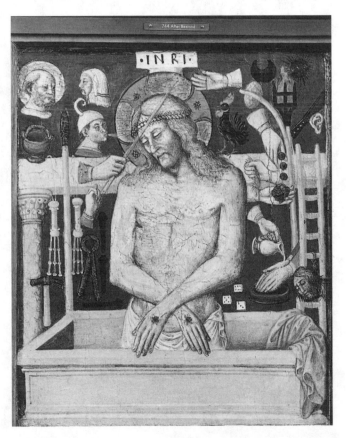

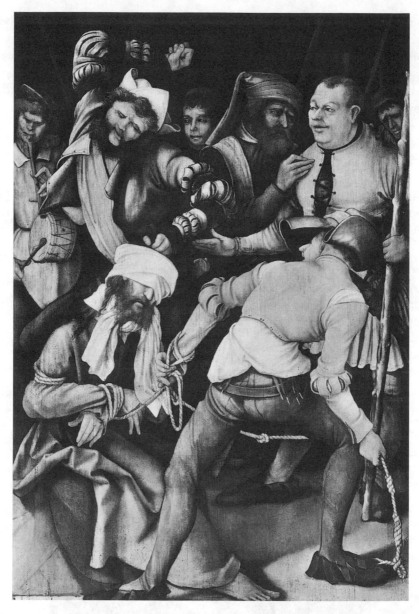

FIGURE 9.10. Matthias Grünewald, *The Mocking of Christ*, ca. 1504–1505. Reproduced with permission of Bayerische Staatsgemäldesammlungen, Munich.

FIGURE 9.11. Sigmund Holbein, *The Mocking of Christ*, early 16th century. Kisters Collection, Kreuzlingen, Switzerland. Reproduced with permission of the Collection Heinz Kisters.

we explain the difference? Synagoga, we suggested, personified the Jews of the Old Testament who rejected Jesus in their blindness and ignorance but whose unwitting biblical testimony to Christian truth mandated their survival and toleration. Yet by the twelfth and thirteenth centuries, this Christian perception of the Jew as a relic of antiquity had given way to a different one. The Christian world viewed the Jew not as a blindly ignorant unbeliever but as a heretic, one who knew the truth but deliberately rejected it nonetheless. This was not the Old Testament Jew personified by Synagoga, but the con temporary Jew, the Jew of the Talmud, who had knowingly forsaken his biblical heritage rather than admit its fulfillment in Christianity. This Jew offered no positive contribution to the Christian world. Rather, in his deviation from authentic Judaism, he constituted a clear and present threat to the order and welfare of Christian society, which, as we have seen, churchmen compared to the body of Christ. Such a Jew, who knew that Christianity was true and yet continued to reject it, was a pernicious enemy of that body. As we saw in chapter 4, no longer did the church consider him one who blindly killed his savior and God in ignorance of his true identity. By the thirteenth century, some of the most revered Christian theologians concluded that the Jews responsible for the Crucifixion killed Christ intentionally and maliciously, well understanding the magnitude of their crime.

The works of art considered here vent this new hostility toward the Jew in a number of ways. They leave no doubt as to the avid enthusiasm and malicious intentions of the Jews who crucified Jesus. If Synagoga embodied the blind, stubborn adherence of Jews to the Law, the Jewish Christ killer of late medieval art expressed a new Christian perception of the Jewish minority: Directed at Christ and everything Christian, the hostility of the Jew was irrational and uncompromising. Quite apart from the guilt for Jesus' execution that they inherited from their first-century ancestors, these medieval Jews continually expressed their enmity toward Christ in their daily lives. No wonder the later iconography depicts these Jewish Christ killers in medieval garb. No wonder it portrays them as perpetrating even those acts of hostility toward Christ that Scripture remembered as Roman acts. No wonder its imaginative visualization of the Secret Passion narrative placed the Jews at center stage at virtually every moment of Jesus' suffering.

## THE DEMONIZED JEW

Most staggering of all, no doubt, was the new conviction that the Jews recognized Jesus for who he really was and killed him precisely for that reason. Ultimately, they chose to kill their God. Thomas Aquinas, who may have tempered his words for fear of appearing to contradict the earlier judgment of St. Augustine, nevertheless came to this conclusion. "They beheld the blatant signs of his divinity, but they corrupted them out of hatred and jealousy of Christ; and *they wished not to believe* his words, by which he proclaimed himself to be the Son of God."[9] What kind of rational human being would behave in such an evil, self-defeating manner? The answer, of course, is no rational human being at all. Thus the deliberate Jewish Christ killer of late medieval art appears ever more inhuman—grotesque, animal-like, and demonic.

This Satanic nature of the Jew, which led medieval Christian lore to link the Jewish Christ killer with an array of inhuman, heinous crimes against Christian society—slanders and libels that we encountered in chapter 5—led to the same connection in the art of the period. Reviewing three groups of these accusations, I turned first to the ritual murder libel, and to mid-twelfth-century English Jews' alleged slaying of William of Norwich in particular. The impact of the Norwich libel, as we noted, extended far and wide, and in 1493, more than three hundred years later, it was the subject of a German woodblock print (fig. 9.12). Testifying to the realities of his own day, the artist has placed Jewish ringed badges on the clothing of the twelfth-century William's crucifiers, even though European Jews did not have to wear them before the thirteenth century. Just as Christian iconography of the Middle Ages typically portrayed the Crucifixion as occurring now, in the present, so does this print portray the ritual murder of William of Norwich. The Jewish danger and hostility have an enduring immediacy. Thomas of Monmouth, we recall, did this in his book about William by representing Jewish ritual murder as a well-planned event masterminded annually by an international conspiracy of Jewish leaders who convened in the city of Narbonne. Thomas intensified his appeal to the minds and emotions of his readers by weaving together both the visible and the invisible in his story—that is, by blending what *did* happen in Norwich in 1144 with what Thomas, writing several years later, concluded *must* have happened. We find this strategy, too, in visual illustrations of ritual murder, like that which

**FIGURE 9.12.** Michael Wolgemut (or the Wolgemut and Pleydenwurff workshop in Nuremberg), William of Norwich, woodcut in Hartmann Schedel, *Liber chronicarum* 1493, f. 201v. Courtesy of the Division of Rare and Manuscript Collections, Cornell University Library.

depicts a ritual murder in the Swiss city of Bern in 1294 (fig. 9.13). As the viewer can readily see through the walls of the house and beholds the Jews torturing their innocent victim inside, the Christian townsmen outside (at the right of the picture) cannot. Ever-present, whether visible or not, the deicidal evil of the Jews imperiled the bodies of Christian faithful.

Christian society, we saw, soon included Christ himself among the victims of the *contemporary* Jewish peril, as it accused Jews of desecrating the Eucharist after its consecration (and miraculous transformation into the body of Christ) by a priest during mass. Illustrations of the Host-desecration libel are plentiful, and here I offer only one, dating to around 1400, from a Spanish (Catalonian) altarpiece (fig. 9.14). We see the desecrating Jew, his wife and child beside him, torturing the bleeding Host. As many of these stories related, he then threw the Host into a boiling pot, from which we see that the Christ child himself has emerged. At the altar, the connection between Jesus' Passion and the Jews' recurring desecration of the Host is emphasized by the placement of this picture next to one of the Last Supper, where we read in the Gospels that Jesus took the unleavened Passover *matzah*, blessed it, gave it to

FIGURE 9.13. Ritual Murder in Bern (1294), ca. 1478–1483, miniature in Diebold
Schilling, *Amtliche Berner Chronik* (Burgerbibliothek Bern, Mss. h.h. l 1 p. 44).
Courtesy of Burgerbibliothek Bern.

his disciples, and said, "Take; this is my body." And above these two scenes,
the altarpiece includes a scene of the Crucifixion.[10]

The medieval mind also imagined Jewish crimes of ritual cannibalism,
in which murderous Jews used the blood of their victims in their Passover
bread or for some other ritual purpose. The 1475 blood libel surrounding
Simon of Trent (see chapter 5) found expression in numerous illustrations of
the late fifteenth, sixteenth, and seventeenth centuries, printed illustrations
that circulated among an extremely wide general public. In many of them (see
fig. 9.15), the figure of Simon reminds us of Jesus on the cross. So too, many
Spanish artists depicted the Jewish execution of the Holy Child of La Guardia,
whose alleged murder, we recall, blended motifs of ritual crucifixion, Host
desecration, and ritual cannibalism.

Yet the very impulse that propelled the Christian imagination from the
Jew as deliberate killer of Christ to the Jew as perpetrator of the most heinous possible crimes against humanity also led to the portrayal of the Jew as
inhuman, satanic, animal-like, and monstrous. We have already witnessed
this tendency in some of the works, written and visual, discussed here, but
the demonization of the Jew proceeded further still. Popular traditions of the
later Middle Ages, for example, characterize Jews as having a distinctive foul

FIGURE 9.14. Jaime Sierra, Desecration of the Host, ca. 1400, detail of Sijena monastery altarpiece. © MNAC-Museu Nacional d'Art de Catalunya, Barcelona. 2005. Photographers: Calveras/Mérida/Sagristà.

odor. Jewish men were commonly thought to suffer from a bloody flux much like a woman's menstrual period. The monstrosity and perversity of the Jew likewise found expression in art, as in a sixteenth-century painting of *Ecce homo* (Pilate's cry of "Behold the man" [John 19:5]) by the Flemish artist Hieronymus Bosch or one of his students (fig. 9.16).[11] Here the artist may well have drawn on Psalm 22, which Christian writers from the first century on read as a prophesy of the Crucifixion and which speaks of lions, bulls, dogs, and ruffians that surround and threaten God's servant. But the anti-Jewish imagery is blatant here no less: the pointed hats, grotesque features (including "large mouth, large lips, flaring nostrils, tightly curled frizzy hair"[12])

FIGURE 9.15. Michael Wolgemut (or the Wolgemut and Pleydenwurff workshop in Nuremberg), Simon of Trent Murdered by the Jews, woodcut in Hartmann Schedel, *Liber chronicarum* 1493, f. 254v. Courtesy of the Division of Rare and Manuscript Collections, Cornell University Library.

of those in the angry mob. Of special interest is the insect on the patch of one of the men in the lower right corner of the painting and on the pennant in the lower left. Some art historians have identified the creature as a scorpion (albeit a deformed one, lacking the classic scorpion's tail), which itself commonly served as a symbol of the venomous, treacherous Jew. The lack of a tail has led others to discern a beetle, not a scorpion, as in one especially fascinating description of the painting:

> With the exception of Christ, the bodies, faces, garments and head-covering of the figures are distorted and transformed into those of insect-like beings, and it is no accident that a beetle appears as an emblem on the banner at lower left, and on the shoulder of one of

**FIGURE 9.16.** Hieronymus Bosch (or a disciple), *Ecce homo*, 16th century. J#352, John G. Johnson Collection, Philadelphia Museum of Art, 1917. Courtesy of the Philadelphia Museum of Art.

the soldiers at lower right. Their arms and hands are like the limbs of insects, and the cudgels and halberds are stylized so that they look like antennae.

As this writer keenly observes,

one gets the impression of an army of noxious insects. They move about quickly and seem to be agitated like insects swarming around a light. The strange transformation of men into insects indicates that the artist intended to describe them not as people taking part in a historical event but as phantoms.[13]

By all accounts, the bestiality of the Jew climaxed in the image of the *Judensau*, the portrayal of Jews along with a female pig—symbolic of filth, impurity, and the taboo that biblical Jews were meant to abhor—riding her in a provocative, bestial, and prurient manner, suckling at her teats, and eating her excrement. Dozens of Judensaus survive from the sculpture, woodwork, and printed illustrations of the late medieval and early modern periods, and they, too, intersect with the portrayal of the Jew as Christ killer. Various illustrations of the murder of Simon of Trent blended images of the Judensau, the devil, the murder of little Simon himself, and the Crucifixion. In the seventeenth-century engraving from Frankfurt reproduced here (fig. 9.17), a well-dressed, very contemporary-looking Jew has mounted the sow backward and holds up her tail, while a second Jew sucks at her milk and a third eats her feces. The horned devil, himself wearing a Jewish badge, looks on, and the butchered Simon, splayed as if on a cross, appears in a panel above. Another Frankfurt Judensau from the same period appeared in a poster-size portrayal of "The Jewish Synagogue," accompanied by a bawdy and derisive poem:

*Arawenos the learned fool*
*Shows the purse and the letters,*
*To instruct the point-heads,*
*How they should excrete on the Christians.*
*Butzmann the gallow-worthy thief,*
*Sticks the tube right up in the arse.*
*Cuntzmann (Trickster) licks his lips, waits anxiously,*
*For the sow to excrete into his mouth . . .*
*Fortzfresser (Fart-glutton) begin! Gobble up quickly,*
*It is good for our health.*
*Gumbel excretes into the sow's trough,*
*Surely one sow smells the other . . .*
*Judas betrayed Christ swiftly,*
*And also the child in Trent.*
*Krotzebeisser stands leisurely,*
*Looks at the (Golden) Calf on the column . . .*
*So stay as you are,*
*And may the Devil ride you.*
*When need presses an honorable Christian,*
*The Jew sings,*
*The devil jumps and springs,*
*And in the end the fire of hell burns.*[14]

Whereas the career of the Judensau lived on—especially in books, pamphlets, posters, playing cards, and ornaments—into the nineteenth century, and libels of ritual murder and ritual cannibalism have been heard even in the twentieth and twenty-first centuries, the prominence of the Jew in the iconography of the Passion waned in the sixteenth century. Historians have

FIGURE 9.17. The Frankfurt Judensau, 17th century. Reproduced with permission of Historisches Museum Frankfurt/Main. Repro-Photographer: Ursula Seitz-Gray.

judiciously called attention to the "erosion" of stereotypes from among those we have discussed here, and one should guard against simply assuming an uninterrupted continuity between medieval anti-Judaism and modern anti-Semitism in every conceivable mode of religious expression.[15] Yet the Christ-killer myth has reared its head in other artistic media, and I will focus on two of them in the next chapters: the stage and the screen.

# THE PASSION ON STAGE: OBERAMMERGAU

A century after Martin Luther launched the Protestant Reformation, just as the iconography of the Crucifixion had passed its heyday, one of the most long-lived, acclaimed, and controversial portrayals of the Passion narrative entered the history of Western culture. Tradition has it that early in the autumn of 1633, plague ravaged the Bavarian countryside in southern Germany. In Oberammergau, a small village some sixty-five miles southwest of Munich, the efforts of the townsfolk to quarantine themselves proved futile, and between September 25 and October 28, eighty-one people perished. The residents of the town then vowed to produce a Passion play every ten years if God would spare them further losses, and, when no one else died, they staged the first Oberammergau Passion Play in 1634. From then until 2000, the play has run during forty seasons, most of them at the turn of the decade. Unquestionably the world's most famous Passion play, the Oberammergau *Passionsspiel* captures and develops many of the central themes of this book. Bridging the gap between classical and contemporary Christianity, Scripture and stage, clergy and common folk, theologian and townsman, the play offers remarkable testimony to the power and problems of the Christ-killer myth.

## FROM PASSION NARRATIVE TO PASSION PLAY

If the iconography of the Passion allowed Catholics to understand the meaning of Jesus' crucifixion by visualizing it, religious drama brought life, movement, sound, and human activity into art in a way that painting or sculpture could not. Furthermore, dramatizations of the Passion readily transformed viewers into participants. In churches as well as on the stages of small towns and villages, dramatic renditions of the Crucifixion story allowed laypersons to join members of the clergy in reliving the events and the emotions of Jesus' last days, whether as actors or as an involved audience. Just as many Jews, heeding the charge to see themselves as present during the Exodus, still include props and movements in their celebration of the Passover seder, so have Christians sought ways to participate in the founding miracle of their redemption by reenacting it themselves. Participation in the Crucifixion story fortifies one's inclusion in its wondrous gift to those who will believe.

However one explains the origins of religious drama in medieval Europe—and historians of the theater differ widely in their views—one cannot overlook the almost natural progression from the liturgy of the Christian church to the dramatization of sacred events, especially those of the Passion narrative. At the heart of Christian communal worship lies the mass, which fathers of the church understood as a veritable reenactment of Jesus' Passion. With its miraculous transubstantiation of wine and bread into the blood and body of Christ, the mass relives Jesus' suffering and his death on the cross, offering the salvation that arises from the Passion to all who partake of the sacrament. As Pope Gregory the Great explained at the end of the sixth century, in the mass Jesus is "immolated for us again in this mystery of the sacred oblation. For His body is eaten there, His flesh is distributed among the people unto salvation, His blood is poured out, no longer in the hands of the faithless but in the mouth of the faithful." The sacrifice of the mass, he concluded, "is in constant representation of the suffering of the only begotten Son, for the sake of our forgiveness."[1]

Beyond such understanding of this most basic Christian ritual, which reenacts the Passion on a daily basis, additional factors contributed to the development of Passion drama as time wore on. Holy Week (leading up to Easter Sunday) commemorates Jesus' last days, and the gospel readings for the mass during that week (traditionally from the Passion narrative in John's Gospel) quite naturally found dramatic expression in the ceremonies, pageants, and processions that marked this most sacred of times. As the Christian culture of the later Middle Ages focused on the transubstantiation of the Eucharist (see chapters 5 and 6), these ritualized public spectacles extended beyond Easter, typically into the late spring and summer when the weather proved more congenial. And as Christian piety concentrated ever more fervently on the humanity and suffering of the crucified Christ, acting out the events of the Passion, whether in one's mind or with one's body, allowed one to identify with Jesus by experiencing what he experienced. *The Garden of Prayer*, a fifteenth-century devotional handbook originally written for Italian girls, instructed its readers in precisely this spirit:

> The better to impress the story of the Passion on your mind, and to memorize each action of it more easily, it is helpful and necessary to fix the places and people in your mind: a city, for example, which will be the city of Jerusalem—taking for this purpose a city that is well known to you. In this city find the principal places in which all the episodes of the Passion would have taken place—for instance, a palace with the supper-room where Christ had the Last Supper . . . , the room where He was brought before Caiaphas and mocked and

beaten. . . . Also the site of Mount Calvary, where he was put on the Cross; and other like places.

The writer's instructions extended even to the characters of the biblical story.

And then too you must shape in your mind some people, people well-known to you, to represent for you the people involved in the Passion—the person of Jesus Himself, of the Virgin, Saint Peter, Saint John the Evangelist, Saint Mary Magdalen, Annas, Caiaphas, Pilate, Judas and the others, every one of whom you will fashion in your mind.[2]

Against this sort of background, Passion plays proliferated throughout Christian Europe during the later Middle Ages, moving gradually from monastery and church into the streets and onto the stage, planting deep roots in the social and cultural lives of many a community that produced them. Alongside manuals for meditating on the Passion and the iconography that visualized it, dramatizing Jesus' suffering became a highly effective tool for representing the pain and tortures inflicted upon him. Texts of late medieval Passion plays refer to elaborate props and complicated dramatic techniques that show the religious imagination enthusiastically at work: from sponges, caps, and wigs for dramatizing Jesus' crowning with thorns, to liquids that would appear to flow from his wounds, to ingenious devices for securing him to the cross. Moreover, the Passion play infused a sense of solidarity and purpose into a Christian community that had now established an active, collective, enduring framework for the ultimate expression of its piety. Celebrating the physical sacrifice of Christ's body as it did, the Passion play must also have fortified a community's relationship with its savior, buttressing the medieval idea of the church of God's faithful as the *corpus mysticum Christi*, the mystical body of Christ. In the well-known cycles of pageant plays produced in English towns such as Chester, Coventry, and York for the June feast of Corpus Christi, different craft guilds took responsibility for a series of biblical scenes from creation to doomsday, with particular attention devoted to the life and death of Jesus. At Chester, for example, the bakers staged the Last Supper; the bow, arrow, and barrel-makers the trial and the flagellation; the "ironmongers" (metalworkers) the Crucifixion itself. Recognizing different roles and functions within a pageant that integrated the entire community as it celebrated the unity of Christian history, Corpus Christi plays became part of the process of self-definition whereby Christians could present themselves in relation to the outside world. Depicting the entire community in its identification with the body of Christ, its symbolic system expressed wholeness and solidarity above all else.

Alongside its heroes and its wonders, the Passion narrative has its villains, whose wickedness likewise takes on life and immediacy on the stage.

Self-definition on the part of a community asserting its integrity all too often celebrates the inclusion of insiders through the exclusion of an outsider, whom the insiders stereotype as malignant. The Jew typically played the role of that outsider in the Christian mentality. Especially when Christian society understood its integrity in terms of the body of Christ, the Christ-killing Jew proved a most appropriate villain. Long after the expulsion of the Jews from many European lands during the later Middle Ages, the Jew retained an important presence in the religious mind-set and on the religious stage of Western Christendom. Although the Jews had been expelled from England in 1290, the fifteenth-century British mystic Margery Kempe had no trouble visualizing them as she dramatized the Crucifixion in her own imagination.

> She beheld how the cruel Jews laid his precious body to the cross and afterward took a long nail, rough and huge, and set it to his one hand and with great violence and cruelness they drove it through his hand. . . . Then saw she with her ghostly eye how the Jews fastened ropes on the other hand, for the sinews and veins were so shrunken with pain that it might not come to the hole that they had marked for it, and drew thereon to make it meet with the hole. . . . And afterward they drew his blissful feet in the same manner. And then she thought in her soul she heard our Lady say to the Jews, "Alas, you cruel Jews, why fare you so with my sweet son and did he you never any harm? You fill my heart full of sorrow." And then she thought the Jews spoke again violently to our Lady and put her away from her son. Then [Margery] . . . thought that she cried out on the Jews and said, "You cursed Jews, why slay you my Lord Jesus Christ? Slay me rather, and let him go."[3]

Typically pitted against the body of Christian faithful and, by extension, the body of Christ itself, the body of the Jew embodied the tension between insider and outsider in the Christian world in a way that the theater—and perhaps the Passion play above all—proved uniquely well equipped to illustrate.

## THE OBERAMMERGAU *PASSIONSSPIEL*

The seventeenth-century Passion play at Oberammergau emerged in this context. It largely resembled German Passion plays of earlier generations, and, in celebrating the town's redemption from the plague, it certainly affirmed the unity of the Christian town as its participants identified with the suffering of Jesus. It too demonized Jesus' Jewish enemies on stage. Thus it enhanced the solidarity of this community of believers, who attributed their salvation to Jesus' own self-sacrifice on the cross. The ensuing career of the play carries the discussion of the Christ-killer myth from the Middle Ages forward into modern times, capturing the depth and complexity of problems at the heart of Jewish-Christian relations even today. Long before this book appeared in print, the town of Oberammergau had already begun work on the production for 2010.

The Oberammergau Passion Play has developed considerably over the course of its nearly four-hundred-year-long history. Responding to various pressures, preferences, and changing tastes, the script of the play—and the music that accompanied it from early on in its career—have repeatedly undergone revision. Recent versions of the script derive from the text prepared by Joseph Alois Daisenberger in 1860, the music from that composed by Rochus Dedler early in the nineteenth century. So, too, has the relationship between the Oberammergau production and the higher authorities of church and state wavered over the years. Responding to a campaign of the Catholic Church to restrict popular dramatizations of the life of Jesus, Maximillian Joseph, elector of Bavaria, banned the performance of the Oberammergau play in 1770. Adolf Hitler viewed the production twice, first in 1930 and again upon the play's tercentenary in 1934, one year after his election as chancellor of the German Reich. The local leadership at Oberammergau, the text of the play itself, and even the entries in a competition for preparing posters to publicize the 1934 production (fig. 10.1) all fell in line behind the new Nazi regime. Recalling the play, Hitler himself reflected years later:

> One of our most important tasks will be . . . to remain forever watchful in the knowledge of the menace of Jewry. For this reason alone it is vital that the Passion Play be continued at Oberammergau; for never has the menace of Jewry been so convincingly portrayed as in the presentation of what happened in the times of the Romans. There one sees in Pontius Pilate a Roman racially and intellectually so superior, that he stands out like a firm, clean rock in the middle of the whole muck and mire of Jewry.[4]

In 1949 and 1959, Catholic cardinals offered the residents of Oberammergau the official blessing of the church as they looked forward to the productions of the succeeding years. By the end of the 1960s, however, the spirit of the Second Vatican Council had changed the climate of opinion yet again, and the church did not extend the same official blessing again. Since the promulgation of the *Nostra Aetate* decree in 1966, in fact, an array of Jewish "defense" organizations—the Anti-Defamation League, the American Jewish Congress, and the American Jewish Committee—have persistently battled for sweeping change in the text and staging of the Oberammergau play. Though the Oberammergau leadership at first resisted these calls for reform, an American-Jewish–led boycott of the 1970 production coupled with pressure from

FIGURE 10.1. Oberammergau 1934 production poster.
Reproduction from *Gebrauchsgraphik*: *International
Advertising Art* 10 (October 1933), 33.

within the Catholic Church itself resulted in successive rounds of revision in
the scripts used in 1980, 1984, 1990, and 2000.

The impassioned controversy surrounding the play at Oberammergau
constitutes a fascinating story unto itself, but that story is not ours to tell.
Still, before delving into the substance of the play, I would offer two observations that might help to illuminate the complexity of the debate and the
persistence of the problem. First, from the understandable perspective of the
citizens of Oberammergau, criticism of their Passion play strikes not merely
at the integrity of a theatrical production but at the heart and soul of their
existence. With some two thousand of the five thousand Oberammergauers
performing on stage, the social and cultural life of the town has for centuries
centered on the play above all else. The play has steered the course of critical
life decisions, from negotiating family matters and choosing a vocation to

planning for the years ahead, from one performance season to the next. Even more important, the play has stood at the center of the town's economy, especially once visitors began to pay for admission late in the eighteenth century. Thirteen thousand people viewed the play in 1830. A century later, in 1934, the number reached some 410,000, and a half million saw the play during the most recent seasons. Ticket prices have risen steadily, too. Between the cost of tickets and other income generated by the influx of theatergoers—packages including a seat at the play, accommodations, and meals range in price from hundreds of dollars to well over $1,000—staging the Passion of Christ at Oberammergau brings in millions of dollars each year. (One cannot help noting the irony: The play itself begins its tale of the Passion with Jesus' heated rebuke of Jewish merchants, profit-mongers who exploit the worship of God in the temple for their own personal gain.) Quite naturally, the play also dominates local politics, with divisions between religious and secular, traditionalists and reformers, relating chiefly to issues of the play, its production, and its reception in the world at large. An anthropological study of modern Oberammergau has followed the gradual shift in the character of the Passion play "from a strictly religious tradition motivated primarily by the desire to fulfill the ancient vow" to a vital economic and political concern. Simply put, Oberammergauers' concern for their Passion play amounts to nothing less than concern for their own survival.[5] Albeit in different circumstances, the play originated out of that very concern some four hundred years ago.

Second, the controversy surrounding Oberammergau in recent decades also affords interesting insight into the Jewish side of the Jewish-Christian encounter. Jewish organizations—propelled by memories of the Holocaust, encouraged by the spirit of Vatican II, on the lookout for expressions of anti-Semitism in postwar Germany, concerned by the Oberammergau play's enduring career, and mindful that North Americans (not a few of them Jewish) form the majority of Oberammergau's theatergoers—have made this particular Passion play a cause célèbre. (If debate over Mel Gibson's film *The Passion* has temporarily overshadowed that over Oberammergau, I predict that the spotlight will return to Oberammergau well in advance of its 2010 production and that the public will rapidly forget the Gibson movie.) At times, various Jewish groups have been at loggerheads over priorities and tactics in confronting both the Catholic Church and the Oberammergau community. Although such tensions may occasionally betray the ambitions of specific individuals, they surely reflect Jews' deeply ingrained sensitivity to the charge that they killed Christ. No less than in ancient and medieval times, the Christ-killer myth continues to elicit a knee-jerk reaction from Jews. Though their strategies for refuting this indictment varied (as we saw in chapter 7), they have consistently regarded the deicide charge as the most dangerous in the entire arsenal of accusations leveled against them in the Christian world.

## JEWS AND JUDAISM IN THE PASSION PLAY

Until the last season at Oberammergau, the various renditions of the Daisen-berger script divided the Passion play into sixteen to eighteen acts, beginning with Jesus' final entry into Jerusalem and concluding with his resurrection. The revised text for the 2000 season reduced the number to eleven. Here the point is neither to praise nor condemn the Passion play for its treatment of the Jews or to take sides in the controversy that has surrounded it. This chapter's concern is the play and its significance, not the attempts to change it, and I have therefore drawn both from the more traditional version of the play and from the most recent one.

Using the acts of the more traditional script as signposts, one can see how the drama progresses on stage:

1. The Entry of Christ into Jerusalem
2. The Plot of the High Council
3. The Visit to Bethany
4. The Last Journey into Jerusalem
5. The Holy Evening Meal
6. The Betrayer
7. Jesus at the Mount of Olives
8. Jesus before Annas
9. Jesus before Caiaphas
10. The Despair of Judas
11. Christ before Pilate
12. Christ before Herod
13. Christ Is Scourged, and Crowned with Thorns
14. Jesus Is Condemned to Be Crucified
15. The Way of the Cross
16. Jesus at Golgotha
17. The Resurrection

As one quickly realizes, the plot of the Passion play highlights the confrontation between Jesus and his Jewish enemies. But not only does the play offer its viewers a particular picture of the Jews. It also frames that picture within a particular perspective on Judaism and its relationship to Christianity. Interspersed throughout the events of Jesus' last days, scenes from Hebrew Scripture (often called freezes or *tableaux*), embellished with music, prologues, and choruses, illustrate how events of the Old Testament prefigure the drama of salvation recorded in the New. It is important to see precisely how these tableaux worked to create a certain image of the Jew.

A blatantly anti-Jewish tableau prefaced the staging of Jesus' final entry into Jerusalem (Act 4), until it was cut from the Oberammergau script after 1970. It portrays the opening of the biblical story of Purim related in the Book of Esther, when the Persian king Ahasuerus replaces his irreparably disobedient wife Vashti with the Jewish heroine Esther. The stage directions say: "King Ahasuerus casts Vashti from him and exalts Esther. (Esther 1–2) Queen Vashti, the proud, symbolizes Jerusalem and Judaism, while Esther typifies Christianity." As this scene silently ensues on stage, the narrator explains to the audience:

> Here, typified in Vashti's fall, behold
> God's purpose to the synagogue unfold.
> "Be far from me and from my throne,
> Woman unworthy of my crown. . . .
> The time of grace is past and gone,
> This people proud no more I own;
> And, as I live," so spake the Lord,
> "A people, who will walk aright
> I choose, and will with them unite,
> As Ahasuerus Esther wed."

The chorus then reinforces the significance of this message by recalling Jesus' scathing attack on the Pharisees for murdering their own prophets (Matthew 23:37, Luke 13:34):

> Jerusalem! Jerusalem . . . !
> O murderess of the prophets, thou
> Thy giddy, shameful path pursuest now;
> "Therefore," thus speaks the Voice Divine,
> "This people shall no more be Mine."[6]

Pressure from critics in the wake of Vatican II understandably led to the removal of this freeze from the Oberammergau script, along with several other tableaux viewed as offensive. Among these was the biblical scene of Joseph's own brothers plotting against him (Act 2), which the narrator explained in no uncertain terms: "As against Joseph, Jacob's sons conspire—so shall we from the viper brood hear the loud cry for Jesu's blood."[7] Instead, one now finds less inflammatory tableaux, as in the likening of the despairing Judas (Act 10, or Act 7 in the 2000 text) to Cain, condemned by God for murdering his brother, Abel, grieving over his destiny of aimless, endless wandering. A 1984 edition of the Daisenberger text still noted: "Abel, the upright, was hated by his brother Cain, even as Christ was despised by His brothers, the Jews. Even as Cain became a fugitive so the Jewish Nation shall be expelled from its kingdom and dispersed over the whole earth."[8] The narrator and chorus then underscore the eternal punishments shared by Cain and Judas for their similar crimes. Though it retains the same Old Testament episode, the 2000 Oberammergau text makes no reference to the Jews here. It concludes with a kinder prayer that God grant forgiveness to all people, "those in despair and those guilty of betrayal, the victims and the perpetrators" alike.[9]

Whether in their traditional or in their most recently revised format, the Oberammergau tableaux resort to the same sort of Christian typology employed by the second-century church father Melito of Sardis in order to celebrate the Passion of Christ (see chapter 3). There, as here in Oberammergau, such a typological approach to the stories of the Old Testament had three important dimensions to it: (1) it affirmed the literal, historical truth of the Old Testament in its own time and its value as a model of greater, Christian things to come; (2) now that the events and observances prefigured in the Old Testament had found fulfillment in the New, it rendered those events obsolete; and (3) it not only allowed for the reenactment of a past event, but, as Melito's *On Pascha* and the Oberammergau Esther tableau demonstrate, it also could result in a reversal of roles as that historical drama recurred. Recall that in Melito's Easter poem, when the crucified Jesus became the true paschal lamb, and when those who believed in him became the new Israel, the Jews forfeited their status as Israel. Instead, they assumed the role of Pharaoh and the Egyptians who had persecuted God's chosen people long ago—and whom God had destroyed as a result. So, too, in the Esther tableau do the Jews forfeit the very status of God's chosen people that their holiday of Purim came to celebrate.

But even in the more "kosher," uncontroversial tableaux that still remain in the latest Oberammergau script, one need not search too strenuously to arrive at a similar, albeit somewhat muted, conclusion. Cain, depicted as a prototype of Judas, typically represented the deicidal Jewish people in the church fathers' reading of the Bible. No less a spokesman for Christianity than Augustine saw the biblical figure of Cain fulfilled in the history and destiny of Israel.

> Now behold, who cannot see, who cannot recognize how, throughout the world, wherever that people [of Israel] has been scattered, it wails in sorrow for its lost kingdom and trembles in fear of the innumerable Christian peoples . . . ? [Like Cain] the nation of impious, carnal Jews will not die a bodily death. For whoever so destroys them will suffer the sevenfold punishment with which they have been burdened for their guilt in the murder of Christ.[10]

The linkage between Cain, Judas, and the Christ-killing Jew remains. And although the more congenial tableaux in the most recent Oberammergau script focus chiefly on "positive" figures in the Hebrew Bible, they, too, nourish the same underlying typological message. For just as the church fathers identified the rejected and the villains of the Old Testament (Cain, Hagar, Ishmael, Esau) with the Jews, so did they "appropriate" its righteous heroes for the church, depicting Abel, Abraham and Isaac, Joseph, Moses, Job, and Daniel, along with others who appear on the Oberammergau stage, as forerunners of Christianity. With or without the latest revisions in the text of the play, one cannot but conclude that the gospel has replaced and fulfilled the Torah. In the divine "economy" of salvation, Christ's enemies in the New Testament have assumed the roles of God's enemies in the Old, just as the church has replaced the Jews as the chosen people of Israel.

Furthermore, as one sees in the case of Melito's Easter poetry, the lessons of typology extend to the present. The story of the Exodus, the Israelite *Pesach*, surely served as a model for the salvation brought by the *Pascha*, the crucified Jesus, the ultimate paschal lamb of God. Yet its significance did not stop there. The same drama of oppression and salvation recurred every time Christians celebrated their Easter/Pascha (as they did in Melito's Sardis), thereby rejecting the rituals and meaning of the Jewish Passover/Pesach. The Jews, though themselves oppressed and then miraculously saved in Egypt, had crucified Jesus in Jerusalem and continued to do so in a symbolic way at their Passover seder ever since. Understood against the historical and theological background surveyed here, the Oberammergau tableaux transmit similar messages. Judas followed in the footsteps of Cain, fulfilling the potential in his character and sharing, therefore, in his fate. The same would appear to apply to the Jews at large. They spurn their God, join in murdering their brother, and wander endlessly in punishment for their crime.

Set against these tableaux, how have the Jews fared on stage in Oberammergau? Not in a favorable light, to put it mildly. In 1860, a Scottish Christian viewer of the play marveled at the hatred with which it portrayed Jesus' Jewish enemies. For the first time, he wrote, he understood how and why this hatred has provoked "cruelties and barbarities unrivalled in history."[11] In 1900, Rabbi Joseph Krauskopf of Philadelphia traveled to Oberammergau to see the play, and he disclosed his impressions in a series of sermons upon returning home. In a word, Krauskopf was overwhelmed, both by the characters of the Jews that appeared on stage and by the injustice that such characterization entailed. Krauskopf declared that if the Jews had in fact done what the play condemned them for doing, he himself would have no choice but to convert to Christianity.

> If all that was enacted last summer in the Passion Play at Oberammergau be true, we have no right to continue as Jews. If all the villanies we are charged with in that play, or in the New Testament, whence that play derives its text and theme, be true, then the sooner we ac-

knowledge our guilt, the sooner we call down the everlasting curse of God upon our ancestors for their heinous crimes against the Virgin-born, Death-resurrected, Heaven-ascended, Only-begotten Son of God, the sooner we crawl to the Cross and there pour out our very souls in contrition, the better will it be for our honesty and for our future salvation.[12]

In the end, however, Krauskopf's review and analysis of the play led him not to the baptismal font, but to a drastically different conclusion.

We have analyzed text and theme, plot and scheme, and we have found precious truths and infamous falsehoods—blessed truths, the gift of the Jew, and falsehoods, the contribution of the anti-Jew, partly due to imagination and hallucination, partly to irrational dogma, partly to malice, mostly to policy and selfishness—the ac-cursed parents of most of the crime and misery on earth. We have dissected with the most approved instruments of history, logic, sci-ence, and we have found in these gospel stories much that is sound but more that is diseased, that is congested with a poison that has not only cursed the life of the Jew, eighteen hundred years long, but now also threatens the very life of the Christian. . . . This life-and love-vitiating poison festers on the very surface of the gospel stories. The future of Christianity demands its eradication; justice to the Jew compels it.[13]

Yet despite the zeal with which Krauskopf reacted to the charges of deicide leveled against the Jews at Oberammergau, his idealism—and perhaps his trust in the culture of his native Germany—proved stronger. He believed profoundly that the modern world, committed to history, logic, and science, as he put it, would exonerate the Jew once it heard his story, accepting him with open arms as a true brother of Jesus. With this truth established, he poignantly exclaimed, "Many a dark cloud will disappear, many a grievous error will vanish, many a long-enduring wrong will be righted."[14] Joseph Krauskopf died in 1923, and his hopes were not fulfilled. During the years that followed his death, his German fatherland purged itself not of its hatred of Jews, but of its Jews themselves. Christianity did not renounce its belief in the truth of the Passion narrative, and the Oberammergau Passion Play continued to flour-ish, throughout Germany's Nazi era and postwar reconstruction alike. In the wake of the Second Vatican Council, both Jewish and Christian researchers listed dozens of problems in the text and staging of the Play, whose correc-tion, to their mind, constituted a minimum of compliance with the decree of *Nostra Aetate.*

These criticisms can be organized under several major headings.

## THE JEWS AND THEIR FAITH

The Jewish people received scathing treatment at Oberammergau two, three, even four decades after the Holocaust. The first Jewish characters to express themselves in the play are the "Priests, Pharisees, and Moneychangers within the portico of the Temple," as the 1970 script labeled them.[15] Jesus calls them "children of Mammon," rebuking them for desecrating the house of God with their pursuit of monetary profit.[16] One of the moneychangers is labeled "Rabbi." Many of them bear biblical names (Joshua, Ezekiel, Zadok, Boaz, etc.), suggesting that the confrontation between them and Jesus echoes the more basic contrasts between material and spiritual, law and grace, hate and love, and, at the bottom line, Old Testament and New. "Moses is our prophet," they proclaim as they march off to denounce Jesus before the Sanhedrin.[17] Again, sealing their pact with the high priests to conspire against Jesus: "Our life for the Law of Moses and to the Holy Sanhedrin!"[18] And Caiaphas himself, as the Sanhedrin determines that Jesus must be killed: "Until he is dead, there can be no peace in Israel, no safety for the Law of Moses."[19] True to this model, Judas distinguishes himself among the disciples with his concern for money, even as Jesus suggests that he must soon leave them forever. Jesus' warning that "the tempter not overcome you"[20] hardly curbs his devilish lust for wealth and honor, and Judas accepts the high priests' offer to betray his master for thirty pieces of silver.

As the events of the Passion unfold, the stark, negative characterization of the Jews only intensifies. Words of hate, contempt, and malice abound, and they readily translate into the enthusiasm with which the high priests' henchmen physically abuse Jesus on the night of his arrest. Just before the Sanhedrin condemns him to death, attention returns to Judas, who, now regretting his treachery, reflects tragically, all-knowingly, on the conspiracy:

> O, thou Synagogue! thou hast, through thy deceiving messengers, concealed thy murderous designs, else hast thou never had Him in thy claws. No part will I have in the blood of the innocent.[21]

Yet the pulse of the plot against Jesus does not abate. As viewers and readers of the play have already noted, the priests and then the Jewish mob insist repeatedly over the course of several scenes, literally dozens of times, that Jesus must die.[22] The tempo enters a crescendo in Act 14 (on the list above), when Jesus is condemned to die on the cross. Following a tableau that likens Jesus to the scapegoat of the Book of Leviticus, the biblical sacrifice that assumed the people's sins and brought them atonement on Yom Kippur, the Jewish mob argues with the chorus over whether Pilate should have Jesus crucified.

> *People*: To the cross with Him! To the cross with him!
> *Chorus*: Ah, see Him there the Holy One!
>          What evil hath He ever done?

*People*: If thou this felon shouldst let free,
    Thou couldst not friend to Caesar be.
*Chorus*: Jerusalem, Jerusalem!
    If for His blood—should God for vengeance call—
*People*: "On us and on our children may it fall."
*Chorus*: On you and on your children *will* it fall.[23]

*On you and on your children will it fall!* Justifying the chorus's ominous curse, the next scene highlights the solidarity of the Jewish people, clergy and common folk alike, in their determination to have Jesus killed.

*Nathanael*: Moses, your Prophet, has bidden you hither. The Holy
    law cries for vengeance.
*1st Crowd*: We will have Moses. We will ever be followers of
    Moses, and of our Law.
*4th People*: We will be free from the false teacher, the Nazarene!
*The Four Leaders*: Your fathers' God will again receive you; you
    will be again His chosen people.
*All the People*: You are our true friends. Long live the High
    Sanhedrim. Long live our Priests and Teachers!
*Annas*: And death to the Galilean!
*Caiaphas*: Come, let us hasten to Pilate.
*Nathanael and Ezekiel*: Let us demand His death—His blood!
*All the People*: Let us go at once to Pilate. The Nazarene shall die!
*The Leaders*: He has falsified the law. He has despised Moses and
    the Prophets. He has blasphemed God!
*All the People*: Death to the false Prophet.
*2nd Crowd*: The death of the cross!
*2nd and 3rd Crowds*: Pilate must crucify Him!
*The Leaders*: He shall expiate His offences on the cross!
*3rd and 4th Crowds*: We will not rest, until the sentence is
    spoken. . . .
*All the People*: Long live the High Council! Death to the Nazarene!
*Priests and Pharisees*: Cursed be he, who does not consent to His
    death!
*People*: We demand that He dies.
*Caiaphas*: Let Him be thrust out from the presence of our Fathers.
*People*: Let Him be thrust out!
*Caiaphas*: Pilate will give you the choice between this blasphemer
    and Barabbas. Let us demand that Barabbas be let go
    free.
*People*: Barabbas must be saved! Down with the Nazarane . . . !

*Caiaphas*: Happy day for the Children of Israel. Children, be
     steadfast!
*Priests and Pharisees*: This day gives back honour to the Syna-
     gogue, freedom to the Children of Israel.
*People (tumultuously)*: We demand the blood of our enemy . . . !
*People*: The Nazarene shall die. . . .
*All*: Pilate must say his death sentence. . . .
*All*: We demand the death of the Nazarene.[24]

Finally, in the scene that follows, when Pilate forswears responsibility for Jesus'
death, the people repeat the damning words of Matthew 27:25: "We take it
on us. His blood upon us and our children!" To which Pilate himself responds:
"It shall be on you, and on your children." And then the priests and the people
reiterate yet again, "It shall fall on us, and on our children."[25] The Gospel of
Matthew mentions this cry but once, the traditional Oberammergau script
no less than four times. Repeating these words again and again, the Passion
play renders them a refrain.

    The curse of the Jews could not but resound in the memories of its view-
ers. Mary Frances Drew, the first translator of the Oberammergau play into
English who saw the play in 1880, in fact recalled that these two scenes were
"each magnificent in the highest degree." Arranged with "the utmost splendor," the stage accommodated hundreds of players, led by the priests and
Pharisees, hurrying in from every direction to press for Jesus' death. The leaders incited the people, and these eagerly cooperated. As the crowd united at
the front of the stage, in her words, "as one man they act, rage, and cry."[26]

## THE CHARACTER OF PILATE

Critics have charged that in presenting Pilate as essentially enlightened, scrupulous in his dedication to justice, and even merciful in his manner toward
Jesus, the play distorts the picture of the rash, brutal, and dreadfully irrespon-
sible Roman presented in the writings of Josephus and other historical records.
In so doing, the Oberammergau script aggravates its anti-Jewish message
further. For as Pilate washes his hands of responsibility for Jesus' execution,
both literally and figuratively, the picture of the malicious, bloodthirsty Jews
darkens commensurately.

    Indeed, Pilate consistently rejects the Jewish priests' charges that Jesus
has rebelled against Rome. He surely would know better than the priests if Jesus
had fomented opposition to Caesar. After conversing with Jesus, he admires
him for the "nobility in his countenance . . . , frankness in his speech . . . , such
high endowments," and his understanding, too great for the Jews, "who cannot bear the weight of His wisdom." Even if Jesus presented himself as a king,

Pilate would not deem him guilty of treason, for among the Romans, the governor waxes eloquently, "every philosopher is a king."[27] As the drama unfolds, the tension between Pilate and the priests only mounts. Finding Jesus not guilty, he orders Jesus scourged simply to appease them somewhat. Yet they insist: "To death with Him!" To which he retorts: "Is your hatred against the Man so deep and vile, that even the blood of his wounds will not quench it . . . ? An unworthy resentment draws you on, caused by the people preferring His teaching to yours."[28] Only when he fears that he might lose control to the angry mob does he give in. "I am constrained, by your fury, to consent to your desire. Take ye Him, and crucify Him! But behold! I wash my hands—I am innocent of the blood of this just man."[29]

## JESUS THE JEW

Finally, in the wake of the Holocaust as well as Vatican II, ecumenically minded Jews and Christians alike have also criticized the Oberammergau play for obscuring the Jewishness of Jesus. Though Jesus and his disciples all lived and died as Jews, they have noted, the Oberammergau script highlights the polar opposition between them, leading the viewer to appreciate the conflict as transpiring between "us and them." Though first-century Judaism included many different sects and ideologies, the Oberammergau drama presents all Jews as identical in their hatred of Jesus. Jesus seems to have nothing in common with his coreligionists. The traditional script refers to his character as Christ, rather than use his Jewish name, Jesus, or Yeshua in Hebrew.

The Oberammergau community has struggled with these criticisms; hence the revisions in the play for each of the last five seasons (1970, 1980, 1984, 1990, 2000), including the reduction in the number of acts to eleven with the removal of particularly hostile tableaux. The blood curse of Matthew 27:25 was first limited to but one exclamation of the people and priests, then eliminated altogether. One now hears more voices supporting Jesus within the crowd in Jerusalem. Pilate appears less admirable than he did previously. Politics, more than greed, motivates Judas. Many disparaging references to the Jews, the synagogue, and the Law of Moses have disappeared. Jesus now identifies straightforwardly with his Judaism, wearing a *kippah* or skullcap (even though the yarmulke may well date from a much later period) and clearly observing the rituals of the Passover seder at his Last Supper. Columbia University professor James Shapiro, who viewed rehearsals of the play before the 2000 season began, recounted in his book on Oberammergau how he helped teach the actors playing Jesus to recite the blessing over the wine (*Baruch atah Adonai, Eloheinu melekh ha-olam, bore peri ha-gafen*) in clear, ungarbled Hebrew. Recalling Oberammergau's resident Jew on the eve of the Holocaust, Shapiro then concludes his fascinating investigation with a poignantly candid thought. "It had been sixty-one years since "Jud" Meyer had been packed off to Dachau in Oberammergau's own *Judenaktion*. I walked away wondering what he would have made of this encounter."[30]

Have these and other changes cleansed the Oberammergau play of its hatred of Jews? Or does the Passion play, perhaps invariably, still give expression to the Christ-killer myth? Preparing for the production of 2000, the villagers of Oberammergau clearly felt that they had come far enough, especially inasmuch as they had returned the final say over the contents of the play to the Catholic Church. In addition, they embarked on a worldwide public relations campaign to secure the blessing of both Jewish and Christian religious leaders, and they commissioned an Austrian-American, herself (though Catholic) a victim of Nazi medical barbarities, to prepare the authorized English translation. Highlighting the extensive efforts to rid the Oberammergau play of its anti-Judaism, the introduction to the official text of the play in 2000 declares that "the Passion Play is in no way meant to find a specific person or group guilty."[31] It contends that key figures in the American Jewish Committee and Anti-Defamation League have come to see the play in a new, more positive light, and it casts the production in a more ecumenical vein, proclaiming the value of the Passion story, a story of understanding and love, for all people: Oberammergauer and foreigner, insider and outsider, Christian and Jew.

Yet across both sides of the Jewish-Christian divide, there remain many who still withhold their blessing. At the end of the day, Judas still betrays Jesus. The high priests still conspire against him and compel a reluctant Pilate to condemn him. The priests and the overwhelming majority of the crowd in Jerusalem still cry out, "Crucify him!" And this conflict between Jesus and his Jewish enemies, from Jesus' initial confrontation with the merchants to his crucifixion, still dominates the play from beginning to end. As recently as 1990, the official text of the Oberammergau play included a New Testament scholar's defense of the controversial blood curse of "His blood be upon us and upon our children." His rationale for retaining this line in the text rivals the gospel itself in its implications: "It was not ignorant Gentiles who were mainly responsible for the death of Jesus, but members of the nation whom God had chosen."[32] In 2000, James Shapiro reported that the village-appointed Catholic translator left the rehearsals in tears over the hatred that still remained. More revealing is Shapiro's own reflection on what he saw:

> I had badly wanted the text to be better than this. I knew that there were elements introduced to counterbalance the effect, small groups onstage who would indicate to the audience that not all the Jews were bloodthirsty or sought Jesus' death. Maybe the problem was that the actors sharing the roles of Caiaphas and Annas were so overpowering; this left the indelible impression that the Jewish leaders were the

implacable foes of Jesus, relentlessly pressing for his death. All the assurances that Pilate would be a far darker character, one more deeply implicated in the sentencing of Jesus, made little difference. This was between the Jewish leaders and Jesus. The blood curse was gone, and no death decree was issued by the Sanhedrin. Yet these omissions hardly mattered. [The] Daisenberger [script] was a run-away train: all the brakes, all the safeguards, all the changes made to prevent anti-Judaism from taking over, had barely slowed it down.[33]

What verdict should the jury return? Fortunately, that question need not concern us here. The merits or demerits of the Oberammergau play today bear little on the story I have set out to tell. Rather, this chapter draws to a close in emphasizing the issue that still lies at the heart of the question. Oberammergauers have always believed that their play adheres to the Passion narrative in Holy Scripture, and now, having recovered the blessing of the Catholic Church for their production, they make this claim with renewed self-assurance.[34] I believe that many Jewish leaders at the forefront of the Oberammergau controversy would tend to agree. The crux of the matter lies less in this particular Passion play than in the Crucifixion story underlying every Passion play.

The Oberammergau Passion Play hardly invented the Christ-killer myth. Based on the Passion narrative in the Gospels, armed with the biblical typology of the church fathers, nourished by the same overriding concern with Jesus' suffering that nourished religious devotion and popular piety in the Middle Ages, it transmitted that myth to posterity, bridging ancient, medieval, and modern periods. The words of another American viewer of the 2000 production in Oberammergau, one who represents neither "side" in the controversy surrounding the play, prove unusually insightful in this regard. Deeply moved by the nigh miraculous power of the Passion play over Christians who watch it, she notes that "it has a special poignancy in a land where six million of Jesus' own people later suffered a similar fate." And thus she concludes:

> To *tell* Jesus' painful, joyful story entails the need to *repeat* Jesus' story. . . . The passion play genre is based on the premise that, like the Doubting Thomases we are, we forever need to *see* his wounds, to act and reenact his wounding/death/rebirth. . . . The Oberammergau Passion play tacitly assumes its audience to be co-participants—Christian co-participants—in the greatest story ever ritually retold. As a work of art, that is both its sin and its salvation.[35]

The influence of the Oberammergau Passion Play has ranged far and wide, well beyond the Bavarian countryside. Inspired by what he saw in Oberammergau in 1900, a French priest from Nancy produced a Passion play in his hometown four years later, and it has been performed repeatedly since. Of the dozens of Passion plays produced in North America, that of Union City, New Jersey, bills itself as "America's Oberammergau, the oldest Passion Play in America." Openly accused of virulent anti-Semitism, the *Great Passion Play* of Eureka Springs, Arkansas, established by Gerald L. K. Smith in 1968, has had the site of its performances renamed "Mt. Oberammergau." And just weeks before I finished writing this book, I saw a Washington, D.C., production of Sarah Ruhl's *Passion Play: A Cycle*, which graphically links the Oberammergau Passion Play with one still produced in Spearfish, South Dakota.

It appears that Oberammergau set a standard, owing to its history, its power, and its notoriety. Moreover, the questions raised by the dramatization of the Crucifixion story reach far beyond the play at Oberammergau itself. Many of these questions recur, often with greater urgency, when the medium for dramatizing the Passion narrative switches from the stage to the screen.

# CRUCIFIXION ON THE SCREEN

Our story of the Christ-killer myth, which began in the Bible, culminates in the cinema, and perhaps appropriately so. If Holy Scripture dominated the thoroughly religious culture of Western societies for many centuries, nothing typifies the "culture industry" of our own day more than the movies. Film unquestionably ranks alongside the visual and dramatic arts discussed in preceding chapters. Its production and "consumption" echo the very heartbeat of our civilization: the values, the priorities, and the tastes of our society and culture. Over the past several decades, film history has emerged as a legitimate field for academic research. Teachers use film as an invaluable teaching tool in the classroom. Like the written records of history, film can serve to transmit information about past events; so too does it help shape the meaning of those events for those who remember them.

The motion picture industry marked its hundredth birthday during the last decade of the twentieth century, and, from its beginnings, the Bible ranked (alongside sex) among the most popular themes that repeatedly have been brought to the screen. More than sixty films dealing with Jesus have since been produced, and dozens more—what some writers prefer to call "Christ films"—include Christlike characters and Christological themes in various modern guises and stories. Starting with *The Oberammergau Passion Play* film of 1897 (actually shot on a New York City rooftop), numerous films have focused in one way or another on Jesus' last days, and these, too, must find a place in the history of the Christ-killer myth—both for the messages that they convey and, in some cases, for the reactions that they have elicited. This chapter turns to five noteworthy Jesus films produced during the last half-century, examining the ways in which they portray the involvement of Jews in the Crucifixion. How do they adhere to and depart from the Passion narrative of the four Gospels? How should one appreciate their significance against the backdrop of traditional Christian belief, the history of Jewish-Christian relations, and the late-twentieth-century Western culture that gave rise to them?

Experts in each field—religion and cinema—have struggled to define the most appropriate criteria for evaluating contemporary films on biblical subjects. When it comes to films on Jesus and the Passion, the traditional nature of the subject matter clearly stands in opposition to the decisively modern character of the art form. On the one hand, portrayals of the Crucifixion in film can be viewed as yet another expression of religious devotion. That is, one can focus chiefly on the ways in which they make age-old biblical teaching palatable and meaningful for modern screenwriters, producers, and moviegoers. One American critic has thus likened Mel Gibson's *The Passion of the Christ* to the Oberammergau Passion Play. Each has proved controversial, especially in recent years, drawing scathing criticism for its treatment of the Jews and Judaism. Yet each constitutes a dramatic, multisensory "witnessing experience," an experience that renders the audience "Christian co-participants in the greatest story ever told."[1] On the other hand, the production, marketing, and consumption of motion pictures epitomize the secularism, the technology, and the commercialism of our modern society. They reflect a value system that is worlds apart from the Christian piety expressed in traditional religious art and drama. As a recent book on "religious values in the movies" has suggested, Passion-centered devotion of the Middle Ages (or in seventeenth-century Oberammergau) sought to involve the Christian actively in the experience of the suffering Christ. But thoughtful moviegoers today must normally detach themselves from the experiences that they behold on the screen—however glorified or attractive those experiences may appear.[2] What seeing the Crucifixion on screen means to a modern audience is very different from what viewing the Crucifixion in plays or icons meant to audiences hundreds of years ago.

A personal note before turning to the five Jesus films: just as the type of material considered in this chapter differs from the materials discussed earlier, so is my vantage point different. Researchers cannot, and needn't try to, keep their cultural selves from shaping their understanding of the past, however ancient or arcane the evidence under discussion. Born into the modern secular Western world, however, I invariably confront recent films far differently from the way in which I would approach sources of any kind from earlier periods. Because I belong to the same cultural context in which these films emerged, I relate to them as their consumer no less than as their investigator. The messages that they impart directly to me, wearing the glasses that I do, must bear on my understanding of their significance.

## THE BIBLE ON THE BIG SCREEN

Do the Gospels lend themselves to the modern screenplay? I turn first to two films whose scripts derive entirely from the Bible. How do their portrayals of the Passion narrative differ from earlier readings of the New Testament, and from one another as well?

*Il Vangelo secondo Matteo* (The Gospel according to Saint Matthew), created and directed by the controversial Italian writer and filmmaker Pier Paolo Pasolini, appeared in 1964, during the very years of the Second Vatican Council. Despite Pasolini's Marxism and his antielitism (directed against those who ruled over church and state alike), the film evidently received financial support from the Catholic Church, and Pasolini dedicated it to none other than Pope John XXIII.

The film relates the story of Jesus found in Matthew's Gospel, setting it in the rustic Italian countryside and relying on the local population to portray most of the characters depicted on screen. Shot in black and white, the film makes no pretense of re-creating the social or cultural realities of Jesus' own day. On the contrary, Pasolini's *Matthew* flaunts its anachronism. Jesus comes to offer a new life and a new world to an oppressed, poverty-stricken Italian peasantry. He preaches basic values of love, charity, and selflessness— toward God and human being—as he attacks the moral and spiritual bankruptcy of the ruling political and religious establishment (Romans, Pharisees, priests).

Pasolini's film offers a wonderful example of modern-day midrash. On the one hand, it pays homage to Scripture. Its script is entirely biblical, its characters flat, transparent, utterly lacking in depth and complexity. Albeit with conviction, Enrique Irazoqui (who plays Jesus) often recites his lines without appearing to assume the character that he represents—or any character at all. One hardly understands what distinguishes good people from villains; one simply knows that they are such. On the other hand, speaking primarily to those already familiar with Jesus and his story, those who look to the gospel to find meaning and salvation, it uses a variety of techniques in order to address them directly. Pasolini omits some scenes from Matthew's Gospel and rearranges the order of others. The soundtrack draws from a variety of cultures and genres, including the "Missa Luba" musical mass from the Congo, Gregorian chant, the African-American spiritual "Sometimes I Feel Like a Motherless Child," and Bach's *St. Matthew Passion*. The camera, at times handheld, often wanders and lingers at length, leaving extended intervals of silence between spoken lines. It focuses suggestively on the faces of those who suffer painfully—Jesus, Mary, the disciples, the poor—contrasting them with the insensitive appearances of the rich, the oppressive, the hypocritical, the evil. One never understands why Herod Antipas's young stepdaughter asks him for the head of John the Baptist as a prize for performing impressively at her dance recital. But here, perhaps more than anywhere else in the film, the viewer confronts the immensity of the gap between those in power and those not, thereby appreciating the social and economic revolution that Jesus' kingdom will bring about. Apocalyptic hopes are all these people have to live for. Pasolini's Jesus, as he describes the heavenly king-dom and the violent upheaval yet to come, airs this Marxist message well.

Alone of all the Gospels, we recall, Matthew's version of the Passion narrative includes the infamous blood curse that the Jews impose among themselves: "His blood be on us and on our children." How, if at all, does Pasolini's film cast the Jews as the killers of Christ? Various critics and reviewers have singled out *The Gospel according to Saint Matthew* for its negative portrayal of Jews and Judaism. Several have called it the "most disturbing" aspect of the film;[3] another has charged that "no Jesus film more exclusively places the responsibility for Jesus' death on the Jewish religious authorities."[4] Pasolini's Jesus capitalizes on every opportunity to lash out at the Pharisees and chief priests in a strident tone of voice. At the same time, although Matthew's Jesus emphasizes repeatedly that he has come to save the people of Israel before all others, one hears none of this in the film. Nor does one sense Jesus' rootedness in Jewish life, the extent to which he frequented the synagogue, worshiped, preached, and felt at home there. One hardly appreciates that Jesus lived his life as an observant Jew, that he taught and prayed in a style much like that of the Pharisees themselves—all of which one *can* sense by reading the gospel in Scripture. The film does not deviate from the traditional story line that the fraudulent charges of blasphemy trumped up against Jesus by the Jewish religious leadership led to his crucifixion. Though produced during the years of Vatican II, it also retains the blood curse of Matthew 27:25. And, after Jesus has been nailed to the cross, after one hears him cry out in agony, after Mary collapses and the camera prolongs its focus on her misery, the screen blackens and the narrator utters the prophecy of Isaiah 6:9–10 concerning the obstinate people of Israel:

> Hear and hear, but do not understand; see and see, but do not per-ceive. Make the heart of this people fat, and their ears heavy, and shut their eyes; lest they see with their eyes, and hear with their ears, and understand with their hearts, and turn and be healed.

In Matthew's Gospel (13:14–15), Jesus recites these verses to his disciples long before the Passion narrative commences, to explain why he teaches in parables. Pasolini, however, has inserted them at the climax of the Crucifixion, as if they belong in Matthew 27. The film may well suggest that the responsibility for Jesus' death extends to the entire Jewish nation. "This people" would hardly appear to refer to the Romans.

Nonetheless, *The Gospel according to Saint Matthew* did not strike me as particularly anti-Jewish. One cannot fault a film version of Matthew's Gos-pel for remaining faithful to Matthew's Gospel, blood curse and all. Moreover, Pasolini may actually have sought to minimize the effect of Matthew's attack on the Jews. Though Matthew relates that the Jewish crowd in Jerusalem cried out, "His blood be on us and on our children," a lone, unidentified voice does so in the film, and the curse is hardly what convinces Pilate to go ahead with Jesus' crucifixion, as it is in the gospel. Neither does Pasolini's Pilate wash his hands of responsibility for his actions (as in Matthew 27:24), nor does the Roman centurion assigned to watch the crucified Jesus admit (as in Matthew 27:54), "Truly this was the Son of God!"

But more important still, Pasolini's film did not impress me as a film about Jews at all. Pasolini himself acknowledges that he set out to re-create the Jesus story "by analogy." His film presents a delocalized, departicularized, and, in Pasolini's own words, "re-mythicized" interpretation of Matthew,[5] which, paradoxically, may well be the most Jewish of all the Gospels. Its drama transpires in a place resembling Pasolini's Italian countryside more than Jesus' Judea—and at a time closer to Pasolini's twentieth century than Matthew's first. While praying, the peasants hold their hands together as Christians traditionally do, not Jews. John the Baptist baptizes in a manner more like Christian sacramental ritual than the traditional Jewish immersion of the entire body in the "living waters" of the river or ritual bath. Herod Antipas and his family more closely resemble Italian patricians than first-century Jewish aristocrats. And the Jewish authorities whom Jesus rebukes, alienates, and incites could just as well be bishops and priests securely ensconced in the Catholic hierarchy. Though Jesus was in fact a Jew living in a Jewish world, there is nothing noticeably Jewish about Pasolini's Jesus, his society, or his universal message of redemption for the underprivileged.

With one possible exception: The camera lingers on the bread that Jesus distributes at the Last Supper, highlighting its resemblance to the unleavened *matzah* that Jews eat at their Passover seder, calling it "the bread of affliction," as they recall their slavery in Egypt. Precisely as viewers focus on the *matzah*, the music switches to the famous *Kol Nidre* declaration that begins the Jewish worship service on Yom Kippur, the most solemn day in the Jewish religious calendar. Inasmuch at it pleads for the annulment of vows, Jewish memory typically associates the *Kol Nidre* with Jews of the Middle Ages, persecuted and forcibly converted to other religions by their non-Jewish oppressors. So long as Jews were victims of slavery, suffering, and persecution, perhaps Pasolini found some room for them, too, in the messianic kingdom that Jesus came to establish. Alluding to the Nazi concentration camps and what he termed "the Jews' tendency towards masochism and self-exclusion," Pasolini declared quite openly:

I have always loved the Jews because they have been excluded, because they are objects of racial hatred, because they have been forced to be separate from society. But once they've founded their own state they are not different, they're not a minority, they're not excluded:

they are the majority, they are the norm. They, who had always been the champions of difference, of martyrdom, of the fight of the other against the normal had now become the majority and the normal and that was something I found a bit hard to swallow.[6]

For Pasolini, both on screen and off, the Jews have evidently forsaken the miserable role assigned them in the Christian scheme of things, a role that according to tradition resulted directly from their guilt in the death of Jesus.

Nearly forty years elapsed between the release of Pasolini's *Matthew* and the 2003 production of *The Gospel of John*, directed by Philip Saville, a film that left me with remarkably different impressions. Visual Bible International, a "faith-based" Canadian media company that has since entered court-imposed receivership,[7] released *John* at selected American theaters, most of them in the southern "Bible Belt," during the height of the controversy over Mel Gibson's *The Passion of the Christ,* which had not yet been released. Thus overshadowed, the film has hardly received the attention that it rightfully deserved.

*The Gospel of John* surpasses even Pasolini's *Matthew* in its adherence to Scripture. Apart from the omission of lead-ins to spoken words ("he said," "they said," and the like)—omissions that usually have little bearing on the significance of the drama—the script reproduces the entire text of the Gospel of John, from beginning to end. Unlike the several reviewers who complained that the film was therefore boring or tedious, I found it both credible and gripping, nothing less than a tour de force. *John* brings John's Gospel to life. It acknowledges the first-century setting of the story at the same time as it appeals to a present-day audience with its own, distinctly modern tastes and sensitivities. Much of the film was shot in Spain, and the terrain substituted convincingly for the Holy Land. A capable cast of seventy-five actors, along with some two thousand extras, depicts the life of Jesus with thoughtfulness and sensitivity. As one listens to the words of the biblical text, one appreciates the filmmakers' creativity primarily in the use of the camera, secondarily, perhaps, in the soundtrack. Yet their own interpretation of the gospel did not stop there. Tone of voice joins visual expression in conveying particular messages. When specific individual characters speak lines that the gospel (noting, for instance, "they said") did not assign to any particular person, or when the narrator simply recites those words that he says were spoken by angels or a voice from heaven—without the viewer ever hearing those voices—choices are being made, value judgments expressed. In all, it creates a very deliberate contemporary reading of the ancient text. As *Variety* magazine's film critic noted perceptively:

The Jesus most commonly imagined in drama and legend—the health-restoring, inspirational and selfless itinerant rabbi who met a painful end, then presented his resurrected body to his disciples on his journey home to his Father—is entirely present. But so is a complexity that allows for multiple sides of this most influential and conjectured-about figure: the provocateur, the showman, the pre-ordained victim, the self-proclaimed deity. And all this within the restraining confines of the most extreme and contentious of the gospels.[8]

Indeed, John is usually considered to be the most extreme and contentious of all four Gospels, especially in its repeated, often damning references to "the Jews" and in the distance that the evangelist creates between Jesus and the mainstream of the Jewish community. Yet *The Gospel of John* evidently seeks to dispel that impression on screen. Whereas Pasolini showed minimal interest in Christianity's Jewish origins, even though Matthew's Jesus appears more rooted in contemporary Judaism than he does anywhere else in the New Testament, *John*'s director Saville restores Jesus to a decisively Jewish context. Except for the Greeks and Romans in the story, all the characters appear to belong to the first-century Jewish community of the land of Israel. They dress, they wear their hair and beards, and they speak as the filmmakers think viewers should imagine first-century Judean Jews. Among both Jesus' followers and his opponents, many men wear skullcaps. Many—not only the condemnable chief priests and Pharisees—wear fringed prayer shawls, or shawls clearly meant to look like Jewish ritual garments. One of Jesus' disciples wears *tefillin* (leather phylacteries) as he prays. When Jesus comes to Jerusalem for the fall holiday of Sukkot (the Festival of Booths), people hold clusters of palm, myrtle, and willow branches as traditional Jews still do today. John the Baptist baptizes his penitents in a much more Jewish fashion than in Pasolini's film. When Jesus preaches in the synagogue in Capernaum, a Torah scroll is situated on the table in the center of the hall. It hardly matters if some of these details—the shape of the Torah scroll or that of the prayer shawls, perhaps—are anachronistic. *John*'s Jesus, maybe even more than John's Jesus, belongs to the Jewish world in which he lived, preached, and died. The film's academic advisory board, which included two Jewish professors, clearly exerted its influence.

Jesus' Jewishness drastically alters one's appreciation of his conflict with "the Jews," which looms so prominently throughout the Gospel of John. Saville's film portrays it as a conflict *within* the Jewish community, a Jewish community that had room for many different points of view. One encounters not the slightest hint of a dispute between Jews and Christians, or Judaism and Christianity. When the Greek text of John refers to *Ioudaioi*, Jews or Judeans, the film follows the Good News Translation of the Bible, which generally speaks of "the Jewish authorities." More noteworthy still, despite the sympathetic—even glorious—light in which viewers behold Jesus throughout the movie, one can clearly understand the hostility that he elicited among his opponents. Jesus is impetuous, vindictive, scathing in his rebuke of the Jewish authorities. He lambastes the Pharisees and chief priests for their refusal to love God and acknowledge Jesus as God's son. Long before they conspire against him, *he* condemns *them* to eternal death and damnation. "I am telling you the truth," Jesus declares over and over and over again throughout the course of the film, and one certainly comes to feel warmly for his disciples, who extol him and follow him even if they, too, hardly grasp the full implications of his teaching. The narrator, for his part, reminds the audience repeatedly that Jesus is the Son of God. But can one truly fault those Jews for not accepting Jesus as he desecrated the Sabbath, showed contempt for priests and sages alike, and bordered on blasphemy as he spoke about himself, especially in a culture in which what posed as miracle might well be magic, and black magic at that? The film, I believe, raises this question. And it definitely raises doubts about the answer.

In keeping with these doubts, *The Gospel of John* tends to deemphasize the responsibility of the Jews for the Crucifixion, certainly the responsibility of "the Jews" in a collective sense. Though some Jews, led by the chief priests, initially approach Pilate to clamor for Jesus' execution, some do not. The crowd that gathers to watch the Crucifixion is noticeably small. Joseph of Arimathaea and Nicodemus, the two who bury Jesus, are dressed in prayer shawls and black cloaks, just as the Pharisees who opposed Jesus dressed. Unlike many other attempts to visualize the Passion, *John* has no one strike Jesus as he makes his way to the house of Annas the priest after his arrest, from Annas to Caiaphas, from Caiaphas to Pilate, and finally, bearing the cross, to Golgotha. Neither do we see or hear Jesus as he is flogged, nor do we watch the Roman soldiers nail him to the cross. Though genuine, his suffering is contained, precisely at those moments when the camera could have portrayed otherwise, without altering the text of the gospel in any way. *John* appears to know nothing of the "Secret Passion" that intrigued Christian mystics, poets, and artists at the end of the Middle Ages.

In the final analysis, however, not even this rendition of the Gospel of John can do away with the anti-Jewish messages imbued so deeply ingrained in its teaching. The gospel condemns the Jews for rejecting and killing Jesus. So too, inevitably, does the film. But even beyond what one reads in the biblical text, Good News Translation and all, overtones of anti-Judaism color the direction of the film and its cinematography. When Pilate presents Jesus to the crowd with his famous declaration, "Here is the man," the gospel text reports that "when the chief priests and temple guards saw him, they shouted, 'Crucify him, crucify him'" (John 19:5–6). Curiously, however, the film omits the Gospel's lead-in that mentions the chief priests and guards. On screen, immediately after Pilate presents Jesus, the entire crowd chimes in with vigor, crying "Crucify him" more than twice. And so again, several verses later, when the people shout, "Kill him! Kill him! Crucify him!" the crowd appears close to mass hysteria.

Yet perhaps more striking than that, the film internalizes the cosmic struggle between good and evil, light and darkness, which, according to the gospel, underlies the conflict between Jesus and his enemies. Though there are exceptions to this pattern, Jesus and his disciples dress in lighter colors than their opponents, especially the Pharisees. And throughout much of the film (corresponding to chapters 5–19 of the gospel), one figure in particular dominates the campaign of the Jewish leadership against Jesus: a formidable individual with long dark hair, long dark beard, and long dark side locks, clad in jet-black robes and turban, who resembles the Hasidic Jews often considered extremists in the Jewish world today. This nameless individual, simply dubbed "Leading Pharisee" in the credits at the end of the film, functions as Jesus' nemesis. He speaks alternatively for "the Jews," "the Jewish authorities," the chief priests, and the Pharisees in their hostile confrontations with Jesus—from his initial entry into Jerusalem through his condemnation to the cross.

Let us follow the appearances of this rather haunting individual. After Jesus heals a lame man in Jerusalem, this nameless villain numbers among "the Jews" ("the Jewish authorities" in the Good News Translation) who reprove Jesus for desecrating the Sabbath (John 5). As Jesus turns upon them, the camera focuses repeatedly upon him. Jesus and his nemesis then approach one another, they stand face to face, and Jesus looks him directly in the eye, explaining how "those who have done evil will rise and be condemned," and how "you have no love for God in your hearts." By the time Jesus secretly enters Jerusalem during the next Sukkot festival (John 7), his archrival is directing the efforts of "the Jews" to locate, arrest, and kill him. Confronted, Jesus focuses on him when he asks, "Why are you trying to kill me?" Throughout this scene, this man repeatedly voices the accusations against Jesus that the gospel simply attributes to "the Jews." Immediately thereafter the same individual, trying to entrap Jesus, engineers the indictment of a woman caught in an act of adultery (John 8). Looking at him directly, Jesus declares: "You belong to this world here below . . . , you will die in your sins . . . , I have much to say about you, much to condemn you for." After Jesus then heals a blind man on the Sabbath (John 9), the chief villain presides over the proceedings against Jesus, speaking the words that the gospel assigns to the Pharisees, the Jews, and the Jewish authorities. He commands center stage at the meeting of the Sanhedrin (John 11) that resolves to kill Jesus. To him does Caiaphas exclaim: "It is better for you to have one man die for the people, instead of having the whole nation destroyed." Eventually (John 18–19), this villain appears in the front lines of those pressing Pilate to crucify Jesus. He shouts for the release of Barabbas. He voices the final cry of "Crucify him" following Pilate's presentation of "Here is the man." When the entire mob thirsted for Jesus' blood, this unsavory figure stood at the head of the pack.

In this despicable character above all else does *The Gospel of John* retain the anti-Judaism of the Gospel of John. Jesus and he appear to engage one another in a protracted duel, reflecting the cosmic struggle—and triumph—of God and his Son against the forces of evil and sin. This man, Jesus underscores on several occasions, represents the Law of Moses; Jesus himself must clearly represent a different law. Owing to the markedly Jewish setting in which the screenplay unfolds, one can hardly suggest that the film's nameless villain exemplifies the Jews and Judaism in general. Yet it certainly nourishes this gospel's contention that the cosmic evil against which Jesus came to do battle was evil embodied by traditional Judaism.

We might well close our discussion of *The Gospel of John* by returning to its very beginning. Before the moviegoer hears the first words of the gospel, the following lines appear on the screen:

> The Gospel of John was written two generations after the crucifixion of Jesus Christ. It is set in a time when the Roman Empire controlled Jerusalem. Although crucifixion was the preferred method of Roman punishment, it was not one sanctioned by Jewish law. Jesus and all his early followers were Jewish. The Gospel presents a period of unprecedented polemic and antagonism between the emerging church and the religious establishment of the Jewish people. This film is a faithful representation of that Gospel.

Intended, perhaps, to deflect charges of anti-Semitism that the film might awaken among its critics, these words echo ideas that figured prominently earlier in this book: Given that any conflict that ensued between Jesus and other Jewish leaders in his day was an internal Jewish conflict, one that involved and concerned Jews living within the same Jewish society, the notion that "the Jews killed Christ" is rooted in Christian myth, not in Jewish history. Moreover, the social and cultural context underlying that myth was essentially that of the second half of the first century, not the first half. This was not the period of Jesus' life and death, but the period when the Gospels and their Passion narrative took shape, set against the background of polemic and antagonism between Jews and Christians of various sorts. The Christ-killer myth originates in the gospel, and it is the gospel that *John* claims to represent faithfully.

## QUESTING FOR JESUS

Pasolini's *Matthew* and Saville's *John* represent one important direction taken by modern readers of the New Testament. Focusing on individual books of

Scripture as they do, they remind us that each of the Gospels constitutes an entity unto itself, that each gospel presents but one of many possible understandings of Jesus' life and death. Yet other concerns of modern biblical scholars have also reached the screen, among them the drive to penetrate and illuminate the puzzling character of Jesus, who frequently appears one-dimensional, uninteresting, and altogether "flat" in dramatizations of gospel stories. At the very beginning of the twentieth century, in his *Quest for the Historical Jesus*, Albert Schweitzer established just how elusive the "real Jesus" truly is and how Christians have repeatedly refashioned Jesus in their own image. As Schweitzer's "quest" itself has evolved through various stages and the search for the historical Jesus has not abated, filmmakers too have strived to make Jesus more accessible to our own world and culture.

Martin Scorsese's *The Last Temptation of Christ* (1988) proved especially innovative among Jesus films, and many reacted to it with an array of superlatives: the most provocative, the most violent, the most controversial, the most daring in its explanation of the origins of Christianity, the most iconoclastic in its portrayal of Jesus' humanity. As one treatment of *The Last Temptation* concluded, "In no other Hollywood film about Jesus has it really been possible for audiences so forcefully to feel that, for all his charisma and inspirational heroism, Jesus may simply not have been the Son of God."[9] Acknowledging that its Jesus depends no less on the artist's imagination than on history, the film opens with words from the prologue of the novel by Nikos Kazantzakis on which it is based:

> The dual substance of Christ—the yearning, so human, so superhuman, of man to attain to God, or more exactly, to return to God and identify himself with him—has always been a deep inscrutable mystery to me. . . . My principal anguish and the source of all my joys and sorrows from my youth onward has been the incessant, merciless battle between the spirit and the flesh. . . .
>
> This film is not based upon the Gospels but upon this fictional exploration of the eternal spiritual conflict.

The contents of *The Last Temptation* have little to add to the story told in this book. Granted, the film does contrast the message preached by Jesus with the traditional Jewish culture that nurtured him, at times presenting this Jewish culture in an uncomplimentary way. When Jesus arrives at the wedding in Cana (where he changes water into wine) with Mary Magdalene by his side, someone reproaches him for bringing a prostitute to a wedding and thus violating Jewish purity law, and Jesus quickly retorts, "Then the law's against my heart." When Jesus overturns the tables of the moneychangers in the temple courtyard, one gold coin flies into the hand of the high priest wearing a prayer shawl, whose colleague beside him also wears *tefillin*. Both in this scene and in that of Passover eve, the whores, merchants, and bloody sacrifices themselves really do make the temple appear more like a den of iniquity than a house of God. And when the priests challenge Jesus concerning his violation of the law and his blasphemy, he brazenly rebukes them: "I'm throwing away the law. . . . I have a new law and a new hope. . . . I'm the end of the Old Law and the beginning of the new one. . . . I'm the saint of blasphemy."

Nevertheless, one barely senses that this conflict between Jesus and the Jews or their religious establishment underlies the Crucifixion. On the contrary, *The Last Temptation* conscientiously shies away from the Christ-killer myth at the heart of the Gospels' Passion narrative. One neither sees nor hears of a Jewish conspiracy against Jesus, Jewish judicial proceedings against him, Jewish pressure on Pilate to execute Jesus, or the damning Jewish cry of "His blood be on us and on our children." Pilate views Jesus as part of the Jewish political opposition against Rome that he must suppress, a struggle in which Judas is actively involved. Judas alone, in fact, enables Jesus' role as savior. He betrays Jesus because Jesus has prevailed upon him to do so. He has the resilience, the idealism, and the determination to wage war on Rome that Jesus seems to lack. "I struggle," he initially chides Jesus (a carpenter who makes crosses for Roman crucifixions of his fellow Jews), whereas "you collaborate," and much of the story that follows bears this out. Otherwise, the film situates the Jesus story in a setting that appears more Arab and Middle Eastern than Jewish. Aside from Saul of Tarsus/Paul the Apostle, who insists he must have a crucified (and resurrected) Christ in order to save the world as he intends, Jews seem to have little role or interest in bringing Jesus to his death.

And yet, if what appears on screen has little bearing on our story, the storm of controversy that surrounded *The Last Temptation* does deserve attention. Christian groups condemned the film on numerous grounds. Jesus' humanity and self-doubt (played out on screen in Jesus' sexual and adulterous liaisons and fantasies), his inclination to trade in the savior's cross for a normal family life, and the "positive" roles given Judas and Paul in prevailing on Jesus to accept his destiny all struck many as blasphemous. One might say that in bringing Kazantzakis's (and Scorsese's) Jesus of Nazareth to life, *The Last Temptation* replaces Jesus Christ, God's son and the messiah who has come to redeem all of humankind from sin, with a weak, self-centered, obsessive mortal who has little to offer those around him. Tempers flared in the wake of the film's release, and the controversy soon evoked the very anti-Jewish expressions that the film had avoided on the screen. To a certain extent the storm may have been predictable: When Kazantzakis first published *The Last Temptation* in 1955, the Greek Orthodox Church excommunicated him, and the Roman Catholic Church banned his book. Though Scorsese and

Kazantzakis were both Christians, some church officials, including the Greek Orthodox bishop of Pittsburgh, honed in on the film's producers. Bishop Maximos wrote the clergy and laity in his diocese:

> I trust that none of you will honor a movie that dishonors Christianity and the Leader of our faith, falling prey to the greed of its blasphemous producers. By the way, you may wish to know that these last ones, the producers, are aligned with those who first crucified Christ. Now they attempt it a second time![10]

It appeared that Christ's crucifiers were at work once again.[11] Not on screen but, so it appeared, in the person of *The Last Temptation*'s producers at Universal Studios, whose parent company, MCA, was chaired by the Jewish Lew Wasserman. A week before the film's release, Italian filmmaker Franco Zeffirelli reportedly linked it to "that Jewish cultural scum of Los Angeles which is always spoiling for a chance to attack the Christian world."[12] Others accused Wasserman of fomenting the anti-Jewish slander associated with the film, perhaps to discredit the film's opponents. As several critics have pointed out, the controversy surrounding *The Last Temptation* demonstrates that even in contemporary America, Jesus Christ is a "cultural icon" whose significance and complexity far exceed the difficulties of working a book into a film.[13] The Christ-killer myth still contributes to that significance and complexity.

*The Last Temptation*, then, hoped to find Jesus—and to understand him—in the mind and misgivings of a conflicted first-century Jew. Appearing less than one year later, Denys Arcand's *Jesus of Montreal* (1989) searched for him among a troupe of present-day avant-garde (and rather unfulfilled) actors, commissioned by a Catholic priest to revitalize his parish's traditional Passion play that had long since proven uninspiring. The actors set out to resurrect the historical Jesus, pursuing him through library research and in consultation with a biblical scholar at a Catholic university who, fearing for his job, refuses to go "on record" with his critical insights. As they develop and perform their rendition of the Passion story, however, the actors gradually become the characters they set out to portray: Mary the mother of Jesus (Constance, the mistress of the priest who commissions the play), Mary Magdalene (Mireille, a sexy model whose agent has told her, "Your talent is all in your ass"), two of the disciples (Martin, who dubs pornographic movies, and Rene, obsessed with human mortality as he narrates a film on the Big Bang and galactic origins), and, of course, Jesus himself (Daniel, an unknown, unemployed actor doggedly in search of himself). In living their new roles both on and off stage, they quickly find themselves rebelling against the morally and spiritually bankrupt institutions of the world around them. Recalling Jesus' rescue of the adulterous woman, Daniel rescues Mireille from an audition for a beer commercial in which she must bare her breasts. He

then overturns the tables of the advertisers and smashes their expensive au-
diovisual equipment, much as Jesus behaved in the temple. Upon the initial
success of Daniel and company's new Passion play, a rich lawyer tries to induce Daniel to "go commercial," recalling Jesus' temptations by the devil.
Most important of all, the actors clash with the very church authorities who
enlisted their services in the first place. Because the new play deviates from
traditional doctrine and casts doubt on the importance of the church in bringing believers to Christ, the parish priest attempts first to rewrite it and then
to shut it down altogether. At the third and final performance, the audience
riots when the church's security guards try to stop the show in the middle.
Already crucified, Jesus (and the cross) topple over. Daniel suffers severe injury and, after leaving one hospital and collapsing again in the subway, eventually dies in another hospital. His transplanted heart and eyes then bring
new life and vision to those who receive them.

As *Jesus of Montreal* blurs the boundaries between the narrative of the
Passion play and the story of the actors themselves, symbolism, metaphor,
and allegory abound. The film is full of double and even triple entendres, and
at times it leaves the viewer confused as to how to interpret what happens.
Which reenactment of the Passion, that of the actors in the church play or
that of the present-day characters on screen, is truly the real one? Where does
onstage give way to offstage—when do the actors stop acting and begin giving genuine expression to their true selves? Who qualifies as the real Jesus:
the first-century Jesus, Jesus of the older Passion play, Jesus of the new Passion play, Daniel? We shall return to these questions momentarily. But we
should first take note that the symbolism of this movie does more than reenact the Gospels' account of Jesus in the lives of the actors at the same time as
they reenact it on stage. As one New Testament scholar has aptly noted, it
drastically alters the essence of Jesus' teaching, not only by rephrasing it in
contemporary language but also by adjusting it to contemporary values. The
satanic lawyer represents the values of the contemporary, profit-seeking commercial establishment rather than some superhuman enemy. The mayhem that
Daniel causes at Mireille's audition does not precipitate an eschatological crisis
but cries out against the commercially motivated sexual exploitation of women.
Jesus' transplanted organs offer people new physical life in this world, not
some eternal spiritual existence in the next.[14] Jesus' message has become that
of a late-twentieth-century French Canadian counterculture.

For our purposes, *Jesus of Montreal* proves most impressive in the power
that it finds in the *story* of the Passion. The actors' efforts to refashion Jesus
according to historical scholarship count for very little. What poses as historical fact is not entirely accurate. Rather, what matters most is the ability
of the Passion play to inspire, to create a genuine Passion experience—for
the actors, for their audience, and, presumably, for viewers of the film. As

some have suggested, *Jesus of Montreal* is "a story about how to tell the story of Christ in a society that has lost the ability to represent God in a coherent way."[15] Where, ultimately, should one look for Jesus, and for the road to liberation and spiritual fulfillment?

I believe that the film hints at an answer. During the first performance of the Passion play, at the moment that the crucified Jesus expires, Mary Magdalene (Mireille) explains, "Artists began painting the Crucifixion five centuries later." The Passion play then shifts to its final scene in the catacombs underneath the church, where the players, reflecting upon their loss, hear from Mireille that she has seen him, although he now looks different. Jesus' mother and one disciple (Constance and Martin) then encounter a hooded figure who gives them bread, and they joyfully acknowledge him as Jesus, their Lord. The players reflect on how Jesus and his message live on as people implement his ethical teaching and thereby continue to realize his presence among themselves. "Jesus is alive, we have seen him," they declare. "Love one another." "Seek salvation within yourselves." "Peace be with you and with your spirit." The play then ends, as Daniel, absent from this scene until now, descends from above ground to take a bow with his colleagues.

At first blush, such a conclusion might appear nice, appropriate, heart-warming—just what one might expect. On second thought, however, it raises questions: Why the reference to artists living centuries later at the moment Jesus dies, leading directly to the final scene that deals with Jesus' resurrected presence? Why does the Jesus whom Mireille swears to have seen look so different? And, most startling, when Daniel descends at the final moment of the play, the audience realizes that the figure whom Constance and Martin recognized as their Lord was not he. Perhaps the film suggests that artists' varying renditions of Jesus and the Passion in subsequent ages demonstrate precisely how everyone can internalize them, how all people, as the players say, must seek salvation within themselves. Once Jesus has died, his followers, like the artists of centuries later, leave his physical person behind. As they continue to encounter him, he appears markedly different (to Mireille). He and his mission appear (to Constance and Martin) in the body of an entirely different person. Ultimately, each and every individual can find him, salvation, and peace in a countless number of different ways. The key, it appears, would lie in one's ability to resurrect Jesus for oneself, and thus to enjoy the gifts that Christ has to offer.

*Jesus of Montreal* proclaims that art, the art of the stage in particular, and the Passion play above all allow people to find themselves in the "greatest story ever told." The Passion play collapses the distance between Jesus the Jew of first-century Judea and the rebellious, nonconformist Christ of present-day Montreal. Actors and spectators alike quickly lose their ability to distinguish between one and the other. The film asserts the power of the

Crucifixion story *as a story*, which serves as the catalyst for spiritual renewal and liberation. Paradoxically, it is only when Jesus cannot remain on the cross, when the players can no longer perform their roles, that Daniel suffers and dies. In other words, when the church authorities put an end to the play, they bring the player who has made the Passion narrative come to life—the one who, more than anyone else, allows Jesus to function as Christ—to his miserable death. Most appropriately, at the very end of the film, Daniel's friends memorialize him in an endowment fund for offbeat theater. In the final seconds of the movie, as the credits begin to appear on screen, the soundtrack concludes with the same choral music of the mass that played at the beginning of the film. The movie opened, however, with shots of the church of Mount Royal, its traditional ecclesiastical artwork, and its priest meeting with Daniel. Now, at the end of the film, the same singers sound the message of the gospel in the Montreal subway where Daniel collapsed, bringing it to the world at large and collecting alms, as a commercial billboard looms behind them.

If, as I suggest, Arcand's film hinges on the paradox that the *story* of the Crucifixion brings Christ (and others who participate in it) to life, while preventing the retelling of the story leads to his demise, who bears the responsibility for killing Christ in *Jesus of Montreal*? Not the Jews. Daniel's Passion play shows no conspiracy of Jewish leaders against Jesus, no pact between the chief priests and Judas, no Jewish mob clamoring for Jesus' death. During the first performance of the play, although Caiaphas warns Pilate about the dangers that Jesus poses, Pilate hardly protests. He certainly does not disclaim responsibility. At the second performance, Jesus condemns the Jewish leaders of his day for their hypocrisy.

> Beware of priests who desire to walk in long robes and love greetings in the markets, the highest seats in temples, the best rooms at feasts, who devour widows' houses, pretending prayer. They shall receive a greater damnation. [Luke 20:46–47]

But at the moment when Daniel proclaims, "they shall receive a greater damnation," he approaches and gazes belligerently at the very Catholic priest who seeks to ban his play, now wearing his clerical collar and accompanied by two priestly colleagues. Nor does Daniel suffice with that. "Do not be called Rabbi" (Matthew 23:8), he rails at these clergymen, and then adds, as if Jesus himself spoke these words, "or Reverend Father or Your Grace or Your Eminence." Those condemned for engineering Jesus' downfall in this movie are none other than the leaders of the established church!

As for the Jews, their role as "crucifiers" is entirely benign. After Daniel collapses in the wake of his fall from the cross, Constance and Mireille rush him by ambulance to St. Mark's Hospital, where the staff, who seem to care more about insurance and paperwork than healing the sick, have no time to tend to him. They leave when Daniel revives, but he soon collapses again. This time they take him to Montreal's Jewish Hospital, where the staff (all wearing Stars of David on their uniforms) receive him—and his companions— quickly and with compassion. Yet Daniel dies, and the attending physician laments that "*we* lost him," explaining that he arrived a mere thirty minutes too late to be saved. Had he received the necessary treatment at the Catholic St. Mark's Hospital, would he have lived? One can only surmise. Constance and Mireille donate Daniel's organs for transplant, and the Jewish surgeon lays Daniel/Jesus out in the shape of a cross, piercing him and extracting his heart, which then becomes a source of new life. Is Arcand offering a subtle commentary on the Christ-killer myth? Perhaps he too has recognized that the story of Jesus' crucifixion requires its Jewish Christ killers in order to exert its power and have its desired effect.

## FROM THE GOSPELS TO GIBSON

Mel Gibson's *The Passion of the Christ*, which brings the chronological sweep of our story to a close, had its day in the sun as I planned and wrote this book. From the announcement of the production in the making, through the heated controversy that followed, to the screening of the film and its bedazzling financial success, one can see the fascinating interplay of religious tradition with cultural politics and social psychology. *The Passion of the Christ* does not boast of the subtlety found in the other Jesus films. It hardly beckons the viewer to contribute to a process of theological interpretation. Rather, unlike any of the other movies discussed here, it does claim to document what actually happened to Jesus during the last day of his life. All told, *The Passion* underscores just how profoundly the story of Jesus' crucifixion remains a burning issue in our civilization nearly two thousand years after it took shape.

   Debate over the film ran wild in advance of its release, as theologians, preachers, academics, public figures, the news media, and Web masters appeared to know no limits. Does *The Passion* recklessly distort the Gospels' account of Jesus' death, or is it "a compelling piece of art"? Does it fan the flames of the age-old Christ-killer myth, or, with its shot of Mel Gibson's own left hand holding one of the nails about to be driven into Jesus' body, does it hold all sinners responsible for the Crucifixion? While one evangelical leader called the filmmaker "the Michelangelo of this generation," a leading Christian magazine questioned, "Is Mel Gibson plotting the death of the Jews?" The Anti-Defamation League of B'nai B'rith struggled against the film. It joined the United States Conference of Catholic Bishops in convening a board of scholars and theologians, Christians and Jews, who expressed serious doubts and concerns over the script that they reviewed. Many lashed back at these critics, and some accused the scholarly review board of obtaining the script unethically, if not illegally. Jewish voices then charged these counter-critics with fomenting anti-Semitism, and they responded in kind.

Beneath the impassioned, often ugly rhetoric of the controversy, one can define several interesting issues worthy of further study in their own right. News of the film commandeered public attention far beyond its creators' intentions, and the broad spectrum of opinion—along which Christians and Jews of all denominations divided in almost every possible combination—underscored the stake that people believed they had in the debate and its outcome. Many voices in the controversy championed both the "literal" meaning of the biblical text and the need for historical accuracy, often weighing them one against the other. Precisely what is the relationship between Scripture and history? What responsibility does an artist have to either or both?

Ironically, liberal Catholic scholars attacked the film because, they declared, it did not adhere to the official teachings of the church today, whereas Gibson, a Traditionalist Catholic opposed to the leadership of recent popes, claimed to have recaptured the unadulterated truth of the Gospels. Strangely enough, he thus found himself allied with many evangelical Protestants, who reject the Catholic Church's claim of exclusive authority to interpret and mediate the truth of Scripture. In this debate over how to portray the death of Jesus, Gibson and his Christian critics really battled over who is an authentic Catholic and a genuine Christian.

Jews, too, found themselves divided. With explicit or veiled allusions to the Holocaust and its roots in Christian tradition, many truly feared that portrayals of "bloodthirsty, vengeful, and money-hungry Jews" and their "implacable hatred of Jesus" would provoke incidents of anti-Semitism, perhaps even violence against Jews.[16] Others, however, demanded that Jews committed to democracy not call for curtailing the freedom of speech or expression. Still others expressed admiration for the film. One outspoken critic called it "the most effective cinematic adaptation of a biblical story I have ever seen."[17] Discussions of the film also raised the question of whether religion and art must yield to modern political and social sensitivities. As one newspaper editorial writer quipped, "there is no Christianity without the Crucifixion, and there is no Crucifixion narrative without the Jews."[18] In this post-Holocaust age, how must Christian theology define the "gospel truth" of the Christ-killer motif? Must we, remembering Auschwitz, circumscribe the freedom of artistic expression? What if Bach's *St. Matthew Passion* in centuries past conveyed messages very similar to those of Gibson's *Passion* today? Should good, responsible souls have suppressed it?

Fortunately or not, the film finally appeared. What people had said about *The Passion of the Christ* before its release now mattered little compared to what they saw on screen. And in this enactment of the Passion narrative, Jews play a major role. The chief priests who engineer Jesus' downfall seem to wear prayer shawls. They and Judas appear to have great concern for money, gold, silver, and jewels. Not only do crowds of hostile Jews cry out against Jesus, but even the young Jewish urchins who pursue and taunt Judas appear unusually menacing, if not demonic. The film does much to exonerate Pilate, who, at the urging of his wife, would very much like to save Jesus. The Jews, however, seem inspired by Satan himself, who appears periodically throughout the movie, from its opening scene in the Garden of Gethsemane, through the various beatings of Jesus over the course of his last hours, to the Crucifixion at Golgotha itself. The film regularly focuses on Mary, whose maternal love and compassion for Jesus contrasts sharply with the inexplicable malice that his foes display toward him. The blood curse of "His blood be on us and on our children" does not appear amid the English subtitles on screen, but one can hear it in the Aramaic being spoken. Mary treats her son as she does, the Jews their children as they do.

Yet the most remarkable feature of *The Passion* lies in its violence. Gibson has overlooked no opportunity to depict the spiteful, malignant, bloody, excruciatingly painful treatment of Jesus: upon his arrest on his way to the high priest's house, during his sham nighttime trial before the Jewish authorities, during his scourging by Pilate's soldiers, en route to Golgotha with his cross in tow, and then as he is beaten, kicked, hoisted, and nailed onto the cross. The camera—like the microphone—leaves virtually nothing to the imagination but presents everything, flauntingly, right before the viewer's eyes. In *The Gospel of John,* Jesus is led away rather calmly following his arrest; in *The Passion,* he is beaten and dropped down over a ledge into a ravine. *John* depicts several cracks of the Roman whip as Pilate has Jesus scourged, but the viewer neither sees nor hears Jesus himself. *The Passion* prolongs the agony for a full ten minutes, as sadistic soldiers beat Jesus to a pulp, to the approval of the Jewish crowds. Likewise, Jesus is flogged gratuitously, suffering under the weight of his cross on the way to his execution, and the Crucifixion is presented in vivid detail. *John* shows almost none of this.

I have no desire to take sides in the debates surrounding this film, but rather to consider *The Passion*'s place in the career of the Crucifixion story—and the Jews' role within it. Nearly a year before the film reached movie theaters, Gibson made his claim for its accuracy: "We've done the research. I'm telling the story as the Bible tells it. I think the story, as it really happened, speaks for itself. The Gospel is a complete script, and that's what we're filming."[19] Whatever Gibson's intention, the film is far from the story as the Bible tells it, or at least not the texts of the Gospels as they stand alone, free of selection, embellishment, and interpretation that have developed over time. On the one hand, *The Passion* omits much from the New Testament account of Jesus' end. It begins only in the Garden of Gethsemane, minutes before Jesus' arrest, and contains but the briefest of flashbacks to earlier scenes in Jesus' life. This film gives almost nothing of Jesus' earlier career: his sermons; his clashes with Pharisees, scribes, and priests; his entry into Jerusalem or the mayhem that he caused in the temple. One sees nothing of any earlier rift between Jesus and Judas. Except for several seconds of flashback, one sees nothing of the Last Supper. And one sees nothing of the Jewish conspiracy against Jesus: neither the priests conspiring against Jesus nor their enlistment of Judas to betray his master. In other words, the viewer has no basis whatsoever for understanding—not condoning, which the Gospels surely do not do, but simply for comprehending—the hostility of the Jewish leadership and the Jewish mob toward Jesus. One therefore sees that hostility not as misguided, not as misdirected, but simply as gratuitous, malicious, and evil.

On the other hand, *The Passion* embellishes its story with much that is not in the Gospels: from the compassion of the women on screen (Mary; Mary Magdalene; Pilate's wife, Claudia; and Veronica, who wipes Jesus' brow as he struggles toward Golgotha bearing the weight of the cross) to much of the prolonged violence inflicted on Jesus' body. The film would seem to testify to the late medieval artistic tradition sometimes called the Secret Passion of Christ (see chapter 9), which added extensively to the Gospels' list of tortures and humiliations that Jesus endured. In fact, when Pilate presents Jesus to the crowd ("*Ecce homo*—here is the man"), hoping that the Jews will accept his offer to release him, the malicious, almost grotesque-looking crowd immediately reminded me of the caricatures in the art of Hieronymus Bosch and his school centuries earlier (fig. 9.16). Despite Gibson's avowed intention to adhere to the letter of the gospel, the film incorporates much from subsequent Christian tradition, and it even relies, heavily and directly, on *The Dolorous Passion of Our Lord Jesus Christ* by the nineteenth-century nun Anne Catherine Emmerich (see chapter 6).

As far as I am concerned, *The Passion's* blend of Scripture and tradition warrants neither praise nor criticism. As we have seen repeatedly, blending the two is a common, even natural tendency in the history of the Christ-killer myth. But it does enable one to situate Gibson's film with regard to several developments considered earlier in this book. First, in focusing entirely on Jesus' suffering, *The Passion* must clearly take a place beside medieval works of Passion-centered devotion, instructions for meditating on the agonies that Jesus endured during his last hours. As we have seen, graphic, detailed descriptions of the violence inflicted on Jesus forged a bond between meditating Christians and their savior: Focusing on this violence and the pain that it caused allowed the faithful to identify with a very human Jesus, to internalize the experience of his Passion, and thereby to achieve an uplifting, cathartic sense of liberation that only the Crucifixion had the power to offer them.

Catherine of Siena instructed her readers to make their home in Jesus' wounds. Ludolph of Saxony begged God to let him suffer pain and humiliation as Jesus had, all for the greater glory of God's name. Christianity teaches that Jesus was a sacrificial lamb without blemish, without the slightest taint of sin. The greater the violence in his crucifixion, therefore, the more powerful and effective his sacrifice: Precisely because his death entails truly gratuitous violence and murder, it yields atonement, rebirth, and salvation to all who would acknowledge its power. The distance between the meditations of Angela of Foligno, a medieval laywoman who meditated extensively on the flesh driven out of Christ's hand by the nail that crucified him, and *The Passion of the Christ* does not appear great at all.[20] In such a context, those who killed Christ cannot but figure prominently. *The Passion* invariably exacerbates a sense of polar opposition—us versus them—between believer and unbeliever.

Second, Gibson's movie very much resembles a Passion play. Several reviewers of the film have noted how the camera draws viewers into the crowd, so that they witness the Crucifixion on screen today from the very perspective of those who, presumably, witnessed it in Jesus' day. As noted regarding the play at Oberammergau, religious drama strives to involve the audience in the performance, to overcome the distinction between passive spectator and active player. Those who have seen the Oberammergau play typically report that the power of the drama lies precisely in that ability to involve them.[21] If nothing else, the regalia, the viewing guides, and the promotional material for *The Passion* testify to a similar goal, and this is probably not coincidence. The introduction to *A Guide to the Passion*, published by the Catholic Exchange, expresses the hope that the film might "set us in a direction of positive change and authentic conversion . . . , a path toward recognizing and pursuing the specific mission God has ordained for us."[22] Does the film succeed? One can only decide for oneself.

Third, and finally, *The Passion* appeared on the big screen some four decades after the Second Vatican Council, in its decree of *Nostra Aetate*, ruled that one cannot hold all Jews responsible for the death of Jesus. How do film and filmmaker appear against the background of Vatican II? Despite his own upbringing and his identification with Traditionalist Catholics who deem the reforms of Vatican II a perversion of authentic Catholic beliefs, Gibson has disclaimed any hatred of Jews—either in his own worldview or in the messages of his film. Though I have no interest in passing judgment, official Catholic reactions to the film are pertinent here. During the months before the film's release, rumors circulated far and wide that Pope John Paul II had effectively endorsed the film, stating that "it is as it was," but Vatican officials soon declared that he said nothing of the sort. More instructively, the scholarly committee established by the United States Conference of Catholic Bishops (USCCB), together with the Anti-Defamation League, to review the script of the film before its release evidently issued grave warnings concerning the implications of the film, especially in view of its deviation from the spirit of *Nostra Aetate*. John T. Pawlikowski, a distinguished Catholic theologian and priest, summarized the committee's consensus thus:

> Certainly films can present Jesus' suffering and death in a powerful way. But they must remain faithful to the church's current understanding. "The Passion of the Christ" does not. Gibson, in fact, rejects those teachings as well as modern biblical scholarship and thus stands outside of official Catholicism today.[23]

Father Pawlikowski's statement certainly reads like a condemnation, and one can easily understand why. Within the framework of its program for implementing the lessons of *Nostra Aetate* in Catholic institutions, the USCCB had issued a list of guidelines for Passion plays in 1988: "Criteria for the Evaluation of Dramatizations of the Passion." *The Passion of the Christ* deviates from these guidelines on numerous counts: in mixing and matching between the various gospel accounts of the Passion in a way that highlights the negative role of the Jews; in failing to present the Judaism of Jesus' day in a sufficiently complex and favorable light; and in whitewashing Pilate. Two weeks before the release of the film, Eugene Fisher, the USCCB's senior expert on Jewish-Christian relations, echoed the substance of these guidelines in the Catholic weekly *America*.[24] But once the film reached the movie theaters, the USCCB backed off—to the dismay of various Jewish leaders who had looked to it as a partner in ecumenical dialogue. In its official review of the movie, the USCCB criticized the overly harsh treatment of Jewish leadership, but it concluded that the Jews were not singled out for blame in the Crucifixion and that the film makes it "abundantly clear that it is the Romans who are Christ's executioners."[25] Dr. Fisher himself revisited *America* six weeks after the film opened and wrote: "Underneath the hype, 'The Passion of the Christ' has given Catholic-Jewish relations in this country a great boost" by actually promoting dialogue between Catholics and Jews. And thus Fisher proposed "to join the rabbi who, after seeing the movie in one such group, commented, 'I want to thank Mel Gibson for bringing us all together.'"[26] Why the change of heart? I cannot answer that question, but the question still stands.

*The Passion of the Christ*, a product of the twenty-first century and the third millennium, offers several concluding insights into the Christ-killer myth and its history. If the story of the Crucifixion touches a nerve among Christians and others who reflect on the Crucifixion in our own day, why should we have different expectations of those who remembered the Crucifixion in generations gone by? Surely one cannot imagine that Jesus' death touched them any less. Conversely, the major issues raised by the earliest Passion narratives remain. They simply refuse to go away. Though they express themselves in present-day idiom and perhaps reflect present-day concerns, recent renditions of the Passion are *interpretations* of fundamental and foundational Christian beliefs, precisely as the earliest Passion narratives were. Neither one nor the other constitutes raw data, documentary evidence as to what "really" transpired in Jerusalem on the day that Jesus of Nazareth met his maker.

Accordingly, strict correspondence to the gospel accounts of the Crucifixion—which Gibson has claimed for his production, just as the Oberammergau community claimed for its own—is largely beside the point. It hardly removes a particular text or work of art from the mythology of the Christ-killer. At the end of the day, *The Passion of the Christ* is more noteworthy for adhering to classical Christian tradition than for departing from it.

# CONCLUSION: "JUDAS ISCARIOT, WHO BETRAYED HIM" (MARK 3:19)

I have mentioned Judas in passing, but I cannot conclude this study of the Christ-killer myth without turning to him directly. Archenemy of Jesus, Judas lurks in the background of the entire Passion narrative, contributing roundly to its tension, its suspense, and its messages. As one writer has suggested, Judas actually *frames* the Gospels' accounts of Jesus' last days. Without him, the story simply would not work, and some have therefore criticized *Jesus of Montreal* for staging the Passion without a villain such as Judas.

Despite Judas's notoriety, we know virtually nothing about his identity or his background. No one has conclusively unlocked the puzzle of his name "Iscariot." Yet Christians have had little doubt as to his villainy. At the end of the *Inferno*,[1] when Dante arrives at the final round of the lowest, darkest circle of hell, a region named Judecca, he encounters those sinners eternally encased in ice for having betrayed their masters. Looming before him stands a three-faced Satan.

> *Within each mouth he used it like a grinder*
> *with gnashing teeth he tore to bits a sinner,*
> *so that he brought much pain to three at once.*

And then Dante identifies the most despicable traitor of all.

> *That soul up there who has to suffer most,*
> *my master said: Judas Iscariot,*
> *his head inside, he jerks his legs without.*

Even more than heroes, villains sometimes entice us to let our imaginations roam freely, and the character of Judas proves a wonderful case in point. From late antiquity to the present, Judas has figured prominently in folklore, literature, art, theater, and film. In dramatic productions ranging from medieval mystery plays to the Oberammergau Passion play to *Jesus Christ, Superstar*, Judas usually proves a more complicated and intriguing character than Jesus. And this interest has not abated. In the past decades, an array of scholarly books have studied him, both as he plays a central role in the Passion narrative and as he has lived on in the annals of Western culture—with much additional color and embellishment. At the same time, various authors have tried their hand at reconstructing Judas's voice, allowing him, as it were, to retell the events of Jesus' last days as he understood them.

The fascinating career of Judas overlaps extensively with that of the crucifixion story, as the myths of Judas Iscariot and the Jewish Christ killer share strikingly similar essential features. The fanfare surrounding the recent publication of the gnostic Gospel of Judas—which, like Kazantzakis's *Last Temptation of Christ*, casts Judas's betrayal of Jesus in a positive, even heroic light—testifies well to the stake that our culture still has in the Passion narrative. Like Jesus, Judas gives expression to the values of those that remember him and retell his story, a story with weighty consequences indeed.

How does the character of Judas take shape in canonical gospels of the New Testament? All four Gospels note that he numbered among the twelve original apostles. Mark, Matthew, and Luke place Judas last in their lists of Jesus' disciples, adding "who betrayed him" (Mark 3:19 and Matthew 10:4) or "who became a traitor" (Luke 6:16) to his name. The synoptic Gospels then go on to report that Judas betrayed Jesus to the chief priests, that they promised him money in return, that he arrived with the crowd of priests and elders that came to arrest Jesus, and that he identified Jesus for them with his treacherous kiss. Matthew subsequently mentions that Judas repented of his treachery. Returning the money he had received from the priests, he left the temple and hanged himself. Earlier, as Judas prepares to turn to the priests with his deceitful proposition, Luke (22:3) adds, "Then Satan entered into Judas called Iscariot."

All this, however, might not amount to a terribly damning indictment, especially when it is unclear why the chief priests needed Judas's collaboration at all. If Jesus, owing to his growing popularity, posed a threat to their authority, shouldn't they have been able to locate—or at least identify—him on their own? Only in the Gospel of John does the character of Judas begin to fill out and make more sense. Early in the gospel, John presents Judas as lacking the essential belief that, as Jesus himself explains, holds the key to salvation:

> "It is the spirit that gives life, the flesh is of no avail; the words that I have spoken to you are spirit and life. But there are some of you that do not believe. Did I not choose you, the twelve, and one of you is a devil?" He spoke of Judas the son of Simon Iscariot, for he, one of the twelve, was to betray him. (John 6:63–71)

Judas later objects when Mary (Martha's sister) anoints Jesus with a costly salve at Bethany (John 12:5–6). "Why was this ointment not sold for three hundred denarii and given to the poor?" Yet he said this, the gospel explains, not because "he cared for the poor but because he was a thief, and as he had the money box he used to take what was put into it." By the time of the Last

Supper, "the devil had already put it into the heart of Judas Iscariot, Simon's son, to betray" Jesus (13:2), and Satan entered into Judas immediately after he ate the morsel of bread that Jesus gave him. Finally, the Book of Acts relates that Judas did not return the priests' money (as in Matthew), but that he used it to buy a field, where "falling headlong, he burst open in the middle and all his bowels gushed out" (Acts 1:18).

How should one make sense of the Judas story? The possibilities recall those for evaluating the account of the Crucifixion itself. Some scholars highlight the similarities between the tale of Judas and earlier ancient Near Eastern myths of combat, betrayal, and cosmic struggle between the powers of good and evil. Viewed from this perspective, Judas amounts to a fictitious dimension of the Passion narrative that early Christianity imported from outside the Jewish world. Some, however, wrestle with the basic story line of the Passion narrative, speculating as to the kernel of historical "truth" underlying the character of Judas. Perhaps he simply arranged a meeting between Jesus and the chief priests, thinking that Jesus should confront his Jewish rivals more openly and directly. Perhaps, to the contrary, he considered Jesus overly involved in the affairs of this world. Other investigators have argued that the story of Judas depends no less on precedents in the Hebrew Bible, traditions that already "belonged" to Judaism at the time that the Gospels took shape. And with considerably more concrete evidence at their disposal, scholars have tracked the rich career of Judas in medieval and modern works of theology, literature, and art. Cautiously on some occasions but daringly on others, readers of the New Testament in later generations refashioned Judas as they saw fit, much as they refashioned Jesus. In Judas's case, however, they transformed him, as one writer has shown, into an obscure object of curiosity, a horrific arch-sinner, a hateful villain, a tragic hero worthy of sympathy and even admiration, and a hopeful, even exemplary penitent.[2] *The Dictionary of Words and Idioms Associated with Judas Iscariot* contains hundreds of entries.[3]

Above all else, Judas Iscariot epitomizes the Jewish Christ killer, illuminating the monstrosity of the crime against Jesus on the one hand, and the guilt of the Jews on the other hand. Judas has come to embody so many of those hateful characteristics with which Jews have been stereotyped over time. The Gospels themselves cast him as dishonest, greedy, entrepreneurial, faithless, jealous, treacherous, and (in the case of Luke and John) satanic. Even if he executed a plan predetermined by God, this hardly eliminates his own guilt and responsibility for betraying Jesus; it hardly lessens the extent of his evil. Later readers of the Gospels amplified these *Jewish* characteristics of Judas and rounded out the list with others: red hair, a crooked nose, a forked beard, allegiance to the devil (see fig. C.1), and more. Medieval legend depicted Judas as an Oedipus-type figure: he killed his father, married his mother, and

FIGURE C.1. Judas at the Last Supper, 12th century. Austrian illumination. Ms. Munich Clm 15903, f. 13r. Reproduced with permission of Bayerische Staatsbibliothek, Munich.

died a miserable death. With a fiendish sexual lust and a cruel streak that erupted into the most heinous of human crimes, such legend demonstrated how incurably sinful the Jewish Judas really was. Most telling of all, the very name of Judas or Judah (*Yehudah* in Hebrew) signifies the entire Jewish people, in the language of Scripture and in subsequent writings, too. As the ultimate expression of evil and betrayal, the character of Judas resides within each and every Jew (*Yehudi*).

Modern voices, both Christian and Jewish, echo this tragic association of Judas and Jew in revealing ways. Despite his repudiation of anti-Semitism and his outspoken opposition to Nazism, the acclaimed twentieth-century Protestant theologian Karl Barth affirmed the essential equivalence of Judas and Jewry.[4]

> Who is this Judas, the man who will maintain his freedom in face of Jesus for the sake of something better, the man for whom Jesus is for sale ... ? Obviously he does not bear this name for nothing. Within the apostolic group ... he obviously represents the Jews ... , he merely does that which Israel has always done in relation to Yahweh. He merely does that which has always made Yahweh's rejection of His chosen people inevitable. ... Israel always tried to buy off Yahweh with thirty pieces of silver.

And as Barth makes unmistakably clear, the dire implications of the Judas-Jewry equivalence still play an operative role in his biblical theology.

> These thirty pieces of silver are not a surprise. ... Judas and all Israel, Judas and in and with him the Jews as such! Like Esau, the rejected of God, they sold their birthright for a mess of pottage. They did not do so with closed but with open eyes. ... They can now live and die in their Judaism, their Yahweh-religion without Yahweh. They can make the best of it. They can call it a gain—and enjoy it as such—that they are the people of God, and yet do not have to believe in God or obey Him.

*Judas and all Israel, Judas and in and with him the Jews as such!* Where do words like these place Barth on the map of Jewish-Christian relations? One Christian writer, who in other respects appears to view Barth as his mentor, cannot suppress his knee-jerk reaction to the passages quoted above. "This is not sadness at some people's rejection of the Christian message but undisguised and ugly hatred for a race that the author believes has 'always' and 'obviously' been unreprobate, ungrateful, and wicked for their entire history. The anger and revulsion that many readers feel for the character Judas, Barth has transferred and even intensified onto the entire people of Israel."[5] Simply put, the basic building blocks of Christian anti-Judaism still figure prominently in modern Christian theology, even in the words of a

Karl Barth. Superseded by Christianity, Judaism is now a Godless religion. Like Esau, the Jews forsook the promise of their ancestral heritage in their pursuit of worldly gain. Like Judas, all Israel—"the Jews as such"—have betrayed their God.

For a modern-day Jewish intellectual like George Steiner, the Judas myth's effects could not have been more horrific. As he rereads the Gospel of John's account of the Last Supper, Steiner reflects on Jesus' instruction to Judas (John 13:27), "What you are going to do, do quickly," after which Judas departed immediately into the night. According to the gospel, the other disciples did not understand the point of Jesus' words. But Jesus, like Judas, knew what lay in store. For Steiner, Judas's quick departure into the night sealed the fate of the Jews in Christian history.

> Judas goes into a never-ending night of collective guilt. It is the sober truth to say that his exit is the door to the Shoah. The "final solution" proposed, enacted by National Socialism in this twentieth century is the perfectly logical, axiomatic conclusion to the Judas-identification of the Jew. . . . That utter darkness, that night within night, into which Judas is dispatched and commanded to perform "quickly," is already that of the death ovens. Who, precisely, has betrayed whom?[6]

For a Jew such as Steiner writing in the wake of the Holocaust, the road from the Gospels to Gibson that we have followed in this book was nothing other than a road from Judas to genocide. This road might not have reached its destination as quickly as Judas departed from the Last Supper into the night. But it surely and unavoidably reached that destination in due course.

Yet I would like to conclude our story on a slightly different note. For there remains yet another aspect to the role of Judas—and the Jews—in the Passion narrative. Even as they condemn Judas, the Gospels accentuate his importance. The undeserved murder of the ultimately innocent victim requires a villain worthy of such an act. No less than the punishment, the one—or those—punished must fit such a crime. Some have speculated that the earliest accounts of Jesus' crucifixion made no mention of Judas at all.[7] But the Passion narrative would not work without an arch-enemy of Jesus for a Christ killer. The story of Jesus' death desperately *needed* its Judas, and he therefore took shape in order to meet this need. And, once he had been created, the range of possibilities for his development as a character was virtually limitless.

This book began by disclaiming any intent to determine who in fact bore the responsibility for the Crucifixion, who *really* killed Jesus. I still have no conclusive answer to this question, and I doubt that the countless perennial attempts to formulate such an answer change the way most people think. Instead, I chose to tell the story of the story and to explore how and why the

Jews emerged as Christ killers in Christian tradition: how and why this identification became ingrained in the Western mind and in Western culture. We
have tracked the Christ-killer myth from its earliest appearances among Christians of the mid- to late first century. We have traveled various roads along
which the idea of the Jews as Christ killers developed, matured, and changed
over the centuries. We have seen that, without struggling too hard, one can
find this idea alive and well in different corners of our world today.

Where should one go from here? Theologians on either side of the Jewish-
Christian divide might wrestle with George Steiner's concluding question:
"Who, precisely, has betrayed whom?" Some might belabor the need for
educational reform that would help to overcome prejudice and shape healthier
attitudes toward "others" in our society. Religious leaders in various quarters might work to implement these changes. Yet the historian, this historian
at any rate, must rest his case. I have tried to illustrate the historical career
and importance of a biblical story, an importance that does not depend on
its factual accuracy. In this case, I submit that the story has had paramount
historical importance. For indeed, in Western society and culture, this story
became "the greatest story ever told."

# SUGGESTIONS FOR FURTHER READING AND NOTES

## INTRODUCTION

1. Fredriksen, *Jesus of Nazareth*, pp. 8–9.
2. http://switch5.castup.net/frames/20050503_yadvashem/video-2.asp (accessed 11 November 2005).
3. Carroll, *Constantine's Sword*, p. 391.

## CHAPTER 1

### Suggestions for Further Reading

Among the many works on the Gospels and their Passion narratives that I have consulted, the following have proved particularly useful, thought-provoking, and accessible: Brown, *Death of the Messiah*; Crossan, *Who Killed Jesus?*; Pagels, *Origin of Satan*; Flusser, *Jesus*; Sloyan, *Crucifixion of Jesus*; Carroll et al., *Death of Jesus*; Chilton and Evans, *Studying the Historical Jesus*; Farmer, *Anti-Judaism and the Gospels*; Fredriksen, *From Jesus to Christ* and *Jesus of Nazareth*; Stanton, *Gospels and Jesus*; F. Davis, *Jews and Deicide*; Meeks, *First Urban Christians*; and Hengel, *Atonement*. On the nature of myth, see the articles on "Myth" in the *Dictionary of the History of Ideas*, 3:272–318, and Dundes, *Sacred Narrative*, among many others. On the cognitive dissonance of the first Christians, see, above all, Gager, *Kingdom and Community*; the collected responses to Gager in *Zygon: Journal of Religion and Science* 13 (1978), 109ff.; and Dudley and Hilgert, *New Testament Tensions*. And on the Gospel of John in particular, see the broad array of viewpoints and further references amassed in Bieringer et al., *Anti-Judaism and the Fourth Gospel*.

### Notes

1. Kudasiewicz, *Synoptic Gospels Today*, p. 55.
2. Houlden, *Strange Story of the Gospels*, pp. 2–3.
3. Aristotle, *Poetics* 9, http://classics.mit.edu/Aristotle/poetics.1.1.html (accessed 15 August 2005; emphasis mine).
4. Thucydides, *Peloponnesian War*, p. 24. (See also http://classics.mit.edu/Thucydides/pelopwar.1.first.html.)
5. Yerushalmi, *Zakhor*, p. 16.
6. Lovejoy, "Entangling Alliance," p. 269.
7. G. Spiegel, "History, Historicism, and the Social Logic of the Text."
8. Brown, *Death of the Messiah*, p. 386.
9. Crossan, *Who Killed Jesus?*, p. 35.
10. Brown, p. 4.
11. Brown, p. 13.
12. Brown, p. 14.
13. Brown, p. 18 (and see his n. 24).

14. Brown, p. 586 (and see the detailed indictment in Crossan, *Who Killed Jesus?*, pp. 36–37).
15. Brown, p. 721.
16. Brown, p. 19.
17. http://www.vatican.va/archive/hist_councils/ii_vatican_council/documents/vat-ii_const_19651118_dei-verbum_en.html (27 July 2005).
18. Crossan, *Who Killed Jesus?*, p. 2.
19. Crossan, p. 159.
20. Crossan, pp. 12, 106.
21. Crossan, pp. 35–37.
22. For example, Brandon, *Trial of Jesus*.
23. Dudley and Hilgert, pp. 76–77.
24. Funk et al., *Five Gospels*, p. 138.
25. Funk, p. 233.
26. Funk, p. 244f.
27. See Garland, *Intention of Matthew 23*, pp. 171–209; Newport, *Sources and Sitz im Leben of Matthew 23*; and Strack and Billerbeck, *Kommentar zum neuen Testament*, 1:934ff.
28. Kampling, *Blut Christi und die Juden*, pp. 34–36.
29. Quoted in Kampling, p. 55.
30. Kampling, p. 170.
31. See the examples brought by Strack and Billerbeck, 1:1033, and Lachs, *Rabbinic Commentary*, p. 429.
32. Bieringer et al., *Anti-Judaism and the Fourth Gospel*, p. 39.

## Chapter 2

### Suggestions for Further Reading

Among many works on the binding of Isaac (Akedah) in Jewish and Christian traditions, see S. Spiegel, *Last Trial*; Daly, "Soteriological Significance"; Vermes, *Scripture and Tradition*, ch. 8; Davies and Chilton, "Aqedah"; Wilken, "Melito"; Saldarini, "Interpretation of the *Akedah*"; Segal, *Other Judaisms*, pp. 108–30, and "Akedah"; Levenson, "Abusing Abraham" and *Death and Resurrection* (and the round-table discussion of this book in *Dialog: A Journal of Theology* 34 [1995], 52–66); Manns, *Sacrifice of Isaac*; Fisk, "Offering Isaac Again and Again"; and Noort and Tigchelaar, *The Sacrifice of Isaac* (with extensive bibliography). On Isaac imagery in the New Testament, see Wood, "Isaac Typology"; Swetnam, *Jesus and Isaac*; and Beckwith, "Death of Christ." And on the Akedah in art, see Jensen, "Binding or Sacrifice of Isaac"; Kessler, "The Sacrifice of Isaac"; and Van den Brink, "Abraham's Sacrifice."

On the Passover sacrifice and the saving power of its blood, see Bahr, "Seder of Passover"; Haran, "Passover Sacrifice"; Davies, "Passover and the Dating of the Aqedah"; Bokser, *Origins of the Seder*; Saldarini, *Jesus and Passover*; Bergant, "Anthropological Approach"; Buckley, "Matter of Urgency"; Vervenne, "'Blood Is the Life'"; Tabory, *Passover Ritual*, and "Crucifixion of the Paschal Lamb"; Alexander,

"Passover Sacrifice"; and Yuval, *Two Nations in Your Womb.*" On Moses, circumcision, and Zipporah's "bridegroom of blood" in particular, see Hoffman, *Covenant of Blood*; Propp, "That Bloody Bridegroom" and *Exodus 1–18*, pp. 233–40; and Haberman, "Foreskin Sacrifice."

Much has been written on the connection between Isaiah's Suffering Servant and Jesus. See, for instance: North, *Suffering Servant*; Orlinksky, "So-Called 'Servant of the Lord,'" and "So-Called 'Suffering Servant'"; Kapelrud, "Identity of the Suffering Servant"; Wilcox, "Servant Songs"; Johnson, "Christ the Servant"; and Hugenberger, "Servant of the Lord."

On Psalm 22, see Stuhlmueller, "Psalm 22"; Kselman, "'Why Have You Abandoned Me?'"; E. Davis, "Exploding the Limits"; Robbins, "Reversed Contextualization"; Koltun-Fromm, "Psalm 22's Christological Interpretive Tradition"; Menn, "No Ordinary Lament"; and Dorival, *David, Jésus et la reine Esther.*

## Notes

1. *Epistle of Barnabas* 7.3, http://www.earlychristianwritings.com/text/barnabas-lake.html (accessed on 31 July 2005).

2. Irenaeus of Lyon, *Adversus Haereses* 4.5.4 http://www.ccel.org/fathers2/ANF-01/anf01-62.htm#P8040_2216168 (accessed on 31 July 2005).

3. Tertullian, *Adversus Judaeos* 10. Available at http://www.earlychristianwritings.com/text/tertullian08.html (accessed on 31 July 2005).

4. Clement of Alexandria, *Paedagogus* 1.5.23.1–2, available at http://www.earlychristianwritings.com/text/clement-instructor-book1.html (accessed on 31 July 2005), emphasis added.

5. Melito of Sardis, *On Pascha*, pp. 74–75.

6. Athanasius of Alexandria, *Epistula festales* 6.8, available at http://www.ccel.org/ccel/schaff/npnf204.xxv.iii.iii.vi.html#fnb_xxv.iii.iii.vi-p44.3 (accessed on 31 July 2005).

7. Quoted in Manns, *Sacrifice of Isaac*, p. 63.

8. Birnbaum, *High Holyday Prayer Book*, p. 390.

9. Etheridge, *Targums*, 1:480–81 (translation modified).

10. Lauterbach, *Mekilta*, 1:57.

11. See Tosafot on Babylonian Talmud, *Ta'anit* 15b, and other rabbinic sources discussed in Niehoff, "The Return of Myth," and Segal, "Other Judaisms," p. 129.

12. Birnbaum, *Birnbaum Haggadah*, p. 94.

13. Justin Martyr, *Dialogue with Trypho* 40, available at http://www.earlychristianwritings.com/text/justinmartyr-dialoguetrypho.html (accessed on 31 July 2005); and see Tabory, "Crucifixion."

14. Routledge, *Passover and Last Supper*, p. 221.

15. Propp, "That Bloody Bridegroom," pp. 496–98.

16. Lauterbach, *Mekhilta*, 1:33–34.

17. Following the translation in *TANAKH: A New Translation.*

18. *Pirke de-Rabbi Eliezer* 29, quoted in Hoffman, p. 102.

CHAPTER 3

### Suggestions for Further Reading

With the generous permission of the editor, I have quoted freely from Melito, *On Pascha*, ed. Stuart G. Hall; stanza numbers appear in parentheses throughout the chapter, and I have on occasion deviated slightly from Hall's translation. I am grateful to Professor Hall for his permission to quote extensively from his work. Helpful studies of Melito and his poem *On Pascha* include: Lieu, *Image and Reality*, ch. 6; Stewart-Sykes, *Lamb's High Feast*; Cohick, "Melito of Sardis's *Peri Pascha*" and *Peri Pascha*; Hall, "Melito"; S. G. Wilson, "Passover, Easter, and Anti-Judaism"; and MacLennan, "Christian Self-Definition." For deicidal accusations against the Jews in the works of other church fathers, see Kampling, *Blut Christi*; and Sloyan, *Crucifixion*, ch. 3. On Jews and Christians in Sardis, the excavations there, and the evaluation of the archeological evidence, see also: Hanfmann, *Letters from Sardis*; Hanfmann et al., *Sardis from Prehistoric to Roman Times*; Kraabel, "Melito the Bishop," "Paganism and Judaism," "Social Systems," and "The Synagogue at Sardis"; Norris, "Melito's Motivation"; Trebilko, *Jewish Communities*; and Rajak, *Jewish Dialogue*, ch. 22. On Pesach and Pascha, see the essays collected in Bradshaw and Hoffman, *Passover and Easter*, and works cited in chapter 2. And on typology in the writings of the church fathers, see Young, "Typology," which includes numerous additional references.

### Notes

1. Justin Martyr, *Dialogue with Trypho* 32, available at http://www .earlychristianwritings.com/text/justinmartyr-dialoguetrypho.html (accessed on 1 August 2005); compare also chs. 67 and 76.
2. John Chrysostom, *Sermons against the Jews* 1.6, translated in Meeks and Wilken, *Jews and Christians*, p. 97.
3. For example: Werner, "Melito of Sardis."
4. See Cohick, *Peri Pascha*, pp. 1ff.
5. Eusebius, *Historia Ecclesiastica* 5.24.2–6, quoted in Melito, *On Pascha*, p. xi.
6. Kraabel and Seager, "Synagogue and the Jewish Community," p. 190.
7. Melito, *On Pascha*, pp. 74–75.
8. Wilken, "Something Greater than the Temple," pp. 190–91.
9. *Birnbaum Haggadah*, p. 97.
10. *Birnbaum Haggadah*, p. 93 (translation modified slightly).

CHAPTER 4

### Suggestions for Further Reading

I have considered the themes and texts discussed in this chapter at greater length in *Friars and the Jews,* "Jews as the Killers of Christ," and *Living Letters of the Law* (with extensive notes and bibliography). See also Watt, "Parisian Theologians"; and Resnick, "Talmud, 'talmudisti,' and Albert the Great."

## Notes

1. Augustine, *Enarrationes in Psalmos* 63.4, available at http://www.ccel .org/ccel/schaff/npnf108.pdf (64.4 in translation edition).
2. Kampling, *Blut Christi*, pp. 174–96.
3. Augustine, *Tractatus in Iohannem* 17.16, available at http://www.ccel .org/ccel/schaff/npnf107.pdf (accessed on 2 August 2005).
4. Augustine, *Tractatus in Iohannem* 18.2 (my translation, but compare text available at http://www.ccel.org/ccel/schaff/npnf107.pdf.
5. Anselm, *Cur Deus homo* 1.9, available at http://oll.libertyfund.org/ Texts/StAnselm0238/Proslogium/PDFs/0578_Pt05_CurDeus.pdf (accessed on 11 June 2006).
6. Peter Alfonsi, *Dialogue against the Jews* 10, pp. 220–238; I am grateful to Irven Resnick for sharing his translation with me in advance of its publication.
7. Abelard, *Ethics*, pp. 54–57 (translation modified slightly).
8. Abelard, *Ethics*, pp. 66–67.
9. Abelard, *Ethics*, pp. 62–63.
10. Available at http://www.fordham.edu/halsall/source/medievalstudentsongs .html (accessed on 2 August 2005).
11. Thomas Aquinas, *Summa theologica* 3.47.5 (my translation, but compare text at http://www.newadvent.org/summa/404705.htm); and see the additional passages quoted in Jeremy Cohen, *Living Letters of the Law*, pp. 374–75.
12. Duns Scotus, *In librum tertium Sententiarum*, d. 20, ad 5, cited in Jeremy Cohen, "Jews as the Killers of Christ," p. 20 n. 58.
13. Quoted in Linder, *Jews in Roman Imperial Legislation*, p. 190.
14. Augustine, *De civitate Dei* 18.46, my translation, but compare text at http://www.ccel.org/ccel/schaff/npnf102.pdf (accessed on 2 August 2005).
15. Augustine, *Enarrationes in Psalmos* 56.9, cited in Jeremy Cohen, *Living Letters*, p. 36 n. 34.
16. Grayzel, *Church and the Jews*, p. 275.
17. Grayzel, p. 115.
18. Shatzmiller, *Deuxième Controverse*, p. 54. See also Rajacs, *Zweite Talmudsdisputation*, pp. 222ff.
19. Raymond Martin, *Pugio fidei*, prooemium 5–9.
20. Raymond Martin, *Capistrum Iudaeorum*, 2:286–88.

## Chapter 5

### Suggestions for Further Reading

On the anti-Jewish libels of the Middle Ages, see, above all, the various essays in Langmuir, *Toward a Definition*; Hsia, *Myth of Ritual Murder*; Dundes, *Blood Libel Legend*; Yuval, *Two Nations*; Patterson, "Living Witnesses"; Ocker, "Ritual Murder";

and Buttaroni and Musial, *Ritual Murder*. On William of Norwich and Thomas of Monmouth, see also: Hillaby, "Ritual-Child-Murder Accusation"; McCulloh, "Jewish Ritual Murder"; and Jeffrey Cohen, "Flow of Blood." On Host-desecration charges: Browe, "Hostienschändungen der Juden"; Despina, "Accusations de profanation"; Rubin, *Corpus Christi* and *Gentile Tales*; Langmuir, "Tortures"; and Tanner, "Eucharist in the Ecumenical Councils." On the Holy Child of La Guardia: Fita, "Inquisición y el santo niño" and "Memoria del santo niño"; Lea, "El Santo Niño"; Baer, *History of the Jews*, 2:398–423; J. Edwards, *Jews in Western Europe*, pp. 104–16, and "Ritual Murder"; and Haliczer, "Jew as Witch." And on Jewish attitudes toward Christian holy objects and these charges against them: Horowitz, "'And It Was Reversed,'" "Medieval Jews," and *Reckless Rites*; and Yuval, "Language and Symbols" and "'They Tell Lies.'"

### Notes

1. Thomas of Monmouth, *Life and Miracles*, p. 10.
2. Thomas of Monmouth, *Life and Miracles*, p. 14.
3. Thomas of Monmouth, *Life and Miracles*, pp. 15–16 (translation modified).
4. Thomas of Monmouth, *Life and Miracles*, pp. 17–18.
5. Thomas of Monmouth, *Life and Miracles*, p. 18.
6. Thomas of Monmouth, *Life and Miracles*, p. 19.
7. Thomas of Monmouth, *Life and Miracles*, pp. 16ff.
8. Thomas of Monmouth, *Life and Miracles*, pp. 19–22 (translation modified).
9. Thomas of Monmouth, *Life and Miracles*, pp. 93–94.
10. Cohn, *Warrant for Genocide*.
11. Thomas of Monmouth, *Life and Miracles*, p. 22.
12. Thomas of Monmouth, *Life and Miracles*, pp. 24–25.
13. Thomas of Monmouth, *Life and Miracles*, p. 35.
14. Thomas of Monmouth, *Life and Miracles*, p. 88.
15. "William of Norwich," available at http://www.newadvent.org/cathen/15635a.htm (accessed on 03 August 2005).
16. Flannery, *Anguish of the Jews*, p. 100: "Some students of the question concede the possible existence of cases of ritual murder in the wide sense, as might happen in cases of aberration. It is not impossible that anti-Christian fanaticism and addiction to sorcery on the part of a Jew by chance converged and resulted in the murder of a Christian."
17. Anderson, *Saint at Stake*, ch. 9; and see Langmuir, *Toward a Definition*, pp. 292–93.
18. Langmuir, *Toward a Definition*, p. 296.
19. Cited in Ocker, "Ritual Murder," p. 176.
20. See Rubin, *Gentile Tales*, 45.
21. Grayzel, *Church and the Jews*, pp. 108–9 (emphasis added); see also p. 34 with n. 70.
22. Gregory of Tours, *Glory of the Martyrs*, pp. 29–30. See also the late

medieval illumination at http://www.chd.dk/gui/thott547_HV_gui.html (accessed on 25 June 2006).

23. Bynum, *Holy Feast*, p. 67.

24. http://home.inreach.com/bstanley/themass.htm (accessed on 31 March 2005).

25. http://www.piar.hu/councils/ecum12.htm#Confession%20of%20Faith (accessed on 3 August 2005).

26. "Dogma," http://www.newadvent.org/cathen/05089a.htm (accessed on 3 August 2005).

27. Grayzel, *Church and the Jews*, pp. 114–15.

28. See Baumgarten, *Mothers and Children*, esp. pp. 136–138.

29. Langmuir, "Tortures," pp. 303ff. (quotation on p. 307).

30. Lampert, "Once and Future Jew," p. 249.

31. Cited in Vauchez, "Laity in the Middle Ages," p. 148.

32. Hsia, *Trent 1475*, p. 89.

33. Ghetta, *Fra Bernadino Tomitano*, pp. 40–45, and see Hsia, pp. 53–56.

34. Hsia, *Trent 1475*, p. 90.

35. Grayzel, *Church and the Jews*, pp. 108–9.

36. Trachtenberg, *Devil and the Jews*, pp. 132–33.

37. Grayzel, *Church and the Jews*, pp. 270–71.

38. Grayzel, *Church and the Jews*, pp. 274–75.

39. Dr. Umayma Ahmad Al-Jalahma of King Faysal University in Al-Dammam, "The Jewish Holiday of Purim," *Ar-Riyadh* (Saudi government daily), March 10 and March 12, 2002, available at http://www.adl.org/Anti_semitism/arab/saudi_blood_l.asp.

## CHAPTER 6

### Suggestions for Further Reading

On the Crusades and the massacres of Jews that accompanied them, see: Riley-Smith, "First Crusade"; Abulafia, "Invectives against Christianity"; Chazan, *European Jewry* and *God, Humanity, and History*; Yuval, "Language and Symbols" and *Two Nations*; and Jeremy Cohen, *Sanctifying the Name*. On crusading sermons in particular: Cole, *Preaching of the Crusades*; and Maier, *Crusade Propaganda*.

On Passion-centered piety and religious devotion, among numerous others: Pelikan, *Jesus through the Centuries*; Kieckhefer, *Unquiet Souls* and "Major Currents"; Hundersmarck, "Preaching the Passion"; Despres, "Ghostly Sights"; Bestul, *Texts of the Passion*; Aers and Staley, *Powers of the Holy*; Hodapp, "Sacred Time and Sacred Space"; Swanson, "Passion and Practice"; Fulton, *From Judgment to Passion*; and Baraz, "Coincidence or Inescapable Development" and *Medieval Cruelty*.

On Luther, see M. Edwards, *Luther's Last Battles*; and Oberman, *Roots of Anti-Semitism*. On the Dreyfus Affair: Bredin, *Affair*; Stephen Wilson, *Ideology and Experience*; Kleeblatt, *Dreyfus Affair*; Lindemann, *Jew Accused*; Safran, "Dreyfus Affair"; and Forth, "Bodies of Christ" and *Dreyfus Affair*. And on the *Protocols of the Elders of Zion*: Cohn, *Warrant for Genocide*; Segel, *Lie and a Libel*; Vogt, *Historien om et Image*, esp. pp. 93–134; and Ben-Itto, *The Lie That Wouldn't Die*.

*Notes*

1. Morris, "Propaganda for War," p. 84.
2. Baldric of Bourgueil, *Historia Jerosolimitana*, quoted in Riley-Smith, "First Crusade," pp. 68–69.
3. Habermann, *Gezerot Ashkenaz ve-Tzarefat*, p. 93, trans. Eidelberg, *Jews and the Crusaders*, p. 99 (translation modified, emphasis added).
4. Benton, *Self and Society*, p. 134.
5. Habermann, *Gezerot Ashkenaz ve-Tzarefat*, p. 121; Eidelberg, *Jews and the Crusaders*, p. 130; and see Marcus, "Jews and Christians," pp. 212ff.
6. Habermann, *Gezerot Ashkenaz ve-Tzarefat*, p. 27.
7. Habermann, p. 43.
8. Peter the Venerable, *Letters*, 1:327–30.
9. Peter the Venerable, "Sermones tres," pp. 232–54.
10. Maier, *Crusade Propaganda and Ideology*, p. 187.
11. Quoted in Maier, pp. 204–5 (with parallels in the writings of Ambrose and Innocent III cited in n. 6).
12. Maier, pp. 206–7; see also Cole, *Preaching of the Crusades*.
13. Aers and Staley, *Powers of the Holy*, p. 17 (citing, but taking issue with, Rubin, *Corpus Christi*).
14. Bestul, *Texts of the Passion*, p. 84.
15. Bestul, p. 87, translation modified.
16. Bonaventure, *Works*, 1:116.
17. Bonaventure, 1:120.
18. Bonaventure, 1:158.
19. Bonaventure, 1:196.
20. Ragusa and Green, *Meditations on the Life of Christ*, p. 291.
21. *Meditations*, p. 298.
22. *Meditations*, p. 302.
23. *Meditations*, pp. 318–19.
24. *Meditations*, p. 5.
25. http://www.jesus-passion.com/THE_PASSION.htm#CHAPTER%20VIII (accessed on 4 August 2004), p. 158.
26. http://www.jesus-passion.com/THE_PASSION3 .htm#CHAPTER%20XXVIII (translation modified), p. 225.
27. Bonaventure, 1:97.
28. Bonaventure, 1:162.
29. Ragusa and Green, *Meditations on the Life of Christ*, p. 5.
30. See Henderson, "Flagellant Movement," p. 157.
31. Catherine of Siena, *Selected Writings*, p. 120.
32. Ragusa and Green, *Meditations on the Life of Christ*, p. 318.
33. Ludolph, *Praying the Life of Christ*, pp. 145–46.
34. Ludolph, pp. 155–56.
35. Kay, "Sublime Body."
36. Catherine of Siena, *Selected Writings*, p. 172.

37. Sloyan, *Crucifixion of Jesus*, pp. 1–2.
38. Luther, *Sermons on the Passion*, p. 72.
39. Luther, p. 49.
40. Luther, p. 75.
41. Luther, p. 137.
42. Among others, see McBride, "Gender and Judaism."
43. Hertzberg, *French Enlightenment*, p. 250.
44. See Paléologue, *My Secret Diary*, p. 43; Barrès, *Scènes et doctrines*, pp. 135–37 ("La Parade de Judas").
45. Barberot, "Pas de Juifs."
46. Paléologue, *My Secret Diary*, p. 105.
47. Meurin, *La franc-maçonnerie*, p. 165; Stephen Wilson, *Ideology and Experience*, p. 513.
48. Kedward, *Dreyfus Affair*, pp. 58, 77; Griffiths, *Use of Abuse*, ch. 6.
49. Stephen Wilson, *Ideology and Experience*, p. 148 n. 134; Quillard, *Monument Henry*, p. 498.
50. Larkin, *Church and State*, p. 77.
51. Christensen, "Cross of Gold." See also Koenig, *Bryan*; and C. M. Wilson, "Cross of Gold." On the anti-Jewish overtones of Bryan's rhetoric, see Handlin, *Adventure in Freedom*, p. 186, and Hofstadter, *Age of Reform*, pp. 77–82; but compare the opposing view of Nugent, *Tolerant Populists*, pp. 14–21.
52. Cohn, *Warrant for Genocide*, pp. 269ff.
53. *Protocols*, pp. 100, 127–28.

## CHAPTER 7

### Suggestions for Further Reading

This chapter develops themes I discussed previously in "Crucified Jesus." On Jewish attitudes toward Jesus and his Passion in classical and medieval sources, see: Krauss, *Das Leben Jesu*; Herford, *Christianity in Talmud and Midrash*; Lauterbach, *Rabbinic Essays* ("Jesus in the Talmud"); Horbury, "Trial of Jesus"; Berger, "On the Uses of History"; and Shinan, *Jesus through Jewish Eyes*. On Passover and the Haggadah, see the works cited in chapter 2, above all Yuval, *Two Nations*. On the Jewish martyrs of the First Crusade, see the citations in chapter 6, especially Jeremy Cohen, *Sanctifying the Name*. On attitudes toward Jesus and the Passion in the works of modern Jewish writers, see also Jacob, *Christianity through Jewish Eyes*; Weiss-Rosmarin, *Jewish Expressions on Jesus*; Berger, "Religion, Nationalism, and Historiography"; Catchpole, *Trial of Jesus*; and Rothschild, *Jewish Perspectives*. On the Jewish reclamation of Jesus in particular, see Croly, *Tarry Thou till I Come*; Lindeskog, *Jesusfrage im neuzeitlichen Judentum*; Lapide, *Israelis, Jews, and Jesus*; Hagner, *Jewish Reclamation*; Roskies, *Against the Apocalypse*, ch. 10; Berlin, *Defending the Faith*; and Heschel. *Abraham Geiger*. Compare also the material on various websites, including: www.shalom.org.uk/testimonies/jewsjesus.htm and www.jfjonline.org/pub/issues/04–05/jesusart.htm.

On Jesus in modern Jewish art—and especially in the work of Marc Chagall—see, above all, the work of Amishai-Meisels: "Origins of the Jewish Jesus," "Jewish Jesus," "Christological Symbolism," "Chagall's 'White Crucifixion,'" "Chagall's *Dedicated to Christ*," and *Depiction and Interpretation*, ch. 3. See also: Meyer, *Marc Chagall*; Cassou, *Chagall*, esp. ch. 8; Kagan, *Marc Chagall*, esp. ch. 5; and Simon, "Pedagogy and the Call to Witness," among many others. Finally, on the dynamics of Jewish acculturation and assimilation in a Christian environment, see Marcus, "Medieval Jewish Studies," "Jews and Christians," and *Rituals of Childhood,* which relate directly to the European Middle Ages but shed light on other periods as well.

## Notes

1. Available at http://www.adl.org/PresRele/ASUS_12/4291_12.htm (accessed 4 August 2005).
2. Shatzmiller, *Deuxième controverse*, p. 56.
3. Maitland, "Deacon and the Jewess," pp. 399–400.
4. Babylonian Talmud, *Sanhedrin* 43a.
5. Krauss, *Das Leben Jesu,* pp. 43–45; trans. Meier, "Polemical Function," pp. 27–28.
6. Berger, *Jewish-Christian Debate*, p. 136. See also Ben-Shalom, "Between Official and Private Dispute," pp. 24–29.
7. Lasker and Stroumsa, *Polemic of Nestor*, p. 102.
8. Kimhi, *Book of the Covenant*, pp. 76–77 (translation modified slightly).
9. Kimhi, pp. 77–78.
10. I thank Prof. Haggai Ben-Shammai for his suggestion.
11. Berger, *Jewish-Christian Debate*, p. 153.
12. Graetz, *History of the Jews*, 2:164–65.
13. Klausner, *Jesus of Nazareth*, p. 348.
14. Zeitlin, *Who Crucified Jesus?*, p. 172.
15. Rivkin, *What Crucified Jesus?*, pp. 116–17.
16. Hirsch, *Crucifixion*, pp. 61–62.
17. Goodman, *Synagogue and the Church*, p. 284.
18. Wise, *Martyrdom of Jesus*, pp. 132–33.
19. Habermann, *Gezerot Ashkenaz ve-Tzarefat*, p. 34.
20. Habermann, p. 32.
21. Habermann, p. 51.
22. Habermann, p. 39.
23. Horowitz, "'And It Was Reversed,'" pp. 141–42. See also his "Medieval Jews" and *Reckless Rites*.
24. S. Spiegel, *Last Trial*, pp. 148–49.
25. Asch, *Children of Abraham*, pp. 66–67.
26. Quoted in Roskies, *Against the Apocalypse,* p. 268. I am grateful to Simcha Davidovich for his help with the original Yiddish of this poem.
27. Quoted in Valencia, "Vision of Zion," p. 170 n. 30.
28. Quoted in Lapide, *Israelis, Jews, and Jesus*, pp. 12–13.
29. Hameiri, *Selected Stories*, pp. 72–88.

30. For photographs of Antokolsky's *Ecce homo* and the passages from the sculptor's letters quoted below, see Amishai-Meisels, "Jewish Jesus," pp. 92–95. The steep reproduction fees of the Tretyakov Gallery in Moscow prevented my including the image here.
31. Meyer, *Marc Chagall*, pp. 414–15.
32. Amishai-Meisels, "Jewish Jesus," pp. 102–3.

## CHAPTER 8

### Suggestions for Further Reading

Among the many pieces written on *Nostra Aetate* and the new Catholic attitude toward the Jewish role in the Crucifixion that the decree epitomized, see especially: Oesterreicher, "Declaration on the Relationship"; Herschcopf, "Church and the Jews"; Croner, *Stepping-Stones* and *More Stepping-Stones*; and Ruokanen, *Catholic Doctrine*. On the implementation and effectiveness of the *Nostra Aetate* doctrine, see also Klein, *Anti-Judaism in Christian Theology*, pp. 92–126, 150–55; Wigoder, "Jewish Reaction"; Van Eijk, "Jewish People"; Prusak, "Jews and the Death of Jesus"; O'Connor, "Universality of Salvation"; and Hayes, "From *Nostra Aetate* to 'We Remember,'" among others.

### Notes

1. http://www.vatican.va/archive/hist_councils/ii_vatican_council/ documents/vat-ii_decl_19651028_nostra-aetate_en.html (accessed on 25 July 2005).
2. I have traced the developing interpretation of this passage in "The Mystery of Israel's Salvation."
3. Oesterreicher, "Declaration on the Relationship," pp. 2–4 n. 2.
4. Bishop, "How Catholics Look at Jews," pp. 12–15; and see also Herschcopf, "Church and the Jews" (1965), pp. 106–7.
5. Glock and Stark, *Christian Beliefs*, p. 54.
6. Pawlikowski, "Shoah: Its Challenges," p. 444.
7. Littell, "'Christendom' and the Holocaust," p. 83.
8. Littell, *Crucifixion of the Jews*, pp. 40–41.
9. James O'Gara, quoted in Herschcopf, "Church and the Jews" (1965), p. 108.
10. Herschcopf, "Church and the Jews" (1965), p. 106.
11. http://www.jcrelations.net/en/?id=1489 (accessed on 8 August 2005).
12. http://www.jcrelations.net/en/?id=1492 (accessed on 8 August 2005).
13. Quoted in Herschcopf, "Church and the Jews" (1965), p. 111.
14. Herschcopf, "Church and the Jews" (1965), p. 135.
15. Quoted in Oesterreicher, "Declaration on the Relationship," p. 102.
16. The evolution of the Vatican decree through its stages can be followed in Oesterreicher, "Declaration on the Relationship"; Herschcopf, "Church and the Jews"; and Ruokanen, *Catholic Doctrine*, pp. 35–44, 121–31.

17. Herschcopf, "Church and the Jews" (1966), p. 57.
18. http://www.vatican.va/roman_curia/pontifical_councils/chrstuni/relations-jews-docs/rc_pc_chrstuni_doc_19741201_nostra-aetate_en.html (accessed on 25 July 2005).
19. Quoted in Croner, *More Stepping-Stones*, p. 86.
20. Croner, *More Stepping-Stones*, p. 70.
21. http://www.vatican.va/roman_curia/pontifical_councils/chrstuni/relations-jews-docs/rc_pc_chrstuni_doc_19820306_jews-judaism_en.html (accessed on 25 July 2005).
22. http://www.bc.edu/bc_org/research/cjl/Documents/John_Paul_II/romesynagogue.htm (accessed on 8 August 2005).
23. Herschcopf, "Church and the Jews" (1966), p. 67.
24. Brunett, "Crossing the Threshold," p. 378.
25. Fisher, "Evolution of a Tradition," p. 41.
26. http://academics.smcvt.edu/pcouture/Interview%20with%20Eugene%20Fisher.htm (accessed on 27 December 2004).
27. http://www.kensmen.com/catholic/jewsvaticanii.html (accessed on 27 December 2004).
28. http://www.crc-internet.org/lib3main.htm (accessed on 27 December 2004).
29. http://www.the-pope.com/church02.html (accessed on 27 December 2004).
30. Carroll, *Constantine's Sword*, p. 552.
31. Fisher, review of Carroll, *Constantine's Sword*, and Cohen, *Living Letters of the Law*, pp. 302–3.
32. Eugene Carson Blake, quoted in Herschcopf, "Church and the Jews" (1966), p. 71.
33. Polish, "Very Small Lever"; see also Riegner, "Twenty Years of *Nostra Aetate*."
34. Klenicki, "From Argument to Dialogue," p. 89.
35. Dietrich, "Nostra Aetate."
36. Quoted in *New York Times*, 8 April 1965, p. 2.
37. Bea, *Church and the Jewish People*, p. 68.
38. Bea, pp. 68–70.
39. Bea, pp. 100–101.
40. See the discussion of Jesus' Jewish crucifiers' intentions in chapter 4.
41. Bea, p. 159.
42. Bristow, *No Religion Is an Island*, pp. 56–99 (quotations on pp. 67 and 79).

CHAPTER 9

*Suggestions for Further Reading*

This chapter draws extensively from Blumenkranz, *Juif médiéval*; Seiferth, *Synagogue and Church*; Schreckenberg, *Jews in Christian Art*; Mellinkoff, *Outcasts*; Shachar,

*Judensau*; Marrow, *Passion Iconography*; Rubin, *Gentile Tales*; and Strickland, *Saracens, Demons, and Jews.* On the development and function of early Christian art, see also Grabar, *Christian Iconography*; Duggan, "Was Art Really the 'Book of the Illiterate'?"; Hahn, "*Visio Dei*"; Caviness, "Biblical Stories"; Jensen, *Understanding Early Christian Art*; and Chazelle, *Crucified God.* And on Passion-centered religious devotion, see Derbes, *Picturing the Passion*, along with works cited in the notes to chapter 6.

### Notes

1. Clark, *Moments of Vision*, p. 40.
2. Both the Latin original and an English translation of Gregory's letters appear in Chazelle, "Pictures, Books, and the Illiterate," pp. 139–40; I have deviated very slightly from Chazelle's translation. See Kessler, "Pictorial Narrative," pp. 76, 89, for precedents to Gregory's statements.
3. See Blumenkranz, *Juif médiéval*, p. 38. (Regrettably, I was not able to secure permission to reproduce this image.)
4. For instance, Mellinkoff, *Outcasts*, pl. i.44.
5. Schreckenberg, *Jews in Christian Art*, pp. 160, 164; Mellinkoff, *Outcasts*, pl. i.49.
6. Pickering, *Essays on Medieval German Literature*, p. 3.
7. See esp. Marrow, *Passion Iconography*, ch. 4.
8. Mellinkoff, *Outcasts*, pl. viii.5.
9. See chapter 4, n. 11 (emphasis mine).
10. See the description in Rubin, *Gentile Tales*, pp. 155–60.
11. On the attribution of the painting, see Mellinkoff, *Outcasts*, 1:297 n. 110.
12. Mellinkoff, *Outcasts*, 1:157.
13. De Tolnay, *Hieronymus Bosch*, p. 352. On the beetles (or scorpions) in particular, see Linfert, *Hieronymus Bosch*, p. 70; and Bulard, *Scorpion*, pp. 147, 299. I am grateful to Lilah Mittelstaedt, reference librarian of the Philadelphia Museum of Art, for her guidance in this regard.
14. Shachar, *Judensau*, pp. 93–94 (with slight modifications in the translation).
15. See, for example, Jordan, "Last Tormentor" and "Erosion of the Stereotype"; Rohrbacher, "Charge of Deicide"; and, more generally, Nirenberg, *Communities of Violence.*

## CHAPTER 10

### Suggestions for Further Reading

On the origins of the Passion play and its development over the course of the Middle Ages, the following have proved helpful: Hardison, *Christian Rite*; Flanigan, "Roman Rite"; James, "Ritual, Drama, and Social Body"; Warning, "On the Alterity of Medieval Religious Drama"; Vince, *Ancient and Medieval Theatre*; Harris, *Medieval Theatre*; Muir, *Biblical Drama*; and, especially with regard to the dramatization of physical pain and torture, Plesch, "*Etalage complaisant?*" and "Notes for the Staging," and

Sponsler, *Drama and Resistance*, ch. 6. On the portrayal of Jews in medieval Passion plays, see Dox, "Representation without Referent"; Jones, "The Place of the Jews"; Enders, "Dramatic Memories and Tortured Spaces," *Death by Drama*, and "Theater Makes History"; and Martin, *Representations of Jews*.

For the text of the play at Oberammergau, I have quoted from Drew, *Passion Play of Ober-Ammergau*; and Lane and Brenson, *Oberammergau: A Passion Play*. On the play's development, analysis, and influence, see Heaton, *Oberammergau Passion Play*; Friedman, *Oberammergau Passion Play*; Shapiro, *Oberammergau*; Sponsler, *Ritual Imports*, ch. 8; and Laws, "Witness to/for the Persecution." On the anti-Judaism of the play, see also Tanenbaum, *Oberammergau 1960 and 1970*; Swidler and Sloyan, *Commentary on the Oberammergau Passionsspiel, Oberammergau Passionsspiel*, and "Passion of the Jew Jesus"; Klein, "Gospel Distorted"; Kelley, "Progress and Problems"; and Mork, "1984 Oberammergau Passion Play," "Oberammergau Passion Play," and "Wicked Jews."

### Notes

1. http://home.inreach.com/bstanley/themass.htm (accessed on 8 August 2005).
2. Quoted in Baxandall, *Painting and Experience*, p. 46.
3. Stanley, *Book of Margery Kempe*, pp. 139–40.
4. Quoted in Friedman, *Oberammergau Passion Play*, p. 117.
5. Kissel, "Politics and Play Reform."
6. Drew, *Passion Play of Ober-Ammergau*, p. 23.
7. Drew, p. 6.
8. Lane and Brenson, *Oberammergau: A Passion Play*, p. 112.
9. Shafer, *Oberammergau Passion Play*, p. 65.
10. Augustine, *Contra Faustum* 12.12–13 (my translation). Compare also http://www.ccel.org/ccel/schaff/npnf104.iv.ix.XII.html#iv.ix.XII-Page_187 (accessed on 8 August 2005).
11. Sellar, "The Passion Play," p. 392, cited in Shapiro, *Oberammergau*, p. 77. Sellar's ensuing comments (pp. 393–95) on Judas and on his own perspective as a white Anglo-Saxon Protestant on the staging of the Passion are no less interesting.
12. Krauskopf, *Rabbi's Impressions*, p. 60.
13. Krauskopf, pp. 132–33.
14. Krauskopf, p. 36.
15. Lane and Brenson, *Oberammergau: A Passion Play*, p. 39.
16. Drew, *Passion Play of Ober-Ammergau*, p. 3.
17. Drew, p. 6.
18. Drew, p. 12.
19. Drew, p. 42.
20. Drew, p. 26.
21. Drew, p. 72.
22. See Friedman, *Oberammergau Passion Play*, pp. 89ff.

23. Drew, *Passion Play of Ober-Ammergau*, p. 98.
24. Drew, pp. 99–101.
25. Drew, p. 105.
26. Drew, p. 99 n.
27. Drew, p. 85.
28. Drew, p. 94.
29. Drew, p. 105.
30. Shapiro, *Oberammergau*, p. 223.
31. Shafer, *Oberammergau Passion Play*, p. 7.
32. Shapiro, *Oberammergau*, p. 83.
33. Shapiro, p. 218.
34. See, for example, the assertion of Heaton, *Oberammergau Passion Play*, p. 115, that only three lines in the play are not grounded in Scripture.
35. Laws, "Power and the Glory," p. 100.

## CHAPTER 11

### Suggestions for Further Reading

On the portrayal of biblical themes and issues in film, see Miles, *Seeing and Believing*; Marsh and Ortiz, *Explorations in Theology and Film*; Plate, "Religion/Literature/Film"; and Reinhartz, *Scripture on the Silver Screen*—among many others. Valuable studies of the Passion story on screen include: Singer, "Cinema Savior"; Hurley, "Cinematic Transfigurations of Jesus"; Telford, "New Testament in Fiction and Film" and "Jesus Christ Movie Star"; Kreitzer, *New Testament in Fiction and Film* and *Gospel Images in Fiction and Film*; Babington and Evans, *Biblical Epics*; Stern et al., *Savior on the Silver Screen*; Tatum, *Jesus at the Movies*; Mahan, "Celluloid Savior"; and Walsh, *Reading the Gospels in the Dark*. I have benefited considerably from the essays of Reinhartz: "Jesus in Film," "Scripture on the Silver Screen," "Jesus of Hollywood," "From D. W. Griffith to Mel Gibson," and "Passion-ate Moments." On Mel Gibson's *Passion* and its reception in the community, I have drawn from the insightful studies of Berger, "Jews, Christians, and 'The Passion'"; Silk, "Gibson's Passion"; Hollywood, "Kill Jesus"; Ohad-Karny, "'Anticipating' Gibson's *The Passion*"; and Laws, "Witness to/for the Persecution."

### Notes

1. Laws, "Witness to/for the Persecution."
2. Miles, *Seeing and Believing*, pp. 30ff.
3. Stern et al., *Savior on the Silver Screen*, p. 105.
4. Tatum, *Jesus at the Movies*, p. 112.
5. Stack, *Pasolini on Pasolini*, p. 83.
6. Stack, p. 76.
7. http://biz.yahoo.com/ic/116/116730.html (accessed on 26 May 2005).
8. McCarthy, "*The Gospel of John*," p. 24.
9. Babington and Evans, *Biblical Epics*, p. 168.

10. Years ago, I secured a copy of the letter (dated 22 August 1988) from the offices of the Anti-Defamation League in Columbus, Ohio.
11. According to the *Pittsburgh Press*, 3 September 1988, Maximos explained several days after distributing his letter that he did not intend to refer to the Jews but to the novelist Nikos Kazantzakis, author of *The Last Temptation*.
12. *New York Times*, 5 August 1988, p. C13.
13. Stern et al., *Savior on the Silver Screen*, p. 287f.
14. Reinhartz, "Jesus in Film," par. 28.
15. Stern et al., *Savior on the Silver Screen*, p. 325.
16. http://www.ncsj.org/AuxPages/061303JWeek_MGibson_Passion.shtml (accessed on 9 August 2005).
17. Michael Medved in *USA Today*, 22 July 2003, p. A13.
18. *Jerusalem Post* editorial, 24 August 2003, p. 6.
19. http://www.bible.com/jesus/PassionMelQuotes.html (accessed on 12 June 2005).
20. See Angela of Foligno, *Complete Works*, pp. 230ff., 268ff.
21. Laws, "Witness," has suggested a direct influence of the Oberammergau play on the Gibson film.
22. *Guide to the Passion*, p. 3.
23. http://www.ctu.edu/WhatWeHaveToSay/Passion_Catholic.htm (accessed on 8 June 2005).
24. Fisher, "The Bible, the Jews, and the Passion."
25. http://www.usccb.org/movies/p/thepassionofthechrist.htm (accessed on 8 June 2005).
26. Fisher, "After the Maelstrom."

## CONCLUSION

### Suggestions for Further Reading

The works on Judas and his career from which I have drawn include: Halas, *Judas Iscariot*; Lüthi, *Judas Iskarioth*; Dieckmann, *Judas als Sündenbock*; Vogler, *Judas Iskarioth*; Hughes, "Framing Judas"; Maccoby, *Judas Iscariot*; Ohly, *Damned and the Elect*; Klassen, *Judas*; Paffenroth, *Judas*; Kasser et al., *The Gospel of Judas*. On biblical and mythological precedents for the character of Judas, see also Forsyth, *Old Enemy*; and Briskin, "Foretold, Fulfilled, Copied" and "Tanakh Sources." On Judas in medieval literature, folklore, and art: Baum, "Medieval Legend"; Mellinkoff, "Judas's Red Hair"; Wolf, "Judas Legend"; Axton, "Interpretations of Judas"; Morey, "Adam and Judas"; Braswell, "Chaucer's Palimpsest"; Paffenroth, "Film Depictions of Judas"; Pyper, "Modern Gospels of Judas"; Weber, "The Hanged Judas"; and Limor and Yuval, "Oedipus in Christian Garb."

### Notes

1. Dante, *Divine Comedy: Inferno* 34:55–63, available at http://www.divinecomedy.org/divine_comedy.html.

2. See Paffenroth, *Judas*.
3. Barth, *Church Dogmatics*, 2,2:464–65.
4. Barth, *Church Dogmatics*, 2:464–65.
5. Paffenroth, *Judas*, p. 53, but compare pp. 139–42.
6. Steiner, *No Passion Spent*, p. 417.
7. Kermode, *Genesis of Secrecy*, pp. 84–95.

# BIBLIOGRAPHY

Abelard, Peter. *Ethics*. Ed. D. E. Luscombe. Oxford, 1971.

Abulafia, Anna Sapir. "Invectives against Christianity in the Hebrew Chronicles of the First Crusade." In *Crusade and Settlement*, pp. 66–72. Ed. P. W. Edbury. Cardiff, 1985.

Aers, David, and Lynn Staley. *The Powers of the Holy: Religion, Politics, and Gender in Late Medieval English Culture*. University Park, Pa., 1996.

Alexander, T. Desmond. "The Passover Sacrifice." In *Sacrifice in the Bible*, pp. 1–24. Ed. Roger T. Beckwith and Martin J. Selman. Carlisle, Eng., 1995.

Amishai-Maisels, Ziva. "Chagall's *Dedicated to Christ*: Sources and Meanings." *Jewish Art* 21–22 (1995), 69–94.

———. "Chagall's 'White Crucifixion.'" *Art Institute of Chicago: Museum Studies* 17 (1991), 139–153.

———. "Christological Symbolism of the Holocaust." *Holocaust and Genocide Studies* 3 (1988), 457–481.

———. *Depiction and Interpretation: The Influence of the Holocaust on the Visual Arts*. Oxford, 1993.

———. "The Jewish Jesus." *Journal of Jewish Art* 9 (1982), 84–104.

———. "Origins of the Jewish Jesus." In *Complex Identities: Jewish Consciousness and Modern Art*, pp. 51–86. Ed. Matthew Baigell and Milly Heyd. New Brunswick, N.J., 2001.

Anderson, M. D. *A Saint at Stake: The Strange Death of William of Norwich, 1144*. London, 1964.

Angela of Foligno. *Complete Works*. Ed. Paul Lachance. New York, 1993.

Asch, Sholem. *The Children of Abraham: The Short Stories of Sholem Asch*. Trans. Maurice Samuel. New York, 1942.

Axton, Richard. "Interpretations of Judas in Middle English Literature." In *Religion in the Poetry and Drama of the Late Middle Ages in England*, pp. 179–197. Ed. Piero Boitani and Anna Torti. Woodbridge, Eng., 1990.

Babington, Bruce, and Peter William Evans. *Biblical Epics: Sacred Narrative in the Hollywood Cinema*. Manchester, Eng., 1993.

Baer, Yitzhak. *A History of the Jews in Christian Spain*. Trans. Louis Schoffman et al. 2 vols. Philadelphia, 1961–1966.

Bahr, Gordon J. "The Seder of Passover and the Eucharistic Words." *Novum Testamentum* 12 (1970), 181–202.

Baraz, Daniel. "Coincidence or Inescapable Development: The Cruelty of Jews in Christian Eyes, 12th–15th Centuries" [in Hebrew]. *Historia* (2002), 95–115.

———. *Medieval Cruelty: Changing Perceptions, Late Antiquity to the Early Modern Period*. Ithaca, N.Y., 2003.

Barberot, O. "Pas de Juifs dans les rangs." *La libre parole* 2:75 (15 December 1894), 4.

Barrès, Maurice. *Scènes et doctrines du nationalisme*. Paris, 1902.

Barth, Karl. *Church Dogmatics*. Trans. G. T. Thomson et al. Ed. G. W. Bromiley and T. F. Torrance. 2 vols. in 4 pts. Edinburgh, 1956–1969.

Baum, Paul Franklin. "The Medieval Legend of Judas Iscariot." *Publications of the Modern Language Association* 31 (1916), 481–631.

Baumgarten, Elisheva. *Mothers and Children: Jewish Family Life in Medieval Europe.* Princeton, N.J., 2004.

Baxandall, Michael. *Painting and Experience in Fifteenth-Century Italy: A Primer in the Social History of Pictorial Style.* 2nd ed. Oxford, 1988.

Bea, Augustin. *The Church and the Jewish People.* Trans. Philip Loretz. New York, 1966.

Beckwith, Roger T. "The Death of Christ as a Sacrifice in the Teaching of Paul and Hebrews." In *Sacrifice in the Bible*, pp. 130–135. Ed. Roger T. Beckwith and Martin J. Selman. Carlisle, Eng., 1995.

Ben-Itto, Hadassah. *The Lie That Wouldn't Die: The Protocols of the Elders of Zion.* London, 2005.

Ben-Shalom, Ram. "Between Official and Private Dispute: The Case of Christian Spain and Provence in the Middle Ages." *AJS Review* 27 (2003), 23–72.

Benton, John F., ed. *Self and Society in Medieval France: The Memoirs of Abbot Guibert of Nogent.* New York, 1970.

Bergant, Dianne. "An Anthropological Approach to Biblical Interpretation: The Passover Supper in Exodus 12:1–20 as a Case Study." *Semeia* 67 (1994), 43–62.

Berger, David. "Jews, Christians, and 'The Passion.'" *Commentary* 117 (2004), 23–31.

———. "On the Uses of History in Medieval Jewish Polemic against Christianity: The Quest for the Historical Jesus." In *Jewish History and Jewish Memory Essays in Honor of Yosef Hayim Yerushalmi*, pp. 25–39. Ed. Elisheva Carlebach, John M. Efron, and David N. Myers. Hanover and London, 1998.

———. "Religion, Nationalism, and Historiography: Yehezkel Kaufmann's Account of Jesus and Early Christianity." In *Scholars and Scholarship: The Interaction between Judaism and other Cultures*, pp. 149–168. Ed. Leo Landman. New York, 1990.

Berger, David, ed. *The Jewish-Christian Debate in the High Middle Ages: A Critical Edition of the* Nizzahon Vetus. Philadelphia, 1979.

Berlin, George L. *Defending the Faith: Nineteenth-Century American Jewish Writings on Christianity and Jesus.* Albany, N.Y., 1989.

Bestul, Thomas H. *Texts of the Passion: Latin Devotional Literature and Medieval Society.* Philadelphia, 1996.

Bieringer, Reimund, et al., eds. *Anti-Judaism and the Fourth Gospel: Papers of the Leuven Colloquium, 2000.* Assen, 2001.

Birnbaum, Philip, ed. *The Birnbaum Haggadah.* New York, 1953.

———. *High Holyday Prayer Book.* New York, 1951.

Bishop, Claire Huchet. *How Catholics Look at Jews: Inquiries into Italian, Spanish, and French Teaching Materials.* New York, 1974.

Blumenkranz, Bernhard. *Le Juif médiéval au miroir de l'art chrétien.* Paris, 1966.

Bokser, Baruch M. *The Origins of the Seder: The Passover Rite and Early Rabbinic Judaism.* Berkeley, 1984.

Bonaventure. *The Works of Bonaventure.* Ed. José de Vinck. 5 vols. Paterson, N.J., 1960–1970.

Bradshaw, Paul, and Lawrence A. Hoffman, eds. *Passover and Easter: Origin and History to Modern Times*. Notre Dame, Ind., 1999.

Brandon, S. G. F. *The Trial of Jesus*. London, 1968.

Braswell, Mary Flowers. "Chaucer's Palimpsest: Judas Iscariot and the *Pardoner's Tale.*" *Chaucer Review* 29 (1995), 303–310.

Bredin, Jean-Denis. *The Affair: The Case of Alfred Dreyfus*. Trans. Jeffrey Mehlman. London, 1987.

Briskin, Lawrence. "Foretold, Fulfilled, Copied." *Jewish Bible Quarterly* 31 (2003), 117–125.

———. "Tanakh Sources of Judas Iscariot." *Jewish Bible Quarterly* 32 (2004), 189–197.

Bristow, Edward, ed. *No Religion Is an Island: The Nostre Aetate Dialogues*. New York, 1998.

Browe, Peter. "Die Hostienschändungen der Juden im Mittelalter." *Römische Quartalschrift für christliche Altertumskunde und für Kirchengeschichte* 34 (1926), 167–197.

Brown, Raymond E. *The Death of the Messiah: From Gethsemane to the Grave*. 2 vols. New York, 1994.

Brunett, Alexander J. "Crossing the Threshold of Catholic-Jewish Relations." *Journal of Ecumenical Studies* 34 (1997), 377–383.

Buckley, Jorunn Jacobsen. "A Matter of Urgency: A Response to 'The Passover Supper in Exodus 12:1–20.'" *Semeia* 67 (1994), 63–71.

Bulard, Marcel. *Le scorpion: Symbole du peuple juif dans l'art religieux des xiv^e, xv^e, xvi^e siècles*. Paris, 1935.

Burridge, Kenelm. *New Heaven, New Earth: A Study of Millenarian Activities*. Oxford, 1969.

Buttaroni, Susanna, and Stanislaw Musial, eds. *Ritual Murder: Legend in European History*. Cracow, 2003.

Bynum, Caroline Walker. *Holy Feast and Holy Fast: The Religious Significance of Food to Medieval Women*. Berkeley, Calif., 1987.

Carroll, James. *Constantine's Sword: The Church and the Jews, a History*. Boston, 2001.

Carroll, John T., Joel B. Green, et al. *The Death of Jesus in Early Christianity*. Peabody, Mass., 1995.

Cassou, Jean. *Chagall*. New York, 1965.

Catchpole, David R. *The Trial of Jesus: A Study in the Gospels and Jewish Historiography from 1770 to the Present Day*. Leiden, 1971.

Catherine of Siena. *Selected Writings of St Catherine of Siena*. Ed. Kenelm Foster. London, 1980.

Caviness, Madeline H. "Biblical Stories in Windows: Were They Bibles for the Poor?" In *The Bible in the Middle Ages: Its Influence in Literature and Art*, pp. 103–147. Ed. Bernard S. Levy. Binghamton, N.Y., 1992.

Chazan, Robert. *European Jewry and the First Crusade*. Berkeley, Calif., 1987.

———. *God, Humanity, and History: The Hebrew First Crusade Narratives*. Berkeley, Calif., 2000.

Chazelle, Celia M. *The Crucified God in the Carolingian Era*. Cambridge, Eng., 2001.
———. "Pictures, Books, and the Illiterate: Pope Gregory I's Letters to Serenus of Marseilles." *Word and Image* 6 (1990), 138–153.
Chilton, Bruce and Craig A. Evans, eds. *Studying the Historical Jesus: Evaluations of the State of Current Research*. Leiden, 1998.
Christensen, William E. "The Cross of Gold Reburnished: A Contemporary Account of the 1896 Democratic Convention." *Nebraska History* 77 (1996), 119–123.
Clark, Kenneth. *Moments of Vision and Other Essays*. New York, 1981.
Cohen, Jeffrey Jerome. "The Flow of Blood in Medieval Norwich." *Speculum* 79 (2004), 26–65.
Cohen, Jeremy. "The Crucified Jesus, Jewish Memory, and Counter-History" [in Hebrew]. *Zmanim* 68–69 (1999), 12–29.
———. *The Friars and the Jews: The Evolution of Medieval Anti-Judaism*. Ithaca, N.Y., 1982.
———. "The Jews as the Killers of Christ in the Latin Tradition, from Augustine to the Friars." *Traditio* 39 (1983), 1–27.
———. *Living Letters of the Law: Ideas of the Jew in Medieval Christianity*. Berkeley, Calif., 1999.
———. "The Mystery of Israel's Salvation: Romans 11:25–26 in Patristic and Medieval Exegesis." *Harvard Theological Review* 98 (2005), 247–81.
———. *Sanctifying the Name of God: Jewish Martyrs and Jewish Memories of the First Crusade*. Philadelphia, 2004.
Cohick, Lynn H. "Melito of Sardis's *Peri Pascha* and Its 'Israel.'" *Harvard Theological Review* 91 (1998), 351–372.
———. *The* Peri Pascha *Attributed to Melito of Sardis: Setting, Purpose, and Sources*. Providence, R.I., 2000.
Cohn, Norman. *Warrant for Genocide: The Myth of the Jewish World Conspiracy and the Protocols of the Elders of Zion*. London, 1967.
Cole, Penny J. *The Preaching of the Crusades to the Holy Land, 1095–1270*. Cambridge, Mass., 1991.
Croly, George. *Tarry Thou till I Come: Or Salthiel, the Wandering Jew*. New York, 1901.
Croner, Helga, ed. *More Stepping-Stones to Jewish-Christian Relations: An Unabridged Collection of Christian Documents 1975–1983*. New York, 1985.
———. *Stepping-Stones to Further Jewish-Christian Relations*. London, 1977.
Crossan, John Dominic. *Who Killed Jesus? Exposing the Roots of Anti-Semitism in the Gospel Story of the Death of Jesus*. San Francisco, 1995.
Daly, Robert J. "The Soteriological Significance of the Sacrifice of Isaac." *Catholic Biblical Quarterly* 39 (1977), 45–75.
Davies, Philip R. "Passover and the Dating of the Aqedah." *Journal of Jewish Studies* 30 (1979), 59–67.
Davies, Philip R., and Bruce D. Chilton. "The Aqedah: A Revised Tradition-History." *Catholic Biblical Quarterly* 40 (1978), 514–546.
Davis, Ellen F. "Exploding the Limits: Form and Function in Psalm 22." *Journal for the Study of the Old Testament* 53 (1992), 93–105.

Davis, Frederick B. *The Jew and Deicide: The Origin of an Archetype.* Lanham, Md., 2003.

Derbes, Anne. *Picturing the Passion in Late Medieval Italy: Narrative Painting, Franciscan Ideologies, and the Levant.* Cambridge, Eng., 1996.

Despina, Marie. "Les accusations de profanation contre d'hosties portées contre les Juifs." *Rencontre: Chrétiens et Juifs* 5 (1971), 150–191.

Despres, Denise. *Ghostly Sights: Visual Meditation in Late-Medieval Literature.* Norman, Okla., 1989.

De Tolnay, Charles. *Hieronymus Bosch.* Trans. Michael Bullock and Henry Mins. London, 1966.

*Dictionary of the History of Ideas.* 5 vols. New York, 1973–1974.

Dieckmann, Bernhard. *Judas als Sündenbock: Ene verhängnisvolle Geschichte von Angst und Vergeltung.* Munich, 1991.

Dietrich, Wendell. "Nostra Aetate: A Typology of Theological Tendencies." In *Unanswered Questions: Theological Views of Jewish-Catholic Relations,* pp. 70–81. Ed. Roger Brooks. Notre Dame, Ind., 1988.

Dorival, Gilles, et al. *David, Jésus et la reine Esther: Recherches sur le Psaume 21 (22 TM).* Paris, 2002.

Dox, Donnalee. "Representation without Referent: The Jew in Medieval English Drama." Ph.D. diss., University of Minnesota, 1995.

Drew, Mary Frances, ed. *The Passion Play of Ober-Ammergau: The Great Atonement at Golgotha.* London, 1910.

Dudley, Carl S., and Earle Hilgert. *New Testament Tensions and the Contemporary Church.* Philadelphia, 1987.

Duggan, Lawrence G. "Was Art Really the 'Book of the Illiterate'?" *Word and Image* 5 (1989), 227–251.

Dundes, Alan, ed. *The Blood Libel Legend: A Casebook in Anti-Semitic Folklore.* Madison, Wisc., 1991.

———. *Sacred Narrative: Readings in the Theory of Myth.* Berkeley, Calif., 1984.

Edwards, John. "Ritual Murder in the Siglo de Oro: Lope de Vega's *El niño inocente de La Guardia.*" In *The Proceedings of the Tenth British Conference on Judeo-Spanish Studies,* pp. 73–88. Ed. Annette Benaim. London, 1999.

———, ed. *The Jews in Western Europe, 1400–1600.* Manchester, Eng., 1994.

Edwards, Mark U. *Luther's Last Battles: Politics and Polemics, 1531–46.* Ithaca, N.Y., 1983.

Eidelberg, Shlomo, ed. *The Jews and the Crusaders.* Madison, Wisc., 1977.

Enders, Jody. *Death by Drama and Other Medieval Urban Legends.* Chicago, 2002.

———. "Dramatic Memories and Tortured Spaces in the Mistere de Sainte Hostie." In *Medieval Practices of Space,* pp. 199–222. Ed. Barabara A. Hanawalt and Michal Kobialka. Minneapolis, 2000.

———. "Theater Makes History: Ritual Murder by Proxy in the *Mistere de la Sainte Hostie.*" *Speculum* 79 (2004), 991–1016.

Etheridge, J. W., ed. The Targums of Onkelos and Jonathan ben Uzziel on the Pentateuch. 2 vols. in 1. New York, 1968.

Farmer, William, ed. *Anti-Judaism and the Gospels.* Harrisburg, Pa., 1999.

Festinger, Leon, Henry W. Riecken, and Stanley Schacter. *When Prophecy Fails*. Minneapolis, 1956.

Fisher, Eugene J. "After the Maelstrom." *America* 190:12 (2004), 12–14.

———. "The Bible, the Jews, and the Passion." *America* 190:5 (2004), 7–9.

———. "The Evolution of a Tradition: From *Nostra Aetate* to the 'Notes.'" *Christian Jewish Relations* 18 (1985), 32–47.

———. Review of James Carroll, *Constantine's Sword*, and Jeremy Cohen, *Living Letters of the Law*, in *Catholic Historical Review* 87 (2001), 302–3.

Fisk, Bruce N. "Offering Isaac Again and Again: Pseudo-Philo's Use of the Akedah as Intertext." *Catholic Biblical Quarterly* 63 (2000), 481–507.

Fita, Fidel. "La Inquisición y el santo niño de La Guardia." *Boletín de la Real Academia de la Historia* 11 (1887), 7–134.

———. "Memoria del santo niño de la Gurdia." *Boletín de la Real Academia de la Historia* 11 (1887), 135–160.

Flanigan, C. Clifford. "The Roman Rite and the Origins of the Liturgical Drama." *University of Toronto Quarterly* 43 (1974), 263–284.

Flannery, Edward. *Anguish of the Jews*. New York, 1965.

Flusser, David, in collaboration with R. Steven Notley. *Jesus*. Jerusalem, 1997.

Forsyth, Neil. *The Old Enemy: Satan and the Combat Myth*. Princeton, N.J., 1987.

Forth, Christopher E. "Bodies of Christ: Gender, Jewishness, and Religious Imagery in the Dreyfus Affair." *History Workshop Journal* 48 (1999), 16–39.

———. *The Dreyfus Affair and the Crisis of French Manhood*. Baltimore, 2004.

Fredriksen, Paula. *From Jesus to Christ: The Origins of the New Testament Images of Jesus*. 2nd ed. New Haven, Conn., 2000.

———. *Jesus of Nazareth, King of the Jews*. New York, 1999.

Friedman, Saul S. *The Oberammergau Passion Play: A Lance against Civilization*. Carbondale, Ill., 1984.

Fulton, Rachel. *From Judgment to Passion: Devotion to Christ and the Virgin Mary, 800–1200*. New York, 2002.

Funk, Robert W., et al., eds. *The Five Gospels: The Search for the Authentic Words of Jesus*. San Francisco, 1993.

Gager, John G. *Kingdom and Community: The Social World of Early Christianity*. Englewood Cliffs, N.J., 1975.

Garland, David E. *The Intention of Matthew 23*. Leiden, 1979.

Ghetta, Frumenzio. *Fra Bernardino Tomitano da Feltre e gli ebrei di Trento nel 1475*. Trent, 1986.

Glock, Charles Y., and Rodney Stark. *Christian Beliefs and Anti-Semitism*. New York, 1966.

Goodman, Paul. *The Synagogue and the Church, Being a Contribution to the Apologetics of Judaism*. London, 1908.

Grabar, André. *Christian Iconography: A Study of Its Origins*. Princeton, N.J., 1968.

Graetz, Heinrich. *History of the Jews*. 6 vols. Philadelphia, 1891–1898.

Grayzel, Solomon. *The Church and the Jews in the Thirteenth Century*. Rev. ed. New York, 1966.

Gregory of Tours. *Glory of the Martyrs*. Trans. Raymond van Dam. Liverpool, 1988.

Griffiths, Richard. *The Use of Abuse: The Polemics of the Dreyfus Affair and Its Aftermath*. New York, 1991.

*A Guide to the Passion: 100 Questions Asked about* The Passion of the Christ. West Chester, Penn., 2004.

Haberman, Bonna Devora. "Foreskin Sacrifice: Zipporah's Ritual and the Bloody Bridegroom." In *The Covenant of Circumcision: New Perspectives on an Ancient Jewish Rite*, pp. 18–29. Ed. Elizabeth Wyner Mark. Hanover, N.H., 2003.

Habermann, A. M., ed. *Sefer Gezerot Ashkenaz ve-Tzarefat*. Jerusalem, 1945.

Hagner, Donald A. *The Jewish Reclamation of Jesus: An Analysis and Critique of Modern Jewish Study of Jesus*. Grand Rapids, Mich., 1984.

Hahn, Cynthia. "*Visio Dei*: Changes in Medieval Visuality." In *Visuality before and beyond the Renaissance: Seeing as Others Saw*, pp. 169–196. Ed. Robert S. Nelson. Cambridge, Eng., 2000.

Halas, Roman B. *Judas Iscariot: A Scriptural and Theological Study of His Person, His Deeds and his Eternal Lot*. Washington, D.C., 1946.

Haliczer, Stephen. "The Jew as Witch: Displaced Aggression and the Myth of the Santo Niño de La Guardia." In *Cultural Encounters: The Impact of the Inquisition in Spain and the New World*, pp. 146–156. Ed. Mary Elizabeth Perry and Anne J. Cruz. Berkeley, Calif., 1991.

Hall, Stuart G. "Melito in the Light of the Passover Haggadah." *Journal of Theological Studies* 22 (1971), 29–46.

Hameiri, Avigdor. *Selected Stories* [in Hebrew]. Tel Aviv, 1954.

Hand, Wayland D. "A Dictionary of Words and Idioms Associated with Judas Iscariot." *University of California Publications in Modern Philology* 24 (1942), 289–356.

Handlin, Oscar. *Adventure in Freedom: Three Hundred Years of Jewish Life in America*. New York, 1954.

Hanfmann, George M. A. *Letters from Sardis*. Cambridge, Mass., 1972.

Hanfmann, George M. A., et al. *Sardis from Prehistoric to Roman Times*. Cambridge, Mass., 1983.

Haran, Menahem. "The Passover Sacrifice." *Supplements to Vetus Testamentum* 23 (1972), 86–116.

Hardison, O. B., Jr. *Christian Rite and Christian Drama in the Middle Ages: Essays in the Origin and Early History of Modern Drama*. Baltimore, 1965.

Harris, John Wesley. *Medieval Theatre in Context: An Introduction*. London, 1992.

Hayes, Michael A. "From *Nostre Aetate* to 'We Remember: A Reflection on the *Shoah*.'" In *Christian-Jewish Relations through the Centuries*, pp. 426–445. Ed. Stanley E. Porter and Brook W. R. Pearson. Sheffield, Eng., 2000.

Heaton, Vernon. *The Oberammergau Passion Play*. 3rd ed. London, 1983.

Henderson, John. "The Flagellant Movement and Flagellant Confraternities in Central Italy, 1260–1400." In *Religious Motivation: Biographical and Sociological Problems for the Church Historian*, pp. 147–160. Ed. Derek Baker. Oxford, 1978.

Hengel, Martin. *The Atonement: The Origins of the Doctrine in the New Testament*. Philadelphia, 1981.

Herford, R. Travers. *Christianity in Talmud and Midrash*. London, 1903.

Herschcopf, Judith. "The Church and the Jews: The Struggle at Vatican Council II."
    *American Jewish Year Book* 66 (1965), 99–136; 67 (1966), 45–77.
Hertzberg, Arthur. *The French Enlightenment and the Jews.* New York, 1968.
Heschel, Susannah. *Abraham Geiger and the Jewish Jesus.* Chicago, 1998.
Hillaby, Joe. "The Ritual-Child-Murder Accusation: Its Dissemination and Harold of
    Gloucester." *Transactions of the Jewish Historical Society of England* 34 (1994),
    69–107.
Hirsch, Emil G. *The Crucifixion: Viewed from a Jewish Standpoint.* 3rd ed. New York,
    1921.
Hodapp, William F. "Sacred Time and Sacred Space: Drama and Ritual in Late Medi-
    eval Affective Passion Meditations." *Downside Review* 115 (1997), 235–248.
Hoffman, Lawrence A. *Covenant of Blood: Circumcision and Gender in Rabbinic
    Judaism.* Chicago, 1996.
Hofstadter, Richard. *The Age of Reform: From Bryan to F.D.R.* New York, 1955.
Hollywood, Amy. "Kill Jesus." *Harvard Divinity Bulletin* 32 (2004).
Horbury, William. "The Trial of Jesus in Jewish Tradition." In *The Trial of Jesus:
    Cambridge Studies in Honour of C.F.D. Moule,* pp. 103–121. Ed. Ernst Bammel.
    Naperville, Ill., 1970.
Horowitz, Elliott. "'And It Was Reversed': Jews and Their Enemies in the Festivities
    of Purim" [in Hebrew]. *Zion* 59 (1994), 129–168.
———. "Medieval Jews Face the Cross" [in Hebrew]. In *Facing the Cross: The Perse-
    cutions of 1096 in History and Historiography,* pp. 118–140. Ed. Yom Tov Assis
    et al. Jerusalem, 2000.
———. *Reckless Rites: Purim and the Legacy of Jewish Violence.* Princeton, N.J., 2006.
Houlden, Leslie. *The Strange Story of the Gospels: Finding Doctrine through Narra-
    tive.* London, 2002.
Hsia, R. Po-Chia. *The Myth of Ritual Murder: Jews and Magic in Reformation Ger-
    many.* New Haven, Conn., 2004.
———. *Trent 1475: Stories of a Ritual Murder Trial.* New Haven, Conn., 1992.
Hugenberger, G. P. "The Servant of the Lord in the 'Servant Songs' of Isaiah: A Sec-
    ond Moses Figure." In *The Lord's Anointed: Interpretation of Old Testament
    Messianic Texts,* pp. 105–139. Ed. Philip E. Satterthwaite et al. Carlisle, Eng., 1995.
Hughes, Kirk T. "Framing Judas." *Semeia* 54 (1991), 223–238.
Hundersmarck, Lawrence F. "Preaching the Passion: Late Medieval 'Lives of Christ'
    as Sermon Vehicles." In *De Ore Domini: Preacher and Word in the Middle Ages,*
    pp. 147–167. Ed. Thomas L. Amos et al. Kalamazoo, Mich., 1989.
Hurley, Neil P. "Cinematic Transfigurations of Jesus." In *Religion in Film,* pp. 61–
    78. Ed. John R. May and Michael Bird. Knoxville, Tenn., 1982.
Jacob, Walter. *Christianity through Jewish Eyes: The Quest for Common Ground.*
    Cincinnati, Ohio, 1974.
James, Marvyn. "Ritual, Drama and Social Body in the Late Medieval English Town."
    *Past and Present* 98 (1983), 3–29.
Jensen, Robin M. "The Binding or Sacrifice of Isaac: How Jews and Christians See
    Differently." *Bible Review* 9.5 (1993), 42–51.
———. *Understanding Early Christian Art.* London, 2000.

Johnson, R. Frank. "Christ the Servant of the Lord." In *The Old and New Testaments: Their Relationship and the "Intertestamental" Literature*, pp. 107–136. Ed. James H. Charlesworth and Walter P. Weaver. Valley Forge, Pa., 1993.

Jones, Michael. "'The Place of the Jews': Anti-Judaism and Theatricality in Medieval Culture." *Exemplaria* 12 (2000), 327–357.

Jordan, William Chester. "The Erosion of the Stereotype of the Last Tormentor of Christ." *Jewish Quarterly Review* 81 (1990), 13–44.

———. "The Last Tormentor of Christ: An Image of the Jew in Ancient and Medieval Exegesis, Art, and Drama." *Jewish Quarterly Review* 78 (1987), 21–47.

Kagan, Andrew. *Marc Chagall*. New York, 1989.

Kampling, Rainer. *Das Blut Christi und die Juden: Mt 27,25 bei den lateinischsprachigen christlichen Autoren bis zu Leo dem Grossen*. Münster, 1984.

Kapelrud, Arvid S. "The Identity of the Suffering Servant." In *Near Eastern Studies in Honor of William Foxwell Albright*, pp. 307–314. Ed. Hans Goedicke. Baltimore, 1971.

Kasser, Rodolphe, et al., eds. *The Gospel of Judas*. Washington, D.C., 2006.

Kay, Sarah. "The Sublime Body of the Martyr: Violence in Early Romance Saints' Lives." In *Violence in Medieval Society*, pp. 3–20. Ed. Richard W. Kaeuper. Woodbridge, Eng., 2000.

Kedward, Harry Roderick. *The Dreyfus Affair: Catalyst for Tensions in French Society*. London, 1965.

Kelley, John J. "Progress and Problems in Passion Plays." *Christian Jewish Relations* 21 (1988), 18–27.

Kermode, Frank. *The Genesis of Secrecy: On the Interpretation of Narrative*. Cambridge, Mass., 1979.

Kessler, Edward. "The Sacrifice of Isaac (the *Akedah*) in Christian and Jewish Tradition: Artistic Representations." In *Borders, Boundaries and the Bible*, pp. 74–98. Ed. Martin O'Kane. London, 2002.

Kessler, Herbert L. "Pictorial Narrative and Church Mission in Sixth-Century Gaul." In *Pictorial Narrative in Antiquity and the Middle Ages*, pp. 75–91. Ed. Herbert L. Kessler and Mariana Shreve Simpson. Washington, D.C., 1985.

Kieckhefer, Richard. "Major Currents in Late Medieval Devotion." In *Christian Spirituality: High Middle Ages and Reformation*, pp. 75–108. Ed. Jill Raitt. New York, 1988.

———. *Unquiet Souls: Fourteenth-Century Saints and Their Religious Milieu*. Chicago, 1984.

Kimhi, Joseph. *The Book of the Covenant*. Trans. Frank Talmage. Toronto, 1972.

Kissel, David L. "Politics and Play Reform in Oberammergau." *Face to Face* 12 (1985), 10–15.

Klassen, William. *Judas: Betrayer or Friend of Jesus?* Minneapolis, 1996.

Klausner, Joseph. *Jesus of Nazareth: His Life, Times, and Teaching*. Trans. Herbert Danby. New York, 1925.

Kleeblatt, Norman L., ed. *The Dreyfus Affair: Art, Truth, and Justice*. Berkeley, Calif., 1987.

Klein, Charlotte L. *Anti-Judaism in Christian Theology*. Philadelphia, 1975.

————. "'The Gospel Distorted' in the Oberammergau Passion Play." *Christian Jewish Relations* 17 (1984), 61–63.

Klenicki, Leon. "From Argument to Dialogue: *Nostra Aetate* Twenty-Five Years Later." In *In Our Time: The Flowering of Jewish-Catholic Dialogue*, pp. 77–103. Ed. Eugene J. Fisher and Leon Klenicki. New York, 1990.

Koenig, Louis W. *Bryan: A Political Biography of William Jennings Bryan*. New York, 1971.

Koltun-Fromm, Naomi. "Psalm 22's Christological Interpretive Tradition in Light of Christian Anti-Jewish Polemic." *Journal of Early Christian Studies* 6 (1998), 37–57.

Kraabel, A. Thomas. "Melito the Bishop and the Synagogue at Sardis: Text and Context." In *Studies Presented to George M.A. Hanfmann*, pp. 77–84. Ed. David Gordon Mitten et al. Mainz, 1971.

————. "Paganism and Judaism: The Sardis Evidence." In *Diaspora Jews and Judaism: Essays in Honor of, and in Dialogue with, A. Thomas Kraabel*, pp. 237–255. Ed. J. Andrew Overman and Robert S. MacLennan. Atlanta, 1992.

————. "Social Systems of Six Diaspora Synagogues." In *Diaspora Jews and Judaism: Essays in Honor of, and in Dialogue with, A. Thomas Kraabel*, pp. 257–267. Ed. J. Andrew Overman and Robert S. MacLennan. Atlanta, 1992.

————. "The Synagogue at Sardis: Jews and Christians." In *Diaspora Jews and Judaism: Essays in Honor of, and in Dialogue with, A. Thomas Kraabel*, pp. 225–236. Ed. J. Andrew Overman and Robert S. MacLennan. Atlanta, 1992.

Kraabel, A. Thomas, and Andrew R. Seager. "The Synagogue and the Jewish Community." In *Sardis from Prehistoric to Roman Times: Results of the Archaeological Exploration of Sardis, 1958–1975*, pp. 168–190, 284–285. Ed. George M. A. Hanfmann. Cambridge, Mass., 1983.

Krauskopf, Joseph. *A Rabbi's Impressions of the Oberammergau Passion Play*. Philadelphia, 1901.

Krauss, Samuel, ed. *Das Leben Jesu nach jüdischen Quellen*. Berlin, 1902.

Kreitzer, Larry J. *Gospel Images in Fiction and Film: On Reversing the Hermeneutical Flow*. London, 2002.

————. *The New Testament in Fiction and Film: On Reversing the Hermeneutical Flow*. Sheffield, Eng., 1993.

Kselman, John S. "'Why Have You Abandoned Me?' A Rhetorical Study of Psalm 22." In *Art and Meaning: Rhetoric in Biblical Literature*, pp. 172–198. Ed. David J. A. Clines et al. Sheffield, Eng., 1982.

Kudasiewicz, Joseph. *The Synoptic Gospels Today*. Trans. Sergius Wroblewski. New York, 1996.

Lachs, Samuel Tobias. *A Rabbinic Commentary on the New Testament: The Gospels of Matthew, Mark, and Luke*. Hoboken, N.J., 1987.

Lampert, Lisa. "The Once and Future Jew: The Croxton *Play of the Sacrament*, Little Robert of Bury and Historical Memory." *Jewish History* 15 (2001), 235–255.

Lane, Eric, and Ian Brenson, eds. *Oberammergau: A Passion Play*. London, 1984.

Langmuir, Gavin I. "The Tortures of the Body of Christ." In *Christendom and Its Discontents: Exclusion, Persecution, and Rebellion, 1000–1500*, pp. 287–309. Ed. Scott L. Waugh and Peter D. Diehl. Cambridge, Eng., 1996.

———.*Toward a Definition of Antisemitism.* Berkeley, Calif., 1990.

Lapide, Pinchas. *Israelis, Jews, and Jesus.* New York, 1979.

Larkin, Maurice. *Church and State after the Dreyfus Affair: The Separation Issue in France.* London, 1974.

Lasker, Daniel J., and Sarah Stroumsa, eds. *The Polemic of Nestor the Priest.* 2 vols. Jerusalem, 1996.

Lauterbach, Jacob Z. *Rabbinic Essays.* Cincinnati, 1951.

———, ed. *Mekilta de-Rabbi Ishmael.* 3 vols. Philadelphia, 1933–1935.

Laws, Page. "The Power and the Glory." *American Theatre* 17 (2000), 34–38, 100.

———. "Witness to/for the Persecution." *Arbeiten aus Anglistik und Amerikanistik* 30 (2005), 53–75.

Lea, Henry Charles. "El Santo Niño de la Guardia." *English Historical Review* 4 (1889), 229–250.

Levenson, Jon D. "Abusing Abraham: Traditions, Religious Histories, and Modern Misinterpretations." *Judaism* 47 (1998), 259–277.

———. *The Death and Resurrection of the Beloved Son: The Transformation of Child Sacrifice in Judaism and Christianity.* New Haven, Conn., 1993.

Lieu, Judith M. *Image and Reality: The Jews in the World of the Christians in the Second Century.* Edinburgh, 1996.

Limor, Ora, and Israel Jacob Yuval. "Oedipus in Christian Garb: The Legend of Judas Iscariot" [in Hebrew]. *Zmanim* 21 (2005), 12–21.

Lindemann, Albert S. *The Jew Accused: Three Anti-Semitic Affairs (Dreyfus, Beilis, Frank), 1894–1915.* Cambridge, Eng., 2004.

Linder, Amnon, ed. *The Jews in Roman Imperial Legislation.* Detroit, Mich., 1987.

Lindeskog, Gosta. *Die Jesusfrage im neuzeitlichen Judentum: Ein Beitrag zur Geschichte der Leben-Jesu-Forschung.* Leipzig, 1938.

Linfert, Carl. *Hieronymus Bosch.* Trans. Robert Erich Wolf. New York, 1971.

Littell, Franklin H. "'Christendom' and the Holocaust." In *What Kind of God? Essays in Honor of Richard L. Rubenstein,* pp. 83–174. Ed. Betty Rubenstein Rogers and Michael Berenbaum. Lanham, Md., 1995.

———. *The Crucifixion of the Jews.* New York, 1975.

Lovejoy, Arthur O. "The Entangling Alliance of Religion and History." *Hibbert Journal* 5 (1907), 258–276.

Ludolph of Saxony. *Praying the Life of Christ.* Ed. Mary Immaculate Bodenstedt. Salzburg, 1973.

Luther, Martin. *Sermons on the Passion of Christ.* Trans. E. Smid and J. T. Isensee. Rock Island, Ill., 1956.

Lüthi, Kurt. *Judas Iskarioth in der Geschichte des Auslegung von der Reformation bis zur Gegenwart.* Zurich, 1955.

Maccoby, Hyam. *Judas Iscariot and the Myth of Jewish Evil.* New York, 1992.

MacLennan, Robert S. "Christian Self-Definition in the *Adversus Judaeos* Preachers in the Second Century." In *Diaspora Jews and Judaism: Essays in Honor of, and in Dialogue with, A. Thomas Kraabel,* pp. 209–224. Ed. J. Andrew Overman and Robert S. MacLennan. Atlanta, 1992.

Mahan, Jeffrey H. "Celluloid Savior: Jesus in the Movies." *Journal of Religion and Film* 6 (2002).

Maier, Christoph T. *Crusade Propaganda and Ideology: Model Sermons for the Preaching of the Cross.* Cambridge, Eng., 2000.

Maitland, Frederic William. "The Deacon and the Jewess; or, Apostasy at Common Law." In *The Collected Papers of Frederic William Maitland*, 1:385–406. Ed. H. A. L. Fisher. 3 vols. Cambridge, Eng., 1911.

Manns, Frederic. "The Binding of Isaac in Jewish Liturgy." In *The Sacrifice of Isaac in the Three Monotheistic Religions*, pp. 59–67. Ed. Frederic Manns. Jerusalem, 1995.

———, ed. *The Sacrifice of Isaac in the Three Monotheistic Religions.* Jerusalem, 1995.

Marcus, Ivan G. "Jews and Christians Imagining the Other in Medieval Europe." *Prooftexts* 15 (1995), 209–226.

———. "Medieval Jewish Studies: Toward an Anthropological History of the Jews." In *Jewish Studies: The State of the Field*, pp. 113–127. Ed. Shaye J. D. Cohen and Edward Greenstein. Detroit, Mich., 1990.

———. *Rituals of Childhood: Jewish Acculturation in Medieval Europe.* New Haven, Conn., 1996.

Marrow, James H. *Passion Iconography in Northern European Art of the Late Middle Ages and Early Renaissance.* Kortrijk, Belgium, 1979.

Marsh, Clive, and Gaye Ortiz, eds. *Explorations in Theology and Film: Movies and Meaning.* Oxford, 1997.

Martin, John D. *Representations of Jews in Late Medieval and Early Modern German Literature.* Oxford, 2004.

McBride, Kari Boyd. "Gender and Judaism in Meditations on the Passion: Middleton, Southwell, Lanyer, and Fletcher." In *Discovering and (Re)Covering the Seventeenth Century Religious Lyric*, pp. 17–40. Ed. Eugene R. Cunnar and Jeffrey Johnson. Pittsburgh, Pa., 2001.

McCarthy, Todd. "*The Gospel of John.*" *Variety* 392 (2003), 24.

McCulloh, John M. "Jewish Ritual Murder: William of Norwich, Thomas of Monmouth, and the Early Dissemination of the Myth." *Speculum* 72 (1997), 698–740.

Meeks, Wayne A. *The First Urban Christians: The Social World of the Apostle Paul.* New Haven, Conn., 1983.

Meeks, Wayne A., and Robert L. Wilken. *Jews and Christians in Antioch in the First Four Centuries of the Common Era.* Missoula, Mont., 1978.

Meier, Joyce Raynor. "The Polemical Function of the Toldoth Yeshu." M.A. thesis, University of Judaism, 1977.

Melito of Sardis. On Pascha *and Fragments.* Ed. Stuart G. Hall. Oxford, 1979.

Mellinkoff, Ruth. "Judas's Red Hair and the Jews." *Journal of Jewish Art* 9 (1992), 31–46.

———. *Outcasts: Signs of Otherness in Northern European Art of the Late Middle Ages.* 2 vols. Berkeley, Calif., 1993.

Menn, Esther M. "No Ordinary Lament: Relecture and the Identity of the Distressed in Psalm 22." *Harvard Theological Review* 93 (2000), 301–341.

Meurin, Leon. *La franc-maconnerie, synagogue de Satan.* Paris, 1893.

Meyer, Franz. *Marc Chagall.* New York, 1964.

Miles, Margaret R. *Seeing and Believing: Religion and Values in the Movies.* Boston, 1996.

Morey, James H. "Adam and Judas in the Old English *Christ and Satan.*" *Studies in Philology* 87 (1990), 397–409.

Mork, Gordon R. "The 1984 Oberammergau Passion Play in Historical Perspective." *Face to Face* 12 (1985), 15–21.

———. "The Oberammergau Passion Play and Modern Anti-Semitism." *Shofar* 3 (1985), 52–61.

———. "'Wicked Jews' and 'Suffering Christians' in the Oberammergau Passion Play." In *Representations of Jews through the Ages,* pp. 153–169. Ed. Leonard J. Greenspoon and Bryan F. le Beau. Omaha, Neb., 1996.

Morris, Colin. "Propaganda for War: The Dissemination of the Crusading Ideal in the Twelfth Century." In *The Church and War,* pp. 79–101. Ed. W. J. Sheils. Oxford, 1983.

Muir, Lynette R. *The Biblical Drama of Medieval Europe.* Cambridge, Eng., 1995.

Newport, Kenneth G. C. *The Sources and* Sitz im Leben *of Matthew 23.* Sheffield, Eng., 1995.

Niehoff, Maren Ruth. "The Return of Myth in Genesis Rabbah on the Akedah." *Journal of Jewish Studies* 46 (1995), 69–87.

Nirenberg, David. *Communities of Violence: Persecution of Minorities in the Middle Ages.* Princeton, N.J., 1996.

Noort, Ed, and Eibert Tigchelaar, eds. *The Sacrifice of Isaac: The Aqedah (Genesis 22) and Its Interpretations.* Leiden, 2002.

Norris, Frederick W. "Melito's Motivation." *Anglican Theological Review* 68 (1986), 16–24.

North, Christopher R. *The Suffering Servant in Deutero-Isaiah: An Historical and Critical Study.* 2nd ed. Oxford, 1956.

Nugent, Walter T. K. *The Tolerant Populists: Kansas Populism and Nativism.* Chicago, 1963.

Oberman, Heiko A. *The Roots of Anti-Semitism in the Age of Renaissance and Reformation.* Trans. James I. Porter. Philadelphia, 1984.

Ocker, Christopher. "Ritual Murder and the Subjectivity of Christ: A Choice in Medieval Christianity." *Harvard Theological Review* 91 (1998), 153–192.

O'Connor, Michael Patrick. "The Universality of Salvation: Christianity, Judaism, and Other Religions in Dante, 'Nostra aetate,' and the New Catechism." *Journal of Ecumenical Studies* 33 (1996), 487–511.

Oesterreicher, John M. "Declaration on the Relationship of the Church to Non-Christian Religions." In *Commentary on the Documents of Vatican II,* pp. 1–136. Ed. Herbert Vorgrimler. London, 1967.

Ohad-Karny, Yael. "'Anticipating' Gibson's *The Passion of the Christ*: The Controversy over Cecil B. DeMille's *The King of Kings.*" *Jewish History* 19 (2005), 189–210.

Ohly, Friedrich. *The Damned and the Elect.* Trans. Linda Archibald. Cambridge, Eng., 1992.

Orlinsky, Harry M. "The So-Called 'Servant of the Lord' and 'Suffering Servant' in Second Isaiah." *Supplements to Vetus Testasmentum* 14 (1967), 1–133.

———. "The So-Called 'Suffering Servant' in Isaiah 53." In *Interpreting the Prophetic Tradition: The Goldenson Lectures, 1955–1966,* pp. 225–273. Ed. Harry M. Orlinsky. Cincinnati, Ohio, 1969.

Paffenroth, Kim. "Film Depictions of Judas." *Journal of Religion and Film* 5:2 (2001).

———. *Judas: Images of the Lost Disciple.* Louisville, Ky., 2001.

Pagels, Elaine. *The Origin of Satan.* New York, 1995.

Paléologue, Maurice. *My Secret Diary of the Dreyfus Case, 1894–1899.* Trans. Eric Mosbacher. London, 1957.

Patterson, Lee. "'The Living Witnesses of Our Redemption': Martyrdom and Imitation in Chaucer's *Prioress's Tale.*" *Journal of Medieval and Early Modern Studies* 31 (2001), 507–560.

Pawlikowski, John T. "The Shoah: Its Challenges for Religious and Secular Ethics." *Holocaust and Genocide Studies* 3 (1988), 443–455.

Pelikan, Jaroslav. *Jesus through the Centuries: His Place in the History of Culture.* New Haven, Conn., 1985.

Peter Alfonsi. *Dialogue Against the Jews.* Trans. Irven Resnick. Fathers of the Church, Medieval Continuation, 8. Washington D.C., 2006.

Peter the Venerable. *Letters.* Ed. Giles Constable. 2 vols. Cambridge, Mass., 1967.

———. "Sermones tres." Ed. Giles Constable. *Revue Bénédictine* 64 (1954), 224–272.

Pickering, F. P. *Essays on Medieval German Literature and Iconography.* Cambridge, Eng., 1980.

Plate, S. Brent. "Religion/Literature/Film: Toward a Religious Visuality of Film." *Literature and Theology* 12 (1998), 16–38.

Plesch, Veronique. "*Etalage complaisant?* The Torments of Christ in French Passion Plays." *Comparative Drama* 28 (1995), 458–485.

———. "Notes for the Staging of a Late Medieval Passion Play." In *Medieval Culture and Medieval Drama,* pp. 75–102. Ed. Clifford Davidson. Kalamazoo, Mich., 1999.

Polish, Daniel F. "A Very Small Lever Can Move the Entire World." In *Unanswered Questions: Theological Views of Jewish-Catholic Relations,* pp. 82–102. Ed. Roger Brooks. Notre Dame, Ind., 1988.

Propp, William H. *Exodus 1–18: A New Translation with Introduction and Commentary.* Garden City, N.Y., 1998.

———. "That Bloody Bridegroom (Exodus IV 24–6)." *Vetus Testamentum* 43 (1993), 495–518.

*The Protocols of the Wise Men of Zion.* New York, 1920.

Prusak, Bernard P. "Jews and the Death of Jesus in Post-Vatican II Christologies." *Journal of Ecumenical Studies* 28 (1991), 581–625.

Pyper, Hugh S. "Modern Gospels of Judas: Canon and Betrayal." *Literature and Theology* 15 (1991), 111–122.

Quillard, Pierre. *Le Monument Henry: Listes des souscripteurs classés méthodiquement et selon l'ordre alphabétique.* Paris, 1899.

Ragusa, Isa, and Rosalie Green, eds. *Meditations on the Life of Christ.* Princeton, N.J., 1961.

Rajak, Tessa. *The Jewish Dialogue with Greece and Rome: Studies in Cultural and Social Interaction.* Leiden, 2001.

Raymond Martin. *Capistrum Iudaeorum.* Ed. Adolfo Robles Sierra. 2 vols. Würzburg, 1990–1993.

———. *Pugio fidei.* Farnborough, Eng., 1687.

Reinhartz, Adele. "From D.W. Griffith to Mel Gibson: Jesus of Hollywood." Available at http://people.cas.sc.edu/rosati/ttp.jesusofhollywood.nr.3804.htm. 2004.

———. "Jesus in Film: Hollywood Perspectives on the Jewishness of Jesus." *Journal of Religion and Film* 2 (1998).

———. "Jesus of Hollywood: A Jewish Perspective." In *The Historical Jesus through Catholic and Jewish Eyes*, pp. 131–146. Ed. Bryan F. le Beau et al. Harrisburg, Pa., 2000.

———. "Passion-ate Moments in the Jesus Film Genre." *Journal of Religion and Film* 8 (2004).

———. "Scripture on the Silver Screen." *Journal of Religion and Film* 3 (1999).

———. *Scripture on the Silver Screen.* Louisville, Ky., 2003.

Resnick, Irven M. "Talmud, 'talmudisti,' and Albert the Great." *Viator* 33 (2002), 69–86.

Riegner, Gerhart M. "Twenty Years of *Nostra Aetate*." *Christian Jewish Relations* 18 (1985), 17–31.

Riley-Smith, Jonathan. *The First Crusade and the Idea of Crusading.* London, 1986.

———. "The First Crusade and the Persecution of the Jews." In *Persecution and Toleration*, pp. 51–72. Ed. W. J. Sheils. Oxford, 1984.

Rivkin, Ellis. *What Crucified Jesus? The Political Execution of a Charismatic.* Nashville, Tenn., 1984.

Robbins, Vernon K. "The Reversed Contextualization of Psalm 22 in the Markan Crucifixion: A Socio-Rhetorical Analysis." In *The Four Gospels 1992: Festschrift Frans Neirynck*, pp. 1161–1183. Ed. F. van Segbroeck et al. Leuven, 1992.

Rohrbacher, Stefan. "The Charge of Deicide: An Anti-Jewish Motif in Medieval Christian Art." *Journal of Medieval History* 17 (1991), 297–321.

Roskies, David G. *Against the Apocalypse: Responses to Catastrophe in Modern Jewish Culture.* Cambridge, Mass., 1984.

Rothschild, Fritz A., ed. *Jewish Perspectives on Christianity: Leo Baeck, Martin Buber, Franz Rosenzweig, Will Herberg, Abraham J. Heschel.* New York, 2000.

Routledge, Robin. "Passover and Last Supper." *Tyndale Bulletin* 53 (2002), 203–221.

Rubin, Miri. *Corpus Christi: The Eucharist in Late Medieval Culture.* Cambridge, Eng., 1991.

———. *Gentile Tales: The Narrative Assault on Late Medieval Jews.* New Haven, Conn., 1999.

Ruokanen, Miikka. *The Catholic Doctrine of Non-Christian Religions according to the Second Vatican Council.* Leiden, 1992.

Safran, William. "The Dreyfus Affair, Political Consciousness, and the Jews: A Centennial Retrospective." *Contemporary French Civilization* 19 (1995), 1–32.

Saldarini, Anthony J. "The Interpretation of the *Akedah* in Rabbinic Literature." In

*The Biblical Mosaic: Changing Perspectives*, pp. 149–165. Ed. Robert Polzin and Eugene Rothman. Philadelphia, 1982.

———. *Jesus and Passover*. New York, 1984.

Schreckenberg, Heinz. *The Jews in Christian Art: An Illustrated History*. New York, 1996.

Segal, Alan F. "The Akedah: Some Reconsiderations." In *Geschichte—Tradition—Reflexion: Festschrift für Martin Hengel zum 70. Geburtstag*, 1:99–116. Ed. Hubert Cancik et al. Tübingen, 1996.

———. *The Other Judaisms of Late Antiquity*. Atlanta, 1987.

Segel, Binjamin W. *A Lie and a Libel: The History of the Protocols of the Elders of Zion*. Ed. Richard S. Levy. Lincoln, Neb., 1995.

Seiferth, Wolfgang S. *Synagogue and Church in the Middle Ages: Two Symbols in Art and Literature*. Trans. Lee Chadeayne and Paul Gottwald. New York, 1970.

Shachar, Isaiah. *The* Judensau: *A Medieval Anti-Jewish Motif and Its History*. London, 1974.

Shafer, Ingrid, trans. *Obrammergau Passion Play 2000*. Oberammergau, 2000.

Shapiro, James. *Oberammergau: The Troubling Story of the World's Most Famous Passion Play*. New York, 2000.

Shatzmiller, Joseph. *La deuxième controverse de Paris: Un chapitre dans la polémique entre Chrétiens et Juifs au Moyen Age*. Paris, 1994.

Shinan, Avigdor. *Jesus through Jewish Eyes*. Tel Aviv, 1999.

Silk, Mark. "Gibson's Passion: A Case Study in Media Manipulation?" *Journal of Religion and Film* 8 (2004).

Simon, Roger I. "Pedagogy and the Call to Witness in Marc Chagall's *White Crucifixion*." *The Review of Education/ Pedagogy/ Cultural Studies* 19 (1997), 169–192.

Singer, Michael. "Cinema Savior." *Film Comment* 24 (1988), 44–49.

Sloyan, Gerard S. *The Crucifixion of Jesus: History, Myth, Faith*. Minneapolis, Minn., 1995.

Spiegel, Gabrielle M. "History, Historicism, and the Social Logic of the Text in the Middle Ages." *Speculum* 65 (1990), 59–86.

Spiegel, Shalom. *The Last Trial: On the Legends and Lore of the Command to Abraham to Offer Isaac as a Sacrifice—The Akedah*. Trans. Judah Goldin. New York, 1967.

Sponsler, Claire. *Drama and Resistance: Bodies, Goods, and Theatricality in Late Medieval England*. Minneapolis, 1997.

———. *Ritual Imports: Performing Medieval Drama in America*. Ithaca, N.Y., 2004.

Stack, Oswald. *Pasolini on Pasolini*. Bloomington, Ind., 1969.

Stanley, Lynn, ed. *The Book of Margery Kempe*. New York, 2001.

Stanton, Graham. *The Gospels and Jesus*. 2nd ed. Oxford, 2002.

Steiner, George. *No Passion Spent: Essays, 1978–1996*. London, 1996.

Stern, Richard C., et al. *Savior on the Silver Screen*. New York, 1999.

Stewart-Sykes, Alistair. *The Lamb's High Feast: Melito, Peri Pascha and the Quartodeciman Paschal Liturgy at Sardis*. Leiden, 1998.

Strack, Hermann L., and Paul Billerbeck. *Kommentar zum neuen Testament aus Talmud und Midrasch*. 6 vols. in 7 pts. Munich, 1922–1961.

Strickland, Debra Higgs. *Saracens, Demons, and Jews: Making Monsters in Medieval Art*. Princeton, N.J., 2003.

Stuhlmueller, Carroll. "Psalm 22: The Deaf and Silent God of Mysticism and Liturgy." *Biblical Theology Bulletin* 12 (1982), 86–90.

Swanson, R. N. "Passion and Practice: The Social and Ecclesiastical Implications of Passion Devotion in the Late Middle Ages." In *The Broken Body: Passion Devotion in Late-Medieval Culture*, pp. 1–30. Ed. A. A. MacDonald et al. Groningen, The Netherlands, 1998.

Swetnam, James. *Jesus and Isaac: A Study of the Epistle to the Hebrews in the Light of the Aqedah*. Rome, 1981.

Swidler, Leonard, and Gerard S. Sloyan. *A Commentary on the Oberammergau Passionsspiel in Regard to Its Image of Jews and Judaism*. New York, 1978.

———. "The Passion of the Jew Jesus: Recommended Changes in the Oberammergau Passion Play after 1984." *Face to Face* 12 (1985), 24–35.

———, eds. *The Oberammergau Passionsspiel 1984*. New York, 1980.

Tabory, Joseph. "The Crucifixion of the Paschal Lamb." *Jewish Quarterly Review* 86 (1996), 395–406.

———. The *Passover Ritual throughout the Generations* [in Hebrew]. Tel Aviv, 1996.

Tanenbaum, Marc H. *Oberammergau 1960 and 1970: A Study in Religious Anti-Semitism*. New York, 1970.

Tanner, Norman. "The Eucharist in the Ecumenical Councils." *Gregorianum* 82 (2001), 37–49.

Tatum, W. Barnes. *Jesus at the Movies: A Guide to the First Hundred Years*. Rev. ed. Santa Rosa, Calif., 2004.

Telford, William R. "Jesus Christ Movie Star: The Depiction of Jesus in the Cinema." In *Explorations in Theology and Film*, pp. 115–139. Ed. Clive Marsh and Gaye Ortiz. Oxford, 1997.

———. "The New Testament in Fiction and Film: A Biblical Scholar's Perspective." In *Words Remembered, Texts Renewed: Essays in Honour of John F.A. Sawyer*, pp. 360–394. Ed. Jon Davies et al. Sheffield, Eng., 1995.

Thomas of Monmouth. *The Life and Miracles of St. William of Norwich*. Ed. Augustus Jessop and Montague Rhodes James. Cambridge, Eng., 1896.

Thucydides. *The Peloponnesian War*. Trans. Rex Warner. Melbourne, 1954.

Trachtenberg, Joshua. *The Devil and the Jews: The Medieval Conception of the Jew and Its Relation to Modern Anti-Semitism*. New Haven, Conn., 1943.

Trebilco, Paul R. *Jewish Communities in Asia Minor*. Cambridge, Eng., 1991.

Valencia, Heather. "The Vision of Zion from the 'Kingdom of the Cross': Uri Tsvi Grinberg's *Albatros* in Berlin (1923)." In *Berlin–Wien–Prag: Modernity, Minorities, and Migration in the Inter-war Period*, pp. 159–174. Ed. Susanne Marten-Finnis and Matthias Ücker. Bern, 2001.

Van den Brink, Eddy. "Abraham's Sacrifice in Early Jewish and Early Christian Art." In *The Sacrifice of Isaac: The Aqedah (Genesis 22) and Its Interpretations*, pp. 130–151. Ed. Ed Noort and Eibert Tigchelaar. Leiden, 2002.

Van Eijk, A. H. C. "The Jewish People and the Church's Self-Understanding." *Bijdragen* 50 (1989), 373–393.

Vauchez, André. *The Laity in the Middle Ages: Religious Beliefs and Devotional Practices*. Ed. Daniel E. Bornstein; trans. Margery J. Schneider. Notre Dame, Ind., 1993.

Vermes, Geza. *Scripture and Tradition in Judaism: Haggadic Studies.* 2nd ed. Leiden, 1973.

Vervenne, M. "'The Blood Is the Life and the Life Is the Blood': Blood as Symbol of Life an Death in Biblical Tradition (Gen. 9.4)." In *Ritual and Sacrifice in the Ancient Near East*, pp. 451–470. Ed. J. Quaegebeur. Leuven, 1993.

Vince, Ronald W. *Ancient and Medieval Theatre: A Historiographical Handbook.* Westport, Conn., 1984.

Vogler, Werner. *Judas Iskarioth: Untersuchungen zu Tradition und Redaktion von Texten des Neuen Testaments und ausserkanonischer Schriften.* Berlin, 1983.

Vogt, Judith. *Historien om et Image.* Copenhagen, 1978.

Walsh, Richard. *Reading the Gospels in the Dark: Portrayals of Jesus in Film.* Harrisburg, Pa., 2003.

Warning, Rainer. "On the Alterity of Medieval Religious Drama." *New Literary History* 10 (1979), 265–292.

Watt, Jack. "Parisian Theologians and the Jews: Peter Lombard and Peter Cantor." In *The Medieval Church: Universities, Heresy, and the Religious Life: Essays in Honour of Gordon Leff*, pp. 55–76. Ed. Peter Biller and Barrie Dobson. Woodbridge, Eng., 1999.

Weber, Annette. "The Hanged Judas of Freiburg Cathedral: Sources and Interpretations." In *Imagining the Self, Imagining the Other: Visual Representation and Jewish-Christian Dynamics in the Middle Ages and Early Modern Period*, pp. 165–188. Ed. Eva Frojmovik. Leiden, 2002.

Weiss-Rosmarin, Trude, ed. *Jewish Expressions on Jesus: An Anthology.* New York, 1977.

Werner, Eric. "Melito of Sardis, First Poet of Deicide." *Hebrew Union College Annual* 37 (1966), 191–210.

Wigoder, Geoffrey. "A Jewish Reaction to the 'Notes.'" *Immanuel* 20 (1986), 67–83.

Wilcox, Peter. "The Servant Songs in Deutero-Isaiah." *Journal for the Study of the Old Testament* 42 (1988), 79–102.

Wilken, Robert L. "Melito, the Jewish Community at Sardis, and the Sacrifice of Isaac." *Theological Studies* 37 (1976), 53–69.

———. "Something Greater than the Temple." In *Anti-Judaism and the Gospels*, pp. 176–202. Ed. William Farmer. Harrisburg, Pa., 1999.

Wilson, Charles M. "A Cross of Gold." *American History Illustrated*, 5.8 (1970), 4–11, 43–48.

Wilson, S. G. "Passover, Easter, and Anti-Judaism: Melito of Sardis and Others." In *"To See Ourselves as Others See Us": Christians, Jews, "Others" in Late Antiquity*, pp. 337–355. Ed. Jacob Neusner and Ernest S. Frerichs. Chico, Calif., 1985.

Wilson, Stephen. *Ideology and Experience: Antisemitism in France at the Time of the Dreyfus Affair.* Rutherford, N.J., 1982.

Wise, Isaac Mayer. *The Martyrdom of Jesus of Nazareth: A Historic-Critical Treatise on the Last Chapters of the Gospel.* Cincinnati, 1874.

Wolf, Kirsten. "The Judas Legend in Scandinavia." *Journal of English and Germanic Philology* 88 (1989), 463–476.

Wood, J. Edwin. "Isaac Typology in the New Testament." *New Testament Studies* 14 (1968), 583–589.

Yerushalmi, Yosef Hayim. *Zakhor: Jewish History and Jewish Memory.* Seattle, 1982.

Young, Frances. "Typology." In *Crossing the Boundaries: Essays in Biblical Interpretation in Honour of Michael D. Goulder,* pp. 29–48. Ed. Stanley E. Porter et al. Leiden, 1994.

Yuval, Israel Jacob. "The Language and Symbols of the Hebrew Chronicles of the Crusades." In *Facing the Cross: The Persecutions of 1096 in History and Historiography,* pp. 101–117. Ed. Yom Tov Assis et al. Jerusalem, 2000.

———. "'They Tell Lies: You Ate the Man': Jewish Reactions to Ritual Murder Accusations." In *Religious Violence between Christians and Jews: Medieval Roots, Modern Perspectives,* pp. 86–106. Ed. Anna Sapir Abulafia. Hampshire, Eng., 2002.

———. *Two Nations in Your Womb: Perceptions of Jews and Christians in Late Antiquity and the Middle Ages.* Trans. Barbara Harshav and Jonathan Chipman. Berkeley, Calif., 2006.

Zeitlin, Solomon. *Who Crucified Jesus?* New York, 1942.

# INDEX

*Italicized page numbers refer to illustrations.*